THE

CONTROL

FREAKS

How New Labour Gets Its Own Way

NICHOLAS JONES

First published in hardback 2001
This edition published in 2002
Politico's Publishing
8 Artillery Row
Westminster
London
SW1P 1RZ
www.politicos.co.uk/publishing

A catalogue record for this book is available from the British Library.

ISBN 1 902301 83 8

Printed and bound in Great Britain by Bookmarque

CONTENTS

PREFACE

Finally, in July 2000, Tony Blair's patience with the news media snapped. So angered was he at the way his government's reputation as open and above board had been traduced by newspaper reports about animosity within the cabinet and infighting between rival ministers and their supporters that he issued a direct challenge to all political correspondents and commentators. They should either name their 'sources' or stop writing news stories based on nothing more than unattributed quotations or the views of unidentified politicians. If anyone could identity a source close to him who was briefing against a member of the government, the Prime Minister was ready to deal with the culprit: 'Well, go on, make my day, name the source and it will be my pleasure to sack them.'

His ultimatum failed to produce the confrontation he desired, and damaging revelations from 'senior sources' and an array of 'friends' and 'insiders' continued to appear in newspapers and books throughout the summer and autumn of 2000. Although many of the accounts which were said to be causing the government grief did seem to throw up far greater circumstantial evidence than before that ministers and their advisers had co-operated with journalists and were providing off-the-record briefings, Blair said that without proof such stories were nothing more than the 'usual froth . . . just recycled tittle tattle'. He was equally forthright in denying that his administration had come to be dominated by 'control freaks' whose overriding compulsion was to manipulate the media and spin their way out of trouble.

Whenever I write about the machinations of media manipulation I do endeavour to source my material. Here, as in my previous books, I strive to give a fair and honest account of what might have occurred or what was said. Notwithstanding Blair's insistence that journalists should 'name names', I suspect some of the MPs, civil servants, political advisers and party workers who are featured in *The Control Freaks* might be aggrieved to find they have been quoted and identified; but I am reluctant to apologise for doing so, for those most likely to be the loudest in their protestations draw their salaries either from the public purse or from a political party, and in my opinion they should not expect, let alone demand, to have their relationship with the news media shrouded in a cloak of secrecy and anonymity. I believe journalists and authors should be held to account for what they write. Broadcasters are subjected to far more stringent controls than those who work in the printed media, and, as the BBC's records will testify, when politicians and their propagandists have been dissatisfied with the standard of my own reporting or behaviour they have not been slow to avail themselves of the Corporation's complaints procedures. My interest in seeking to illuminate through my books the hidden seven-eighths of the iceberg world of media manipulation is of long standing. I try to be open and upfront in the pursuit of my objective. To those who might consider that their remarks have been reproduced and sourced without their knowledge or approval, I would suggest that a wider understanding of the complex relationship between politicians and the news media is a matter of legitimate public interest.

INTRODUCTION

When the pollster and strategist Philip Gould revealed in a memo
leaked in July 2000 that the 'New Labour brand' had become 'badly
contaminated', he confirmed what had been widely suspected for
months. Disquiet about the government was being fuelled not by
catastrophic political failure but by a growing sense of unease among
party members and the broader electorate about the tactics being
employed by Tony Blair's close colleagues and advisers. As the memo
put it with such clarity, a dependence on presentation and spin,
combined with a perceived lack of integrity, had made New Labour
the 'object of constant criticism and, even worse, ridicule'. Gould
could hardly have provided me with a better starting-point for *The
Control Freaks*, which seeks to explore the fallout from the practices
which transformed the Labour Party in opposition and which have
since been replicated within government.

Gould's soul-searching was meant for the private consumption of
Blair's inner circle, and it has been in sharp contrast to the public
pronouncements of the Prime Minister and his press secretary,
Alastair Campbell. They have denied interfering needlessly in party
affairs or having allowed their preoccupation with presentation to
become so intense that it has destabilised and damaged the government. Their protestations notwithstanding, the powers and resources
acquired by Blair and his media advisers have been unprecedented,
and their ability to control events from Downing Street and to
manipulate the political messages which they have sought to promote
has been far greater than that of any previous government.

These changes have provoked considerable debate. Parliamentarians have become alarmed by procedures that they contend have
made it far harder for MPs to hold ministers to account. Party
members and trade unionists have complained bitterly about a sense
of disengagement and the lack of influence they have been able to
exercise on policy-making. Of far wider concern has been a fear that
the emphasis the Blair regime has placed on presentation and
publicity has added to a general sense of cynicism about politics and

a mistrust of politicians. My aim in this book has been to chart the steps the Labour government has taken to impose control; to examine the machinery that has been established to co-ordinate the way in which the administration publicises information; and then to assess whether these structures have served the public interest.

My fascination with the process of political communication and the shadowy interface between the promoters and reporters of politics has made my previous work a target for criticism by Labour's spin doctors. They say that by immersing myself in the hour-by-hour minutiae of their tortuous daily contact with journalists, and by becoming starry-eyed about the presentational wizardry of New Labour, I have lost sight of Blair's political objectives. In their judgement, what matters ultimately is the success or failure of a policy, not the process by which it was agreed or the means by which it was communicated to the public and then reported by newspapers, television and radio. Their argument is that the froth and trivia of the news media's daily output can largely be discounted because ultimately the government will be judged on its achievements and by its record in delivering what was promised to the electorate.

Yet I believe lessons can be learned from the way in which Peter Mandelson and Alastair Campbell have refashioned the mechanisms used by the Labour Party and the government to control and disseminate information during the nearly four years that have elapsed since Labour's landslide victory in the 1997 general election. It is my contention that the techniques they have introduced have been applied with scant regard to the twin requirements to uphold parliamentary accountability and to safeguard the political impartiality of the civil service. Another disturbing consequence of the new procedures that have been imposed on the government's information service is that, by their conduct, Labour's spin doctors appear to have precipitated a further decline in the standard of political reporting. Instead of creating a level playing field for journalists and trying to encourage a balanced coverage of politics, the government has fuelled those competitive pressures within the industry that have tended to sacrifice accuracy and reliability for the sake of headline-grabbing exclusives. Blair has complained vociferously about the growth in political news stories for which there is no attribution, while conveniently overlooking the fact that it is Mandelson's masterly use of unsourced news stories when the party was in opposition that has been copied so assiduously by another generation of up-and-coming young spin doctors. Having been accused in the past of being mesmerised by Labour's day-to-day relationship with the news media, I thought it was time to stand back, to look at the reasons why the leadership's fixation with presentation and publicity became so dominant in the first place, and to assess the repercussions of this phenomenon for politicians, civil servants and journalists.

Unlike previous Labour prime ministers, Blair succeeded in remodelling his party before winning power. The foundations for a root-and-branch restructuring were laid long before he was elected leader and, with the backing of the party conference, he saw through to fruition the fundamental reforms of which the architects of New Labour had dreamed for so long. Once in Downing Street, the Blairites brooked no opposition. Although they had established a system of command and control that was the envy of their political opponents, they lacked the confidence to encourage or even allow open debate and disagreement; instead, they stifled dissent. I had seen at first hand the turmoil that had engulfed the Labour Party during the 1980s, when the trade unions and constituency parties challenged and defeated the leadership, and I understood why the modernisers recoiled from the memory of those turbulent and divisive years. However, despite all the many justified complaints about rank-and-file militancy and the undue levels of union influence on the party machine, the local parties and the unions supplied not only the money Labour needed to fight general elections but also a constant stream of policies and ideas. Under New Labour, many of the channels for voicing criticism and challenging the leadership were either closed down or rendered ineffective. My study of control freakery starts with an assessment of the impact these sweeping changes have had on the party's organisation and policy-making processes.

I have to admit that I was caught slightly off guard by the sheer ferocity of the backlash, which evidently caused so much anguish to Philip Gould and which has so tarnished the good name of New Labour. I had not appreciated the speed with which this would occur.

4 / THE CONTROL FREAKS

I had always thought the government would pay a penalty for its obsession with spin, but I did not foresee the possibility that it was the one word that had the potential to become as damaging to Blair as 'sleaze' was for his predecessor, John Major; nor did I imagine that 'control freakery' would emerge quite so quickly as a worthy entry for the next dictionary of political jargon. If spin is to be successful, the first prerequisite is effective control. The task of deciding 'the line to take' is often the easy part; the far harder assignment is to ensure that the agreed message is imposed and then adhered to. When the leadership went too far in trying to control the party's procedures for selecting local candidates to represent Labour, the results damaged party morale. The setbacks Blair suffered over the elections for the Scottish Parliament, Welsh Assembly and Mayor of London were all blamed on unacceptable interference from Downing Street. Officials in No. 10 had been gripped by a desperate fear of the adverse publicity that might be generated if party activists were allowed to select candidates who were prepared to exhibit a degree of independence. At Westminster, the loyalty shown by Labour's 183 new MPs seemed initially to know no bounds; indeed, they were mocked for the dutiful way in which they responded to the pager messages sent out by Millbank Tower and for their willingness to parrot the party lines that were faxed to their offices each morning in the *Daily Brief*. Ministers and MPs alike remained in a state of high alert, as if they were in still in opposition, constantly fighting an election; any word of censure had to be challenged, and if a parliamentary attack was mounted by their political opponents or by dissident Labour MPs it had to be defeated.

So great was the overriding urge to rebut all criticism that ministers participated in retaliatory action, which damaged the government's reputation for fair dealing in Parliament. Rather than take steps to enhance the independence of the select committees of the House of Commons, the government has thwarted their work by undermining the authority of their reports and rubbishing their findings. Another blatant abuse encouraged by the control freak tendency is the cavalier way in which No. 10 has flouted the long-established parliamentary convention that policy announcements should be made first to MPs rather than publicised in advance. In the three years that she held office under the Blair government, the former Speaker, Miss Betty Boothroyd, issued six separate rulings against ministers for disclosing information to the news media before statements had been made in the House.

Perhaps the greatest manifestation of the command and control culture that has become the hallmark of New Labour has been the emergence of a little understood but highly influential new élite. Even before Labour won the 1997 election, discreet preparations were being made for an unprecedented infusion of political appointees who would inhabit the ill-defined interface between ministers and their civil servants. Blair and his cabinet colleagues took with them into government the aides who had assisted them in opposition; many more were transferred directly from party headquarters to Whitehall departments. Westminster had never seen anything like it. By December 2000, Blair had authorised the appointment of seventy-nine politically appointed special advisers, twice the number employed by the Conservatives; twenty-six of them were based in No. 10, three times as many as under John Major. Not only have their numbers increased: so have their authority and range of work. Alastair Campbell and Blair's new chief of staff Jonathan Powell were both given executive powers immediately Labour took office; some of Downing Street's special advisers were hired for newly created units that provide back-up for the Downing Street press office and co-ordinate the presentation of government policy. Special advisers have the status of temporary civil servants, but they are allowed to assist ministers to present the government's affairs in a political context, and they can perform other party functions; their combined salary bill of well over £4 million a year is met by the taxpayer. However, their duties are not clearly defined, and there have been repeated calls for the model contract under which they are employed to be replaced with a separate code of conduct that should impose tight regulations on their activities and be enforced with greater vigour. Much of this book is devoted to an examination of the role that has been filled by this new political breed. I offer my assessment of the influence that special advisers have exercised over civil servants and the impact of other far-reaching changes that Blair has sanctioned over the way government information is communicated to the public.

In attempting to secure the tightest possible control over the dissemination of information, Campbell took on a challenge that had defeated previous administrations. His aim was to ensure that a disparate array of government officials and party representatives spoke with a single voice. A year after his appointment as Downing Street press secretary, he appeared as a witness before the Select Committee on Public Administration. He gave numerous undertakings as to his own conduct and that of the many other political appointees who have responsibility for the government's relationship with the news media. Sir Richard Wilson, the Cabinet Secretary and head of the civil service, has reinforced those assurances and has repeatedly told MPs that he has monitored the activities of the Downing Street press office. Nevertheless, in pursuit of his ambitious objectives Campbell has cast aside long-standing checks and balances, and has succeeded in refashioning to Labour's advantage the traditional dividing lines between the responsibilities of civil service information officers and those of political appointees, whether special advisers or party press officers. One of my objectives in writing *The Control Freaks* has been to analyse Campbell's *modus operandi* and to assess his achievements.

I quite understand why most of my fellow political correspondents have been reluctant to hold Blair's official spokesman to account. His argument that he is a mere servant of No. 10 has been persuasive, and the collective view within the lobby has been that the deciding factor for journalists in judging his effectiveness should be the degree of authority with which he, as a Downing Street spokesman, can speak on behalf of the Prime Minister of the day: a test in which Campbell has continued to acquit himself with flying colours. Yet, notwithstanding the trepidation of some of my colleagues, I believe there is every justification for taking a detailed look at the strategies Campbell has employed on Blair's behalf. Campbell has said repeatedly that his job is to do all he can to communicate government policy, and that he intends to do this by making full use of every available media outlet. Nevertheless, if at the same time he has the temporary status of a civil servant and draws an annual salary from the state of £96,275, he should not mock those who might wish to examine the methods he has used to 'grab the agenda', especially on those occasions when, as a self-confessed party propagandist, he has done so in 'a political context'. Downing Street has exercised unprecedented authority over the flow of information to the news media from across Whitehall; this level of control, combined with a deep-seated urge within New Labour to control and manipulate what is said on the party's behalf, raises important ethical and constitutional questions, which need to be addressed.

DRAWING THE
BROTHERS' CLAWS

'Look, it must be very sad being a labour correspondent, reporting all those meaningless resolutions. I do wish you could find a different agenda.'

Tony Blair, Labour Party leader, speaking to Nicholas Jones,

13 September 1995

Whenever Tony Blair has been accused at open meetings of becoming a control freak and of presiding over an autocratic party machine, his response has been brisk and to the point. He has asked the rank and file to remember the indiscipline of the 1980s when Labour was unelectable. In his judgement, the chaotic state of the party during those long years out of office provided every justification for a thorough overhaul; and in order to give the party the required sharp, professional edge, the leadership had to impose tight control over its structure and organisation. Indeed, so great has been the party's wish to escape from the horrors of the past that Blair had little difficulty in his early years as Prime Minister in silencing those voices at Labour gatherings who were starting to express criticism of his leadership. He has spoken frequently of how his own formative years in the party were scarred by the turmoil and strife that kept Labour out of power for so long. He was twenty-nine when he launched his political career, standing as Labour's candidate in the Beaconsfield by-election in May 1982; he lost his deposit. Listening to him speak so evocatively about his own experiences, I have felt considerable sympathy with his argument that the labour and trade union movement stood no chance of winning back the public's respect unless it undertook wholesale reform.

As a labour correspondent for BBC radio at the end of the 1970s, I was one of the journalists who gained national exposure by reporting the industrial turbulence of those years. At a time of considerable press hostility towards both Labour and the unions, my own reports must have made depressing listening for an aspiring politician, and may perhaps have contributed to the damage of which Blair complained. The lurch to the left in the labour movement after Margaret Thatcher's defeat of the Labour government led by James Callaghan was fuelled in no small part by an upsurge in industrial militancy. The numerous pay disputes and strikes that constituted the 1979 'winter of discontent' provided a rollercoaster ride of one fast-moving story after another, and they inflicted deep and lasting wounds to the standing and credibility of the Labour politicians of the day. Then, no sooner had the labour and industrial journalists started adjusting to the change of government than we were back on the picket lines reporting the mayhem that erupted in protest at the Conservatives' trade union and employment reforms. Thatcher was so successful in this arena that she almost managed to destroy the *raison d'être* of the labour and industrial reporters.

Blair finished off what Thatcher started: she smashed the unions' industrial muscle; he all but silenced their political voice. I think I can claim with some justification to be one of the early victims of New Labour's 'control freakery'. Once Blair became Labour's employment spokesman in 1989, and later after he became party leader, he singled me out on more than one occasion to ask why I persisted in reporting the progress of what he thought were pretty pointless trade union motions at Labour's annual conferences. He was clearly annoyed at the way the unions could still, on occasion, set the political agenda. Once in a position to do so, with power in his grasp, Blair wasted no time in controlling and then curbing, at least for some years, a partic-ularly troublesome source of unwelcome news stories.

Whenever he chided me about my persistence in reporting trade union affairs he was always pleasant but forthright. He could not understand why I failed to see the futility of my work. Looking back on those early encounters with him, I realise how my enthusiasm as a labour correspondent must have grated on him and other like-minded young reformers whose political careers so far had seen nothing but defeat and disappointment. The long-drawn-out collapse of the Callaghan government, like the disintegration a couple of decades later of John Major's administration, provided some of the most absorbing years of my career. The months and weeks leading up to those two election defeats bore many similarities. In each case the Prime Minister had effectively lost control; both were overwhelmed by infighting within their cabinets and parties. Labour struggled without success to curb industrial militancy fuelled by inflation and high pay demands; the Conservatives were beset by their own internal dissent over Britain's future relationship with Europe, and were also being dragged down by allegations of financial 'sleaze'. Both prime ministers hung on to the bitter end, and the slow, lingering deaths of their administrations gave journalists something to get their teeth into. We sensed the defeats that were to come; but Callaghan and Major saw no alternative to fighting on, for month after month. The final demise of an ailing government is always unpredictable. Events moved so fast during the countdown to polling day in 1979 and again in 1997 that life for the news media was often a hand-to-mouth existence. Even before they had finished one story, reporters were sent off to the next assignment. Any journalist who was prepared to put in the hours was never short of exposure.

Our fervour in chasing each successive setback must have saddened if not sickened those politicians and party members who would have to pay the price in the longer term for our short-term domination of the headlines. The baleful looks I got from dejected Conservatives in the immediate aftermath of Major's defeat mirrored the downcast demeanour of those Labour MPs who had realised years earlier that they had most to fear from the left's ascendancy. For a time there were many in both parties who could not stomach the company of the journalists who had profited from their misfortune. And indeed, from the journalist's point of view, there was much profit, in terms of career development, to be had, as I discovered myself. In the late 1970s, having been a reporter for BBC radio for several years, I was looking for a chance to move on from general news, and was ready to consider any opportunity to develop some lasting expertise. More and more specialist correspondents were being appointed to help fill the extra airtime being generated by the rapid expansion that was starting to take place in television and radio output, and one section of the newsroom that needed strengthening was industrial reporting. The Conservative government led by Edward Heath had been defeated in the wake of the 1974 miners' strike and the three-day week, and Labour's re-election had done little to curb industrial militancy. The expertise of the BBC's industrial correspondents always seemed to be in demand.

The problems on which they reported, of course, were not new. Strikes in the pits, docks, power stations and car factories had become so commonplace by the late 1950s and early 1960s that the damage they were doing to the economy could no longer be ignored. In 1969 Harold Wilson's government announced plans to fine strikers and trade unions involved in unofficial walk-outs. Callaghan, then Home Secretary, was implacably opposed to the legal sanctions contained in the white paper *In Place of Strife*, for which the Secretary of State for Employment and Productivity, Barbara Castle, had argued so forcefully. Later, after negotiations between Wilson and the TUC, the penalty clauses were withdrawn on the promise of new union rules to curtail unofficial strikes and inter-union disputes. After Wilson's defeat in the 1970 election, legal curbs were introduced by the Conservatives; but the 1971 Industrial Relations Act proved ineffective and, after his own defeat in 1974, Heath blamed Labour for having impeded the battle against inflation by undermining his legislation. On taking office in 1976, Callaghan found that the union militancy which had dogged Labour in the mid-1960s had spread far beyond the traditional industrial workplaces. Disputes were breaking out right across the public sector. Local authorities, schools and hospitals had all become targets for industrial action in protest at years of wage restraint.

My opportunity had arrived: in 1978 an extra correspondent was required to report the protracted public sector pay negotiations, which eventually foundered in one of the most damaging breakdowns in British industrial relations, culminating in Callaghan's election defeat the following year. There had been few volunteers for the task of trying to disentangle the complicated pay machinery of the National Health Service and the local authorities. Many journalists had an intense dislike of labour and industrial reporting because it could so often be both tiresome and unproductive. When there was an agreement, the details could often be confusing and hard to explain; and once a dispute had been settled, newsrooms tended to lose interest. I soon found myself spending day after day standing outside buildings where meetings were being held by union officials and management representatives. During the subsequent decade I would clock up countless hours on the doorsteps of employers' offices and union headquarters waiting for the conclusion of pay talks and other negotiations.

The significance of the 'winter of discontent' was that it drew in union members who had not previously taken industrial action and resulted in disruption to a wide range of services. Refuse collectors, water and sewerage workers, gravediggers, ambulance drivers and hospital porters were just some of those who struck or worked to rule. The management response was made doubly difficult by rivalry between different groups of workers within each local authority or hospital. The unions were also in competition with each other – there were often four or five unions representing the same group of workers – and that produced bitter inter-union disputes. Any attempt by a journalist to summarise a possible outcome to a new or improved offer illustrated the sheer complexity of the problem the government faced: '. . . it is a pay deal that might prove acceptable to members of the Confederation of Health Service Employees, and has attracted some interest from the National and Local Government Officers' Association, but is unlikely to appeal to the National Union of Public Employees and has already been rejected by two of the biggest unions, the Transport and General Workers' Union and the General and Municipal Workers' Union . . .' Eventually the confusing prolif- eration of names and acronyms, which had itself proved such a barrier to clear industrial reporting, was swept away by a succession of union mergers necessitated by a halving in union membership as a result of the events of the next few years.

Margaret Thatcher's victory in 1979 brought about a fundamental change in the nature of industrial action. She was determined to increase the efficiency of the nationalised industries and end decades of compromise by management. Most of the major disputes of the 1980s were about resisting industrial change and protecting jobs, rather than fighting for better wages and conditions. One by one the great industrial heartlands of Britain were torn apart by the imposi- tion of new working practices, by redundancies and ultimately by privatisation. Shipyards, steelworks, the railways, coal mines and the print rooms of the national newspapers all became locations for the set-piece confrontations that resulted from the drive for rationalisation and modernisation.

Thatcher's assault on trade union power was highly politicised and put enormous pressure on the Labour Party. In the early 1980s appeals for solidarity with striking workers, and campaigns against privatisation and closures, tended to dominate the proceedings at party conference. Union leaders were determined to get as much support and publicity as they could for their causes; but there were many within the Labour leadership who resented the way the party was continually getting dragged into damaging and often unpopular disputes. When it came to trying to work out what would happen during these divisive conference debates, the labour and industrial correspondents often had the edge over political journalists, and were sometimes a step ahead of the party's own officials as well. We tended to be well primed as to the likely outcome because we had spent months following the twists and turns of each dispute. We were usually on relatively good terms with the relevant union leaders and knew their true intentions. Our understanding of the arguments surrounding the key policy debates was a source of irritation to party managers concerned that news coverage of the conference should be presented in the best possible light for the party. As we had invariably spent much of the summer visiting the separate annual conferences of the major unions, we had a pretty good idea of the approaches their delegates would take when the votes were held. The understanding we gained of the pivotal role which the union movement could exercise over the Labour Party's affairs was ideal preparation for reporting politics, and indeed, over the years many labour and industrial correspondents moved on to join the lobby at Westminster. I had already spent a period working at the House of Commons in the late 1960s, as a parliamentary reporter for *The Times*, and when I returned to political reporting in January 1988, I found my decade on the industrial beat was put to good use almost immediately.

After his defeat in the 1987 general election, the Labour leader Neil Kinnock embarked on a fundamental policy review, which resulted in his party accepting the vast majority of the employment and trade union laws introduced by the Conservatives. His willingness to take on the unions meant I was fortunate in being able to maintain my long-standing interest in labour affairs, although the news media were now taking far less notice of the subject. By the late 1980s Margaret Thatcher's success in curbing union power had resulted in a sharp reduction in the level of strike action. The union movement was in retreat, and the labour and industrial staff had lost their prominent place in the journalistic hierarchy of most newsrooms, finding that the space and airtime they had once commanded was increasingly being filled by business and financial correspondents, to whom we rather mockingly referred as the 'footsoldiers for popular capitalism'. Their workload had expanded out of all recognition as a result of the competitive forces unleashed by privatisation and the moves to widen share ownership. Although he resented the popularity of many of Thatcher's achievements, and smarted under her continued electoral success, Kinnock recognised that the Conservatives had performed a great service for the Labour leadership: the long war of attrition between unions and government was over. Four prime ministers had spent twenty years grappling with union power; now, finally, the legislation was in place. While the unions might remain a thorn in the flesh of the party, Kinnock knew that no future Labour prime minister was likely to be beaten by brute industrial force; thanks to Thatcherism, his party was free at last from the charge that it was simply the political arm of the union movement.

Although my long background in labour reporting had less relevance now than in previous years, I noticed that my presence at news briefings and other events was always viewed with suspicion by the Labour Party's well-established campaigns and communications director, Peter Mandelson. He had been in charge of the publicity department since October 1985 and, although he had won plaudits for the professionalism of Labour's 1987 election campaign, he agreed with Kinnock that the party still had much to do if it was to win back the trust and support of the electorate. He was anxious to obliterate all reminders of the maulings that party leaders had endured in the past at the hands of the unions, and was intent on doing all he could to thwart attempts by journalists like myself to report Labour's affairs from a union perspective. On one celebrated occasion, not long after my return to Westminster, Mandelson told me to my face that he remained suspicious about my motives: 'I don't trust you. Once a labour correspondent, always a labour correspondent. Never trust labour correspondents.' This remark may have had something to do with an encounter between myself and Tony Blair a few months after his appointment as shadow employment secretary in November 1989. Blair was preparing for the launch in May 1990 of the party's new policy document, *Looking to the Future*, which endorsed much of the Conservatives' employment legislation, including provisions on secret ballots and the sequestration of union funds, restrictions on secondary action and the ban on mass picketing. Mandelson was reluctant to allow me to interview Blair for a report for *Breakfast News,* which was intended to preview the policy launch.

Within weeks of taking on the employment brief Blair had surprised union leaders by the speed with which he had persuaded the party to accept the latest draft of the European Commission's Social Charter, which banned the closed shop. As he had shown such clear resolve in insisting that every worker had to have the freedom 'to join or not to join' a union, I expected him to be pretty positive about the forthcoming policy document. Mandelson clearly had his own ideas about any exchange on the subject, and I sensed trouble when he and Blair arrived for the interview on College Green. Blair's office had already indicated that he wished to withdraw from the arrangement, and Mandelson said he saw no advantage to the party in allowing the shadow employment secretary to participate in what he feared would be one of my 'usual knockabout reports on Labour and the unions'. Although Blair relented and finally agreed to answer one prerecorded question, he obviously shared Mandelson's reservations, and for the first time I came face to face with Blair's masterly control of television and radio interviews. Knowing that I had agreed not to challenge his answer, Blair simply avoided my question – whether his proposals on employment law would damage the party's relationship with the unions – and made no reference to that relationship in his response. Instead, he concentrated on Labour's commitment to training and their plans to meet the skills shortage.

Blair could not have been friendlier and he smiled at Mandelson's parting shot, which amounted to another tirade about my past misrepresentation of Labour's policy and about what he was sure would be another report that amounted to nothing more than a repeat of 'the same old story of Neil Kinnock being kicked around by the unions'.

In subsequent years, whenever I had to report Blair's speeches to union gatherings, I liked to remind myself of that encounter. He had demonstrated an effortless ability to sidestep awkward questions. He had also displayed a resolute determination to distance himself and his party from attempts by the news media to link the Labour Party to the trade unions. Memories of our confrontation on College Green came flooding back a year after Blair was elected party leader, when he addressed the 1995 TUC conference. Blair had some tough words not only for the delegates but also for the labour and industrial correspondents who were there to report his speech. He gave the unions a foretaste of the uncompromising position on employment law he intended to adopt at the 1997 election. There would be no repeal of all the Conservatives' employment laws: 'No mass or flying pickets . . . All those ghosts of time past, it is time to leave them where they lie.' Blair then turned to 'my old friends, those labour correspondents' who liked 'living in a time warp', perpetuating their 'old rituals of winding up the issues' before TUC conferences. No one seriously believed any longer that 'passing resolutions' was going to deflect a Labour government, and there was no point in journalists 'dramatising each event as if the destiny of the nation hung on it'. Blair's press secretary, Alastair Campbell, had told me the day before that he had written much of the speech; and, as he had always been pretty withering about the work of labour and industrial correspondents, I suspected that he had encouraged Blair to put us in our place.

Next morning, before leaving Brighton for London, Blair and Campbell paid a brief visit to a breakfast rally at the Grand Hotel. As they left I thanked them for the name check, but said I was not sure about living in a 'time warp'. Blair laughed and then paused for a moment, taking me slightly to one side. 'Look, it must be very sad being a labour correspondent, reporting all those meaningless resolutions. I do wish you could find a different agenda.' Mulling over later what he had said, I realised that I had been rather foolish in trying to mock his remarks; but what had made the greatest impression on me was his engaging manner. During several previous encounters I had come to realise that he took a far greater interest in the news media than he ever let on publicly, and that he often took the initiative when in the company of journalists. I almost felt that here was an invitation: 'If you are interested, come and join us.' In later years it came as no surprise to me that, once installed as Prime Minister, Blair recruited a succession of leading correspondents and broadcasters to work on his behalf. One of them was Philip Bassett, industrial editor of *The Times*, himself among the correspondents who reported Blair's speech in Brighton. Bassett told me at the time that it was no surprise the labour correspondents had been criticised for being out of touch: at a recent CBI event he had attended, Blair had asked about the identities of the journalists present, and indicated his dislike of the labour and industrial group. Bassett was one of several candidates Blair interviewed as a possible press secretary, and although that job went to Campbell, a former political editor of the *Daily Mirror*, Bassett left *The Times* six months after Labour's election victory to join the staff of Downing Street's newly created strategic communications unit, which opened up a No. 10 website on the Internet, and was given the task of preparing and publishing an annual report for the government.

The planned build-up to Blair's 1995 TUC speech had taken something of a knock because of the publication that morning of a leaked document obtained by the *Guardian*. It was written by a political strategist, Philip Gould, who had been Kinnock's polling adviser and who was now advising Blair on preparations for the 1997 election campaign. Gould proposed a 'unitary command structure leading directly to the party leader' and suggested that Campbell should take the lead in disseminating 'the message'. The document was headed 'The Unfinished Revolution' – a phrase Gould subsequently used as the title for a book published in 1998 that told the story of Labour's election triumph, 'the apotheosis of a revolution within Labour'. When he briefed journalists before Blair's speech, Campbell said the leakage of the document was of no consequence and would not change what he promised would be a 'completely uncompromising defence' of the need to modernise the Labour Party. For the unions, this meant acknowledging that they should no longer be seen as 'instruments of political influence'.

Rodney Bickerstaffe, general secretary of Unison, told me after the speech that it had been 'a pretty chilling message', and he thought the line Blair seemed to be pushing, that 'anything goes to get power', was worrying. It implied that a future Labour government would see itself as being independent from the party. Blair had surprised delegates at the Labour conference the previous year by announcing in his first speech as leader that he wanted to abandon the party's historic commitment, set out in Clause Four of its constitution, to the 'common ownership of the means of production, distribution and exchange'. After hearing his clear exposition at Brighton a year later of the need for the party to speed up the pace of modernisation, I realised that he was deadly serious in his intention to limit the unions' contribution to policy-making and to overhaul what the modernisers considered was an arcane and cumbersome conference procedure for debating policy motions.

I was disappointed by the negative tone Blair had adopted when he spoke so dismissively about my reporting of all those 'meaningless resolutions' from the unions, and I could understand Bickerstaffe's irritation. Blair seemed intent on putting control over the news agenda, and his desire to eliminate stories which he disliked, above the need to maintain channels for genuine debate and for allowing union and party delegates an opportunity to vote for what they believed in. Campaigns that had sometimes succeeded, years later, in changing government policy often gained national publicity for the first time after being taken up by the unions or constituency parties. Labour's 1997 manifesto commitment to introduce a 'sensibly set national minimum wage' was the fruition of years of resolute campaigning by Bickerstaffe and the leaders of other unions representing low-paid workers. It was at the 1982 TUC conference, in his first speech as the new general secretary of the National Union of Public Employees, that Bickerstaffe moved a composite motion calling for a 'vigorous campaign' to get 'government action on minimum wages'. When he spoke again on the subject the following year, more unions backed the campaign because of mounting concern over plans by the Thatcher government to abolish the long-established wages councils, which set minimum rates of pay for low-paid workers in trades like catering and hairdressing. Bickerstaffe's long and initially rather lonely crusade to persuade the party to commit itself to statutory protection for the lowest paid finally achieved success in April 1999 when the government introduced a minimum hourly rate of £3.60 for workers aged twenty-two and over. Other pioneering work from the early 1980s has also stood the test of time. A card vote was required at the 1983 TUC conference to ensure support for the National Union of Seamen's refusal to handle or transport nuclear waste to be dumped in the western approaches to the Atlantic, off Land's End. Within two months of the conference the government had suspended sea dumping. A campaign by the National Union of Agricultural and Allied Workers for controls on the use of dangerous pesticides, in particular the herbicide 245-T, proved far more arduous but no less rewarding.

It seemed that the new leadership was not disposed to set much store by this route of policy evolution. On being elected leader, Blair wasted no time in stepping up the process of internal party reform started by Neil Kinnock and continued by his successor, John Smith. Their hopes were nearly dashed at the 1993 Labour conference when Smith succeeded by only the narrowest of margins in securing approval for the introduction of one member one vote in the procedure for selecting Labour's parliamentary candidates. Some unions were bitterly opposed to the removal of their block votes at constituency level and the debate turned into a cliff-hanger. The majority in favour was 0.2 per cent of the total conference vote. Blair, Mandelson and the other modernisers were shocked to see Smith pitched into a desperate, last-minute struggle to claw back support. The shake-up Blair was now planning would go far further than any previous Labour leader had dared contemplate. Within a year of his election, leading members of the party's ruling national executive committee had attended seminars at the Cranfield School of Management. By January 1996 the executive committee had established the 'party into power project' which a year later published *Labour into Power: A Framework for Partnership*, setting out the changes which would have to be made to ensure there was a 'united, co-operative approach' in the relationship between a future Labour government and the party.

In defending the decision to take action well ahead of the 1997 election, the modernisers cited in their justification the example of Harold Wilson, who, despite winning a majority of ninety-six in the 1966 general election, was in no position to take full advantage of his success.

At that time there were no plans in place to modernise the party's constitution so as to limit the opportunities for internal dissent, an omission for which the reformers believed Wilson paid a heavy price. Blair was anxious to seize his moment long before polling day. At a meeting in January 1997 the national executive approved *Labour into Power* by twenty-two votes to one. In future, policy-making was to take place not on the hoof at conference but over a three-year cycle. Constituency parties and trade unions would no longer be able to submit wide-ranging motions to the annual conference, and the time allocated for debates there would curtailed. Instead, there would be a rolling programme of work to be conducted by the party's national policy forum, which would be enlarged and strengthened. Local policy forums would allow party members to be 'involved in policy debate at an earlier stage through local discussion'. In my report for that evening's news bulletin on BBC radio, I said previous Labour prime ministers and party leaders who had clashed with the conference would have 'jumped at the chance' to make the changes which Tony Blair looked like achieving. Delegates opposed to key policy decisions would no longer be able to disrupt the conference by declaring 'open season' in their criticism of the party. With his blueprint for reform in place, and having already ensured it was backed by the ruling executive committee, the new Prime Minister was in a commanding position when he sought approval at the 1997 conference for the sweeping rule changes contained in the document, which had subsequently been retitled *Partnership in Power*. However, by that time Labour's landslide election victory and Blair's parliamentary majority of 179, rather than assuaging the concerns of the activists, seemed only to have intensified their fears.

Most of the motions on party reform tabled for the conference were opposed to the changes, and over eighty called for a year's delay in implementing them. Left-wing newspapers and magazines campaigned against changes which the Labour MP Tony Benn said would establish a 'top-down party on the American model'. In an interview for *Labour Left Briefing*, Benn predicted that the leadership would end up obtaining 'much firmer control' over the party and that the conference would become like an American convention, where ministers made statements and there was a structured response. The refusal to let local parties take their motions direct to the conference was seen by another long-standing Labour MP, Dennis Skinner, as the likely source of even greater divisions in the future. In an article for *Socialist Campaign Group News*, he said the party had always been proud of holding annual conferences that allowed people 'to speak out', contrasting this with the rallies held by the Conservatives. 'The truth is you can't mechanically stop dissent from finding expression.'

Notwithstanding these prominent expressions of dissent, Blair need have had no fears about the outcome; the conference gave his plan its overwhelming support. Tom Sawyer, the party's general secretary, told those delegates who were seeking to defer the decision that the restructuring had to go ahead to prevent the internal divisions that had opened up under each previous Labour government and that had always ended in defeat at the polls. 'We must never let that happen again.' One concession to the trade unions was that they were allowed to retain a 50 per cent share of any conference votes.

The debate attracted far less publicity than anticipated because of an unexpected boost for the Labour MP Ken Livingstone, who had used an eve-of-conference article in the New Statesman to accuse Blair of exploiting the 'loyalty that accrues to a new government'. In the results announced that afternoon of the election for places on the national executive committee, Livingstone had succeeded in defeating Peter Mandelson, who had spent the first six months of the new government serving in the Cabinet Office as minister without portfolio. Mandelson's decision that summer to campaign for a seat on the executive had caused considerable controversy. His argument for standing was that he was anxious to 'step out of the shadows' and build up his support within the party. There were seven vacancies on the executive and Livingstone took fifth place with 83,669 votes.

Mandelson was the leading runner-up, on 68,023 votes. Needless to say, the defeat of the Prime Minister's close friend and adviser, at Labour's first conference since winning power, dominated the newspapers next morning. 'Activists get their revenge on spin doctor Mandelson' was the headline in the *Daily Express*. Writing in the *Mirror*, Mandelson said he had no regrets. 'A taste of humility is good for everyone, particularly for a politician . . . Many in the media claim that as Labour's arch moderniser, I have no popularity in the party. 68,023 votes proved that wrong.' The left hailed Livingstone's victory as the clearest possible indication that the socialist wing of the party would not be silenced. An editorial in the *Daily Telegraph* said it was Livingstone's 'greatest coup' since his 'glory days' as leader of the former Greater London Council.

For a former labour correspondent like myself, the 1997 Labour conference was a rather nostalgic occasion. Rituals that our group had followed for years were about to disappear. My first duty on the Saturday morning of the conference weekend was to report on the outcome of the 'compositing meeting' where party officials, union representatives and constituency delegates went through the agenda to establish an agreed basis for the various debates. That year the agenda ran to 119 pages and listed 560 motions for debate. Wherever possible, a group of motions on the same issue would be fashioned into a single composite. Sometimes there would be no dispute about the wording, but often it was impossible to find a way to bridge the opposing points of view. If there was no agreement there might have to be two opposing composites; alternatively, some of the original motions could be left on the order paper and put to the conference individually. Arguments over the wording could last all day as rival camps went through the proposed composites line by line, each seeking to protect its position. More often than not, by dint of sheer persistence, it would be delegates from the left of the party who would succeed in inserting a phrase or sub-clause that would come back to haunt the leadership. Party officials were fond of saying that the three essentials required for compositing were patience, a pair of scissors and a pot of paste. Often their work in cobbling together an agreed text would result in long, rambling composites that were not only unintelligible to the lay reader but also contradictory.

Blair and the reformers thought the whole process was absurd and archaic. They believed last-minute bargaining on the eve of conference was an unsatisfactory and dangerous way to make policy. Every year there was a risk of getting caught up in a behind-the-scenes fix which would allow the media to accuse the leadership of indulging in 'horse-trading' and doing deals in 'smoke-filled rooms'. Still, while I would be the first to agree that the leadership were often ambushed and outmanoeuvred by the unions and left-wing activists, the procedure had some strengths. Delegates felt they were directly involved, and although reporters were never allowed access to the compositing meetings, it was heartening to see representatives from constituencies up and down the country arriving ready to put the case for what were perhaps obscure or unpopular positions. Sometimes they would not back down and insisted on forcing a vote. Occasionally a constituency motion that had escaped the compositing process might provide an unexpected rallying point from which delegates could challenge the platform. There were dangers for the leadership in each stage of the process, because once the wording of the composite motions had been agreed, they had to be considered the following Sunday morning at the delegation meetings held by the individual trade unions to work out their responses and decide how they should vote in the week ahead. At this point it could be hard to predict what might happen, and party officials would have to scurry back and forth trying to find out which way the big unions intended to cast their block votes. Political journalists, who enjoyed the traditional political theatre of Labour conferences, marvelled at the dogged perseverance of the labour correspondents in trying to keep up with these byzantine procedures.

At the 1997 conference – excepting Peter Mandelson's setback – there were no policy defeats, and there was little to dent the continuing sense of euphoria following Labour's election victory that May. The theme of Blair's address was that he wanted to modernise Britain in the same way that he had modernised his party. Britain could become 'a beacon to the world' by being the 'best place to live . . . to bring up children . . . to lead a fulfilled life . . . to grow old'. In his closing speech, the Deputy Prime Minister, John Prescott, said the overwhelming vote for *Partnership in Power* meant there was an opportunity for party members across the country to start discussing and shaping the government's future priorities. The aim of the new rolling programme was to ensure that by the 2000 conference the party had considered and approved policy documents that could form a basis for the next manifesto. In addition to the revamped national policy forum, there were eight policy commissions and numerous local forums. When the first reports on health, welfare reform, and crime and justice were presented to the 1998 conference, it was said that 10,000 party members had participated in the discussions. By the time the three-year rolling programme was completed, 40,000 party members were said have attended forums up and down the country. The final reports were considered at a weekend session of the national policy forum held at Exeter University in July 2000 – a far cry from the composite meetings of old. Because the rolling programme was so long-drawn-out and so all-embracing, there were very few focal points to attract the attention of the news media and, as the conference was always going to have the last word, few political journalists thought it was worth going all the way to Exeter. The only significant news story of the weekend was Tony Blair's speech to the forum, and that attracted a certain amount of coverage largely, if not only, because it came at the end of what turned out to be a particularly stressful week for the Prime Minister. After having been criticised for suggesting that drunken louts should be taken to cash machines to pay on-the-spot fines, Blair learned that his sixteen-year-old son Euan had been found drunk and incapable in Leicester Square, for which Euan was subsequently given a reprimand by the police.

I was one of only six journalists who remained in Exeter for the weekend, and although party officials seemed entirely relaxed about the lack of interest in the forum, the absence of reporters was seen by the left as confirming their belief that the leadership had succeeded in their twin objectives of gaining almost total control over the policy-making process and ensuring that it was no longer as newsworthy as it had once been. Mark Seddon, editor of the left-wing newspaper *Tribune*, who served on the forum in his capacity as a member of the national executive, told me that the media had only itself to blame for letting the party get away with it. 'Here in Exeter, where the real decisions are being taken, there are only six journalists and one television crew, but there will be hundreds of reporters at the party conference covering a soap opera which the spin doctors will be manipulating.' There was considerable justification for Seddon's criticism; but except for a handful from the left, few of the forum's 175 representatives were prepared to answer questions posed by those reporters who were there. Cabinet ministers did attend the sessions that covered their areas of responsibility, but except for a few pleasantries they too had little or nothing to say.

Of far greater concern to another of the left's representatives, Christine Shawcroft, was her failure to persuade the forum to allow an amendment to be made to the economic policy document. She wanted to see increases in the state pension linked to the rise in earnings (rather than prices), but her move was ruled out of order because party officials said pensions were covered by the welfare reform document, which had been approved by the 1999 conference. 'I was told there was no way the policy could be challenged or changed. They're just stifling debate. It's obnoxious.' Ms Shawcroft's experience was not uncommon. As each policy document was approved over the three-year programme, the party succeeded in closing off all possibility of its being amended, thus depriving party activists of an opportunity to mount a challenge at conference. The restoration of the link between pensions and earnings, which was broken by the Thatcher government, was an issue that had caused division in previous years and the only remaining chance of getting it debated at the 2000 conference in Brighton was by tabling a contemporary motion. The four to be debated would be chosen in a ballot on the opening day. As there had been mounting criticism all summer over the government's insensitivity that April in granting an annual increase of only 75p a week in the basic state pension, the leadership had already indicated there would be a statement to the conference by the Secretary of State for Social Security, Alistair Darling. Nevertheless, the issue of pensions topped the ballot and without any real warning the party leadership and the journalists found themselves re-entering the 'time warp' about which Blair had complained in 1995. The tight control that had been exercised over the two previous conferences was about to slip away as the leadership lost its grip on the news agenda.

At last the rank and file had found a cause around which to rally; and it could not have come at a more awkward moment for Blair and his cabinet, struggling to regain their composure after a summer of political setbacks. Protests in September by farmers and road hauliers over the duty on petrol and diesel had caught ministers off guard. After a chaotic few days of fuel shortages and disruption, the loss of confidence in the government was so great that for almost a fortnight the Conservatives moved ahead of Labour in the opinion polls, for the first time since John Major's 1992 election victory. Not surprisingly, contrition was the order of the day at the party conference. The first key speech of the week, by the Chancellor of the Exchequer, Gordon Brown, was greeted next morning by the banner headline 'In retreat' across the front page of the *Daily Mail*. The paper said that, after all their 'tough talk', Blair and Brown were 'set to give ground to pension and petrol protesters'. Brown promised that the pre-Budget report he would be delivering within a few weeks of the conference would 'do more' for all pensioners. A new pension credit would be introduced in 2003, and in the meantime there would be 'transitional arrangements to the benefit of all pensioners'. Brown's pledge to 'do more' was seen by political journalists as the clearest possible signal that the government would grant pensioners a rise well above the increases of around £2 a week for single pensioners and £3 for couples that the existing formula seemed likely to produce, once the autumn inflation figures were known.

As soon as Brown had completed his speech, reporters asked for more details. The Chancellor's chief economic adviser, Ed Balls, and his press spokesman, Ian Austin, both went to the media centre; but instead of using the briefing room laid on by the party's director of communications, Lance Price, the two men walked out and spoke to reporters on the steps to the conference hall. During a chaotic ten-minute briefing, which for a moment or two verged on a shouting match, Balls kept repeating the same line when asked if Brown was promising more than £2 and £3 a week: 'Yes, there will be extra help for all pensioners. Yes, it will go beyond those numbers. Yes, pensioners won't be disappointed.' As Balls tried to make himself heard, Austin rushed around the perimeters of the mêlée ordering television crews to stop filming. He said the briefing was off the record and off camera. On returning to the media centre, the journalists tried to work out what Balls' statement had meant. As the Conservatives and Liberal Democrats had already indicated they would give pensioners weekly increases of £5 for single pensioners and £8 for couples, the consensus was that Brown would have at least to match what the opposition parties were offering. Next day *The Times*, *Daily Telegraph*, *Daily Mail*, *Daily Express*, *Sun* and *Mirror* all agreed that the increases could be worth at least £5 and £8 a week. Even before the political editors had filed their stories early that evening, word of the line that they were going to take next morning had reached Dan Hodges, press officer to John Edmonds, general secretary of the GMB union, who was on his way to a now old-fashioned event which was about to start at the conference hotel – a compositing meeting: for there were so many individual contemporary motions on pensions that a composite had to be constructed.

The sticking point, during a process which went on for three days, was a futile struggle to find a form of words that, while not tying the hands of the Chancellor, would allow the conference to express support for a restoration of the link between pensions and earnings. Edmonds was encouraged by what he had heard coming out of the media centre and he told me he understood that, at a later briefing for political editors, the Chancellor's advisers had not challenged the figures of £5 and £8. 'If this speculation is right, then we're making progress and we'll help Gordon create a nice atmosphere, if that's what he wants.' His press officer, Dan Hodges, was explicit about their tactics. 'If the Chancellor isn't prepared to give any figures himself, we'll help him fill in the blanks.' Although Edmonds felt optimistic, the Unison general secretary, Rodney Bickerstaffe, whose union was in a dominant position at the compositing meeting, was nowhere near so confident. On the promise of a statement next morning from the Secretary of State for Social Security, Alistair Darling, the meeting adjourned. Ed Balls and Ian Austin had also got wind of the line the newspapers were taking, and in the middle of the evening I took a telephone call from Austin. He insisted that he and Balls had not given out the figures of £5 and £8. When I asked if the figures were incorrect, he simply said the Chancellor's office had not authorised them. Later, interviewed for *Newsnight*, John Edmonds accepted that there was confusion but said that if the speculation was correct, and if there were similar increases in years two and three, that would very helpful to those unions bound by long-standing policy to vote in favour of restoring the earnings link. Edmonds told me that Brown's advisers were unwise to have given such an inconclusive briefing. 'Ed Balls will talk to journalists but not to the union leaders who are most closely involved – and this is from a government which promised us it had stopped spinning.'

Next day all attention was focused on the Prime Minister's conference speech to see whether he would firm up the Chancellor's assurances. Blair accepted the government had taken a knock in recent weeks. 'It happened on my watch and I take responsibility.' He insisted he had been listening and he realised people were angry over disappointments like the 75p pension increase. 'I tell you now, as Gordon made crystal clear yesterday, we get the message.' However, there was no further clarification during the day over the likely size of future pension increases and, when the compositing meeting reconvened, the struggle continued to come up with a composite with which both the delegates and the Chancellor could live. Rodney Bickerstaffe finally emerged with the text that would be put to the conference next day. As befitted the drama of the occasion, the ghosts of previous compositing sagas seemed to have been there to guide the hand of the wordsmiths as their deliberations drew to a close. Two words – 'for example' – were inserted into the key sentence in the hope that they would give the Chancellor room for manoeuvre and allow him to save face. The composite motion called on the government 'to introduce further measures to reduce pensioner poverty and boost pensioner income by an immediate and substantial increase in the basic state pension and by linking the basic state pension to, for example, average earnings or inflation, whichever is the greater'. Bickerstaffe and Edmonds believed there was sufficient flexibility in this wording to show that the government retained a completely free hand over future increases.

But the Chancellor would have none of it. He had left Brighton the day before, immediately after his speech, in order to attend a meeting of the International Monetary Fund in Prague, and the Treasury had told the BBC the previous week that he would remain there for the next two days. In the event Brown returned to Brighton the following evening and, after being shown the composite motion, asked to see Bickerstaffe and Edmonds early next morning, well ahead of the pensions debate that afternoon. There followed what can only be described as the worst possible nightmare for a New Labour control freak. Reporters, photographers and television crews jammed the foyer of the Metropole Hotel as the drama unfolded. Brown held court in a room upstairs and leading members of the compositing group waited in a private room behind the hotel reception area. Bickerstaffe, Edmonds and a succession of other luminaries went backwards and forwards all morning as Brown tried in vain to persuade them to strike out any mention of a link between pensions and average earnings. As the motion had to be considered by the ruling national executive before it could be debated by the conference, some committee members joined the throng in the hotel foyer.

On seeing Bickerstaffe and Edmonds mount the stairs for yet another meeting with the Chancellor, Margaret Prosser, who represented the Transport and General Workers' Union, said she could not understand what all the fuss was about because it was obvious the government would kick the motion into touch by recalling the national policy forum once the pensions uprating had been announced. 'Rodney and John are under such a lot of pressure they are now in a complete doodah. New Labour have surrounded themselves with all these bright young things but they haven't a clue about managing the party. If needs be we were always able to composite, with a pair of scissors and a pot of glue and paste, something together.' Every time a prominent figure appeared in the foyer there was a media scrum and reporters shouted out demanding the latest news. At one point Ian Austin and Ed Balls emerged to give a briefing. Balls said there was no possibility of Brown accepting a fudge. 'If the conference pushes it to a vote, so be it. There is no question of us accepting the earnings link or pre-empting the pre-Budget report. Yes, this is a hard-line position, there will be no compromise.' A few minutes later Austin re-emerged to emphasise that it had been a 'constructive meeting'. He said Balls' remarks were off the record and must not be sourced to the Chancellor or his staff. Later, a separate briefing was given on behalf of the party by Lance

Price who reaffirmed the line that a conference defeat would not change the Chancellor's mind.

After an inconclusive meeting between Bickerstaffe and Blair, a vote had to be taken. The compositing group decided by eight votes to five to ask for the motion to be remitted – sent back for reconsideration by the party, rather than decided upon by the conference – a move the national executive endorsed by eighteen votes to eight; but Bickerstaffe was told that he was not bound personally by the decision and, as he headed out of the hotel and returned to the conference centre, it was obvious there would be a showdown. Party officials were stony-faced on leaving the meeting. I smiled at the party's general secretary, Margaret McDonagh, as she passed by, and remarked that it was 'just like the old times'; she gave me an icy look in return. Three days of behind-the-scenes negotiations had got nowhere. Bickerstaffe knew that despite the leadership's appeals for support, many union and constituency delegates felt duty bound to make a stand on behalf of pensioners. Mary Turner, who represented the GMB union on the executive, told me the fiasco of the 75p increase illustrated how out of touch New Labour had become. If those at the top of the party had relatives with so little money that they relied on collecting their pensions at the post office every week, they would know how hurt the pensioners were when they saw just 75p a week added to their pension books. The only question mark over the final outcome was the possibility that Bickerstaffe might back down at the last moment. But once the former Labour minister, Lady Castle, one of the staunchest campaigners for the restoration of the earnings link, had delivered her passionate rallying cry behind the motion, the outcome could no longer be in any doubt. When the call went out: 'Would you remit?' Bickerstaffe stood up, ramrod straight, and shouted 'No.'

The leadership lost by almost two to one: 60.2 per cent in favour, 39.8 per cent against. However, it was the block votes of the unions, controlling half the total conference vote, that carried the day. In the union section the vote was 84.2 per cent in favour; but the position was reversed among constituency delegates, 63.7 per cent of whom voted in support of the government's argument that help should be concentrated on the poorest pensioners. The strength of the constituency vote was a great encouragement to party modernisers, who believed it proved that Gordon Brown and Alistair Darling had won the argument among party members and were thwarted only by the unbending block votes of the unions.

Although it was Blair's first significant conference defeat since becoming leader, Alastair Campbell had little difficulty afterwards in holding the line with reporters when he visited the media centre. He said pensioners would do well out of the pre-Budget report and he insisted the government had no intention of restoring the earnings link. When asked by George Pascoe-Watson, deputy political editor of the *Sun*, whether the Chancellor would bring forward the annual uprating, Campbell decided attack was the best line of defence. 'I know the *Sun*'s story line: "Tony Blair rocked by a sensational union revolt last night." So George, calm down.' At this point he was interrupted by George Jones, political editor of the *Daily Telegraph*: 'Alastair, do you want your by-line on that story, as well?' Campbell's light-hearted and rather cynical approach reflected the political reality of the position. A pension uprating was to be announced within weeks; so the government had held the initiative from the beginning. Delegates had known all along that they had little real influence over the decision, and would probably not have been deeply offended if ministers had chosen to play down the conference defeat as nothing more than a passing setback and an embarrassing headline. None the less the labour and trade union movement had decided this was an occasion when it intended to express a collective opinion, and the attempt to twist arms was not appreciated.

The episode had illustrated the inordinate lengths to which the leadership was prepared to go in order to control events and have the last word at the party conference. In previous years there had been pre-conference meetings with Blair and an understanding about how disagreements would be avoided. The animosity that had been generated this year had left union leaders feeling a sense of despair at the self-defeating nature of the exercise. They could not understand why they had been pushed into a corner when ministers knew most unions were bound by long-standing policies to campaign for a link between pensions and earnings. In the event the pension increases that Gordon Brown announced in his pre-Budget statement in November 2000 amounted precisely to the figures the journalists had predicted at the conference – £5 a week for single pensioners and £8 a week for married couples – which made the Chancellor's stand-off with the unions appear all the more surprising.

Bickerstaffe told me the day after the conference vote that he was still mystified as to why Blair and Brown had been so determined to micro-manage the debate and prevent delegates expressing an opinion. 'Why do they want to control everything? Are they saying delegates can never ever tell the leadership what we think? We weren't instructing the Chancellor to do anything. All we wanted to do was to show that we believed in something.' Bickerstaffe sounded bruised by his experience. 'I was under enormous pressure. It went on for hour after hour but I couldn't give way. For some of us, protecting the old age pension is a point of principle.' His disenchantment reflected a wider sense of unease among delegates whom I had known and spoken to over the years. Some seemed bewildered and disillusioned during their stay in Brighton that year. Without the responsibility of having to decide how to respond to a succession of competing policy positions, they did not feel so involved in the affairs of the conference. Nevertheless, they had felt fully engaged in the debate over pensions and, for the constituency representatives, it was one of the few opportunities that week to use one of their card votes. They said that in years gone by they would have attended numerous lunchtime and evening fringe meetings so as to have become fully informed about the opposing arguments. At the two previous annual conferences, and again at Brighton, they had spent much of their time visiting stands in the exhibition areas or enjoying the hospitality provided at the receptions hosted by the many corporate concerns that were only too anxious to bend the ear of the party in power.

Talking to party members from constituencies around the country in the months leading up to the 2000 conference, I had detected a growing sense of disengagement among them. They resented the withdrawal of their right to table two motions and an amendment for one or other of the various policy debates. Previously, once their contributions were printed on the agenda, the constituency parties had felt a sense of ownership about the points they were trying to make, and their delegates were always encouraged by the prospect that one of their motions might get called for debate. Although, at the end of the day, most of the issues that concerned them were invariably absorbed into the composite motions, there was still a sense of achievement at having played a part in the process. One delegate who participated in the final compositing session in 1997 said it was so rewarding to feel there was a link from the conference going all the way back to the constituency and to the very ward that drafted the motion. That connecting thread had now been broken, and although many of the delegates had attended local policy forums, some had come away disappointed, fearing their ideas had got lost in an unwieldy policy-making process which was failing to interest or excite the activists. In their opinion one of the greatest drawbacks to the new system was that, without the focal point of a conference motion, it was harder to get publicity for the causes they supported. Sending a delegate to conference for a week cost each local party around £500 in travel and hotel expenses, and with opportunities for constituency parties to have a direct input reduced, fewer thought it worth being represented. According to calculations by Ann Black, who was elected to the national policy forum on the slate of the centre-left Grassroots Alliance, up to a third of the constituencies had failed to send a delegate to the Brighton conference. 'What's the point in a local party shelling out £500 if there's so little for their delegate to do? While it was the case in the past that most of the constituency motions got mangled up into composites, the constituencies still felt they had a part to play. With the policy forums there is more participation, and the constituencies are told by the leadership their contributions count for far more, but party members feel they have less influence and that has led to disappointment.'

As the 2000 conference drew to a close I was reminded of the drive and enthusiasm of the rank and file I had witnessed so often in the past. The highlight of the final session was a speech by the former President of South Africa, Nelson Mandela. Shortly before he appeared on the platform, the chair, Vernon Hince, appealed to visitors to move forward to fill up the conference floor. Earlier in the week, during the set-piece debates, there had seemed to be far more empty seats than in previous years, reflecting the fall in numbers of constituency delegates. But by the time Tony Blair walked into the conference hall, arm in arm with Mandela, the floor was packed – even if many of the seats had been taken by the stewards in their distinctive red shirts. While waiting for the speech to begin, I read a tribute to Mandela in the conference diary written by Frank Dobson, Labour's defeated candidate in the election for Mayor of London. He recalled how trade unionists and party members had organised meetings, marches, pickets and petitions in support of the African National Congress and their long struggle against apartheid. The campaign to release Mandela, sentenced to life imprisonment in 1964, was a cause taken up by union branches and constituencies throughout the country. I remember from my days as a local newspaper reporter in the late 1960s the deep sense of conviction among those early campaigners and how difficult they found it to get support and publicity for the anti-apartheid cause, long before it built up the momentum that developed in later years. Mandela, who was not released from prison until 1990, told the conference that the solidarity shown in Britain had helped make bearable those long years of exile.

Fighting unpopular and unfashionable causes has long been a forte of union and constituency activists. Blair's reforms have limited the opportunities they once had to use the Labour Party as a platform and vehicle for their campaigns. Control over the party machine and the news agenda has taken precedence, at least for the moment, dissipating some of the drive and energy that motivated so many party members and that explained why for them the party conference had always been the pinnacle of the political year.

CONTROL AND
CONTEMPT

'I'm talking to you off the record . . . Far from criticising me, the committee praises me
for unprecedented openness . . . Remember this conversation didn't take place.'

Robin Cook, Foreign Secretary, speaking to Nicholas Jones, 9 February 1999

Few groups of aspiring politicians have been lampooned so quickly and so comprehensively as the 183 newly elected Labour MPs who joined the record-breaking ranks of the Parliamentary Labour Party in May 1997. Many were the bemused beneficiaries of a landslide election victory that far exceeded the wildest expectations of the party's most optimistic strategists. The roll-call of constituencies commandeered by Labour on election night included numerous seats where the winning candidates were the first to admit they found it almost impossible to comprehend their success and could not believe they really were on their way to the House of Commons. In their first few bewildering months at Westminster, the one bond that united all of the newcomers was a sense of discipline. They owed their good fortune to a party that had drilled into its candidates and supporters the importance of following agreed policy positions and of avoiding the merest hint of dissent. They had fought an election campaign that exploited the Conservatives' disunity and was designed to obliterate all reminders of Labour's dark, divisive days in opposition. The sheer enormity of Labour's overall majority of 179 seats gave the parliamentary party an air of invincibility. Rarely had there been such a large contingent of new MPs who were so anxious to demonstrate loyalty and so keen to allow their responses to be influenced, if not controlled, by the party machine.

These hesitant but obedient new MPs were easy prey for political columnists and parliamentary sketch writers. Soon the caricature had been established. They were the puppets of the party's headquarters in Millbank, their message pagers always to hand, awaiting instructions, ready to parrot the latest line from Labour's spin doctors. As they became accustomed to life at Westminster, the new intake became profoundly annoyed on finding they had become a constant target of ridicule. Nevertheless, although a few broke free and were soon only too eager to display their independence by defying the diktats of Millbank, the vast majority immersed themselves in the rituals of backbench life and the complexities of constituency casework. They had an intense desire to help the government honour Labour's election pledges; most were desperate for promotion; and they were ready to be fashioned into a well-regimented troop of parliamentary foot-soldiers. For many of the new MPs it was not just a case of doing their duty: they felt honour bound to do the leadership's bidding, whatever the potential damage to their own reputations. Repetition of identical phrases in planted questions to the Prime Minister revealed the handiwork of the authors of the *Daily Brief*, which Millbank faxed each morning to the offices of Labour MPs and which gave them the 'line to take' on the key issues of the day. The same cloying lines would be repeated in interviews for television and radio. This was perhaps only to be expected; what often seemed out of place and uncalled for was the belligerent tone they adopted when replying to any attempt to censure the Blair government. Responding instantly to attacks was one of the lessons the new MPs had learned as candidates, and the urge to rebut all criticism was so deeply embedded in the New Labour psyche that for months ministers continued to give the impression they were still fighting an election.

Most of the new MPs were only too well aware that Millbank frowned on unguarded fraternisation with representatives of the news media, and to begin with they shunned almost all contact with the journalists of Westminster. The new intake was so large and so dominant that many of the political correspondents found it difficult to make headway in gaining their acquaintance and, as the months went by, the atmosphere that developed was unlike anything that I or the other reporters had experienced. We had begun to notice a change as soon as Tony Blair was elected party leader in 1994. His predecessor, John Smith, gave every appearance of being at ease in the company of journalists, frequently stopping to chat when he walked through the members' lobby. In the final, tumultuous years of John Major's government the lobby would be packed night after night with various Conservative factions, each desperate to bend the ears of the nearest reporters, to give them a run-down on the detailed ramifications of the latest developments over their interminable preoccupation with Britain's future role in Europe. Time spent in the members' lobby was always rewarding and, in the easier-going regimes of Michael Foot, Neil Kinnock and John Smith, Labour MPs had been just as garrulous and entertaining as their Tory counterparts. Now all this was changing.

In his years as a political editor, Alastair Campbell was assiduous in working the lobby. Most days, straight after lunch, he would take up his position, lounging against the plinths of one of the statues. He rarely had difficulty in attracting the attention of one or other of the prominent politicians who happened to pass through the lobby – often observed by Peter Mandelson, standing in another corner; after his election in 1992 as Labour MP for Hartlepool, Mandelson took a fiendish delight in keeping tabs on the preferred contacts of the various correspondents. Campbell enjoyed holding court. He would have a laugh with MPs and relished the chance to taunt other journalists by rubbishing whatever they had just written or broadcast. Mandelson was far more purposeful and secretive. He invariably stood aside from the throng and could usually be observed deep in conversation with whichever correspondent was currently in his favour – or, alternatively, had incurred his particular displeasure. As the 1997 election approached, Labour's leading players spent far less time in the lobby. As Blair's press secretary, Campbell was ensconced in the offices of the Leader of the Opposition, at the far end of the building; Mandelson was planning Labour's election campaign from his office a short walk away at Millbank. If either of them passed through, there was little time for pleasantries; and the same went for the shadow cabinet. Some would stop and exchange a few words, but there was to be no more loose talk in the lobby. New Labour's relationship with the news media was to be structured and disciplined. Giving a one-to-one briefing to a journalist was no longer to be regarded as a haphazard event; it was a calculated act that was best conducted in privacy or on the telephone, and certainly not in the members' lobby.

When Labour came to power, a further change in the party's relationship with the political correspondents rapidly became apparent: after a few weeks we realised that most secretaries of state were avoiding the lobby altogether. Under previous governments, ministers had often lingered for a few moments before answering questions or making a statement, but under Tony Blair their appearances were few and far between. The only chance journalists had of catching their attention was during a division, either by standing outside in the corridor as MPs passed by or by diving in again once journalists were allowed to return to the lobby. Establishing contact with the many newly elected Labour MPs was just as difficult. Once the hours for House of Commons sittings were changed, in order to reduce the number of late-night sessions and to finish early on Thursdays, there were even fewer opportunities to strike up a conversation. Within a matter of months journalists were no longer devoting the time they once did to making contacts in the lobby. In the mid-1970s, when I spent several years with the BBC at Westminster, there was a rule that we should have at least one correspondent on duty in the lobby at peak moments in the late afternoon and early evening. The great value in standing around was that journalists picked up endless titbits of information about parliamentary procedures, the conduct of MPs or whatever intrigue was afoot. At that time, less and less notice was being taken of the guidance on lobby etiquette, reissued in the 1960s, which stipulated that correspondents should not 'see' anything in the members' lobby and should observe the rule that 'incidents, pleasant or otherwise, should be treated as private'. By the mid-1990s correspondents considered there were no restraints at all on reporting what they had observed. Arguments between Conservative MPs in the lobby, and other indiscretions which reporters had witnessed, made front-page news during the last days of the Major government.

Labour strategists believed the best precaution against a repetition of such damaging publicity under Blair was to exercise as much control as possible over the access political correspondents had to ministers and MPs, and to limit the activity that took place in front of journalists. For our part, by scaling down the time we spent observing MPs outside the chamber, in the lobbies and corridors, we were not perhaps as diligent as we should have been in keeping abreast of the ease with which the government was able to exploit its massive parliamentary majority. We had not understood the full implications of the unquestioning loyalty that ministers commanded, nor had we any real inkling of the risks being taken to ensure that Labour kept one step ahead of the news media. In the long lead-up to the 1997 election nothing seemed to matter more to the party leadership than the task, day after day, of influencing the way Labour was being reported. Once in government, no opportunity would be missed to score a political point, however inconsequential or inept it might appear. There were many willing helpers among the new intake. By asking friendly, rehearsed questions, the new MPs gave ministers a chance to trot out Labour's achievements. But some, unaccustomed to the confusing rules and practices of parliamentary life, had not foreseen how, in choosing to assist their fellow members on the government payroll, they would be transgressing against long-standing conventions of confidentiality and procedure.

The sycophantic behaviour of many new entrants particularly distressed some long-serving Labour MPs who had grown especially uneasy about the way government whips had packed the membership of House of Commons select committees with those of their colleagues whom they believed ministers regarded as being the most trustworthy and the least likely to understand and insist on proper parliamentary scrutiny of measures under consideration. The role of the select committees in challenging the executive had become even more important than in previous parliaments because of the size of Labour's majority. The chain of events that was to unfold in the spring and summer of 1999 revealed a degree of complicity in undermining that independent role of investigating and analysing government affairs which shocked opposition MPs and took political correspondents by surprise. Three Labour MPs were suspended from the Commons for their involvement in supplying leaked draft copies of select committee reports; a fourth Labour committee member resigned; a select committee chairman had to apologise; and there was criticism of three senior members of the cabinet, the Chancellor of the Exchequer, the Foreign Secretary and the Secretary of State for Scotland. When it came to their day of reckoning, the MPs gave no coherent explanation for their breach of confidence, nor was there any apology from the government. None of those who were implicated seemed prepared to acknowledge that they had become the willing servants of Labour's obsessive compulsion to manipulate the news media.

The value to the government of an illicit early copy of a select committee report was that it gave the responsible minister a head start in assessing the likely impact of any criticism. In Labour's rule book of media management 'r' stood for rebuttal, and the best way to fight a damaging report by a select committee was to have the government's defence worked out well in advance. If possible the task of refuting or undermining a committee's findings should begin long before publication. The starting point for my insight into the desperate measures ministers were prepared to take to defend their reputations was the morning of 9 February 1999, just after the 8 a.m. news on BBC Radio Four. One of the items in the bulletin was my preview of the publication at 10 a.m. that day of a long-awaited report of an investigation by the Foreign Affairs Select Committee into the delivery of British arms to Sierra Leone in contravention of a United Nations arms embargo. I said in my report that the committee was understood to be 'scathing in its criticism' and that some of the 'severest criticism is directed at Robin Cook for his refusal to do more to co-operate with the MPs' inquiry'. On returning to the newsroom once the bulletin had finished, I was handed an urgent message and told to ring Robin Cook, the Foreign Secretary, on a direct line.

Cook answered the telephone almost immediately. Once I had identified myself, he insisted that he must not be quoted and, without pausing, before I could stop him or question the terms that he was laying down, began to challenge my broadcast. 'I'm talking to you off the record. You will see that far from criticising me, the committee praises me for unprecedented openness and a quantum leap in the amount of information which I supplied. The committee's gripe is that I should have released that information during their inquiry, but you can't have two inquiries hearing the same witnesses. If you are going to report this in a balanced way, you must refer to the paragraph that welcomes the unparalleled amount of information which

I provided. The committee are wanting to have their cake and eat it. Remember this conversation didn't take place.'

My justification for revealing in this book the contents of that short telephone call is that I do not consider I am under an obligation not to disclose what Cook said. I did not in any way solicit the Foreign Secretary's help, nor did he supply me with any information that could be considered newsworthy or of value. As I saw it, his objective was calculated and straightforward: he wanted to ensure that in any subsequent broadcasts I presented him in a better light. I felt it was rather stretching a point for a cabinet minister to telephone a correspondent, rebuke him for what he had reported and then at the same time insist that his complaint was somehow 'off the record'. Subsequent events were to show, however, that what was most significant about the conversation was not its content but its timing.

I had returned the call immediately after the completion of the 8 a.m. news bulletin, which usually lasts for no more than ten minutes, and the paragraph to which Cook had drawn my attention was no. 99 in a report of 112 paragraphs. At that point I had not seen the report and it was not until two weeks later that I realised the precise import of the timing of his call. Cook told the House of Commons subsequently that copies of the select committee's report, embargoed until publication at 10 a.m., were released to his officials at 8 a.m on 9 February. As Foreign Secretary, he was 'immediately sent a copy'. Bearing in mind our conversation, the timings Cook gave did appear remarkably tight. To have identified a complimentary paragraph about himself on the thirty-ninth page of the report within the space of not much more than ten minutes, and to have been ready to quote it chapter and verse when making a complaint to a political correspondent, did suggest remarkable powers of comprehension. Admittedly, as shadow Foreign Secretary, he had won considerable praise in 1996 for his rapid speed-reading of Sir Richard Scott's voluminous report of his three-and-a-half-year inquiry into the circumstances surrounding defence exports to Iraq after the Iran–Iraq War. On that occasion Cook was locked into a room in Whitehall and given three and a half hours to read the report before rising at the dispatch box to give the opposition's response following its publication at 3.30 p.m. According to the *Mirror*'s calculations, he had to read the 1,800 page report at the rate of 'a page every seven seconds'. In my judgement Cook had embarked on a highly risky course in telephoning me that morning in 1999, although his action was perhaps only to have been expected.

Cook's conduct as Foreign Secretary had attracted sustained press criticism on a number of fronts, and the long-running row over the government's response to the illegal shipment of arms to Sierra Leone had proved to be no exception. Publication of the select committee's report had coincided with renewed diplomatic initiatives following President Milosevic's refusal to accept a NATO-led peacekeeping force in Kosovo, and Cook was on his way that morning to Rambouillet for another foreign ministers' meeting. He was clearly concerned about the way the news media were likely to interpret the committee's findings, and as he was going to be in France at the critical moment he had perhaps understandably grabbed at any chance to influence that reporting. However, our conversation was not an isolated act: the Foreign Secretary's call was part of a concerted attempt that morning to limit the impact of the select committee's criticism. I had spoken an hour earlier to the deputy head of the Foreign Office news department, John Williams, who had apparently taken exception to my first report that morning. After I had been interviewed on *Today* at 6.30 a.m. and given listeners a run-down of the committee's likely conclusions, I was handed a message asking me to ring Williams immediately. I had been quite forthright in predicting that the report would be critical of the Foreign Office because the select committee chairman, the Labour MP Donald Anderson, had given reporters some off-the-record guidance the day before. As there had been press speculation about the committee's likely findings, Anderson was keen to ensure that reporters refrained from making wild predictions. While he would give no indication about the precise nature of the committee's recommendations, he was prepared to confirm that the report would censure the Foreign Office and repeat and reinforce their public criticism of Cook for his refusal to let the committee see diplomatic telegrams and question witnesses from the intelligence services.

When I heard that Williams wanted to speak to me I returned the call immediately. I was still writing my report for the 8 a.m. news bulletin and I was anxious to see if he was volunteering any fresh information on the Foreign Secretary's behalf. Williams, a former *Daily Mirror* political editor, joined the Foreign Office news department the previous year and had worked tirelessly on Cook's behalf. He was always approachable and well informed. When I spoke to him shortly before 7 a.m. he made it clear that the committee's findings would be rejected. He said Cook would not let the select committee's censure of Foreign Office officials 'lie unanswered' as the government considered the committee's criticism 'wholly out of proportion', a phrase that was to be echoed later that morning both by Cook himself and by Blair.

Williams' early-morning call was another reflection of Cook's state of high alert, after having endured months of embarrassment over his handling of events in Sierra Leone. In July 1998 a report by Sir Thomas Legg blamed Foreign Office diplomats and officials for 'repeated and partly systematic failures of communication', which meant that ministers had not been alerted to the shipment of military equipment to President Kabbah without a British licence and in contravention of a United Nations resolution. Although Cook promised to make immediate changes in management and operational procedures within his department, the select committee was not satisfied and continued to proceed with its own inquiry, which it believed the government had impeded by refusing to release the information its members had requested. In its report, published as planned at 10 a.m. on 9 February, the committee concluded that there had been 'an appalling failure' within the Foreign Office and said that in future it should be made 'crystal clear' to the diplomatic staff that they had to act 'only within the confines of policies set by ministers'. As Cook had correctly predicted in his telephone call to me earlier that morning, the committee had welcomed his 'quantum leap' in allowing MPs to read all the relevant telegrams, but remained critical of his earlier refusal to release documents. It recommended that the government should adopt a 'more mature attitude' towards the controlled access to information and recognise that select committees 'must be trusted' to do the job the House of Commons had given them. 'MPs savage Foreign Office' was the front-page headline next morning in the *Guardian*, and the *Daily Express* said the Prime Minister and the Foreign Secretary had been arrogant in being so dismissive of the report and should 'learn a little humility'. Blair's outright rejection of the committee's findings when he was interviewed by Jimmy Young two hours after the report's publication angered the chairman, Donald Anderson, who said he was shocked by the speed with which the government had moved to blunt the impact of their recommendations. Blair's rebuttal left no room for doubt. He told the programme that the committee's 'very harsh criticism' was 'disproportionate and unfair'. His comments were entirely consistent with the two-page minute which Cook had issued immediately after the 10 a.m. embargo, which also said the criticism was 'wholly out of proportion'.

Anderson said he could not believe that Blair had even looked at the committee's report when he rubbished its recommendations on BBC radio. 'I would be surprised if the Prime Minister had even picked up the report, let alone read it, between 8 a.m. and being interviewed by Jimmy Young.' Blair's over-hasty denunciation of the select committee's investigation had also been spotted by the opposition, and at Prime Minister's questions next day the Conservative leader, William Hague, mounted a sustained attack, accusing the government of 'dismissing the report before it had even been published' and of treating the House with 'complete arrogance and contempt'. Blair told MPs that he had promised to 'respond carefully' to the committee's report. When I inquired at the 4 p.m. lobby briefing precisely where and when the Prime Minister had given this undertaking, Alastair Campbell said he did not know but he was sure it had been delivered. When I pointed out that the transcript for the *Jimmy Young Programme* contained no such assurance, he laughed and brushed aside my question: 'I'm sure the Prime Minister said it somewhere . . . Well, all right then, he said it to me.' If Campbell's offhand reply could have been broadcast, it would have confirmed MPs' worst suspicions of a concerted campaign to denigrate the committee's report.

An uncomfortable question time and some critical newspaper headlines might have been an end to the matter if it had not been for the diligence of David Wilshire, one of the Conservative MPs on the committee. He thought the eagerness of the Foreign Secretary and his staff in rebutting the committee's criticism merited further investigation. My 8 a.m. news report had included a line from the guidance Williams had given me shortly before 7 a.m. and which I had attributed to the Foreign Office. I had said that Cook was 'giving his officials his full support' and that he intended to complain about the way the committee had 'subjected diplomats to criticism all over again' after they had been cleared the previous July. Wilshire was puzzled by Cook's ability to respond with such certainty in defending his officials when the embargoed copies of the report were not released until 8 a.m. and, in view of his suspicions, he tabled a series of carefully worded parliamentary questions. He asked if Cook, other ministers or his officials had ever had access to a draft report of the committee's findings and if Cook could publish the text of press briefings that he or his department gave before 8 a.m. on 9 February. At no point had I spoken to Wilshire, nor had I kept abreast of the questions which he and other Conservative MPs had tabled on the order paper; so, as far as I was concerned, the Foreign Secretary's written answer to Wilshire, released on 23 February, came out of the blue. Cook revealed that his office had received a copy of a draft report of the committee's findings in the second week of January and that shortly before publication his department was 'made aware of certain key conclusions in the report', but said that neither he nor any minister, official or special adviser took 'any action to publish or disclose any part of any version of the report'. Although Cook did not say so in as many words, he was in fact admitting for the first time that his department had been receiving leaked information from the committee.

However, it was his answer to Wilshire's second point, about advance briefings, which seemed to fly in the face of my notes of what had happened that morning. The Foreign Secretary could not have been more precise in his written answer: 'In advance of the publication of the report on 9 February, we made no comment to the media about the report, except in response to leaks by others to the press. Copies of the report – embargoed until publication at 10 a.m. – were released to officials from the parliamentary relations department of the Foreign Office at 8 a.m. on 9 February. I was immediately sent a copy. A spokesman subsequently briefed the press orally, under the same embargo, on my initial response to the report.' My first reaction on reading the answer was one of disbelief. Not only had Williams been in touch with me an hour before the report was released but Cook himself had spoken to me nearly two hours before the embargo was lifted. When ministers are put on the spot in Parliament and asked precisely who said what to the news media, they usually find neat ways to sidestep the question. Cook's answer was categoric and went into far greater detail than I would have expected. However, I did not have the chance to give any further thought to the contradictions between my recollection of events on 9 February and Cook's answer, because the story had taken a far more dramatic turn with the announcement that a Labour MP on the committee, Ernie Ross, had resigned after admitting that he had leaked a copy of the report to the Foreign Secretary.

After a short extract from my 8 a.m. news bulletin report was replayed that afternoon on *PM*, the presenter, Chris Lowe, said that it did seem that two hours before the report was published Cook was indicating publicly his intention to reject the committee's findings. David Wilshire told the programme that after hearing the news bulletin on the morning of 9 February he complained to the Speaker, Betty Boothroyd. 'The government were clearly rubbishing a report which they said they hadn't seen. It just didn't add up.' As a result of Wilshire's complaint, the committee agreed to undertake an investigation. Ross resigned when the clerk proposed writing to each MP to ask if he or she was responsible. Ross apologised for 'breaching the confidence' of the committee, an action which he said had been prompted by his concern over the committee's decision to prolong the Sierra Leone investigation. After a succession of points of order that afternoon from Conservative MPs, Cook had no alternative but to make an oral statement next day. He assured the House that neither he nor any other minister 'took any action' on the draft copy supplied by Ross or over the second leak, when Ross informed a special adviser in his department of the key conclusions of the final report. Cook was adamant there had been no impropriety: 'There was no briefing, no leak to the press in advance of publication . . . I have fully complied with the obligations on me as a minister not to impede or obstruct the work of the committee.' Cook's robust defence of himself was backed by the Prime Minister's official spokesman, Alastair Campbell, at the afternoon lobby briefing. He acknowledged that Cook had read the draft copy but said he had 'put it on the shelf' and made no further use of it. John Williams repeated the same point when he was approached by correspondents. He said he was personally aware of what the leaked report contained but did not brief on the basis of the leak, and he insisted that Cook did not see the final printed report until 8 a.m. on the morning of publication.

Attempts by Campbell and Williams to play down the significance of the two leaks did little to convince MPs, and Cook found himself being assailed from all sides. After the select committee called for a wider inquiry and Conservative MPs asked if Cook had breached parliamentary privilege by not returning the leaked document, the Speaker, Betty Boothroyd, took decisive action. She asked the Standards and Privileges Select Committee to give her a ruling on the action MPs should take if they found themselves 'in possession of leaked committee papers'. Two days later, questions tabled by David Wilshire produced further damaging disclosures. In a written answer Cook admitted that the Foreign Office had received two earlier leaks from the Foreign Affairs Select Committee. In December 1998 he and a limited number of officials had seen a leaked copy of the committee's report on human rights, and in January 1999 the minister of state, Ms Joyce Quinn, and a limited number of officials, saw a draft version of the committee's report on European enlargement. Cook defended himself the next morning on *Today*, insisting he had nothing to apologise for. 'We have not interfered with the work of the committee or engaged in the prior disclosure of reports to the news media.' He quoted from the ultimate parliamentary authority, Erskine May, to defend his claim that he could be aware of a committee's deliberations yet stay within the rules: 'Knowledge itself is not an offence. Any use of that knowledge would be an offence.'

Cook's strident protestations prompted a sharp rejoinder from Diane Abbott, one of the Labour MPs on the committee. She told *Today* that the Foreign Secretary had put a lot of obstacles in the way of their inquiry. 'The government see select committees as an irritant that must somehow be brought under their command and control structure.' The former Conservative Prime Minister, John Major, told *Breakfast With Frost* that there would have been an outcry if a Foreign Secretary in his government had owned up to having received so many leaked select committee reports. Spurred on by the controversy, the shadow Foreign Secretary, Michael Howard, carried out further inquiries into Wilshire's suspicions that there had been an early-morning briefing by the Foreign Office in advance of the report's publication. I only became aware of this on reading an interview Howard gave to the *Sunday Times* in which he claimed that transcripts of BBC news bulletins showed that the Foreign Office had 'launched a pre-emptive strike' by briefing BBC journalists. Howard said that although no mention was made in the 7 a.m. news of the Foreign Secretary's likely response, a report at 8 a.m. referred to Cook mounting a strong defence by 'giving his officials his full support', and he suggested it was 'inconceivable' that Cook had not used the leaked draft copy, supplied by a 'nark' on the committee, to 'get his retaliation in first'.

New avenues for attacking the government were opened up by Conservative MPs who started probing other ministers renowned for their mastery of New Labour's repertoire of rebuttal. The Chancellor of the Exchequer, Gordon Brown, was the next to own up to a leak. In a written answer on 16 March he admitted that shortly before the Budget his parliamentary private secretary, the Labour MP Don Touhig, was given a preliminary draft of a report from the Social Security Select Committee on child benefit. Brown said that neither he nor any other Treasury minister was given or read any of the committee's reports before their release. Ten days later the Labour MP David Stewart resigned from the Scottish Affairs Select Committee after admitting that he had supplied extracts from a report to the then Secretary of State for Scotland, the late Donald Dewar. Stewart said he let Dewar see some sections of the report because the contents had already been leaked 'wholly improperly' to the *Herald* in Glasgow and he was anxious that the secretary of state should be able to make his own judgement before responding to the newspaper. Dewar's embarrassment was compounded by an announcement that afternoon from the Speaker about action to curb leaks. She said the Standards and Privileges Committee had ruled that MPs who received leaked reports must not act in a way that impeded a select committee, and they should return such documents without delay. Miss Boothroyd had few words of encouragement for the MPs who had breached the confidence of their committees. She said the Standards and Privileges Committee would consider their conduct once it had completed an investigation into the Sierra Leone leak.

The full extent of that inquiry was not revealed until the committee published its report at the end of June. It recommended that any unauthorised use of unpublished select committee documents should be regarded as a contempt of Parliament. Robin Cook, John Williams and other Foreign Office officials were all questioned by the committee. Ernie Ross, the Labour MP who had leaked the draft report in second week of January, said he wanted to alert Cook and the minister of state, Tony Lloyd, to the fact that the committee intended to make a 'very damning attack on civil servants' who would have no right of reply. In his written evidence Cook said that he personally was not shown the leaked report until eight days before its official publication. It was faxed to his special adviser, Andrew Hood, who showed it to four other members of staff, including John Williams. Cook also revealed that the select committee chairman, Donald Anderson, gave the Foreign Office parliamentary relations department 'a full briefing' the day before publication, making clear that the bulk of the criticism would be aimed at officials. What caught my attention was the Foreign Secretary's reply when asked if the draft or leaked conclusions had been used in briefing the media. Cook's denial was even more explicit than his written answer in February: 'No use was made of either the draft or additional information from Anderson or Ross in briefing the media, nor did the terms of the report give us any reason to do so. Indeed the only contact we had with the media regarding the report in advance of its publication was as a result of reports in the *Independent* and *The Times* who had received a leak of the conclusion of the report from a perspective hostile to the Foreign Office.'

John Williams gave oral evidence and said it 'did not occur' to him that it was wrong to have read the leaked document, made his own copy and kept it. 'I do regret that I focused far too narrowly on this simply as a matter of media strategy.' He explained how 'a week or so away' from the report's publication he discussed the leaked report with the Foreign Secretary and outlined the tactics he proposed to adopt if approached by political journalists who might be following up speculative leaks about the committee's findings. His strategy would be to say to journalists: 'If what you are saying is right, if that is the way the report comes out, Robin Cook will back those officials because he regards this as unfair.' After a leak appeared in the *Independent*, Williams said Cook agreed that he should start giving the response they had worked out together. 'I had subsequent calls from *The Times*, *Daily Telegraph*, *Financial Times* and *Sunday Telegraph*, all claiming to know what was in the report. To all of them I said, "I am interested in what you say. If it is true, he will back those officials because, as you know, he regards it as unfair." ' When asked directly whether knowledge of the leak had helped him rebut those stories, Williams said he sat through the Sierra Leone hearings and knew they had been 'pretty hostile' to Foreign Office officials. 'The Foreign Secretary said right at the beginning of this process that he regarded it as unfair on them that they should be subjected to what he called double jeopardy and I was obviously aware that if I said anything that depended on knowledge of that leak that would be wrong. I did not do so.'

None the less, in my opinion Williams' answers bore out my belief that leaks from select committees had provided ministers with an opportunity to work out the most effective line to take when rebutting a critical report. I was surprised that the Standards and Privileges Committee did not follow up the detailed points raised by David Wilshire and Michael Howard and failed to ask questions about possible Foreign Office briefings on the morning the Sierra Leone report was published. Much was said at the time, not only by the Conservatives but also by influential Labour MPs, about the way Cook and Blair had been so quick off the mark in launching their rebuttal; but the MPs on the committee seemed far more concerned about the potential culpability of the Foreign Office for allowing senior civil servants to hold on to a leaked document for almost a month than in probing the Foreign Secretary's media strategy. In order to deter potential leakers, the committee reinforced its earlier ruling that MPs should return leaked committee papers without delay and called on the Prime Minister to amend the ministerial code to require ministers and their parliamentary private secretaries to comply with the guidance. Similar instructions had already been issued to civil servants and diplomats, and the committee said they should also apply to politically appointed special advisers. Any breach of the rule would be a disciplinary matter. Use by departments of unpublished select committee documents would in future be regarded as a contempt of Parliament.

I made several broadcasts about the committee's new guidance on leaked documents, and shortly after my first report went out on BBC Radio Four, I received a complaint from the Foreign Office news department, which had remained ever vigilant on Cook's behalf. A press officer, Chris Sainty – one of the five officials who saw the leaked Sierra Leone report – disputed my assertion that the committee had 'rebuked' Cook in rejecting as 'mistaken' the grounds that the Foreign Secretary put forward when defending himself. Sainty accepted that Cook had been criticised but he said he did not think it amounted to a rebuke. However, most of next morning's newspapers were in no doubt that Cook had not escaped without blame, and the *Guardian*, *Daily Telegraph* and *Daily Express* said the report did constitute a 'rebuke' for the Foreign Secretary. Most of the coverage concentrated on the fate of Ernie Ross. The committee said his action in leaking the draft report and the key conclusions of the final report amounted to a 'serious interference' with the select committee system and recommended he should be suspended from the House of Commons for ten days. The day after the suspension took effect, the Foreign Affairs Select Committee chairman, Donald Anderson, apologised to the House for giving Foreign Office officials an advance briefing on his committee's report.

Having disposed of the Sierra Leone leak, the Standards and Privileges Committee launched an investigation into the leaked report on child benefit. After the Chancellor's admission in March that his parliamentary private secretary had obtained a photocopy of the report, the Social Security Select Committee had mounted its own inquiry but failed to discover who was responsible: the eleven MPs on the committee had all answered 'no' when asked if they had given Touhig a copy. In view of their responses, the Standards and

Privileges Committee said it could do no more than condemn the conduct of the MP who had failed to tell the truth. Within three days of that conclusion being reached on 20 July, and before it had been made public, the Labour MP Kali Mountford wrote to the Standards Committee to say that she had given Touhig sight of her copy of the draft report. Ms Mountford said that at the time the committee was anxious to persuade the Treasury to give evidence, and in order to explain the significance of their request, when Touhig asked to see the report she had agreed to show it to him. She apologised for her delay in being 'totally forthcoming'. The committee concluded that she had aggravated her original offence by initially denying responsibility and recommended she should be suspended for five days and Touhig suspended for three days. Ms Mountford resigned from the committee and Touhig stood down as Brown's PPS.

These suspensions did not take effect until October, by which time two debates which had taken place underlining the growing unease among senior MPs about the government's failure to respect and defend the independence of select committee members. The Conservative MP Sir Patrick Cormack regarded a certain degree of over-exuberance on the part of new Labour MPs in their desire to please the government as understandable; but he noted that there had been a 'disturbing proliferation' of leaks from the select committees since Labour took power, and suggested that the task of nominating committee members should be taken away from the whips' offices and given to an independent committee of selection. The Liberal Democrat MP Malcolm Bruce said that in Kali Mountford's case there had been 'over-enthusiasm on the part of an inexperienced new MP' and more should be done to ensure that committee membership reflected a balance of experience and parliamentary responsibility. A government with such a large majority did not need 'quislings on select committees to conduct their business', although Bruce did not suggest any MP had behaved in that manner. After the Leader of the House, Margaret Beckett, said she doubted whether much more would be achieved by seeking further to punish those MPs who leaked reports, the Labour MP Dale Campbell-Savours said that leak inquiries should be conducted under oath, as that would ensure MPs were held to account. Tony Blair followed up the debate by publishing the new guidance issued to ministers, parliamentary private secretaries, civil servants and diplomats to ensure they returned leaked reports.

Notwithstanding the introduction of a revised ministerial code, the chairmen of the thirty-three select committees believed the Sierra Leone episode had been a defining moment. They considered the extent of the subterfuge they had uncovered had demonstrated the need for a fundamental shake-up of rules and procedures to strengthen the ability of their committees to hold the executive in check. Within a week of Robin Cook's precipitate rejection of the findings of the Foreign Affairs Select Committee, the various chairmen were asked to start cataloguing instances where ministers had shown arrogance and contempt in responding to their inquiries and reports. The Liaison Committee, which supervised their relations with the government, said that once these observations had been collated it would consider what needed to be done to ensure their work was not impeded. Robert Sheldon, the Labour chairman of the committee, told *The World At One* that the government's pre-emptive strike in rebutting the report into the Sierra Leone arms shipment was 'not very helpful' and showed the danger of ministers making instant pronouncements without studying the recommendations in detail.

Once the chairmen embarked on their review and found themselves caught up in the repercussions of the various leaks, they became convinced that far-reaching safeguards were needed. There seemed to be a general consensus that their inquiries had lost some of their former status and were not having anything like the effect they had achieved under the previous administration. Labour had made great use of critical parliamentary reports when attacking John Major's government, and the publicity the select committees' work attracted had enhanced their overall reputation. I had seen at first hand the discomfort Conservative ministers had been forced to endure when they were called to give evidence. I spent nearly a year presenting *Scrutiny*, a weekly programme on BBC2 that broadcast extracts from the televised evidence-taking sessions. One of the longest inquiries I covered was into the future market for coal; it began in the autumn of 1992, after the House of Commons took the unprecedented step of asking the Trade and Industry Select Committee to mount an investigation after the uproar that followed the thirty-one pit closures announced by the President of the Board of Trade, Michael Heseltine. By making a formal request for an inquiry, the House had strengthened the authority of the committee and its hearings received widespread coverage in the news media. When the committee presented its report, the Labour chairman, Richard Caborn, said the Conservative government had been forced to acknowledge that when faced by dissent on its own back benches a speedy inquiry by a select committee had succeeded in deepening the level of public and parliamentary debate.

Another much-publicised session was the carefully rehearsed appearance in January 1993 of three 'Sir Humphreys' who had to defend the Treasury's decision to sanction the payment of £4,700 towards legal costs incurred by the Chancellor, Norman Lamont, after he discovered that a sex therapist was renting his basement flat. The Public Accounts Committee spent nearly four hours interrogating the Cabinet Secretary, Sir Robin Butler, and two permanent secretaries, Sir Terence Burns and Sir Peter Middleton. Never before had three such senior Whitehall mandarins been questioned publicly in that way, and the television pictures of them sitting together in a row, weighing up their answers, made riveting viewing.

Conservative infighting and the government's fragile majority had given the politics of the early 1990s a certain edge, and the competition for seats on select committees intensified as the standing of their work increased. Televised hearings, which started in 1989, soon began to produce positive feedback and MPs found themselves being praised by their constituents for persisting in their tough questioning of ministers and civil servants. Select committee clerks said they noticed that MPs began spending far more time studying briefing documents for the evidence-taking sessions, and their high level of preparation meant that ministers had to keep up their guard.

Labour had used this high-profile exposure to their advantage while in opposition; once in power, they faced nothing like the threat from select committee investigations that the Conservatives had been forced to face. *Scrutiny* ceased its weekly broadcasts in 1995 and Channel Four dropped its weekly parliamentary programme, *A Week in Politics* after the 1997 general election, leading to a sharp drop in the use of committee footage. Such was the hectic pace of Labour's first year in power that the new ministers had no need to look for additional opportunities to promote their policies, and the much-reduced coverage for the televised hearings hardly made them an attractive or appealing platform. Once the government had established itself, and the select committees started unearthing issues on which Labour ministers were vulnerable, they found it harder than they expected to reassert their authority and attract the media's attention. Some chairmen complained of having been snubbed when they asked ministers to give evidence, and the marginalised nature of their work became all too apparent when figures for the rate of absenteeism showed that the number of MPs failing to turn up for committee sessions had risen to 34 per cent in the parliamentary year to November 1999 from less than 25 per cent in 1996. A cause of even greater concern was the rapid turnover in Labour committee members who saw a short stint on a select committee as a stepping-stone to promotion. Several well-respected committee chairmen had also taken jobs in the government. At the turn of the year the Liaison Committee started to consider how best to stop the government's power outstripping parliamentary control, and it published its blueprint in March 2000.

A hard-hitting report, *Shifting the Balance*, included a raft of proposals to redress the balance and bring the select committees back from the sidelines. The most contentious recommendation was that for the first time since the committees were created in 1979, effective control over their membership should be removed from the whips and handed to a non-partisan select committee panel that would maintain lists of MPs seeking places. Another far-reaching idea was to institute a new select committee half-hour, to take place immediately after questions each Tuesday afternoon, when the House could consider a topical or recent report. When the Leader of the House, Margaret Beckett, delivered the government's response in May the Liaison Committee was dismayed to see that almost all its radical ideas had been rejected. The thirty-three chairmen agreed unanimously that Beckett had given a 'very disappointing reply'. She acknowledged that select committees had been a 'major step in making the executive accountable to Parliament', and asserted that ministers continued to value the role they played; but when it came to the question of their membership ministers were unconvinced that a select committee panel would provide a better alternative as there had to be an incentive for the party of government to ensure there was a 'reasonable' allocation of places for its nominations. The government denied that 'unfettered party management' was exercising a subversive control and producing a 'docile set of select committees'.

As an indication of its disenchantment with this response, the Liaison Committee took the unusual step of asking Mrs Beckett to give evidence so that she could be questioned on the reasons the government had given for its stance. David Davis, Conservative chairman of the Public Accounts Committee, told *The World Tonight* that it heralded the start of a tough summer for the Leader of the House. 'This is the first time the committee chairmen have ever held a public hearing and it will be an historic occasion. It'll be difficult for her to hold her own because she'll be up against Labour MPs who could have been in the cabinet.' Perhaps not surprisingly, Mrs Beckett seemed in no hurry to respond to the request, and as the weeks went by, frustration turned to anger among stalwart supporters of the select committee system who showed no hesitation in attacking the government. Andrew Mackinlay, a Labour member of the Foreign Affairs Select Committee, told Mrs Beckett during her weekly business statement that the pressure he had been under during the Sierra Leone inquiry had been demeaning and unacceptable. 'A government whip came up to me and said without a note of sarcasm, but with genuine incredulity, "Mackinlay, I just cannot understand you. We put you on the principal committee of the House and you insist on asking all these questions. Why don't you just enjoy it?" ' Afterwards Mackinlay told me that the pressure had continued throughout the inquiry and he was asked repeatedly to 'go easy on the witnesses'. After recounting Mackinlay's experiences in his weekly column in the *Independent*, the former Conservative MP Michael Brown predicted that Mrs Beckett would live to regret her 'contemptuous dismissal' of the Liaison Committee's reform package. Brown told the *Westminster Hour* there was nothing new in

Mackinlay's revelations; when he had been a Conservative whip he was under instructions to exercise as much control as possible over the select committee members. 'I had a tame Tory MP on a committee who owed his position to me . . . In the tea bar, that was the moment to seek a draft report from that MP or persuade him to put down an amendment helpful to the government.'

When Mrs Beckett finally appeared before the committee in early July she was adamant that ministers remained resolutely opposed to changing the selection system. She said there was self-nomination and MPs were free to apply to join select committees, but there had to be a balancing process to get some degree of equity between MPs of the governing party and opposition parties. When Archie Kirkwood, Liberal Democrat chairman of the Social Security Select Committee, challenged her to admit that it was the party managers who controlled committee membership, Mrs Beckett accepted they played a role but insisted that the final power of nomination remained with the House itself. Her arguments were rejected in forthright terms when in late July the Liaison Committee published its aptly titled response, *Independence or Control?*. The committee chairmen said there was widespread disquiet about a practice that had not worked and was clearly not independent of the government. 'Those being scrutinised should not have a say in the selection of the scrutineers. We believe that the present system does not, and should not, have the confidence of the House and public.' The modernisation of Parliament had to provide better accountability and tougher scrutiny of the government of the day. 'This is our aim. We believe it is the test by which the public will judge the effectiveness and value of Parliament. This is not something that will go away.' The committee also took grave exception to the way government had tried to put a highly selective gloss on their disagreement. A press release issued by the Cabinet Office said ministers had 'responded positively' to the proposed new powers for the select committees when in fact the government had rejected 'every major recommendation'. The Liaison Committee said that was not the kind of presentation to the news media which the government should employ in its relations with Parliament.

An uneasy stand-off had developed leaving the committee chairmen with no other option but to plan for the day when Mrs

Beckett allocated sufficient parliamentary time to debate their report. David Davis tried to rally support for a full-scale challenge by writing a column in the *Independent* under the headline: 'Let the Commons rise up against the control freaks.' He was convinced that Tony Blair's government was 'probably the worst ever in its obsession for control' and that Labour's 'spin doctors and media manipulators' were trying to thwart the select committees in their 'thorough research, careful and persistent questioning of ministers, and critical but non-partisan reports'. Davis said the leaking of early draft reports from the Foreign Affairs and Social Security Select Committees had allowed government departments to get their retaliation in first. 'That kind of rapid rebuttal can cripple a committee's effectiveness.'

When *Shifting the Balance* and *Independence or Control?* were finally discussed on the floor of the House in November 2000, the government denied MPs a chance to vote on the Liaison Committee's recommendations through the technical device of holding the debate on a motion to adjourn. Mrs Beckett remained resolute in her opposition to proposals that would allow select committees to begin 'to substitute their judgement for that of the government'. She was prepared to consider providing more resources and extra research support, but the changes that had been put forward would 'completely reshape' the work of an MP and take the select committees into government and party politics, which had 'hitherto been anathema to those who have so much admired our select committee structure'. Mrs Beckett justified the government's refusal to allow MPs the chance to vote on the Liaison Committee's rcommendations on the grounds that the proposed shake-up was so far-reaching that it required further debate and could not be decided 'off the cuff'. This did not satisfy the champions of the select committee system, who believed the Prime Minister had reneged on an undertaking he gave to the House in July 2000 that there would be 'a free vote'.

Although the government had succeeded in denying MPs the chance to secure any further reforms until after the next election, the Foreign Affairs Select Committee was determined that the events of Tony Blair's first parliament should not pass unrecorded. In a special report published in January 2001, the committee said its refusal to 'capitulate under pressure' from the Foreign Secretary, Robin Cook, and its insistence on conducting its own inquiry into arms supplies to Sierra Leone, had 'done a service' to all select committees. MPs had shown that when it came to scrutinising the government, 'tenacity has its rewards'; ministers and officials had been reminded that 'the beam of the select committee searchlight may one day swing in their direction, and that they may have to justify their action – or inaction – when subject to intense scrutiny by a committee such as ours, acting on behalf of Parliament and, beyond that, on behalf of a wider public interest.'

My sympathies were with the select committees in their drive to add weapons to their armoury and their wish to remove committee membership from the patronage of the executive and party whips. The committee chairmen had set aside their political differences to demonstrate cross-party support for measures aimed solely at strengthening parliamentary scrutiny. I considered they were justified in many of their fears about the cavalier way in which the Labour government had sought to restrain their influence and independence. Although there were several highly controversial leaks from select committees under the Thatcher and Major governments, there had been nothing on the scale of the rather more systematic breaches of confidentiality exposed during the first half of 1999. Leaving aside any inconsistencies between my recollections about the rebuttal of the Sierra Leone report and the statements Robin Cook and John Williams gave to the Liaison Committee, their evidence showed conclusively that the mindset within the highest reaches of the Foreign Office was that, rather than pausing to reflect on the select committee's conclusions, the report should be instantly discredited. Instead of pulling back and making no immediate comment other than giving an undertaking to study the report, there was to be a knee-jerk rebuttal of the findings. As Williams had openly acknowledged in his evidence, he had focused far too narrowly on the leaked draft 'as a matter of media strategy'. He said his role in the Foreign Office news department was to specialise in 'controversial stories that the lobby are taking a hostile interest in' – which explained why a former *Daily Mirror* political editor, and not a career civil servant, was advising the Foreign Secretary on how to refute a highly critical report on an illegal arms shipment to Sierra Leone.

WHO ARE THE
CONTROL FREAKS?

'They kept on pestering me. Tony said to me: "I want you to do the job." You can't say "no" if you are asked by the Prime Minister.'

Phil Murphy speaking to Nicholas Jones, 26 January 1999, on his appointment as the Labour Party's director of communications

Tony Blair does have a point when he insists that the reliance his cabinet ministers have placed on their political advisers has been no different from that of the last Conservative government. Margaret Thatcher and John Major faced criticism in their day about the growing influence of their politically appointed but publicly funded support staff who were becoming increasingly prominent in Downing Street and the private offices of the secretaries of state. Where Blair has dissembled so blatantly has been in his refusal to acknowledge publicly the changed nature of much of the work these individuals now undertake. He has more than doubled the number of special advisers, expanded and strengthened the Downing Street policy unit and created two new politically staffed departments within No. 10. Some of the advisers hired to assist individual ministers have confined themselves to the policy issues that gave them their specialist status, but many more have been at the sharp end of the hard sell that has characterised New Labour's aggressive approach to the news media. Peter Mandelson and Alastair Campbell have become the role models for a generation of what I see as 'journo-politicos' spawned by the spin-doctoring culture that helped Blair win power.

These men and women are mainly young professionals whose backgrounds have been in the media, publicity or politics, and their habitat is the all-important front line of the vastly expanded interface between politicians and journalists. Demarcation lines have become blurred and the 'journo-politicos' can move around with ease. They can be switched at will between Downing Street and the party's offices in Millbank Tower; one month their salaries as temporary civil servants are funded by the state; next month, back at Labour's headquarters, they are paid for by the party. Their success is judged in terms of their effectiveness in political presentation. Can they deliver when it comes to launching new policies or extricating ministers from unforeseen trouble? Are they prepared to ingratiate themselves with the political correspondents whose assistance they need, or alternatively, can they put the boot in when it comes to browbeating journalists who have overstepped the mark and caused trouble? Blair has always been consistent in defending the need for Labour to embrace the very latest techniques in political communication and to develop a hard-edged attitude towards the media but, like previous prime ministers, he has kept himself above the fray and pleaded ignorance when challenged about some of the more questionable activities undertaken in his name. In recent years the Downing Street press office has been home to several redoubtable political streetfighters. Promoting and defending a prime minister has become one of the most maligned occupations in modern politics and Campbell's instinct to attack first is no different from that of two of his illustrious predecessors, Joe Haines and Bernard Ingham.

For the majority of their long years in opposition Labour faced a largely hostile press. This was a considerable handicap and had a lasting impact on party thinking. Gaining favourable publicity was always an uphill struggle, and although Blair has been criticised for the way he courted Rupert Murdoch, Thatcher enjoyed a much longer and far friendlier relationship with the country's leading newspaper proprietors than anything a Labour prime minister has succeeded in establishing. Close links between government ministers and editorial executives persisted for most of the eighteen years the Conservatives were in power and made life easier for their special advisers. Many were closely involved in devising ways to use press, television and radio to present and promote new policies, and they did have regular contact with journalists. Although there were numerous spectacular disagreements with newspapers and broadcasting organisations, the pace of events did not seem quite so frenetic and – except for their final years in power – Thatcher and

Major did not appear quite so overwhelmed by the siege mentality towards the news media that has afflicted most Labour politicians in both opposition and government. As deadlines have continued to get shorter over the years, broadcasters and newspaper correspondents have placed even greater demands on the special advisers. Their unique status as half party worker and half civil servant has made them an important conduit when journalists are trying to make instant contact with a minister. The massive expansion in rolling news programmes has meant there are many more requests for interviews, and the pressure that builds up for the speedy release of information has been intensified still further by the proliferation of news services on the Internet.

On looking through newspaper cuttings and my notes for the Thatcher and Major years I was struck by how few references there were to conflicts between journalists and special advisers. Much of the news coverage was devoted to exploring the controversial policies the advisers were propounding on behalf of their ministers and to investigating their involvement in doubtful political ventures. According to a calculation made in 1992, a third of the advisers working in the Major government had been recruited from among the Oxbridge graduates hired as political researchers at Conservative Central Office. Some appeared intent on using their stint working for a minister as a way of helping them find lucrative employment in lobbying or public relations, but most of the young advisers saw it as an invaluable stepping-stone towards getting selected as a prospective parliamentary candidate. For example, five of the thirty-five special advisers on the payroll in 1993 went on to win seats as Conservative MPs in the 1997 general election: Crispin Blunt, James Gray, Damian Green, Eleanor Laing and David Ruffley. Some advisers listed that year were well established and had worked for their cabinet ministers in several different departments. They were well connected politically and socially, and were far removed from the foot-in-the-door journalism of tabloid newspapers. Lady Eileen Strathnaver was the long-standing adviser to Michael Heseltine. Tessa Keswick followed the former Conservative Chancellor of the Exchequer, Kenneth Clarke, each step of the way as he was promoted up the cabinet ladder from Secretary of State for Health, to Secretary of State for

Education, to Home Secretary and then to the Treasury. A profile of Mrs Keswick, published in the *Daily Mail* shortly before the 1993 Budget, was headed: 'Mrs Fixit who has the ken to help Clarke.' She was described as a 'feisty, sophisticated mother of three' who had struck up a 'formidable political partnership' with the Chancellor. She said she helped Clarke identify difficult political issues and talked to him when he was dealing with the press so that she could advise him on the different approaches he might take.

I recall discussing the work that the job entailed with Dr Elizabeth Cottrell, who was special adviser to Gillian Shephard, the then Minister for Agriculture, Fisheries and Food. 'Agriculture has been the best ministry so far for Gillian. I think she was glad to get out of Employment and now we really have got something to get our teeth into. I suppose you could describe me as the adviser to an upwardly mobile minister, a political survivor.' Dr Cottrell said the advisers met each Wednesday lunchtime to swap notes. Apparently one of the perils of being assigned to a minister with a topical brief was being asked on Friday afternoon to ghost-write an article for one of the Sunday newspapers. Advisers frequently prepared the speeches which ministers gave at party events and they spent much of their time maintaining contact with party officials and sorting out political problems. My notes of conversations with Dr Cottrell and other advisers did not give me the impression that they considered talking to journalists took precedence over all their other work. They made mention of their role as minders when their ministers were being hassled by reporters and photographers, but their dealings with the media appeared to be just one of their many day-to-day duties rather than their dominant concern.

Perhaps the most marked difference between them and their successors was in their general temperament. They did not seem to be on the constant campaign footing their Labour counterparts have adopted, perpetually promoting the next story or trying desperately to recycle what has already been announced. A former senior civil servant who worked closely with special advisers during the Thatcher and Major years found that many of them just wanted to get selected as for parliamentary candidates. Geoffrey Hollis, an under-secretary at the Ministry of Agriculture, Fisheries and Food until his retirement in 1996, told me that their chief interest seemed to be in studying advance copies of white papers and reports. 'They were anxious to keep up to date on policy issues and I never got the impression they spent much time talking to journalists. We considered most of them were just trainee Conservative MPs.'

When the status and payment of special advisers was formalised by Harold Wilson's government in the 1970s, the aim was to provide ministers with a counterbalance to the power and influence of senior civil servants. The 1968 Fulton Report on the civil service had welcomed the practice of governments bringing in professional experts and advisers but believed it should be put on a 'regular and clearly understood basis'. In a speech in 1975, Wilson described the political adviser as 'an extra pair of hands, ears and eyes and a mind more politically committed and more politically aware' than would be available from the political neutrals in the civil service. In 1974 there were thirty special advisers spread across fifteen departments, including No. 10, and they were most likely to be economists or experts in key areas of social policy like pensions, housing and education. Their appointment was welcomed by many Labour MPs as a way of ensuring that the party's objectives were not wrecked by the traditional conventions of Whitehall. Thatcher and Major both took full advantage of a system that left the taxpayer picking up the bill not only for hiring outside political advice but also for financing what had become an invaluable training ground, providing remunerated employment for the young recruits that every party was desperate to attract. Because Labour spent so many years in opposition, the Conservatives have been the main beneficiaries of the taxpayers' munificence – though there are signs that some catching up is going on. The first ministerial aide of the Blair government to progress to membership of the House of Commons was Hilary Benn, son of Tony Benn. After serving for two years as a special adviser in the Department for Education and Employment, he was chosen as Labour candidate for the Leeds Central by-election, which he won in June 1999. Hilary Benn MP has proved to be a stout defender of his former role in providing political back-up in David Blunkett's department: in a debate in July 2000 he said advisers should have a unique knowledge of the governing party's background that enabled them to provide advice 'which it would be wrong to expect a civil servant to give'. Several special advisers currently working for ministers in the Blair government have added their names to the list of candidates, hoping to be selected in the final run-up to the next general election. So far, Jack Straw is the only prominent Labour politician of his generation to have followed this route right to the top, having risen from the post of special adviser to the Secretary of State for Social Services, Barbara Castle, in 1974 to become Home Secretary in 1997; but Straw's achievement pales into insignificance when set against the massed ranks of Tory high-flyers whose entry to the House of Commons was expedited by the experience and contacts they built up when assigned to cabinet ministers during the long, uninterrupted years of Conservative government.

The roll-call of former special advisers who have made it to high office bears testimony to the efficacy of Harold Wilson's astute political footwork in laying out the ground rules. When Oliver Letwin was appointed a Treasury affairs spokesman in September 2000, he became the third former special adviser to have secured a place in the shadow cabinet, joining the shadow Chancellor, Michael Portillo, and the shadow social security secretary, David Willetts. Other members of the frontbench team, including David Liddington and John Bercow, were also former special advisers, as were John Redwood, head of the Conservatives' parliamentary campaigns unit; Tim Collins, the party's senior vice chairman; John Whittingdale, parliamentary private secretary to William Hague; and Andrew Tyrie, a leading member of the Select Committee on Public Administration. Redwood, Willetts, Letwin, Collins and Damian Green all did service in the Downing Street policy unit, long considered the hothouse for rising political talent. Much of the news media's interest in the work of the Conservatives' special advisers focused on their role inside No. 10 and the scope and influence of the policy unit expanded under both Thatcher and Major.

Redwood, who was appointed head of the policy unit in 1984, was succeeded the following year by Professor Brian Griffiths, who in turn was replaced by Sarah Hogg when Major became Prime Minister in 1990. Mrs Hogg, economics editor of the *Daily Telegraph* and *Sunday Telegraph*, was one of the few former journalists to have served as a special adviser under the Conservatives. Howell James, Major's political secretary for his final three years in No. 10, had extensive experience in broadcasting. He organised outside broadcasts for Capital Radio; helped launch TV-am; served as political adviser to the former Conservative Secretary of State for Employment, Lord Young; was appointed director of corporate affairs for the BBC at the age of thirty-three; and held the same post at Cable and Wireless, before finally heading to Downing Street in 1994. None the less, lack of previous employment or contact with the news media was commonplace and clearly did not constitute a handicap, reflecting no doubt the slightly less fevered relationship with journalists. However, as the demands made by newspapers, television and radio multiplied, ministers found their advisers were of increasing assistance in fielding reporters' questions about party affairs. Civil service guidelines laid down a clear division between party business and work for the government. Calls of a political nature were strictly off limits for government information officers and had to be dealt with by the special advisers, who were also responsible for liaising with Central Office and briefing Conservative MPs.

Sometimes mistakes were made, and disputes over the demarcation line – a source of considerable controversy once Labour gained power – were not unknown under the Conservatives. Six months before the 1997 general election, the Deputy Prime Minister, Michael Heseltine, got embroiled in a row over what Labour claimed was an attempt to politicise the civil service, a charge that would become a far commoner refrain after Tony Blair became Prime Minister. Heseltine had been caught out by a series of leaked letters from the Cabinet Office which showed that he wanted all departments to draw up lists of successful public servants like headteachers, doctors and prison governors, and also the heads of privatised services and agencies, who were prepared to be 'vigorous and attractive proponents' of the government's achievements. Names of suitable people would be 'made known to the media' as the election approached. Heseltine was convinced of the value of his strategy: 'Positive presentation of the facts by a service deliverer . . . carries greater public credibility than any government spokesman can hope for.' Labour accused him of looking for 'cheerleaders' for Tory policies, but he insisted that as soon as he was informed by the Cabinet Secretary, Sir Robin Butler, that work of this nature should not be undertaken by civil servants, he issued 'explicit instructions' to ensure that the task was completed by political advisers.

Labour maintained that Heseltine had been caught 'red handed in a flagrant abuse of power' and that the episode showed that the Conservatives were prepared to breach the political neutrality of civil servants. When accused at question time by John Prescott of 'trying to subvert the impartiality of the civil service', the Deputy Prime Minister insisted that he had left open the question of who would draw up the lists of the prominent public figures he had in mind. Heseltine then hit back at Prescott by claiming that the 'worst and most excessive' example of politicisation was Harold Wilson's appointment in 1969 of a Labour Party sympathiser, Joe Haines, as chief press officer in Downing Street, a precedent that he thought was likely to lead to Alastair Campbell being considered for that post if 'ever a Labour government were re-elected'. Campbell had already completed two years as Blair's press secretary, and getting a name check from the Deputy Prime Minister was a recognition of the damage that New Labour's media offensive had been inflicting on the government. However, Heseltine and the rest of the cabinet had no inkling of the transformation that would take place in the Downing Street press office once Blair was elected.

John Major, like previous Conservative prime ministers, had insisted that his chief press secretary should always be a senior civil servant, and that this was one post which should not become a political appointment. Even so, Major had not escaped criticism over the cost of employing highly paid political advisers at a time of tight spending controls. On becoming Prime Minister he announced that most departments would be limited to one special adviser, and in 1992 four of the thirty-five posts he inherited from Thatcher were left vacant. His resolve was short-lived. By the following year all thirty-five posts were filled, and in response to a question from the Liberal Democrat MP Matthew Taylor he revealed that the annual wage bill was £1.4 million, having doubled in the space of five years. Newspaper leader writers were indignant at the size of the salaries being paid to the advisers. Three earned at least £80,000 a year, which was more than the Prime Minister, and the salaries of another six were up to the level of a cabinet minister. The London *Evening Standard* said the bill for the 'gilt-edged, publicly subsidised pay packets' of these 'pampered political bureaucrats' should go straight to Conservative Central Office. 'Matthew Taylor says that it is just a career fast-track for ambitious young Tories. He's absolutely right.' A similarly caustic line was taken by Mark Seddon, editor of *Tribune*, who accused the Conservatives of abusing the system Harold Wilson created. The typical Tory adviser was a 'very different creature' from that envisaged in the 1960s. Seddon said they were invariably products of private schools and Oxbridge, not one of the thirty-five had worked in the public sector, and their previous employment had been at banks at party headquarters or as lawyers or lobbyists.

Amid all the protestations about the way party hacks had taken advantage of the public purse, there was not a word of complaint from Labour's high command. Successive Labour leaders had seen the benefit the Conservatives had derived from a system that injected influential outside advice into the heart of government and also met the cost of hiring sharp political operators who could give some much-needed back-up to ministers. Tony Blair had certainly not signalled his intentions in advance of the 1997 election, but the alterations and initiatives he planned in the rank and deployment of special advisers would prove to be as far-reaching as the upheaval that resulted from the creation of the Downing Street policy unit in 1974, a step regarded by its first head, Bernard Donoughue, as the 'most important Whitehall institutional innovation' for forty years. Within two days of Blair's taking office, a meeting of the Privy Council approved an order in council giving Blair's chief of staff, Jonathan Powell, and his press secretary, Alastair Campbell, executive powers that were unprecedented for political appointees taking up jobs previously performed by senior civil servants. Both were provided with the authority to instruct civil servants, and Campbell's contract allowed him to present the government's affairs 'in a political context', thus freeing him from civil service rules on political neutrality. Other members of the cabinet, including the Deputy Prime Minister, John Prescott, the Chancellor of the Exchequer,

Gordon Brown, and the Home Secretary, Jack Straw, followed Blair's example and took with them into government the advisers who had been with them in opposition.

Cost-cutting restrictions that John Major had imposed were swept aside. Each department was allowed a minimum of two special advisers; some had three, four or five. By early June 1998 the total had risen to seventy-three, almost double Major's final establishment of thirty-eight. The largest increase of all was in Downing Street, where the number of political appointees had risen to twenty-three. When Major left office there were eight. Most of No. 10's additional special advisers were attached to a much-enlarged policy unit, but two of the new posts resulted from another of Blair's innovations, a newly established strategic communications unit that was told to think long-term about the presentation of future policy announcements. The task of influencing and controlling the news agenda could not be handled simply on a day-to-day basis, and the unit would look ahead to make sure the government was not caught unawares by events that should have been foreseen. Although these structural changes were far-reaching, their impact was dwarfed initially by the aggressive recruitment policy that was instituted by the Prime Minister and his press secretary. Talent scouts were on the look-out not for bright eyed researchers but hardened media hands who could develop and maintain the supremacy New Labour had established in the art of political communication. Press officers who had worked at Millbank during the election campaign were snapped up by ministers as their special advisers; several newspaper journalists who had already revealed privately their support for what was commonly known as 'the project' were soon installed inside No. 10; they were joined by others who had experience of broadcasting, publicity and public affairs. As the months went by the trawl of likely candidates was spread wider and wider.

New opportunities also opened up within the civil service as vacancies arose as a result of a shake-up in government press offices and the hasty departure of numerous directors of information. Lobby correspondents were never quite sure who among their colleagues would be signed up next. The BBC appeared to have become a regular target for the Downing Street raiding party as a succession of senior producers and correspondents left to take up a variety of posts on offer. While some of the early and prominent signings did attract publicity, others passed by almost unnoticed. What struck me particularly forcibly was the way in which many of the real or imagined barriers to free movement between jobs in journalism, politics and government simply melted away. Transfers that would have attracted considerable comment under previous governments were no longer questioned, let alone a source of controversy. Journalists from Labour-sympathising newspapers and former Labour Party press officers had no difficulty in becoming civil servants and in securing some of the most senior posts in the information service. The reverse was also the case: journalists who had taken party appointments but later relinquished them or were sacked appeared to have no difficulty returning to jobs in broadcasting or on newspapers.

Westminster has been enriched over the years by a regular traffic in personnel between the news media and politics. Some of the country's leading politicians started out as journalists, just as some MPs have forsaken Parliament to become celebrated columnists and pundits. All the major parties have been beneficiaries of this two-way flow. However, the presentational techniques developed and deployed by Labour, which have increasingly been copied by their opponents, demanded by their very nature a high level of staffing, and the previous small but steady flow of personnel out of the media, across the divide and into political employment, has become a flood of unparalleled proportions. No longer was it a case of the odd high-flyer being enticed out of a well-paid job in order to work as a publicity director for one or other of the political parties. What transpired under Tony Blair seemed far more calculated. Journalists, producers and researchers have been picked off one by one. Some had established by-lines or were well-known broadcasters; others had middle-ranking jobs; all had skills that were badly needed by the Labour government. Although their newsroom colleagues had known or guessed that most of those who departed probably were Labour supporters or sympathisers, few were regarded as having been highly committed or intent on entering politics full-time. Nevertheless Blair had found a way of enthusing and attracting workers from a profession known for its cynicism. In exploring how this recruitment policy originated and operated, and in assessing the consequences of such a large influx of highly experienced journalists into a politically controlled regime, I do not intend to launch a blanket attack on the motives and integrity of reporters and party workers, with some of whom I have been acquainted for many years. None the less I do believe the phenomenon raises issues worthy of investigation.

Public undertakings were given by Blair and Campbell about the controls that would be put in place to prevent the politicisation of the information service. Special advisers would not be allowed to abuse their status as short-term civil servants by getting the taxpayer to help fund Labour propaganda, nor would political appointees be permitted to use their positions as a platform for attacking the opposition or for pursuing internal party conflicts. Most of the incidents and events I discuss might be explained away as nothing more than misplaced enthusiasm; but I contend that they have to be seen against the background of wider concern about moves towards a more presidential style of government. Constitutionalists and commentators have been charting this development for some years, and in my last book, *Sultans of Spin*, I discussed the safeguards introduced in the United States to police political appointments. Labour were usually so effective in opposition in exposing and exploiting any violations of rules by the Conservatives that Thatcher and Major had to remain ever-watchful, and they always insisted that they did their best to honour the dividing line between work for the party and the state. While many politicians and journalists have continued to question the Conservatives' record, some of the distinctions that separate government publicity from political promotion no longer appear to be quite so clear-cut. The interchangeable status and duties of many of those recruited since 1997 has given a seamless cohesion to the new political cadre that the Prime Minister and his press secretary have created.

Once installed in Downing Street, Campbell was in no doubt about the sea change he wanted to see in the performance levels of the one thousand civil service information officers. In a letter circulated to all Whitehall departments in September 1997, he said the election of a new administration had provided a 'real opportunity for the government information service to raise its game'. Labour had outgunned the Conservatives on every flank during the long propaganda offensive that culminated in Major's defeat, and Campbell had to find ways of preserving that superiority. In their first few months in office ministers had been appalled by the lack of urgency they found within the government's publicity machine, and there was harsh criticism of the heads of the information service for doing so little to keep pace with the challenging, non-stop demands of 24-hour news. These failings were of little consequence initially, because the new administration had been greeted with a blaze of favourable publicity. Campbell and his colleagues had the great satisfaction of seeing most newspapers heap praise on policy announcements that Labour had long planned for in opposition. Most of the special advisers involved in the launch of those early initiatives had worked together for some years and had been welded into a close-knit team of party press officers for the election campaign. Tim Allan and Hilary Coffman, who had been in Blair's office in opposition, joined Campbell in the Downing Street press office; Campbell's partner, Fiona Millar, also acquired the status of special adviser as press officer and personal assistant to Cherie Blair. At the Treasury, the Chancellor, Gordon Brown, had four advisers including his personal press officer, Charlie Whelan, his chief economics adviser, Ed Balls, and Ed Miliband, whose brother David was appointed head of the No. 10 policy unit in 1998. Other newly appointed advisers who were well known to political journalists included Ed Owen, who followed Jack Straw to the Home Office; Conor Ryan, adviser to the Secretary of State for Education, David Blunkett; and Joe McCrea, adviser to the Secretary of State for Health, Frank Dobson.

Campbell had to wait some months before he could start finding openings for the journalists whom he already knew were prepared to work for Blair, or whom he thought might be tempted by a top job in the government or the party. In October 1997 work began on a full evaluation of the future direction of the information service. Robin Mountfield, the permanent secretary for the Office of Public Service, who conducted the review, gave his backing to the creation of the strategic communications unit which was established in Downing

Street in January 1998 with a staff of six, two of whom were senior newspaper correspondents, Philip Bassett and David Bradshaw. Both were prolific writers known for their strong political commitment to New Labour, and they joined the lengthening list of special advisers. Bassett, formerly industrial editor of *The Times*, was one of those interviewed by Blair in 1994 for the post of press secretary; his partner, Baroness Symons, was parliamentary under-secretary of state at the Foreign Office. Bradshaw, a former political correspondent on the *Daily Mirror*, had worked at the party's media centre at Millbank Tower during the election campaign. In May 1998 two more journalists from the *Daily Mirror* took up senior positions, both becoming civil servants in the information service: John Williams, formerly the paper's political editor, joined the Foreign Office as deputy head of news, and Sheree Dodd, a former political correspondent, was signed up as head of news in the Northern Ireland Office, and subsequently became head of media relations at the Department of Social Security. With Campbell in No. 10 there were now four ex-*Mirror* journalists working together; but a far greater infusion of new blood into both the party and the government was about to be provided by the BBC.

One early, short-lived recruit was Joy Johnson, a former BBC political news editor, who was Labour's communications director for almost a year until her resignation in January 1996. The start of what turned into a mini-exodus began in January 1998 when Martin Sixsmith, a former BBC correspondent in Moscow, was appointed director of information at the Department of Social Security, a post he held for a year. In February Tom Kelly, the BBC's chief producer in Belfast, was appointed director of communications in the Northern Ireland Office; he was followed in June 1998 by one of the BBC's political correspondents, Lance Price, who became a special adviser at No. 10 and replaced Tim Allan in deputising for Campbell on political issues. (Allan had been hired by British Sky Broadcasting as its director of corporate communications.) After spending two years in the Downing Street press office, Price moved to Millbank Tower on being appointed the party's director of communications. Price's departure from the BBC was followed within a fortnight by that of another political correspondent, Lorraine Davidson, who was appointed director of communications for the Scottish Labour Party, a post she held for nearly a year before returning to journalism as political editor of the *Scottish Mirror*. In March 1999 Bill Bush, head of BBC research, and his second in command, the research project co-ordinator Catherine Rimmer, both resigned and moved to Downing Street, where Bush took up a new post as head of No.10's newly established research and information unit. Bush's task was to establish a database of factual information on policy issues, research papers and statistics. His arrival in No.10 coincided with speculation that Ken Livingstone might be banned from Labour's shortlist of candidates for Mayor of London. In the early 1980s, before he joined the BBC, Bush was political assistant for the Labour group on the former Greater London Council, when Livingstone was leader, and his political background provoked considerable comment. Livingstone used his weekly column in the *Independent* to compliment the Prime Minister for choosing a researcher who had 'acute political understanding'.

Another recruit from the BBC was Ed Richards, chief policy strategist under the director general John Birt, who became a special adviser in the Downing Street policy unit, joining another former BBC strategist, James Purnell, whose brief at No. 10 included culture, media and sport. Two producers who had previously worked at the BBC's studios in Westminster added their names to the list. Don Brind became press officer for the Parliamentary Labour Party and Adrian Long was appointed special adviser to the Minister of State for Transport, Lord Macdonald. Long was one of five advisers in the Department of the Environment, Transport and the Regions, headed by John Prescott. The new deputy director of the media centre at the Department of Health was another recruit from broadcasting, GMTV's political correspondent, Sian Jarvis.

Blair's approval was needed for all political appointments by ministers, and he also took a keen interest in the choice of senior publicity staff for the party. Joy Johnson told me that before being appointed Labour's communications director in February 1995 she had been given a 'thorough grilling' by Blair. She had been a Labour Party member for twenty years, but she said he insisted on checking out the depth of her commitment to the party, the strength of her determination to see Labour win the election, and whether she could remain resolute and ruthless under fire. Ms Johnson was headhunted for the job after her flair in editing *Conference Live* at the previous year's Labour Party conference had impressed Gordon Brown and several other members of the shadow cabinet. Her experience of being identified and then targeted would be repeated time and again; but once Labour was in government, and having to face an inevitable turnover in staff, the task became harder. Lorraine Davidson had the same high expectations as Ms Johnson on being recruited to work for the Scottish Labour Party. On leaving the post a year later, after the first elections to the new Scottish Parliament, she told me of the efforts that were made to persuade her to accept the job, making no secret of the fact that Blair and Campbell had personally encouraged her to take it. Having done so, she said, she found it an unrewarding occupation. She was constantly bombarded by calls from journalists and, at the same time, she felt under pressure from officials in the government and the party. 'When it comes to trying to promote Labour in Scotland, I have been there, done that and I don't want to do it again.'

In some cases it took a personal appeal from Blair to clinch an appointment. Phil Murphy, another of Labour's short-lived directors of communications, was a long-time target of the New Labour headhunters. He was a well-established political journalist and had spent twelve years in the lobby. After working for the *Newcastle Journal* and then becoming political editor of the *Yorkshire Post*, he was made political editor of the Press Association news agency, a post he relinquished within a year of the 1997 general election on being appointed director of communications for the Arts Council. Murphy's appointment to the Labour Party was confirmed in January 1999 at a regular meeting of the national executive committee in Millbank Tower. Afterwards a briefing for reporters was given by the chief press officer, Adrian McMenamin, who revealed that six applicants had been interviewed. He said one potential candidate was another BBC political correspondent, John Kampfner, who opted not to proceed with his application. In deciding to appoint Murphy, the party had agreed to make him an assistant general secretary, a higher position than that held by previous directors. Murphy turned up on the doorstep a few minutes later and, after I had congratulated him on his appointment, he explained why he had finally agreed to take the job. There had been speculation for months that he was a likely candidate for a post which had been advertised twice and had been vacant for almost a year since the departure of Labour's longest-serving media spokesman, David Hill, who had joined the celebrated lobbyist Sir Tim Bell and become a senior director of Bell Pottinger Good Relations. Murphy said the party's general secretary, Margaret McDonagh, and the Chancellor, Gordon Brown, had both encouraged him to take the job. 'I was minding my own business but once the party got hold of me they wouldn't let go. They kept on pestering me. Tony said to me: "I want you to do the job." You can't say "no" if you are asked by the Prime Minister.'

Murphy was given a public warning that weekend on *The Week in Westminster* about the difficulties he would face. David Hill and the *Mirror*'s political editor, Kevin Maguire, set out what they thought he should do to win the respect of political journalists. Maguire said it was important not to become too closely associated with either the Blair camp or the Brown camp. 'In many ways the job is easier in opposition but in government it is harder because the No. 10 machine and the Treasury machine are both trying to control things and that can make it a minefield.' Hill commiserated with his successor and said Murphy would have to get used to getting up to seventy to eighty messages on his pager every weekend. 'You have to know the journalists you are dealing with and you have to retain your integrity. You must never lie to journalists because you will always get caught out.'

Hill spoke with twenty-five years' experience of working as a middleman between Labour politicians and the media. He started out in 1973 as political assistant to the then shadow education secretary, Roy Hattersley, and became his special adviser when Hattersley was appointed Secretary of State for Prices and Consumer Protection in 1976. Recalling his early days in an interview for the *New Statesman*, he said Hattersley was unusual in realising that he required help in dealing with the news media. 'Roy recognised this earlier than any other politician in opposition . . . politicians do need assistants to communicate on their behalf and journalists require authoritative voices to go to . . . spin doctors are a consequence of that.' Hill said that after spending only ten days as Hattersley's special adviser there were complaints within the Department for Prices and Consumer Protection about his memos having been 'far too political', but Hattersley stood by him. 'The civil service machine had to recognise they were operating in a more political atmosphere.'

Phil Murphy remained at Millbank Tower until June 2000 when he moved to Downing Street as a special adviser. His replacement as communications director at Millbank Tower was Lance Price. Several other key appointments that year indicated the ease with which it was possible to move from party headquarters to jobs at the heart of government. Carl Shoben and Chris McShane, two members of the media monitoring unit that the Labour Party had developed at Millbank, became special advisers in No. 10 where they performed the same role for the press office and drew on the output of the media monitoring unit that the government had established in the Cabinet Office. Their arrival took the total number of special advisers in Downing Street to twenty-six, over three times the number under Major. Another significant new appointment was that of Joe McCrea, who was hired on a short-term civil service contract to help develop another newly launched government service, the 'knowledge network', which was designed to provide ministers and civil servants with an electronic database of up-to-date information on policy briefings, facts and figures. McCrea had served at the Department of Health as special adviser to Frank Dobson until the latter's departure from the cabinet in October 1999 when he entered the contest to become Mayor of London. The forerunner of the new knowledge network had been an information system devised by McCrea at the Department of Health which gave 24-hour access by desktop or laptop computer to the latest 'lines to take' on health service announcements and hospital waiting lists. The intention was to provide the same service for the whole of Whitehall.

McCrea's civil service contract and a range of other appointments secured by former party employees at Millbank Tower illustrated the portable nature of the media skills acquired by party workers and political journalists and what I judged was the increasingly relaxed approach being taken towards the nature of their previous employment. While in opposition Labour had regularly drawn attention to what they suspected was a lack of impartiality in public appointments. Both the BBC and ITN were criticised for having appointed broadcasters and producers who were said to have been past members or supporters of the Conservative Party. Nick Robinson, a BBC political correspondent who had been national chairman of Young Conservatives, told me that during the 1997 election campaign he was aware there had been some misplaced comments about his objectivity among staff at Labour's headquarters. A year after Campbell became Blair's official spokesman he used an afternoon lobby briefing to deliver a pointed reminder to the assembled correspondents that a newly promoted BBC political reporter, Max Cotton, had worked for three weeks as a freelance on the Conservatives' 1992 election campaign. It had been my task to introduce Cotton at his first briefing, and by way of introduction I said he had joined the BBC from the independent London radio station LBC. Campbell added the rejoinder, 'Yes, LBC, via Central Office,' just to leave no one in any doubt that he had marked Cotton's card.

Several former Conservative Party press officers told me that they discovered their previous employment at Central Office could be considered a handicap when they applied for media-related work in the public services because there was a possibility they might find themselves vulnerable to attacks from Labour politicians, and that made prospective employers hesitant about taking them on. The easier-going attitude evident since the change of government provoked considerable comment among former Whitehall directors of information. Nine of the seventeen heads of department in place at the time of the election claimed they had been eased out within a year because they had been considered unsuitable or had failed to establish a working relationship with their incoming ministers. A year later all but two had either been removed or left the government. The interview procedures which had been followed in appointing their successors were stoutly defended by the head of the information service, Mike Granatt, in his 1999 annual report. He said claims that appointments were being made as a result of patronage were completely unwarranted. Certain individuals had been singled out by name in the news media as having been appointed 'for reasons of political sympathy, not merit', but there was no evidence of misbehaviour by any of them. Less than a 'handful' of senior recruits had worked for the Labour Party, and the civil service did not discriminate against candidates because they had worked for or supported a mainstream political party. Ex-Conservative Central Office staff had 'quite properly' worked as information officers and Granatt did not know of 'any significant or indeed any substantiated complaint' against any of his colleagues with former party connections. Civil service commissioners supervised all senior appointments and Granatt had been a member of almost every interview panel.

Notwithstanding this forthright rebuttal, there had been a marked change in the pattern of recruitment. When it came to promotion, career civil servants had lost out consistently as the more senior positions went to journalists, broadcasters, other media professionals and former Labour Party press officers. I considered this to be a clear departure from previous practice and a trend that pointed to a lighter touch with regard to previous employment of a political character. I found my opinion was shared by newly recruited information officers attending the annual study week arranged by the University of Leeds for a postgraduate diploma in public administration. I addressed the course each year and noted that in July 2000 considerable concern was being expressed over the way senior posts were being taken by outside applicants. Several of the younger civil service press officers said the advertisements all seemed to be directed towards recruiting experienced people from the news media and that seemed to have demolished their career structure within the information service.

Three senior appointments that summer indicated the speed with which Mike Granatt and the interview panels had been working. The first involved a former Labour Party press officer, Lyn Bryan, who became chief press officer for the Department for Education and Employment in June 2000. I had known Ms Bryan for nearly twenty years. We first met in the early 1980s when she worked in the private sector and was on the staff of the Engineering Employers' Federation. She then changed course and became a press officer for the National Union of Public Employees, later renamed Unison. In 1997 she was one of several trade union public relations officers who assisted with Labour's general election campaign, after which she resumed her employment with Unison. When I complimented her on yet another career move she smiled and said it was no secret that she had faced quite a tough test and had been asked some pretty searching questions by Mike Granatt. Ms Bryan believed the range of work she had undertaken demonstrated that her communication skills were transferable and she was sure her record in providing accurate information, which she knew was respected by the news media, would have satisfied the civil service interview panel. Two months later it emerged that another former Labour Party press officer, Ian Hepplewhite, had been appointed to head one of the biggest information departments in Whitehall. After spending the two previous years as head of news at the Department for Culture, Media and Sport, he had gained promotion and was to take over as director of news at the Department of Trade and Industry. Hepplewhite would be in contact with an ex-colleague, Jo Moore, a former chief press and broadcasting officer at Millbank Tower, who had become a part-time special adviser to the Secretary of State for Trade and Industry, Stephen Byers. The third appointment was a promotion for the ex-*Mirror* political editor, John Williams, who after serving for over two years as deputy head of news at the Foreign Office had been made head of department, the first non-diplomat to hold the post.

Except for a few paragraphs in several newspaper diary columns, these appointments attracted no immediate adverse comment in the press, nor were there any protests from Conservative MPs, although they had frequently accused Labour of politicising the civil service by doubling the number of special advisers and exerting unfair pressure on government press officers. Some weeks later I asked the Conservatives' spokesman on Cabinet Office affairs, Andrew Lansley, why they had not commented on the latest appointments. He denied there was any inconsistency in their position. Party officials were aware that two ex-*Mirror* journalists and two former Labour Party press officers had got top jobs in the government information service, but the Conservatives had no reason to challenge civil service inter-view procedures and Lansley had no intention of getting involved in personalities. 'Obviously an incoming Conservative administration would want to look at this very carefully and consider any appointments which have been made, but we have to rely on the civil service commissioners fulfilling their responsibility to ensure political impartiality when appointing government information officers.'

Lansley was much more interested in developing the Conservatives' attack on the spiralling cost of the politically appointed special advisers. Earlier in the year he had opened an opposition day debate by accusing the government of wasting public money on its 'growing phalanx' of taxpayer-funded spin doctors. He said they had become a 'malign influence' who were briefing against each other as much as against the Conservatives. He had tried repeatedly to discover more details of their future annual wage bill and in a written answer, published shortly before the summer recess, the Minister for the Cabinet Office, Dr Marjorie Mowlam, revealed that the estimated cost of the salaries of the seventy-nine special advisers on the payroll would rise to £4.6 million during the twelve months to April 2002. A promise to halve government spending on 'political advisers and spin doctors in Whitehall' was one of the guarantees announced by William Hague when he launched the Conservatives' policy document, *The Common Sense Revolution*, at the 1999 annual conference. The pledge was repeated in the party's draft manifesto, *Believing in Britain*, published in September 2000 and reinforced a month later in Hague's address to the party conference. He said that people were 'sick of the spin' from political advisers whose only role was to dream up 'phoney statistics and falsehoods' aimed at winning headlines for the Prime Minister. Hague's attempt to highlight the government's dependence on special advisers was just one facet of his sustained attack on the work of New Labour's spin doctors. 'Spin' was the word the Conservatives were determined to hang round Blair's neck to drag him down, just as Labour had succeeded in pinning 'sleaze' to John Major. Opinion polls conducted during the summer and autumn of 2000 had shown a consistent fall in Blair's approval rating when people were asked if they regarded him as being honest and trustworthy, a finding exploited on every possible occasion by members of the opposition front bench who took delight in the constant repetition of their claim that no one believed any longer in the government's policy announcements or statistics.

Alastair Campbell's tactic when seeking to refute such attacks was to blame journalists for being preoccupied with gossip and trivia and for failing to report the government's achievements. However, he had difficulty sustaining his accusation that political correspondents had become obsessed with spin doctors and the whole process of political communication when some advisers were just as likely to be creating headlines as the ministers they worked for. An even greater threat to the Prime Minister and his press secretary were the advisers who had been forced out of their jobs and had nothing to lose by speaking out against practices that on reflection they believed were unacceptable or counterproductive. In several cases I was highly encouraged by their willingness to recant, especially as I had been on the receiving end of the kind of treatment that these very same individuals now felt able to renounce. The trigger for these frank expositions of the darker side of the New Labour spin machine was the demise of a most unlikely duo, Charlie Whelan and Benjamin Wegg-Prosser, the two special advisers who lost their jobs as a result of the temporary downfall of Blair's long-standing confidant Peter Mandelson, then Secretary of State for Trade and Industry, who resigned in December 1998 after confirming that he had bought a house in Notting Hill with the help of a £373,000 loan from the then Paymaster General, Geoffrey Robinson. Whelan was second only to Alastair Campbell in his notoriety as a spin doctor for the Blair government and in some ways his dedicated support for his patron Gordon Brown seemed far more personal and intense than the rather business-like bond between Campbell and Blair.

Whelan's departure was a messy affair, and although he protested his innocence he was left with no option but to resign after being blamed for leaking details of Mandelson's indebtedness to Robinson. The emergence of the home loan scandal was just one manifestation of a feud that had its roots in Mandelson's decision to abandon Brown in the 1994 leadership election and give covert assistance to Blair, a role that Whelan later exposed. Whelan had been Brown's press officer for five years, through the hard grind of opposition and on into government, and together with Ed Balls, Brown's economics adviser, they often enjoyed Robinson's hospitality at his flat in Park Lane. Their evenings together planning tactics while eating pizza and watching football on television would no doubt have been considered slightly downmarket by Peter Mandelson whose tastefully furnished house in Notting Hill reflected the social ambitions of a newly appointed cabinet minister. Although Wegg-Prosser, who was twenty-four at the time, was younger and far less experienced than Whelan, he worked just as tirelessly, on Mandelson's behalf. None the less the pair's endeavours did not always succeed in promoting the good deeds of their respective ministers or in enhancing the government's relations with the public, because the distrust that lingered on from the Blair–Brown rift, and the deep-seated animosity between rival groups of friends and supporters, had placed Whelan and Wegg-Prosser on opposite sides of a gulf that was not just unbridgeable but getting wider.

Their briefing styles could hardly have provided a sharper contrast. Whelan played on his reputation as a brash loudmouth who would do whatever he thought was necessary to protect Brown and kill off news stories that might damage him. Beneath the bluster was a cunning operator with a sharp mind who understood everything he needed to know about news deadlines and who had no compunction about manipulating the media by playing off newspaper reporters against broadcasters. Wegg-Prosser was more thoughtful and seemed far happier talking to journalists on the telephone than in having to endure the discomfort of a push-and-shove encounter on the doorstep. He was determined to do what he could to elevate his own importance and establish his position in the pecking order of New Labour's special advisers. Often he would spend some minutes at the end of a conversation deciding how his briefing should be attributed: perhaps his guidance should appear as words emanating from Mandelson's 'friends'; alternatively, it might be given the added status of having come from 'a senior source'; or it might even be sourced directly to one of the secretary of state's 'advisers'.

In the emotional aftermath of Mandelson's resignation and the resulting loss of his own job, Wegg-Prosser agonised for some moments as to how I would be allowed to source the guidance he had given me on Mandelson's future plans. One option he had volunteered was that Mandelson might consider putting his name forward as a Labour candidate for Mayor of London and try to follow in the footsteps of his grandfather, Herbert Morrison, who had been leader of London County Council. Wegg-Prosser wanted me to say that this was the advice that 'friends and colleagues' were giving the former cabinet minister. I thanked him for the information and in my report that evening for BBC radio I stated that Mandelson's 'adviser says standing in London is an option'. Needless to say my identification of the source of the story provoked an immediate complaint from Wegg-Prosser, who said that by quoting him directly I was implying that Mandelson was 'already thinking of standing' when this was 'something his friends are suggesting and is an option he will consider'. I could not help smiling while I listened to Wegg-Prosser's contortions as he struggled to bring some clarity to our earlier, convoluted conversation. Mandelson had been playing the same games with me on and off for the previous ten years, and I sensed that his young pupil had discovered to his cost the danger of working for a master who studied every nuance and who must clearly have taken offence at my report.

In his long career as Labour's most eminent spin doctor Mandelson had given so many off-the-record briefings to compliant journalists that he prided himself on being able to detect sufficient clues in reports to give him a good idea as to who was the likeliest source for most of the troublesome and speculative stories he had to contend with. He had the flamboyance and flair of an Hercule Poirot rather than the dogged perseverance of a Sherlock Holmes, and the next time he met an errant correspondent he liked nothing more than to pronounce on the identity of the culprit whom he thought was the source for whatever was the latest mischief that had troubled him and then, before departing, dismiss the matter with a flourish of the hand.

Although Mandelson's brief stint as Secretary of State for Trade and Industry meant Wegg-Prosser spent only five months as a special adviser, he was convinced that his work within the department had been constructive and that much of the criticism of the seventy-nine political advisers was misplaced. In a series of reflective newspaper articles for the *Guardian* he set out the advantages of the system, while at the same time going further than any of his former colleagues to atone for past evasions. Special advisers were 'an aid and resource, not a threat' as they kept officials out of political work; but there was no greater fear for senior civil servants than being bypassed by political appointees who were instrumental in many of the significant decisions taken by Blair's ministers. 'Much of the great progress this government has made since the election would not have happened without the energy and drive of the special advisers.' Wegg-Prosser was at his most revealing when acknowledging that during his stint at the Department of Trade and Industry he had been quoted in the newspapers under all manner of guises, a practice he realised had undermined the government's credibility, by suggesting that ministers were obsessed by spin, and had damaged the reputation of political reporting. Well-sourced anonymous quotes had their uses, but 'some combatants on both sides of the spin frontline' had overstepped the mark. 'If I were still a special adviser I would be happy to be quoted as one, and the days of hiding behind political pseudonyms should now come to an end.' Wegg-Prosser found the experience he had gained as Mandelson's political assistant, and then briefly as his special adviser, was highly marketable. Within days of his patron's downfall he was offered the post of assistant to David Yelland, editor of the *Sun*. Although the offer was later withdrawn, he went on to become corporate communications manager for Pearson, the publishers, and then edited the United Kingdom version of the on-line magazine *Slate* before joining the *Guardian*'s Internet division in September 2000 as publisher of two new websites.

Charlie Whelan provided another illustration of the ease with which political appointees could find employment in the news media. His forthright views and cheeky-chappie demeanour made him an ideal columnist and pundit, and he flourished on a clutch of commissions that included a football column for the *Observer*, writing commentaries for the *New Statesman* and presenting a Radio Five Live political programme, *Sunday Service*. Although Whelan remained a highly partisan supporter of his former boss, Gordon Brown, he was anxious to establish his credentials as a defender of press freedoms, and while his recantation was nowhere near as wholehearted as that of Wegg-Prosser he was prepared to go some way towards recognising the error of his ways. His repudiation of the indefensible duties that special advisers found themselves performing was prompted by a blistering attack on the 'rent boys of politics' by the author Ken Follett, whose wife Barbara was Labour MP for Stevenage.

In an article published in the *Observer* in July 2000 under the headline 'Blair's blackest art', Follett accused the Prime Minister of doing nothing to stop the anonymous briefings being used to denigrate cabinet ministers like Mo Mowlam, who was said to have lost Blair's support. Follett believed the 'floods of vituperative briefings' by 'Downing Street sources' or 'senior cabinet ministers' could be halted if Blair issued that instruction to Campbell and Mandelson and the word then went out to the No. 10 staffers and special advisers. Follett said that off-the-record conversations with journalists were the media equivalent of the 'poison-pen letter', and he feared Blair would be remembered as the Prime Minister who made malicious gossip an everyday tool of modern government. 'The people who do the briefing, who whisper the words of poison into the ears of journalists, are of no consequence. They are the rent boys of politics, and we shudder with disgust when they brush past us in the lobby . . . The polite fiction that the Prime Minister's advisers are responsible is absurd. Control-freak Tony doesn't let Alastair Campbell and Peter Mandelson go around saying anything they like.'

When alerted the previous evening to Follett's imminent attack, Downing Street and the Labour Party launched a furious counteroffensive. After complaining about two inaccuracies in the references to the way he conducted lobby briefings, Campbell persuaded the *Observer* to amend the published version of the article. Campbell told the BBC that Follett's attack was a 'pathetic, self-indulgent rant' that would be treated with the derision it deserved. His denial was followed up by the Labour Party, which said the 'lurid, over-the-top language' showed that Follett had joined the ranks of the 'disappointed and disgruntled' and explained why he was better known for his fiction than his judgement. Undaunted by the strength of the rebuttal, which was quoted at length in the Sunday newspapers and on the morning news bulletins, Follett counterattacked when he appeared on *Breakfast With Frost*. He said Campbell and

Mandelson could not deny all responsibility for the poisonous briefings which took place. 'They are Tweedledum and Tweedledee. If it is not them it is someone who works for them and Tony Blair is responsible.'

In a flurry of publicity that weekend Whelan sprang to Follett's defence and told BBC radio that special advisers had been responsible for anonymous briefings. He was sure that 'a lot of flunkeys' at No. 10 and Labour's headquarters were continuing the practice. 'It's ridiculous to claim this doesn't go on. What Blair and Campbell should be saying is "This has got to stop" rather than saying it does not happen because it clearly does.' Whelan had grown ever more strident in his attacks on Campbell, and next morning's edition of the *Mirror* published opposing columns from the two combatants. Campbell said senior political journalists had never known him say a critical word about a minister. 'I have a golden rule in speaking to journalists: I never say anything bad about anyone in this government . . . People should know the vast bulk of spin comes from what I call journalist spin doctors. When you read about a senior source, please don't imagine it is me or anyone speaking to the Prime Minister. We speak on the record.' Whelan responded by insisting that there was 'an enemy within' whom Blair and his henchmen had to control. 'There isn't one Labour MP or journalist who doesn't believe that people in No. 10 have been rubbishing Mo Mowlam behind her back.'

Whelan's war of attrition with Downing Street had been fuelled by Campbell's decision to take the leading role in a BBC documentary, *News From No. 10*, which was broadcast in mid-July, a fortnight after Follett's outburst. When Whelan agreed in 1997 to allow a television production company to film two fly-on-the-wall documentaries about Gordon Brown's first three months as Chancellor, Campbell berated him and said it was a 'terrible mistake', a reprimand Whelan never forgot. Campbell's argument in favour of allowing television cameras to film several of his briefings for the production of *News From No. 10* was that it would give the public 'a better understanding of the relationship between modern politics and the modern media'. Once most of the filming had been completed, Campbell announced in mid-June that he intended to give fewer lobby briefings so that he could concentrate on long-term strategy work for the Prime Minister. Whelan was highly critical of Campbell's decision to adopt a lower profile and in an article for the *Independent* he warned that if the Prime Minister's press secretary did fewer face-to-face briefings it would lead to more spinning and only encourage journalists to make up their news. 'I do feel that the American system of completely open and attributable briefings has a lot to be said for it. The trouble is that Alastair went only half-way. He did allow himself to be named and become a focus of attention but he didn't go the whole hog and agree to be interviewed on camera in press conferences. If he had taken such a bold decision then, I think that a lot of the negative attention he gets would have dissolved away.' Whelan took another swipe at Campbell in the *Mail on Sunday*, saying Blair's biggest mistake was the order in council that gave Campbell a special status above all the other political advisers. 'It certainly gave Alastair all the authority he wanted. The trouble was that it blurred the lines between whether he was a party appointee or a civil servant, and it set him apart from everyone else.' Whelan then admitted there was an unacceptable side to the regime with which he had been so intimately connected: 'Alastair and I often discussed the problems of our new style of spin, high profile and, yes, sometimes ruthless.'

Whelan revelled in his role as a Radio Five Live presenter and commentator, and I must admit that to begin with I did find it rather disconcerting when working at a BBC computer screen to find that sitting at the next terminal was a former Labour Party apparatchik who in previous years had gone to inordinate lengths to rubbish the accuracy of my news reports and accuse me of underhand behaviour. Nevertheless, in view of his willingness to disown some of his past excesses, I congratulated him on his conversion to the idea of tele-vised lobby briefings, a cause for which I had been campaigning for the previous ten years. Whelan insisted he had always supported the need for lobby briefings to be on the record and agreed it was time to open them up to television and radio. 'Campbell can't write articles in the *Mirror* slagging off political journalists and still insist on maintaining a secret system in the lobby. It just doesn't work.' Whelan was at one with Mandelson's former special adviser in calling for radical action, for Wegg-Prosser had also used his newspaper articles to urge Campbell to give way on the 'ultimate sacred cow' and allow cameras and microphones through the closed doors of lobby briefings on a permanent basis.

I believed that one way to repair the damage caused by the whispering campaigns against ministers and to persuade the public to recognise that they were unauthorised and untrue would have been for Blair to follow the example of the White House in Washington, where there has been a long tradition of televised briefings by those officials who speak on behalf of the President and the United States administration. Unless the Prime Minister's official spokesman was forced to look journalists in the eye when answering their questions, and was seen to be doing so on television, his constant complaints about the inaccuracy and trivialisation of the news media would continue to lack credibility. Blair and Campbell could not ignore the downside of the transformation they had brought about in the size and composition of what in some respects was becoming a new political élite. Labour's special advisers were a far cry from their predecessors. Some were considered to have exercised far greater influence on policy making than was ever permitted under the Conservatives, and most were directly involved in political presentation and had close contact with journalists. On my calculations, of the seventy-nine in post in the autumn of 2000, at least ten were recruited by Blair directly from newspapers and broadcasting organisations; as many again had previously been employed as press officers by the Labour Party or the trade union movement; and altogether well over half of them had extensive experience in the news media or associated areas like public affairs or lobbying. They were highly mobile individuals, and a high turnover among advisers, government information staff and party press officers helped create a vast pool of politically aware contacts on whom journalists could call. Most were more than likely to have maintained their loyalty to whichever minister or faction they worked for, and they were often only too ready to talk to well-placed journalists and give them the inside information being sought.

The wider use of unsourced news stories and the rapid growth in the supply of unattributed quotations were not the only worrying side-effects of the transformation that had taken place. Complaints about an obsession with spin and the bad-mouthing of disaffected ministers had obscured other, far graver concerns. Early on in the government Campbell had given explicit undertakings about the way in which he and the other special advisers would conduct themselves. There had subsequently been repeated assurances by the Cabinet Secretary, Sir Richard Wilson, that these commitments had been honoured and were being policed. My enquiries indicated that Sir Richard's confident assertions were misplaced: special advisers had been engaged in questionable practices; they had used their positions to promote election contests and other internal affairs involving the Labour Party; and their influence had also endangered the political neutrality of the government's information service.

FRAYING AT THE EDGES

'I happen to believe that you can put across the government case in a coherent and co-ordinated way without frankly briefing against anybody . . . I keep reading all this stuff about politicisation. I have never seen a substantive convincing piece of evidence about politicisation.'

Alastair Campbell, chief press secretary to Tony Blair, giving evidence to the House of Commons Select Committee on Public Administration, 23 June 1998

Alastair Campbell's appearance before a House of Commons select committee in the early summer of 1998 was seen as quite a coup by the cross-party group of eleven MPs who had the chance to question him for two and a half hours. They were surprised that he had been so willing to attend and they admired the fact that he had not sought to suggest that the Cabinet Secretary, Sir Richard Wilson, should give evidence in his place – a device Tony Blair adopted in November 2000 when he blocked the committee's attempt to cross-examine the Downing Street chief of staff, Jonathan Powell. Perhaps Campbell's readiness to oblige was not so surprising: after not much more than a year in office, and as one of the final witnesses in a brief inquiry, the Prime Minister's official spokesman had little to fear from a grilling by a group of MPs who had shown by their perfunctory examination of the workings of the Whitehall information service that they had little understanding of the manipulative techniques New Labour had mastered in opposition and which had been transferred all too easily into government.

Campbell laid on a bravura performance, outwitting the MPs at every turn as they tried to catch him out and expose what they suspected might have been his sleights of hand as he denied repeatedly overstepping the mark or misleading journalists. Most of the newspaper coverage of his evidence highlighted the combative way in which he demolished the MPs' questions, and the verdict of the columnists and sketch writers was that he had escaped unscathed. There was one sticky moment when he was challenged as to whether he was responsible for saying that the Chancellor of the Exchequer, Gordon Brown, had 'psychological flaws', but there was little else for the committee to get its teeth into. In June 1998 Blair's lead in the opinion polls increased for the fourth month running, and the pollsters said the 'feelgood factor' was responsible for Labour's unprecedented 25-point lead over the Conservatives. There was some discontent among party members over the leadership's tight grip on the plans for devolution in Scotland, Wales and London; but it was not until later in the year that Blair would be accused of control freakery and of using Downing Street and the No. 10 press office to interfere in Labour's selection procedures for the new devolved institutions. Although the explanations and assurances that Campbell volunteered to the select committee attracted little or no publicity at the time, when pieced together they did constitute a rough and ready set of guidelines. The clear implication was that the standards he had set for himself and his own staff in No. 10 would apply to all the seventy-three political advisers who were then in post.

When the committee published its report in August 1998 it recommended that the government introduce a code of conduct tailored to the work of the advisers, which should set out their obligations during their contacts with the press. Eighteen months later the Committee on Standards in Public Life repeated the call for a new regulatory framework and recommended that a limit be placed on the total number of advisers, to be increased only after an affirmative resolution in both Houses of Parliament. Lord Neill, the committee's chairman, said the 'high public profile' acquired by some of the special advisers had generated a debate as to how they should be regulated, and in addition to a future cap on their numbers, his committee wanted the code of conduct, which would be written into their contracts of employment, to include a requirement to uphold the political impartiality of the civil service when dealing with the news media. Although most of the recommendations were accepted six months later when the government published its response in July 2000, ministers gave no precise indication on timing and said any changes would not take effect until after the next election. An overall limit on the number of advisers would be included in a new bill governing the future employment terms of all civil servants, but no date had been set for this legislation and it would be up to the government of the day to fix the upper limit. A code of conduct would be included in a new model contract for advisers, and that would come into force after the next election. In the meantime the government said it hoped the Select Committee on Public Administration would give further advice on the likely scope of a special advisers' code in a report due early in 2001.

In the absence of any definitive guidance in advance of the next election, Campbell's evidence in June 1998 remained the clearest exposition of the criteria on which he and the other political appointees felt they should be judged. At no subsequent point has he sought to withdraw the undertakings he volunteered to the committee and which he was confident he would honour, and they have not been amended in evidence given to later hearings by the Cabinet Secretary, Sir Richard Wilson, or the Head of the Information Service, Mike Granatt.

The Select Committee's two principal concerns when cross-examining Campbell were to find out whether the government's overhaul of the information service had endangered civil service neutrality by politicising the work of government press officers, and to see if there was any truth in the complaint that the advisers had abused their position by briefing against ministers and engaging in Labour Party infighting. As the questioning proceeded, Campbell remained adamant that the MPs' fears were groundless. There was no need for any new mechanism to either police his heightened powers of control over the information service or to regulate the advisers. The changes Labour had introduced were intended to make the information service more effective, and he described how his responsibility to co-ordinate government announcements had, for example, allowed him to arrange background and on-the-record briefings ahead of the 1998 welfare reform green paper. 'What we did not do is trail the new policy announcements that were being put into the public domain in Parliament.'

When challenged by the Conservative MP David Ruffley about complaints by the Speaker, Betty Boothroyd, that she was fighting a battle over 'ministers' tendency to use the media to outline policy' rather than the House of Commons, Campbell insisted his job was to present government policy in an effective way. 'What I do not do is pre-empt major announcements to Parliament.' He was equally robust in denying that as a highly politicised individual he was somehow contaminating the ethos of the civil servants who worked with him. He believed that the dividing line in Downing Street between political appointees and civil service information officers was clear – and 'much much clearer' than when David Ruffley had been in the Treasury as a political adviser for the Conservatives. 'I keep reading all this stuff about politicisation. I have never seen a substantive convincing piece of evidence about politicisation . . . I want to be the Prime Minister's official spokesman and that is who I am . . . I do not think that means that I politicise the people with whom I work and, as I say, I do try to err on the side of caution. It is often me who actually raises the point about whether this is something the civil service should be getting involved in.' Ruffley challenged Campbell as to whether he had sanctioned briefings against ministers and if he was responsible for telling the *Observer* that Gordon Brown had 'psychological flaws'. After denying that he had briefed 'against any member of the cabinet', he insisted he had no idea who had spoken out against the Chancellor: 'I do not know, I do not know.' Campbell gave a precise undertaking as to his future conduct: 'I happen to believe that you can put across the government case in a coherent and co-ordinated way without frankly briefing against anybody.'

In setting out his ground rules for dealing with political issues, he acknowledged that he had greater freedom than previous Downing Street press secretaries: 'If the Prime Minister is the subject of a political attack I am in a position to rebut it . . . I will never refuse to respond. But I will be reactive in terms of any party political activity, not proactive.' Campbell said that he did not brief journalists on issues relating to the Parliamentary Labour Party or the party's national executive committee, and that such questions would be referred to the party's press officers at Millbank Tower. He was permitted to 'set things in a party political context', and if he helped prepare a speech for a party event or conference, and there was a party political element in what the Prime Minister intended to say or do, then he would brief reporters; but otherwise he had 'got into a habit' of referring such matters to party spokesmen. The guidelines he had volunteered, especially in the 'grey area' between government and party, had added importance in view of the evidence given the week before by the Cabinet Secretary, who had promised the MPs that he would not hesitate to intervene if he believed the press secretary was sanctioning party propaganda or going 'over the top' in attacking the Conservatives. Sir Richard Wilson told the MPs he studied the readout from the daily lobby briefings. 'If there was something I did not like I would go to Campbell and say, "I think you ought to watch that. You are going over the line on that." . . . If needs be, I would go to the Prime Minister.' In its report the committee welcomed Sir Richard's determination to 'remain vigilant' in policing the 'difficult boundary between effective presentation and party political advocacy'.

The MPs gave Campbell a clean bill of health, saying that the arrangements for lobby briefings worked well and that there was no evidence that Blair's official spokesman favoured certain newspapers and provided some journalists with special treatment. The committee shared his view that televised lobby briefings should be rejected because they would undermine ministerial accountability to Parliament. The MPs made no comment on Campbell's undertaking not to brief against individuals, or on his clear delineation of the boundaries of his own responsibilities and his promise that party matters would be referred to Millbank Tower. The discontent that was developing in Scotland, Wales and London would test these undertakings almost to the point of destruction: the Downing Street press office was about to wade deep into the murky waters of party infighting in a desperate attempt to shore up the Prime Minister as he fought a losing battle to control Labour's selection procedures for the new devolved authorities. Within five months of giving MPs an assurance that the Downing Street press office would not take the lead in party affairs, and that lobby briefings would not be used to interfere in party campaigning, Campbell and his staff were to be accused of becoming part of a 'control freak tendency' that was trying to impose Blair's will on the selection of candidates for the Scottish Parliament, the contest to elect a leader in the Welsh

Assembly, and the procedure for choosing Labour's candidate for Mayor of London.

Ken Livingstone began his long and unsuccessful struggle for the Labour nomination in London well before the referendum held in May 1998 to seek approval for a new strategic authority for the capital. An opinion poll published in the *Guardian* in October 1997 showed that Livingstone was in second place to the businessman Richard Branson as Londoners' most popular choice for Mayor. Almost immediately newspapers started predicting that the Labour leadership would bring in a selection procedure to stop 'Red Ken' winning the nomination. Livingstone, however, was in no hurry to declare his hand, and argued that London needed a powerful authority rather than the 'absolutely barmy' idea of a Mayor. Nevertheless he remained a likely contender, and after he indicated he would stand if the authority were granted tax-raising powers, the political editor of *The Times*, Philip Webster, revealed in March 1998 that Blair was planning to veto Livingstone to prevent him becoming 'a running embarrassment to the government'. Within a few weeks Livingstone ended months of speculation and indicated that he would put his name forward, a move the *Guardian*'s political editor, Michael White, said was countered immediately when the 'Labour machine happily provided journalists with a long list of reasons' why Livingstone would have to be blocked. The leadership's tactics were a response to what the *Sunday Telegraph*'s political correspondent, Tom Baldwin, reported were 'signs of panic in No. 10 at the nightmare scenario' of Livingstone winning. 'Downing Street has vowed to stop him. "It cannot be allowed to happen, it must not happen, it will not happen," said one worried prime ministerial aide.' A month later another opinion poll, published in the London *Evening Standard*, showed that 55 per cent of Londoners would vote for him – prompting the headline 'Red Hot Ken' in the *Sun*.

After the London-wide referendum held in May 1998 produced a 'yes' vote of 72 per cent vote in favour of a Mayor and Assembly for the capital on a low turnout of 34 per cent, Livingstone told the *Evening Standard* that he still hoped to secure the Prime Minister's backing, and he urged Blair to tell Peter Mandelson and Alastair Campbell to stop their spin doctors briefing against him. Almost every newspaper story for weeks had included quotes from party 'sources' and 'insiders' explaining how Downing Street would block his nomination. He said he had no intention of standing aside. 'They should have ignored me. Now it's too late.'

Livingstone's interview appeared in the *Evening Standard* a fortnight before Campbell gave his evidence to the select committee. Anger among activists in London over the party's treatment of its maverick member had been mirrored in Scotland after the party announced there would be a selection process for choosing Labour's candidates for the Scottish Parliament, which the *Glasgow Herald* described as a 'loyalty test'. In November 1998, after the management board of the London party agreed to appoint a scrutiny committee to assess the suitability of mayoral candidates, Livingstone joined forces with the left-wing Scottish Labour MP Dennis Canavan, who had been prevented from standing as a Labour candidate for the new Parliament and who was prepared to fight as an independent. Livingstone told the *Evening Standard* that if he was barred by the leadership he would stand and ask voters to 'write in' their support for him. 'If the leadership think it's going to be a three-day row and is going to fade away, they are kidding themselves. I do not crawl away and give up.' The two MPs denounced what they said was the 'control freak tendency' in Downing Street – a charge echoed among party activists in Wales, who were protesting at a parallel move to modify the election rules to choose Labour's leader in the Welsh Assembly in a manner designed to boost the chances of the Secretary of State for Wales, Alun Michael, at the expense of the Labour MP Rhodri Morgan.

Although Blair was thus being assailed on three fronts over issues that had caused widespread unease within the party, his official spokesman did not duck awkward questions at lobby briefings and continued to adopt a robust attitude. When challenged about the attempt to block Livingstone, Campbell said Blair welcomed the new procedure because it would ensure that 'suitable people' represented the party. 'We make no apology about the professionalism of the party, the importance we attach to discipline and the quality of the people who want to represent Labour.' A copy of Campbell's briefing, which at the time was on restricted circulation, was faxed to the headquarters of the London party. Livingstone retaliated in his weekly column in the *Independent*, promising that he would not be silenced by the 'Dalek faction of Labour's Millbank Tendency'; but a fortnight later the *Sunday Telegraph* published the contents of a dossier on Livingstone's 'disloyalty' which it said had been prepared by officials at Millbank Tower.

As Livingstone and the London party dug in for a tit-for-tat war of words that continued for months and developed a momentum of its own, Blair was anxious to focus the party's attention on campaigning for the elections to the Scottish Parliament and the Welsh Assembly, which were to be held in May 1999. Blair answered his critics in an article for the *Independent*, which bore the headline: 'If control freakery means strong leadership, then I plead guilty.' He recognised that a small minority in the party had changed their line of attack from the charge of arrogance to one of control freakery, but would not deny the offence if he thereby ensured the government was successful and Labour did not return to 'factionalism, navel-gazing or feuding'. Blair said the real answer to the control-freak charge was that the systems of proportional representation to be used in the Scottish and Welsh elections, and in elections to the European Parliament in June 1999, would result in Labour 'giving away seats'; and that was a 'funny way' for a prime minister to exercise control. The selection procedure in London was not designed to 'stop one candidate in particular', and he denied that he was leader of a party that was 'desperate to be different'. None the less, disenchantment with the tactics the leadership had pursued was blamed for a sharp fall in Labour's share of the vote in the first elections for the new devolved institutions. In the constituency vote in Scotland, Labour took 38.8 per cent of the vote, down from 45.6 per cent in 1997. Together with its share of votes on the party list, the party took fifty-six of the 129 seats in the Scottish Parliament. Eight days later Labour signed a coalition deal with the Liberal Democrats to form a power-sharing administration. The scale of the rebuff in Wales was far greater: the party's share of the constituency vote in Labour's strongest and most loyal territory dropped to 37.6 per cent, a far cry from the 54.7 per cent secured in the general election. Labour took twenty-eight of the sixty seats in the Welsh Assembly, sufficient to form an executive, and Alun Michael was appointed First Secretary.

Michael's election as leader had split the Welsh Labour Party, and the nationalists were regarded as the beneficiaries. Plaid Cymru achieved their best ever share of the vote and took seventeen seats, including some astonishing Labour scalps in the Welsh valleys. Michael had to shoulder much of the blame for this setback, as he was depicted during the Assembly elections as Blair's man, parachuted into Wales from Westminster simply in order to defeat Rhodri Morgan. The leadership election was held two months before Wales voted and there was uproar when, in contrast to previous contests, the party ruled that trade unions were not required to ballot their members, a move that put Morgan at a disadvantage; he was beaten narrowly by Michael who took 52.7 per cent of the vote. Morgan had the satisfaction of seeing his share of the Assembly vote in his Cardiff West constituency increase over the general election; in Scotland Dennis Canavan, who stood as an independent for the Edinburgh Parliament in Falkirk West, took 55 per cent of the vote, three times the support for the official Labour candidate. The *Evening Standard*'s columnist Peter Kellner said the message for London from two of the most striking victors in Scotland and Wales was that if Blair blocked Livingstone, and Livingstone stood as an independent, he would 'trounce the party's official nominee'. Labour had also lost well over a thousand seats in the May local authority elections. In his weekly column in the *Independent* Livingstone accused the control freaks of the 'Millbank Tendency' of failing to learn the lessons of these setbacks, and warned that Labour remained in danger of losing the mayoral and Assembly elections in May 2000.

Speculation continued throughout the summer as to the nature of the loyalty test that Labour's candidates in London would have to face. Livingstone was undaunted, and in early September 1999 he launched his campaign for the Labour nomination by unveiling a poster and opening a dedicated website on the Internet. A month later, after a frenzy of speculation at the party's annual conference, the Secretary of State for Health, Frank Dobson, finally confirmed that he intended to stand. In being hailed as the Prime Minister's preferred candidate, Dobson found himself at an immediate disadvantage; and his discomfort increased when the party decided to impose an electoral college for candidate selection, as in the leadership contest in Wales, rather than follow the practice of one member one vote under which Blair had been elected. Despite all the dire predictions that he would be barred, the London selection board agreed in November 1999 to allow Livingstone to be included, together with Dobson and Glenda Jackson, in a shortlist of three to go before the electoral college. Blair had recognised that the price Labour would pay for excluding Livingstone was too great; but he took the first opportunity he could to warn party members of his own misgivings. Broadcasting organisations were alerted by the Downing Street press office that there would be a statement from Blair on the subject immediately after he had delivered a speech to the Institute for Public Policy Research. Lance Price, Campbell's deputy on political matters, told the BBC that although reporters could not interview the Prime Minister, he would respond. A party worker from Millbank Tower had been primed to ask a question. Price said that Blair's view was that the modern Labour Party had been created by leaving behind the 'politics of extremism' and Livingstone would have to abide by the rules.

Next day, in a signed article in the *Evening Standard* under the headline 'Why we must stop Ken', Blair explained why he doubted whether Livingstone had changed. 'I was a foot soldier in the Labour Party in Battersea and in Hackney in the early 1980s. I canvassed and campaigned for Labour in London when we were at our lowest ebb. . . At that time the party was a byword for extremism . . . The leading figures were people like Ken Livingstone, Tony Benn and Arthur Scargill.' Livingstone responded in an interview for the *Daily Telegraph* in which he argued that Blair and the rest of New Labour had got a 'completely distorted memory' of the 1980s. 'They believe what they read in the papers, that the late GLC was a reign of red terror . . . I am afraid we were not running the country.'

As the three candidates stepped up their campaigns for support in the run-up to the closing of the electoral college vote in mid-February 2000, one constant source of controversy was the government's plan for the future funding of the London Underground. After Railtrack pulled out of discussions to upgrade and maintain the lines, Livingstone said ministers should abandon their plan to privatise the tube network and finance improvements through a bond issue. At a lobby briefing the next morning Campbell rounded on Livingstone, although to begin with he did not identify him by name, mindful no doubt of the assurance he had given the select committee that he could present the government's case 'without frankly briefing against anybody'. Campbell said there was no question of rolling back from a public–private partnership on the tube, although the argument was moving on to something else 'he has dreamed up'.

Campbell continued: 'We will leave this up to other people who seek to move the goalposts. There has been a deliberate, and because he has so many supporters in the press, a partially successful attempt, to portray this as privatisation . . . On the bond issue, you are asking Londoners to take a very large gamble. You can try to pull the wool over people's eyes, but this is public sector borrowing . . . It is time we went through the changing positions of those people we won't name.' Once I had an opportunity I interrupted Campbell to ask if the 'he' he had referred to was by any chance Ken Livingstone. Campbell paused, gazed around the room for a moment, and then, with a look of absolute pity in his eyes, turned towards me and nodded before answering. 'Wherever government policy is misrepresented I will put forward government policy as it is, not as to how others try to present it.'

Far from being deterred by Campbell's briefings, Livingstone told me in mid-December 1999 that he owed a large debt of gratitude to the Prime Minister's official spokesman. We were discussing his campaign as we walked towards the BBC's studios in Millbank, where Livingstone was to give interviews about his private member's bill to ban hunting with dogs. He had finished eighth in the MPs' annual ballot and outlined his proposals at a packed news conference in the House of Commons. He accepted that foxes could be 'wicked old things', recalling that one had got into his garden in the spring and bitten the head off his tortoise, but stressed that his bill was intended to stop the unnecessary cruelty caused by hunting. On the way to the news conference I had met Don Brind, press officer to the Parliamentary Labour Party, who inquired what was going on. When I explained that Livingstone had jumped in to pick up the private member's bill previously introduced by the Labour MP Michael Foster, Brind shook his head in disbelief. 'Don't tell me. I know, Ken's timing is brilliant.' Subsequently Frank Dobson complained to his supporters about the leadership's failure to spot Livingstone's publicity coup, which could have been avoided by persuading another of the Labour MPs successful in the ballot to promote the bill to ban hunting. Although his position on the list meant there was almost no chance of his bill making progress, Livingstone was pleased with his handiwork and, as we headed towards BBC Westminster, he assured me he was genuinely grateful for the way Downing Street had orchestrated a media campaign against him. 'I never thought I would get so much help from them. If Campbell had ignored me all along, I would never have got such a high profile. No political correspondent could write a story last year without the obligatory paragraph dictated by No. 10 saying that I would not be allowed to stand. They are the people who have kept my name in front of the public.' He thought the leadership had made a mistake in allowing *Panorama* to film a rally in Brixton at which Blair and the former Labour leader, Neil Kinnock, spoke in support of Dobson and denounced Livingstone's campaign. 'Usually you never see Blair doing anything negative like that, getting stuck in and just attacking me. If the roles had been reversed, I would never have allowed *Panorama* to film it. I would have said it was a private meeting.'

Livingstone had told his press officer, Simon Fletcher, never to attack Frank Dobson or Glenda Jackson, and to refrain from being unpleasant to reporters. 'We just don't go around abusing journalists. We try never to make complaints or ask for a right to reply. Labour have now been so rude to so many journalists for so long that they never get any sympathy. I don't want to see Simon's name in the prints, which is why it is all so damaging for Campbell.'

I did not have long to wait before experiencing another illustration of the risks that the Downing Street press office was taking in the attempt to thwart Livingstone, and of the casual disregard shown by Campbell's staff for the undertaking which he had given to MPs that party matters would be referred to Millbank Tower. In mid-January, in the final weeks of campaigning by the candidates, I took a call from the Downing Street press office. Lance Price said he wanted to alert the BBC to an interview by Livingstone in which he was praising the Seattle rioters and saying that if the World Trade Organisation came to London he would make sure there were plenty of things to throw at them. 'It's in *The Face*. I don't suppose you know it, Nick, it's a fashion magazine. We've just been tipped off about it by the *Daily Telegraph* and they're going to run it. Tony Blair has been asking Ken if he's changed. We don't want to see Labour return to gesture politics and Blair would say this is an example of what he has talked about.'

The Face had asked Livingstone a series of questions about his plans for London and for his opinion of the other contenders. Much of the interview was lighthearted, with jokey answers about his favourite Glenda Jackson film and why he thought the Conservatives' candidate Steve Norris appealed to women. When asked how he would respond to another anti-capitalist protest in the City of London or a 'Battle of Seattle-style demo', Livingstone appeared to pull no punches: 'Well, I can make it absolutely clear that if I am Mayor of London we will not be inviting the World Trade Organisation to come here – unless we get vast stocks to put them in so we can throw stuff at them in an organised way. I've always been in favour of direct action. One of my fondest memories was chasing the inspector of the Archway Road inquiry out on to the roof at Central Hall. The barrister representing the government was one Michael Howard who interposed his body, saying "Don't throw him over!" As if I was going to.'

The BBC did not run the story that evening, but it did make the inside pages of some newspapers next morning. 'Ken backs city rioters' was the headline in the *Sun*. The *Daily Mail*'s story, under the headline, 'He's back! Red Ken supports city rioters,' said Livingstone's remarks had caused 'deep unease' in Downing Street. When asked about it next day, Livingstone told the BBC his answer was a joke. 'I have never been in favour of violence. I have been on the record in so many interviews and articles over the past thirty years – you won't find a single time when I have supported violence.' Nevertheless the line that Price gave me, that the interview seemed to signal a return to gesture politics, figured prominently in an all-out public attack on Livingstone mounted by Blair and the Chancellor, Gordon Brown.

'Brown lays into "Wrecker Red Ken"' was the headline over the *Evening Standard*'s front-page splash. In an article inside the paper, the Chancellor asked whether Livingstone still proposed 'an old style back-to-the-Eighties economic agenda that would threaten to hurt Londoners'. Brown said that to attack the very policies that were creating stability and steady growth would 'threaten jobs and put the economy at risk'. The article was aimed at building up interest in a rally in Bloomsbury, which Blair and Brown were to address that evening in support of Dobson. At the morning lobby briefing, Campbell went through Blair's speech and said he would use it to condemn as 'silly and offensive' Livingstone's response to a possible Seattle-style riot. 'Ken says his remarks were all a big joke. He always does. This is no joke. Issues for London like crime and poverty are no joke. Blair will urge people to read Brown's article in the *Evening Standard* and call on party members to think long and hard. So let's not pretend the contest is a joke. It's time to get serious . . . The question to Livingstone has always been whether he has changed. Recent events suggest precious little evidence so far.' Blair would use the rally to stress that Dobson was the right man for London. 'He has experience, he is serious, he is his own man and also a team player.' It was the first time I had heard Campbell use a lobby briefing to promote a sustained, personal attack on Livingstone, and he made no secret of Blair's irritation over the failure of the party leadership to influence the campaign. 'In spite of all the control freak allegations, the Labour Party has a choice and Blair will say that what Gordon is writing is important. So let us have a focused debate. We should not let the media, who have their own motives and appear to be on the side of Ken Livingstone, decide it for us.'

The afternoon lobby briefing touched on another of the issues that had angered Blair and would be raised at the rally. Livingstone had used newspaper interviews to express his willingness to work with independent Assembly members, rather than Labour's candidates, if he were elected Mayor, and Campbell said he thought this was 'a very odd state of affairs'. Advance copies of the speech showed that Blair intended to read out what looked like a charge sheet to explain why party members would regret picking the 'wrong' candidate. The list included the 'silly and offensive' remarks about the Seattle riot and criticism of a call Livingstone had made for the Chancellor to be sacked over his handling of the economy.

At the rally, Blair prefaced his remarks by saying it was not his style to 'go round attacking fellow MPs', but he misjudged the audience and had barely started on his list before he was interrupted by protests and heckling. A report for the *Nine O'Clock News* showed Blair, as he struggled against the jeers, trying to make his point: 'This is a serious election. It matters. If you wonder why I've said the things that I have about Ken Livingstone as the Labour candidate it is because we cannot afford a return to gesture politics.'

All Blair's efforts were in vain; when results of voting in the three sections of the electoral college were announced in mid-February, Livingstone topped the ballots for both party members and trade unionists. However, he still lost the Labour nomination to Dobson, who inched ahead because of the overwhelming support he had obtained from the separate vote of Labour's London MPs, MEPs and candidates for the new Greater London Assembly. The final result, which gave Dobson 51.53 per cent, just ahead of Livingstone on 48.47 per cent, masked the scale of the popular vote among the rank and file. On first preference votes Livingstone secured the support of 19,548 party members, well ahead of the 12,559 for Dobson; once Glenda Jackson's second preferences were allocated, Livingstone's tally had increased to 21,082, again well ahead of Dobson on 14,042 votes. Livingstone immediately called on Dobson to consider whether he intended to accept 'this tainted result' or stand down as candidate. Speaking outside his London home, Livingstone said his 'huge democratic mandate' was a 'ringing endorsement' of the policies he had put forward. Next day, under the front-page headline, 'Go for it Ken, says London,' the *Evening Standard* published an opinion poll which showed that 61 per cent of those questioned believed Livingstone should go it alone and that if he stood as an Independent, 50 per cent of Londoners would vote for him while Dobson, as the official Labour candidate, would get only 22 per cent.

For the next fifteen days there was endless speculation as to whether Livingstone would take the gamble of his political life and face expulsion from the Labour Party. From Millbank Tower came ringing endorsements for Dobson. 'He's the right choice for

London,' said Blair, as the party machine reminded Livingstone of his repeated public undertakings not to stand against an official Labour candidate. When Livingstone finally made his decision, the first journalist he alerted was the political editor of the *Evening Standard*, Charles Reiss, whose coverage of the whole saga had made his newspaper essential reading. 'Let the bloodiest battle commence,' was the headline next day in the *Daily Mail*, which said 'Red Ken risks all to run against Labour' having opened up the 'deepest rift in the party for decades'. Political correspondents at Westminster started digging in for a two-month campaign, which lived up to all their expectations; at the end of it, as had been widely predicted, the combined election for the Mayor and Assembly in May 2000 produced the most damaging electoral setback of Blair's premiership, representing a severe indictment of his political judgement. Livingstone's return to power after fourteen years as a political outcast was a personal triumph. His final tally of first and second preference votes in the London-wide contest was 776,427 (57.92 per cent), well ahead of the Conservative candidate, Steve Norris, on 564,137 votes (42.08 per cent). On the first count Livingstone had secured 667,877 votes, almost three times the number polled by Frank Dobson, who finished in third place with 223,884 votes, well behind Norris on 464,434 votes and only just ahead of the Liberal Democrat, Susan Kramer, on 203,452 votes. Livingstone, never short of a cheeky one-liner, reclaimed control of London with a memorable thank-you after the declaration of the result: 'As I was saying before I was so rudely interrupted fourteen years ago . . . ' Blair, who was attending peace talks in Northern Ireland, insisted that he would seek to co-operate with the new Mayor of London, although he had not changed his views about Livingstone. 'That's in the past, in the sense that the people of London have made their verdict clear, and it's my responsibility to make sure that it now works for London.'

Next day's newspapers made unhappy reading for the party leadership, Livingstone's victory being only one of several humiliating setbacks the press had to report. Labour had failed to win outright control of the new London Assembly; it had lost 568 seats in the local authority elections in England and Wales; and its candidate in the

Romsey by-election, Andrew Howard, had forfeited his deposit. 'Control freak Blair blamed for Labour's nationwide disaster' was the front-page headline of the *Daily Express*. Anonymous friends and former ministerial colleagues of Dobson, quoted by the *Independent*, blamed Downing Street for his humiliation and said that Blair had got the mayoral contest hopelessly wrong, just as he had misjudged the decision to impose Alun Michael as leader of the Wales Labour Party. Michael had been forced to resign as First Secretary in early February, just before he faced a vote of no confidence in the Welsh Assembly, and he had been succeeded with much acclaim among party members by Rhodri Morgan. The indignity of Michael's wounded retreat was compounded ten days later by the embarrassment over the disputed electoral college vote in London, which had underlined Livingstone's popularity, and there was no doubt that these setbacks had been chastening experiences for the Prime Minister and his official spokesman.

A prominent feature of the latter stages of the mayoral campaign was the lack of visible support for Dobson from No. 10, which had become obvious by mid-March. Paul Waugh, writing in the *Independent*, said Downing Street appeared to have written off Dobson's chances of winning because Blair did not want to be associated with his failure. After being asked repeatedly why the Prime Minister had not been campaigning alongside Labour's candidate, Campbell said Blair was confident that Dobson would win provided the news media concentrated on the policies involved and these were understood by London's voters. Shortly before it was finally announced that Blair would show his public support for Dobson by sharing a platform with him in early April, Campbell confirmed publicly that it was his intention to step back from the mayoral campaign. In mid-February the Downing Street press office started to publish extracts from lobby briefings on No. 10's website, and in the entry for 30 March 2000 Campbell set out the policy he intended to pursue during the last few weeks of the contest. He had been asked to comment on a report in the *Daily Mail* that Livingstone was intent on winning the pink vote by establishing a civic register to enable gay couples to formalise their relationships. Campbell said it was not an issue on which Blair had expressed an opinion. The extract continued: 'Pressed further, the PMOS reminded the journalists of his intention not to give a running commentary on the mayoral campaign in government briefings. He added that he thought the London mayor debate had improved since he stopped participating in it.'

I had not been at the briefing that morning, and as the extract was not a transcript of precisely what Campbell had said, it was difficult to decide whether his reference to having stopped 'participating' in the mayoral campaign was meant to be taken seriously or was just a joke. I had noticed for some weeks that Campbell had been highly selective in deciding which items from the lobby briefings would be published on the website. There was no doubt in my mind that he must have hoped his carefully-worded extract would help draw a veil over all his earlier briefings about Livingstone, for which of course there was no transcript, nor any published version, because until mid-February the extracts had been circulated only within Whitehall on a restricted basis and were not available on the Internet.

I considered the role played by Campbell and his colleagues in briefing against Livingstone had breached the undertakings he had given to the select committee. The Downing Street press office had been 'proactive' rather than 'reactive', and it had acted in a calculated and concerted way to support moves to block Livingstone's candidature. It was not until Livingstone decided to stand as an independent on 6 March 2000 that Campbell began to back away and became more circumspect about his involvement. In my view the activities of the Downing Street press office, in helping to orchestrate a media campaign against Livingstone between the spring of 1998 and the declaration of the electoral college vote in February 2000 did, on Campbell's own test, constitute a 'substantive convincing piece of evidence about politicisation'. Labour's selection process for mayoral candidates was an internal party matter which, on the basis of Campbell's undertakings to the select committee, should have been dealt with at all times by staff at Millbank Tower. He had said himself that his intention was to 'err on the side of caution', and yet I did not have to cast my mind back far to find examples of caution being thrown to the wind: to cite just two, the telephone call by Lance Price drawing my attention to Livingstone's interview in *The Face*, and Campbell's two lobby briefings in mid-January at which he promoted both Brown's article in the *Evening Standard* and the attack on Livingstone that Blair intended to make at the Bloomsbury rally.

I accept that most political correspondents would probably have been only too grateful for Price's tip-off and would not consider it exceptional or untoward that Downing Street had mounted a ring-round to alert journalists to what Livingstone had told *The Face*. None the less, Price's attempt to damage Livingstone served only to demonstrate the brazen way in which Campbell operated his press office, and what I considered to be the failure of the Cabinet Secretary, Sir Richard Wilson, to impose the discipline he had promised. Although Price was appointed Labour's communications director within six months of our conversation, he was at the time a special adviser whose salary was paid by the taxpayer, and as a temporary civil servant he was bound by the terms of his contract. Special advisers can assist in the 'effective presentation of the government's policies and achievements' with a degree of 'party political commitment and association which would be impermissible for a permanent civil servant'; however, they are not allowed to take part in the work of the party's national organisation; they must be 'careful not to take any active part' in an election campaign beyond giving specialist or political advice to a minister; and they must not take party in 'political controversy' and should 'avoid personal attacks'. In my opinion, Price's attempt to generate unfavourable publicity for Livingstone during an internal party contest seemed at odds with these conditions and failed to honour Campbell's assurance that the Downing Street press office could present the government's case without 'frankly briefing against anybody'.

There were many complaints in Bernard Ingham's day about the way in which he conducted the Downing Street press office for Margaret Thatcher, not least over his conduct in 1985 when he used a lobby briefing to describe the then Leader of the House, John Biffen, as 'a semi-detached member of the cabinet'. Even so, in my experience, he was always careful when asked about internal party matters to refer the questioners to Conservative Central Office, a practice that I found was followed to the letter by John Major's three press secretaries, Gus O'Donnell, Christopher Meyer and Jonathan Haslam, who, like Ingham, were civil servants.

The timing of the undertaking by the Downing Street press office to refrain from giving 'a running commentary on the mayoral campaign' was not without significance because the Cabinet Secretary, Sir Richard Wilson, had been forced earlier that same month to extricate Campbell from a complaint that he had broken the rules over party political work by acting as a go-between for the former Conservative MP, Shaun Woodward, in publicising his defection to Labour. Woodward was sacked from the opposition front bench in December 1999 for refusing to vote in support of the retention of Section 28 of the 1986 Local Government Act, which prohibits the promotion of 'the teaching in any maintained school of the acceptability of homosexuality as a pretended family relationship. As his party's spokesman on London, Woodward had been at the forefront of the Conservatives' attempts to exploit Blair's embarrassment over Ken Livingstone, and Labour moved swiftly to capitalise on both his sacking and his forthright criticism of William Hague for his failure to curb prejudice and intolerance towards the gay community.

The complaint against Campbell hinged on what happened during the countdown to Woodward's defection, which was timed to cause maximum damage to Hague. Campbell had built his reputation partly on his ability to orchestrate devastating publicity coups against the Conservatives. He had masterminded Alan Howarth's defection to Labour in 1995 with deadly precision. Howarth, formerly Conservative MP for Stratford-upon-Avon, agreed to wait nearly a fortnight before announcing his defection in the Sunday newspapers published on the eve of the Tories' annual conference, which destabilised carefully laid plans to re-establish John Major's authority as Prime Minister. Woodward had supported moves by the Labour MP Ann Keen to get the age of homosexual consent reduced from eighteen to sixteen, and she had warned Campbell about the likelihood of his defection five days after the Conservatives imposed a three-line whip on the Section 28 vote and four days before he was sacked by Hague. The day after his sacking, Woodward saw Blair and Campbell at No. 10 and, following a series of clandestine meetings, he agreed to announce his defection fifteen days later at noon on

Saturday, 18 December, in order to create maximum impact in the Sunday newspapers.

All the forward planning paid off, and the build-up to a bruising weekend for Hague worked like clockwork. A hint of what was to come did appear that morning on the front page of the *Daily Express*, which reported exclusively that Woodward was 'at the centre of intense speculation' that he might defect, but the announcement went ahead as planned. It led the lunchtime and evening bulletins, dominated the weekend news coverage on television and radio, and was a front-page lead for the Sunday newspapers. The *Sunday Mirror*'s coverage of the story included a half-page article by Blair welcoming the defection of a 'politician of courage, principle and judgement' who had stood out against the Conservatives, who were 'increasingly extreme' and had 'lost touch with the priorities of the decent majority of people in our country'. Most of the Sundays published a detailed timetable for the events that led up to Woodward's defection and they were in agreement that the starting point was the advance warning given to Campbell by Ann Keen on 29 November. The evening after his sacking on 2 December, Woodward went to see Campbell at No. 10. They went upstairs to meet Blair and discussed his dismissal and his growing alienation from the Conservatives. The next day, 4 December, Woodward went back to Downing Street for further discussions with Blair and Campbell, who brought Lance Price and Peter Mandelson into the discussion. After spending a week thinking through his position, Woodward decided to defect and began planning the announcement with Campbell and Price. He met them the following Monday, 13 December, and again on Thursday, 16 December, followed by a final meeting with Blair that evening. Most newspapers were able to print detailed insights into the various meetings. Campbell, who had regularly criticised the news media for being obsessed about his work, was happy on this occasion to revel in his exploits and to provide direct quotations.

He gave a graphic account to Jon Craig, political editor of the *Sunday Express*, whose report described what happened when Woodward walked through the gates of Downing Street: 'Eventually Campbell took him upstairs to the PM and they all had a chat. Woodward was offered tea, but asked for coffee. Then the press chief left Woodward and his suitor alone for an hour. "He talked about how he was in politics because he believed it could make a difference and he was concerned about the direction of the Conservative Party, particularly in relation to their views on public services," said Campbell yesterday. The next morning, Woodward was back in Blair's flat. This time the talk was of strategy and the PM and his spokesman were joined by Mandelson. "Peter is an old friend of Shaun's," said Campbell. "He had pretty much decided by then." ' At the final meeting on 16 December, Woodward took his wife Camilla to meet Blair. 'There were handshakes and bottles of Beck's.' In the *Mail on Sunday*'s account, the political editor, Simon Walters, said the 'military precision' of the final countdown was no surprise as Blair and his team were 'almost as expert at pulling off spectacular defections as spy chiefs during the Cold War'. Walters detailed the measures taken in the final week to keep the defection secret. 'Campbell knew it was too risky to meet at No. 10 in case the Tories were tipped off . . . Instead, they met at a friend's house . . . On Thursday night, Woodward met Blair one last time . . . the MP was smuggled into No. 10 through the back door.'

The last three meetings were described in even greater detail by Philip Webster, political editor of *The Times*, who began his story by revealing what happened on Monday 13 December, after Woodward had spent the weekend thinking through his position and had decided to defect. A flat in the former County Hall had been made available for these two secret encounters by one of Lance Price's friends, and Webster made full use of the inside information which he had been given: the two press officers 'walked unnoticed from Downing Street over Westminster Bridge through the crowds taking pictures of the London Eye . . . Over coffee, tea and biscuits the three planned in detail the events of the week . . . The three returned to the flat on Thursday afternoon.'

These detailed reports, together with Campbell's own account of the role he played in the defection, intrigued the Conservative MP Andrew Tyrie, who tried without success in February of the following year to discover from the Cabinet Secretary whether this was a 'legitimate function' of a special adviser. Although Tyrie was prevented from pursuing his cross-examination when Sir Richard Wilson gave evidence to the Select Committee on Public Administration, he persisted with his enquiry and wrote to ask whether Campbell's meetings with Woodward had been consistent with the requirement of a special adviser's contract to 'use discretion and avoid controversy'. Sir Richard, who took a fortnight to reply, gave a version of events which bore little relationship to the sequence of meetings set out in the newspapers and which made no mention of accounts given by Campbell himself.

Sir Richard said it was his understanding that what happened was in line with the contract for special advisers: 'Woodward did not make clear before the first meeting that he wished to discuss a possible move to join the Labour Party, and subsequent meetings took place with the approval of the Prime Minister, away from No. 10, either at lunchtime or outside office hours.' Sir Richard's account differed considerably from the press reports. The newspapers on Sunday and Monday were in agreement that Ann Keen informed Campbell on 29 November that Woodward might defect; some correspondents quoted her directly. Sir Richard's account made no reference to the second meeting inside No. 10 on 4 December, which involved Campbell as well as Blair, Mandelson and Price; nor did he refer to the fact that the final meeting took place on the afternoon of 16 December and was followed by Woodward's third visit to No. 10. Tyrie was unable to probe the official version of events until a hearing of the select committee in November 2000, when Sir Richard stuck firmly to his contention that after the first meeting inside No. 10 all the subsequent conversations which Campbell had with Woodward 'took place off premises and in his own time'. Sir Richard assured MPs they could rely on his eyes and ears: 'My concern is that the resources of the state are not to be used for party political purposes. The taxpayer is paying Alastair Campbell to work for the government as the government, not the Labour Party. My concern therefore is that in his hours at work he is doing work for the government, qua government. What he does in his own time to support the Labour Party is his own business, as he is entitled to do.'

None the less, in my opinion an additional and significant failing in Sir Richard's replies was that he had decided to overlook or ignore the role played by the Downing Street press office in briefing political correspondents about the events leading up to Woodward's defection. Tyrie told Sir Richard at the select committee hearing in February 2000 that the press reports were 'well documented'. In fact, all the newspapers attributed their information to sources at No. 10; most identified Campbell and Price by name; and Campbell was quoted directly by the *Sunday Express*. Sir Richard's failure to make any mention of this was all the more surprising in the light of the evidence Campbell gave to the select committee in June 1998 when he was questioned about his role in the defection to Labour of another senior Conservative MP, Peter Temple-Morris. Unlike Howarth and Woodward, Temple-Morris did not join the Labour Party immediately and sat as an Independent One-Nation Conservative for some weeks after he lost the Tory whip in November 1997. Temple-Morris, MP for Leominster, was one of the Conservatives' much-reduced band of pro-European MPs. He had agonised for months about his future; William Hague withdrew the party whip after accusing him of disloyalty for having had talks about joining Labour in protest at the Conservatives' opposition to the single currency. Three weeks before he crossed the floor of the House he told the *Observer* about his two meetings with Campbell and his lunch with Blair's chief of staff, Jonathan Powell, to discuss Labour's policy on the euro.

When Campbell was asked by the select committee six months later about his involvement in the defection of the MP, he said that he had raised it first in a discussion with the Cabinet Secretary. 'I did specifically put something in front of Sir Richard and said, "Is this the right thing to do?" which was in relation to Temple-Morris. I knew that that was about to happen, I knew what his arguments were going to be. Now, can I go into a briefing and say, "Peter Temple-Morris is about to take the Labour whip and these are the reasons"? I discussed that with Sir Richard. He actually thought it was a greyish area and in the end we decided the best thing to do was put it out through the party network.' In view of the sensitivity that surrounded the defection of Temple-Morris in 1997, I failed to see why Sir Richard had made no mention of the way in which Woodward's defection was presented to the news media. Given his advice to Campbell over Temple-Morris, he should presumably have reached the same conclusion over Woodward and directed that any statements to the news media about this latest defection should have been made by Millbank Tower rather than by Downing Street. On my reading of the newspapers on the Sunday and Monday of Woodward's defection, none of the political correspondents quoted Labour Party sources but relied instead either on what Campbell had said on Saturday or on briefings given on Sunday by Lance Price, who responded to calls left by journalists on Woodward's pager.

Sir Richard's reply to Andrew Tyrie was nevertheless significant because he spelt out in the clearest possible terms the conditions under which special advisers could participate in political activity. The schedule of their contract said that if, with the approval of their minister, they wished to 'assist with party political matters (other than national election campaigning and standing for Parliament) they may do so at times which do not interfere with their normal duties, for example, out of office hours'. Tyrie told *The Times* that, reading between the lines, he thought Sir Richard had made it 'abundantly clear that Campbell had overstepped the mark' in helping to arrange and promote Woodward's defection, but he thought it was 'farcical' to imagine that Campbell could somehow confine his 'highly party political work' to his lunch break. Andrew Lansley, the Conservatives' spokesman on Cabinet Office affairs, told the *PM* programme that Sir Richard appeared to be in a desperate muddle over what to do about the political appointees in the Downing Street press office. 'The idea that Campbell can pop out at lunchtime, turn into a party political animal and then return after lunch as a civil servant is a complete nonsense.' When Campbell gave his evidence to the select committee I had been struck by his utter confidence in rejecting the possibility that there was any danger that his own appointment, and the doubling in the number of special advisers, would in any way put undue political pressure on the government's information officers. He said the dividing line in Downing Street was clear: the civil servants knew what they had to do and the special advisers knew what they were supposed to do.

One member of the committee listening to Campbell's evidence in 1998 who was still uncertain that all was well was the Conservative MP Richard Shepherd, who feared that if the chief press secretary in

Downing Street was 'an essentially overt political individual, highly politicised', that might 'contaminate the ethos' of civil servants in Downing Street and Whitehall in their presentation of government policy. Campbell's assurance that he did not think that his presence would 'politicise the people' with whom he worked was supported by two other witnesses. Mike Granatt, head of the information service, insisted that the separation of roles was clear and would prove to be 'a confidence-building measure' for the civil service. There was an equally unequivocal endorsement from Robin Mountfield, the permanent secretary for the Office of Public Service. He thought that by appointing Campbell to 'an explicitly political role' the Prime Minister had clarified the position and it was 'a more honest position' because the distinction between political appointees and civil servants was transparent. At Blair's request Mountfield had carried out a review of the work done by civil service information officers and his report, published in November 1997, had made wide-ranging recommendations to ensure that the information service did 'raise its game' as Campbell had requested.

Whitehall departments were told to improve their professional and technical standards: press releases should be structured to 'grab the agenda'; as the publication date of white papers and other documents approached, information officers should be poised to start a 'ring-round' of newsrooms in order to stimulate interest; and staff should begin 'trailing the announcement during the previous weekend'. My concern about these instructions, which were set out in a newly revised manual, *Press Office Best Practice*, was that if departments were required to undertake the aggressive selling of the government's policies and decisions, even before they had been announced to the House of Commons, there was a risk that information officers would be asked to use their authority as civil servants to support politically inspired stories which the government was trailing and seeking to exploit. The main reason for doubling the number of special advisers, and bringing in so many political appointees with experience of the news media, had been to ensure that the government became more proactive and drove forward the news agenda. Special advisers were in an ideal position for some astute pump-priming. They had the freedom to excite the Sunday press by starting to trail the decisions that were due to be announced the following week, and I described in *Sultans of Spin* the difficulties I was encountering as a broadcaster when checking out the growing number of unattributed newspaper stories relating to forthcoming government announcements.

I felt the changes agreed to by Mountfield had created difficulties for civil service information officers who were sometimes not quite sure precisely how far they should go in confirming unsourced newspaper speculation that they knew was being fuelled by the special advisers in their departments but which related to parliamentary statements that had not yet been made to MPs. My conclusion in *Sultans of Spin* was that Mountfield had done Campbell's bidding and that civil servants were becoming the spin doctors' accomplices, an opinion that I subsequently discovered was shared by Bernard Ingham, who in his final years as Thatcher's chief press secretary had also taken on the additional role of head of the information service. Sir Bernard told me that he remained in contact with his former colleagues and he had informed Mountfield and Granatt of his concerns over the changes they had agreed to. He believed that by encouraging information officers to start 'trailing' announcements, they had in effect sanctioned the advance leaking of government statements and that had opened the door to the politicisation of the civil service. 'I think Robin Mountfield sold the pass on this and I told him so. Mike Granatt told me that he had written the section in their report on trailing announcements and I said more fool him, because that had given Campbell and his bloated battalion of special advisers precisely what they wanted.' Sir Bernard said the growing frequency with which exclusive stories on the BBC and other television and radio services were sourced to 'leaked' government reports and figures indicated the heightened activity of the special advisers. Many of these news reports were slanted in favour of the government, and he was convinced the information had been leaked on purpose to help prepare the way for ministerial statements.

One minister who authorised his special advisers to brief journalists was the Chancellor, Gordon Brown, and newspapers like *The Times* had been encouraged to promote a bewildering array of projections for his multi-billion-pound increases in public spending. Figures leaked in May 2000, nearly two months ahead of the comprehensive spending review, helped divert attention from the controversy Brown provoked over the failure of Laura Spence, an eighteen-year-old pupil at a North Tyneside comprehensive, to get a place at Oxford University. Laura's rejection by Magdalen College, despite the expectation that she would get five As at A-level, was condemned by Brown in the strongest possible terms. He said it was scandalous that a schoolgirl from North Tyneside with the best qualifications had been turned down by 'an interview system more reminiscent of the old school network and the old school tie than genuine justice'. Lobby correspondents were told by Godric Smith, one of Campbell's deputies, that Blair 'fully endorsed' the criticism; but after an outraged response from the university authorities, who accused the Chancellor of damaging Oxford's efforts to attract more entrants from state schools, Brown seemed anxious to distract the news media. Three days after the speech, the front-page lead in *The Times* on spring bank holiday Monday was an exclusive story by its political editor, Philip Webster, revealing that the Chancellor had told ministers that the baseline for public spending in the 2001/2 financial year would have increased by 'more than £40 billion' by 2003/4.

Webster, who quoted an 'insider', said *The Times* had 'learnt' that Brown would devote another £28 billion to public spending on top of the £13 billion for health that was already committed for the third year of the Treasury's review. I was on duty that bank holiday and knew there was every likelihood that the figure was correct because Brown had given Webster exclusive stories in the past, including a headline-grabbing interview in October 1997 revealing that a referendum on future British membership of the European single currency would not be held until after the next election. However, I was doubtful whether I would be able to get confirmation for the £40 billion figure because the Treasury's information officers had always been resolute in their refusal to give official backing to specu-lative stories in advance of key announcements like the Budget or the comprehensive spending review. To my surprise the Treasury's duty press officer, Vickie Sheriff, suggested that I contact a second infor-mation officer, Francis McGee, who answered questions on statistics. He sounded rather hesitant at first but said he could confirm that

£40 billion was 'in line' with the spending total for 2003 if calculated on the basis of the Budget figures. However, he could give no substance to the breakdown which The Times gave for individual departments and when I inquired about the spending total for 2002/3, he said that had not been worked out, which I thought was rather odd, so I pressed him further: was the Treasury telling the BBC that the figure of at least £40 billion was correct? He hesitated for a moment and then said it was 'authentic within the spending envelope for the final year'.

My conclusion from our conversation was that although he was reluctant to discuss, let alone support, speculation about the contents of the spending review, he had given the Treasury's backing to the figure leaked to The Times. Within a matter of ten minutes or so, I took a call from the Chancellor's personal press spokesman, Ian Austin, who had succeeded Charlie Whelan as one of Brown's four special advisers. He said he understood McGee had already spoken to me and he wanted to reassure me that the £40 billion quoted in The Times was authoritative and 'within the Budget envelope'. Austin and the Treasury press office had obviously co-ordinated their approach when handling reporters' calls that bank holiday Monday, and as they were substantiating the £40 billion figure, which had not previously been revealed by the Treasury, I advised the editor of the Six O'Clock News on BBC Radio Four that it made a newsier top to my story on Brown than the continuing fallout from the row he had generated over Laura Spence. I said in my report that by allowing the Treasury to publicise his future plans so far in advance of the spending review, Brown hoped to 'deflect adverse publicity over his attack on élitism at Oxford University'. Downing Street's press office had spent the bank holiday weekend telling reporters that the Chancellor had never intended to say anything to damage the excellence of Oxford as his intention was to 'take class barriers down, not put them up'. Next day most newspapers followed up what the Guardian had headlined as 'Labour's spending spree', which provided some positive coverage for the Chancellor amid continuing protests over his attack on Oxford's selection procedure.

I was intrigued by the speed with which the figure leaked to The Times had gained acceptance as an accurate projection. Five weeks later, shortly before Brown's statement to MPs, BBC journalists were given a briefing by a group of economists and analysts from the City of London. Their presentation used the £40 billion figure as the projected increase in public spending by 2003/4. When I inquired about the origin of their estimate, David Walton from Goldman Sachs told me they had obtained it from *The Times*. 'It was the first time it had appeared and we checked it out, found it was reliable, as did the Institute of Fiscal Studies, and we think broadly that is the ball park increase for 2003/4.' The accuracy of the figure leaked to *The Times* was finally confirmed by the Chancellor himself in mid-July, when he gave MPs details of his three-year spending review. He said that by the 2003/4 financial year 'an extra £43 billion will be allocated to front-line services.'

In my experience this was the first time Treasury information officers had taken the exceptional step of giving credence to what in previous years they would have said was pure speculation, and I considered the episode a further illustration of the proactive stance that government press officers had been urged to adopt in conjunction with the special advisers assigned to their departments.

Some publicity-conscious ministers who served under Thatcher and Major shared Labour's frustration over the lack of drive that they too had experienced in the information service, and they were privately in awe of the turnround Alastair Campbell had achieved. In June 2000 the former health secretary, Virginia Bottomley, who had worked tirelessly to promote Conservative reforms such as hospital trusts and GP fundholders, told the *Daily Express* how she had tried without success to persuade government press officers to be more energetic. She had debated the point regularly with the then Cabinet Secretary, Sir Robin Butler, and asked him why the information service could not be more professional and sound more committed to the government's achievements. 'Robin used to say that the rules I disliked in government, I would value most in opposition.' Although Mrs Bottomley believed New Labour's 'bullying' had triumphed where she had failed, she considered the information service had been politicised because in her day no civil servant would have dared give different stories to different newspapers.

A few weeks earlier I had witnessed another instructive and ground-breaking example of the assertive way in which information officers were supporting their ministers and how they were getting dragged into the political fray despite Richard Wilson's repeated assurances. John Prescott, the Deputy Prime Minister, had faced sustained opposition from a sizeable group of Labour MPs who were critical of the plans for the partial privatisation of the National Air Traffic Service, and in early May 2000, shortly before the committee stage of the Transport Bill, he appealed for support at a weekly gathering of the Parliamentary Labour Party. The PLP meets in one of the large committee rooms and if political journalists think there is likely to be a story, they line up outside waiting for a briefing from a Labour Party press officer.

Although government information officers are regular visitors to the committee corridor, especially when ministers are giving evidence to MPs, they have never, to my knowledge, been in attendance under any government for what are strictly party meetings, and I was surprised to find Prescott's civil service press secretary, Derek Plews, standing outside ready to brief political correspondents. I asked him why he was present and he told me his task was to explain to journalists on Prescott's behalf why a public–private partnership for air traffic control would enable it to raise the £1 billion needed for investment in new equipment. The meeting had attracted considerable interest because there were predictions that up to sixty Labour MPs might rebel against the government in the vote on the bill, and, as it drew to a close, the group of reporters waiting outside had grown to about a dozen, among them Plews, who had briefed new arrivals. As the MPs began to leave we managed to get the odd word about what had happened inside. Michael Clapham confirmed that some of his fellow MPs had expressed strong feelings against air traffic privatisation. Gordon Prentice said he had personally explained his reservations. Martin Salter, Labour MP for Reading West, and a leading opponent of the sell-off, walked towards us and then suddenly veered away, wagging his finger. Paul Bromley, a political correspondent with Sky News, shouted after another likely critic, Andrew Mackinlay, who surprisingly turned round and came back to talk to us. He said with a mischievous grin that half the MPs had applauded Prescott, the other half had not, and ministers were with the half who had clapped.

Once the meeting had finished and Plews had spoken to Prescott, he told us that the Deputy Prime Minister had managed to allay a lot of the concerns expressed by MPs. Don Brind, press officer for the parliamentary party, brought over Clive Soley, the PLP chairman, who acknowledged that a significant number of MPs remained uneasy about the plan. When the House debated the Transport Bill the following Monday night, forty-seven Labour MPs voted against the public–private partnership. Andrew Mackinlay, who voted with the government, told me afterwards that he was upset about what happened after he spoke to reporters the previous week. 'After telling you lot that half the MPs clapped the Deputy Prime Minister and half hadn't, I got a right old bollocking from him later that afternoon. Prescott called me over and told me that I knew the rules and that I shouldn't have been telling reporters what went on in a private party meeting. When I challenged him to say what he meant, Prescott said he had asked his man outside the meeting to tell him what had happened and Prescott then repeated to me my quote, word for word, so he'd got me banged to rights.' Mackinlay accepted he could not blame anyone but himself. He had presumed everyone in the group was a journalist and he said he would have to be more careful before speaking to us again on the committee corridor.

By taking along a senior government press officer to give him support outside a purely party meeting, the Deputy Prime Minister had in my opinion set something of a precedent. I realise many Labour MPs or political journalists would doubt whether the distinction I make here has much significance: Prescott wanted any questions from reporters about the public–private partnership for the air traffic control service cleared up immediately and, as Alastair Campbell had said repeatedly, the government had every right to make sure its message was properly understood by the news media. Nevertheless, the distinction between party workers and civil servants had been observed religiously under Thatcher and Major, when press officers from Conservative Central Office were always deployed to answer questions relating to ministerial speeches at the 1922 committee, the equivalent grouping for backbench Tory MPs. Now, it seemed to me, the sharp dividing lines of previous years had become blurred, the safeguards of the past were being ignored and, as the political appointees who managed the dissemination of the Labour government's message continued to extend their power and influence, ministers as well as civil servants found themselves being subjected to ever tighter political control over the content and timing of statements and policy announcements.

FALL GUYS, ENFORCERS
AND VOICE OF THE DAY

'I had to apologise to the Speaker but it was No. 10 who took the sports strategy announcement out of my hands . . . Downing Street wanted to control the whole story and I had to take the blame, so don't talk to me about it.'

Kate Hoey, Minister for Sport, speaking to Nicholas Jones, 6 April 2000

'It was all very funny, rather like that scene from the film Annie Hall *where the subtitles show what* Woody Allen and Diane Keaton *are really thinking. Underneath me it should have said, "That's a bloody good question to a cabinet minister and I'm not sure I know the answer."'*

Dr John Reid, Secretary of State for Scotland, speaking to Nicholas Jones, 23 September 2000, about his role as a government spokesman during the fuel protests

P rime Ministers down the years have complained that one of the biggest banes of their life in Downing Street has been the difficulty they faced in trying to make sure their ministers kept to the agreed line when giving speeches, talking to journalists or being interviewed on television or radio. Most recent incumbents of No. 10 managed at some point in their premierships to impose a degree of discipline, but a unified front rarely lasted long, and once solidarity started to dissipate the vitriolic savagery of sacked and disenchanted former ministers knew no bounds and tended ultimately to hasten the demise of the administrations they once supported. Resignation statements by holders of three great offices of state – Foreign Secretary George Brown, Leader of the House Sir Geoffrey Howe and Chancellor of the Exchequer Norman Lamont – were among the direst moments for the governments of Harold Wilson, Margaret Thatcher and John Major respectively.

Although he has yet to experience the full force of the volcanic eruptions that can ensue if a loyal linchpin of the cabinet departs the scene and seeks revenge, Tony Blair, like his predecessors, has had to take the flak and come to terms with the punishment inflicted by several former colleagues. Blair has tried to tackle the problem head-on and has gone far further than any previous prime minister to safeguard his administration from the damage, intended or accidental, that can result from the uncontrolled behaviour of publicity-seekers within his government. He has established new mechanisms to control both the timing and the content of the speeches and broadcast appearances of his cabinet colleagues. Blair has also reinforced his government's ability to defend itself by ensuring that a minister or party stalwart has always been on hand to fill the breach or hold the line, and prepared at all costs to remain on message. Instant rebuttal has become a cornerstone of the armoury for withstanding attack from either the party's political opponents or the news media. Virtually no debasement has been considered beyond the call of duty for the rent-a-quote defenders of New Labour. During the final, gruelling years of his premiership, John Major was fortunate in being able to call on the services of his deputy prime minister, Michael Heseltine. So far none of Heseltine's Labour successors at the Cabinet Office has had the ability, stature or staying power to stand much chance of challenging his enduring accolade as Minister for the *Today* programme. He could be relied on to navigate his way through a succession of difficult interviews, and he had the knack of being able to turn some of the bleakest moments for the Major government into an attack on the Labour Party or his BBC interrogators. Heseltine's nonchalant demeanour and suave delivery often infuriated viewers and listeners, but party managers at Conservative Central Office regarded him as their safest pair of hands, capable not only of closing down the most troublesome news stories but of doing so without falling into the trap of provoking further unexpected controversy.

Blair's first line of defence on becoming Prime Minister, and the foundation for a raft of other measures aimed at co-ordinating the presentation of government policy, was the publication in July 1997 of the *Ministerial Code*, which gave his ministers guidance on their conduct and the procedures they should follow. It was a revamped version of the long-standing rule book for cabinet government,

Questions of Procedures for Ministers, which was updated by successive cabinet secretaries and treated as highly confidential until Major made it public in 1992. Blair's code was several pages longer than the previous guide on the functions of government, and there was much comment at the time over the wording of paragraph 88, which set out the requirement placed on ministers to ensure the effective presentation of government policy:

All major interviews and media appearances, both print and broadcast, should be agreed with the No. 10 press office before any commitments are entered into. The policy content of all major speeches, press releases and new policy initiatives should be cleared in good time with the No. 10 private office; the timing and form of announcements should be cleared with the No. 10 press office. Each department should keep a record of media contacts by both ministers and officials.

The power of command and control that the code vested in the Downing Street press office was plain to see, and the wording of the paragraph came to be regarded as a clear manifestation of the control freakery of which Blair was later accused. However, there was nothing new in his attempt to establish a framework of rules to govern the use ministers made of the news media. Harold Wilson's press secretary Joe Haines wrote to *The Times* to defend the *Ministerial Code* and said every prime minister for the previous thirty years had attempted to establish a 'rational way of co-ordinating government responses to public events'. Haines explained how he had operated a system similar to the one proposed by Blair, and he recalled how he was forced to advise that one minister be forbidden to give a television interview and another refused permission to circulate a speech. Wilson had imposed a further rule in his day that no non-emergency parliamentary statement could be made without being submitted to the press secretary forty-eight hours in advance. None the less Haines, who had also been a political appointee, could not compete with the ability of Blair's press secretary to lead from the centre, because Alastair Campbell had the authority to instruct civil servants as a result of the order in council giving him executive powers. Appropriately enough, the first public indication of the institutional changes that would flow from the *Ministerial Code* was the letter Campbell circulated to all Whitehall departments in September 1997 calling on the government's information service to 'raise its game' and arguing that a media strategy had to be an integral party of the policy-making process in each department.

In the subsequent report on the future working of the information officers, published the following month, Robin Mountfield set out the changes that he believed were needed to strengthen Campbell's leadership role and to establish the machinery that would allow the Downing Street press office to give clear direction from the centre. The principal task of the press secretary was to ensure that the 'essential messages and key themes' which underpinned the government's strategy were 'sustained and not lost in the clamour of events'. If this was to be achieved, there would have to be advance planning to secure a 'timely and well-ordered flow' of information and a requirement that 'actions or announcements' by individual departmental ministers had to 'fit in with and reinforce the political strategy and direction' set by the Prime Minister and the cabinet. In addition to recommending the creation of the new strategic communications unit, which was given the task of co-ordinating the presentation of future initiatives and events in order to 'show their coherence' with the government's main themes, Mountfield gave his support to a structure of daily and weekly meetings that Campbell could use to maintain 'clear and orderly government messages' across the news media.

Michael Heseltine, who took charge of presentation in the final years of the Major government, had relied on a meeting first thing each morning to go through the day's business, and Mountfield believed this was a 'tailor-made forum' for allocating responsibility, agreeing lines to be taken on current stories and, if need be, mounting a rapid response. Under Blair, the daily meeting was at first chaired by the minister without portfolio, Peter Mandelson, who worked in the Cabinet Office for the first twelve months of the Labour government and who had ministerial responsibility for presentation. It is now chaired by Campbell or his deputy and is attended by representatives of the No. 10 policy unit and press office, the Cabinet Office, the Chief Whip's office, the Deputy Prime Minister and the Labour Party press office.

Perhaps more significant are the changes that have taken place in the weekly meeting. Bernard Ingham had placed considerable emphasis during the Thatcher government on a meeting each Monday afternoon with the heads of information from the Whitehall departments, at which the media strategy for the week ahead would be considered. Campbell abandoned this practice and replaced the Monday meeting with one on Thursday afternoon, at which the strategic communications unit took on the task of planning the presentation of events and likely stories during the following week – well in time to take into account the management of stories likely to figure in that weekend's Sunday newspapers. The unit prepared a weekly diary, known as 'the grid', which was intended to integrate important initiatives so as to prevent a clash of events and ensure that positive developments were not blotted out by unwelcome news coverage for announcements that were known to have the potential to damage the government.

A copy of the grid, which had a restricted circulation, was obtained by the *Guardian* in June 2000 and revealed the care which had been taken to draw together the presentation of four key speeches planned for the third week of May. A memo attached to the grid said the Prime Minister was keen that all ministers should be 'referring to each other's work' and the aim was to explain that the government had a 'clear mission and purpose' and was making progress towards achieving its goals. The timetable showed how the speeches were intended to complement each other: Monday, Chancellor, child poverty: 'no child need grow up in poverty'; Tuesday, Prime Minister, economy: 'families are protected from boom and bust and enjoy rising living standards'; Wednesday, Home Secretary, police training and recruitment: 'people need not live in fear'; Thursday, Secretary of State for Health, medical school expansion: 'we can get an NHS fit for the twenty-first century'. The memo underlined the overall message: 'Big goals. Big arguments. Serious government versus opportunistic opposition.'

Given the care and thought that went into planning each week's events, and the strong overall control exercised by the Downing Street press office, Campbell had little patience with ministers who refused to co-operate and who wanted to grab the headlines for themselves. No sooner was the ink dry on the Downing Street press notice, dated 14 January 1998, which announced the creation of the strategic communications unit, than Campbell had the chance to demonstrate his newly enhanced authority to require departmental ministers to toe the line. A memo dated 15 January 1998, which was leaked the following March, revealed his fury at the behaviour of the two feuding ministers who then had responsibility for benefit reform, the Secretary of State for Social Security, Harriet Harman, and the Minister of State for Welfare Reform, Frank Field. Campbell was annoyed by their rival attempts in the newspapers that morning to claim the credit for the 'welfare roadshow' being launched that day by Tony Blair in Dudley. His memo, marked urgent and faxed to them both, said it was time 'facts took over from personalities' and he did not want to see their interpretation of Blair's speech in next day's newspapers. Campbell left them in no doubt as to who was in charge of presentation: 'I will issue the welfare reform focus files at 11.30 a.m. at the morning briefing. I will announce the membership of the welfare group.' He sent the two ministers another memo the following month saying it was important they entered a 'period of pre-budget purdah' and avoided giving interviews because speculation on welfare changes and Budget issues had become 'inextricably linked'. He urged them to show 'extreme caution' if they were asked to have lunch with political journalists and he reprimanded Ms Harman for having given interviews to the *Guardian*, *Woman's Hour* and *The World At One* that were 'not cleared' through his office.

Copies of the two memos were obtained by Simon Walters, political editor of the *Sunday Express*, who said they revealed the 'thuggish methods' used by Blair's 'right-hand man and enforcer' to keep the cabinet in check. The Select Committee on Public Administration, which had already started its inquiry into complaints that the government's information service had been politicised, considered the leak was sufficient justification to ask Campbell to give evidence. The decision to call him as a witness was instigated by the Labour MP Rhodri Morgan who chaired the committee and who later that year launched his campaign to be Labour leader in the Welsh Assembly. He told *The World At One* that he wanted to discover whether the Downing Street press secretary had the Prime Minister's full authority to administer 'a ticking off in this way'. Did

Campbell's status as a temporary civil servant allow him to rebuke ministers who had been 'quarrelling in public' and tell them it was time they stopped? 'There is obviously a control freak tendency in the New Labour government . . . Alastair Campbell is saying in those memos, "There is only one spin doctor round here and that's me" . . . If I had been a minister, I think I would have been pretty upset about the tone of those memos, unless the first line was "Tony Blair has told me to tell you . . ." And if they do have the full authority of the Prime Minister, wouldn't it be better if the memo actually states it?'

Campbell was in robust form defending himself at the afternoon lobby briefing. He dodged questions about the brutal tone he had adopted and said the two memos simply underlined what everyone knew, that No. 10 had to be notified of bids to interview ministers. 'It is a simple act of co-ordination. It is no big deal and you lot know it is no big deal . . . The media should get more interested in the issues but what we have is a media obsessed with itself and with process. You lot are more interested in the process of politics than the policies.' Campbell used the same response whenever political journalists tried to challenge him about the methods being deployed by No. 10, and he would often brush aside a question, even before it was finished, accusing correspondents of being preoccupied with what he later came to describe as the two most boring subjects raised at his briefings, 'processology' and 'spinology'.

Rhodri Morgan's decision to summon him as a witness was given added prominence the following weekend when the *Sunday Times* and *Sunday Telegraph* revealed that Campbell had been attending every meeting of the cabinet. David Ruffley, a Conservative MP on the select committee, said Blair's press secretary had become the twenty-third member of the cabinet but was not accountable to Parliament. Campbell was taken to task by most newspaper columnists for throwing his weight around, although Joe Haines, writing in the *Daily Mail*, thought the only mistake his successor had made was to put his instructions on paper. When Campbell lost his temper, he said, he did so on behalf of the Prime Minister, and 'every Mr Nice needs a Mr Nasty'.

Events were to prove that Campbell could not be faulted on the prescience of his warning shot to Harriet Harman and Frank Field.

Blair had become impatient with their inability to work together, or to develop a coherent strategy for welfare reform. Ms Harman was sacked in the reshuffle of July that year and Field resigned rather than be shunted sideways into another job. Campbell told lobby correspondents that Field had demanded a more senior role but that his talents were 'not best suited to running a government department' and Blair considered it was time to start work on welfare reform and 'not just talk about it'. Once Downing Street had given the stamp of approval to denigration of the former minister, it was a green light to every unattributable briefer in Westminster, and the Sunday newspapers were filled with quotes from unnamed government sources accusing him of being 'childish and pathetic' and a 'failed joke'. On the Monday, Field told the *Jimmy Young Programme* that unless Blair stopped the divisive spinning being done in his name it would become a cancer that would eat away at the very heart of the government.

Later that summer, when he had recovered from his traumatic exit, Field told me that by spinning against him, Campbell had helped restore his reputation as an independent thinker on welfare reform. 'I had no idea Campbell intended to criticise me in a lobby briefing but in the end it gave me credibility, especially when it was clear the spin doctors could not even agree between themselves on the reforms that I was proposing.' Field became a regular columnist for the *Sunday People*, writing under the by-line 'Frank and Fearless', and one of his regular themes was that the government's frantic efforts to promote its own performance were counterproductive. He expanded on his theme in an interview for the *Independent*: 'The electorate don't want to keep being told the same things. They pick up messages very quickly, quicker than some MPs, and they don't need pagers to know what to think.' After getting embroiled in the controversy surrounding Ken Follett's declaration that the Downing Street spin doctors were the 'rent boys of politics', Field revealed in July 2000 that he had written a book about his fifteen months as a minister which he threatened to publish unless Blair stopped the practice of hostile briefings. Field said he had evidence to prove that he was only one of several sacked ministers who had been undermined by anonymous government sources speaking to the press.

Harriet Harman, by contrast, followed Campbell's advice to the lobby to avoid 'processology', and she stuck firmly to policy issues when speaking to journalists. She campaigned regularly on family matters and urged ministers to adopt policies that were more friendly to women. After a radio interview in January 2000, when she insisted that the policy divisions between Labour MPs were nowhere near as great as those among the Conservatives, she apologised to me for being so firmly on message. 'I know I am sounding relentlessly upbeat but I am going to complain one day and I might have something to say.'

When Rhodri Morgan finally had the chance to cross-examine Campbell about his controversial memos at the select committee hearing, he explained that as an ex-civil servant he believed the No. 10 press secretary should have made it clear he was writing with Blair's implicit authority; otherwise there was an implication that the Downing Street spokesman was 'more important than some ministers'. Campbell acknowledged that it might have been better if his memos had been worded differently, but he denied having implied that he was more powerful than a minister. He reminded the MPs that he had responsibility under paragraph 88 of the *Ministerial Code* to co-ordinate announcements. 'In terms of anything that I would say to a minister, it is not me that is speaking, but it is the spokesman of the Prime Minister.'

Campbell was supported by Robin Mountfield, who told the select committee that Blair had made it abundantly clear in opposition that he wanted strong co-ordination at the centre over policy and presentation. A strong centre did not diminish the power of individual secretaries of state, but the 'very special position' of the Prime Minister allowed him to exercise 'a very strong degree of co-ordination' through the No. 10 press office. 'I would express it as co-ordination rather than control, consistent with the principle of collective government.' Mountfield revealed that when the Cabinet Office discovered shortly before the 1997 election that Blair's chief of staff and chief press secretary were to be political appointees, discussions were held with the two main parties about the precise terms of appointment for special advisers. The contract used under the Conservative administration had not been precise and it was agreed there should be 'a rather clearer statement' about their role. Under the order in council, Campbell and Jonathan Powell had been freed from the 'advice-only requirement' placed on other advisers. 'That clearly unlocks to some extent Campbell's ability to operate at the margin. It allows him to operate . . . in a political context.'

Campbell's unique ability as a political appointee to co-ordinate presentation was the subject of prolonged cross-examination by David Ruffley, who believed it had allowed Downing Street to bypass MPs and trail government announcements before they were made to the House. Ruffley tried repeatedly to pin the blame for this on to Downing Street, but Campbell insisted he did not have superhuman powers to stop everyone in government and Whitehall speaking to journalists. 'I do what I can to make sure that government policy is presented in a co-ordinated and effective way. That is my job. What I do not do is pre-empt major announcements to Parliament . . . I have no doubt whatever that people brief the press when they should not, none whatever, and it may annoy the Speaker and it regularly annoys me too . . . I think it is a problem . . . I have said I think she is right.' Correspondents present at the committee hearing were amused by Campbell's show of concern over the complaints by the Speaker, Betty Boothroyd, about policy statements being announced first to the news media. Many political journalists had failed to benefit from the exclusive stories about future announcements, which Campbell had directed towards newspapers favoured by Downing Street, and whenever correspondents mentioned the Speaker's criticism during lobby briefings Campbell treated it as a joke. The previous November, on the eve of the publication of Robin Mountfield's report, when he gave a taster of the changes that were to be made, he was asked if this might offend the Speaker. Campbell grinned and retorted: 'I have never, ever trailed things which should be relayed to Parliament first . . . ' His final words were lost in laughter, but he shrugged it off, asking 'Tell me the last time I did?'

Miss Boothroyd, elected Speaker in 1992, served for the first three years of the Blair government before retiring in July 2000, and she made six separate rulings against ministers for disclosing information to the news media before delivering statements to the House. Her first complaint came in July 1997, a day before the publication of the

Dearing Report, prompted by early morning news reports on BBC Radio Four saying that the government had confirmed that it intended to introduce students' tuition fees. Miss Boothroyd said there had clearly been 'very heavy briefing' before the ministerial statement and she considered that advance briefings by Whitehall sources or ministerial aides had developed progressively to the point where the rights of MPs were in danger of being overlooked. 'The House is rightly jealous of its role in holding ministers to account. If it is to fulfil its function properly, it must be the first to learn of important developments of government policy. I deprecate most strongly any action taken that tends to undermine this important principle.' After a second ruling in February 1998, political columnists took up her complaint and rebuked Blair for ignoring her criticism. Peter Dobbie, writing in the *Mail on Sunday*, said New Labour had turned the House of Commons into 'a disgraceful pastiche of parliamentary democracy' where everything was 'rigged beforehand and nodded through'. Joe Murphy, the paper's political editor, said that after the article appeared Miss Boothroyd rang up the newsroom and spoke to Dobbie because she wanted to discover whether journalists had any ideas for restoring parliamentary authority. After thinking over the issue for some time, she agreed in early April to give an interview to the *Westminster* programme in which she appealed to the Prime Minister to rein in the government's spin doctors. She had already made her views known at the highest level in Whitehall. 'I mean talking to a minister, speaking eyeball to eyeball with a minister . . . It is up to ministers to harness their spin doctors.'

Miss Boothroyd acknowledged that on occasion all governments had briefed the news media before ministers appeared in the House, but said that it had been done 'far more subtly and professionally' since the 1997 election. 'There are probably far too many of what I would term "apparatchiks" who are working in government departments and who have been accustomed, when the party was in opposition, to getting maximum publicity. That's understandable. Now, in government, they have to be harnessed a little more.' She delivered her third ruling later that month after Blair's failure to make a statement in the Commons about a visit to the Middle East. Her disparaging remarks about ministers' disregard for the House were quoted at length by David Ruffley when he cross-examined Campbell in June 1998. The day after the select committee's hearing I had the chance to speak to Miss Boothroyd at the Speaker's annual reception. She told me she welcomed Campbell's acknowledgement that the trailing of government statements had become a problem for the House and she was 'chuffed' that he was taking her criticism seriously. She had only agreed to take the exceptional step of giving a television interview because she was 'really uptight' about the blatant way statements were being leaked in advance to the media. Yet despite Campbell's assurances that he shared her concern, she had to intervene again ten days later in early July after the BBC and several newspapers reported details of the government's plans to overhaul the Child Support Agency three days before a statement to the House. Miss Boothroyd was clearly annoyed that her appeals were still being ignored: 'I cannot deprecate strongly enough the leaks and the briefings that go on, perhaps behind our backs.'

In March 1999 she supported a complaint that the contents of a statement by the Secretary of State for Health, Frank Dobson, announcing an extra £200 million for hospital modernisation, were revealed in the 6 a.m. news on BBC radio. Ann Widdecombe, the shadow health secretary, said the details given in the report about how the money would help reduce the number of hospitals that lacked an admissions ward indicated that the information must have been given out in advance. Miss Widdecombe went on to read out a list of six other announcements that she claimed had all been leaked by the Department of Health, including the nurses' pay award; a statement on mental health leaked to the *Sunday Telegraph* two days before publication; a statement on social services which appeared in the *Independent* and *Guardian* on the morning of publication; and a statement on health spending which appeared in *The Times* on the morning of its delivery in the House. Miss Boothroyd told MPs that she listened avidly to the radio each morning. 'I heard the 6 a.m. report to which Miss Widdecombe referred and every news from then on. I use my Walkman to listen to the news when I take a walk and I hear far too much information that is made public often days before it is revealed at the dispatch box. I shall continue to deprecate that practice for as long as it continues.'

She felt it unnecessary to issue a further rebuke until April 2000, when she reprimanded the Minister for Sport, Kate Hoey, for holding a news conference at 9.45 a.m. to reveal the government's sports strategy when there was no parallel announcement in the House and when copies of the document were not available to MPs until much later that morning. Miss Boothroyd said she had heard Miss Hoey speak about the sports strategy on *Today* and she had subsequently investigated a complaint made by the opposition culture spokesman, Peter Ainsworth. She was forthright in her ruling: 'This is a clear breach of the conventions that apply to announcements of this sort, and it is totally unacceptable to me and the House. It seems to me that there is a situation developing in some departments in which the interest of Parliament is regarded as secondary to media presentation, or is overlooked altogether. I hope that ministers will set in hand a review of procedures right across Whitehall to ensure that the events which took place this morning are never allowed to occur again.' Miss Hoey accepted the ruling immediately and apologised to MPs: 'I appreciate this was not done correctly . . . I believe that the House has been treated discourteously. That point will be made to my department, and I apologise unreservedly on its behalf.'

The build-up to the news conference announcing that £150 million was to be spent on improving sports facilities at schools and community centres had been a text-book example of how to trail a news story. An exclusive in the *Independent on Sunday* had predicted that schools were to get up to £100 million for new sports gyms and equipment. A fuller story appeared in the *Mirror* on the morning of the launch. After her interview on *Today*, Miss Hoey joined the Secretary of State for Culture, Media and Sport, Chris Smith, for a photo-opportunity laid on for the lunchtime bulletins and evening newspapers. They visited a sports centre in north London and went out on the running track with children from a local primary school. Most of the national newspapers carried the photographs next day, and although Miss Hoey's rebuke was reported in full, the boost to school sports got the biggest headlines.

Having to rise at the dispatch box to apologise to the Speaker is a galling experience for any minister, and I felt a slight sense of trepidation the following afternoon on being told that I had to interview

Miss Hoey about the murder of two Leeds United football fans in Turkey. As we walked to the gardens opposite the BBC's studio in Millbank to film the interview, the newsroom alerted me to reports that four horses had been killed during races on the opening day of the Grand National meeting at Aintree; I was asked to get Miss Hoey's reaction. My first two questions were about the death of the Leeds fans, and I then asked if she could comment on the loss of the four horses. She said she could not possibly respond to what had happened at Aintree as she had been in meetings all afternoon. As we packed up to leave, Miss Hoey left me in no doubt that she was annoyed at being thrown the additional question when the BBC had asked originally for an interview on the disturbances involving the football fans in Turkey. I remarked rather flippantly that as I was only an interviewer and not the Speaker, I would not tell her off for not giving an answer.

My tease was clearly a step too far, and the very mention of the Speaker's name provoked an unexpected response: 'It wasn't me. I had to apologise to the Speaker but it was No. 10 who took the sports strategy announcement out of my hands the week before. I didn't do anything. Downing Street wanted to control the whole story and I had to take the blame, so don't talk to me about it.' Miss Hoey's remark could not have made the position any plainer: here was a clear-cut instance where Downing Street's communications strategists had taken control of a significant policy announcement and made presentation to the news media the priority, giving little if any thought to informing Parliament.

Earlier that day I had caught up with another ironic twist to the circumstances surrounding Miss Boothroyd's reprimand. I had been unable to attend the afternoon lobby briefing the previous day, but on reading the extract on the Downing Street website, I saw that at the moment the Speaker was accusing the government of putting media presentation before the interests of Parliament, Campbell was congratulating information officers and special advisers for their effectiveness in operating the procedures she was complaining about. He announced that Paul Martin, head of public affairs at the security service MI5, was to become the new director of communications at the Cabinet Office. Martin had taken a number of steps to improve public awareness of MI5's work and had opened a website for the service. Campbell used the appointment as an opportunity to commend the action which had been taken to improve co-ordination between policy and presentation. He said the 'excellent proposals' in the Mountfield report had made a 'considerable difference' to the government's communications.

Campbell had every reason to feel satisfied with the efforts made by the information service to 'raise its game' and 'grab the agenda'. Praise for the 'swifter co-ordination' being achieved in communicating government policies was prominent in the 1999 annual report on the work of civil service press officers. Mike Granatt, head of the information staff, said they had provided 'a first-class professional service' to ministers. The forward planning being done by the No. 10 strategic communications unit was producing results, and advance publicity for policy decisions often appeared across a wide range of news outlets. Indeed, the trailing of forthcoming announcements was proving so successful that the *Daily Telegraph* had calculated that in the first three years of the Labour government at least forty MPs had complained to the Speaker about occasions when the press had been informed before Parliament.

Miss Boothroyd bided her time, waiting until the day of her departure at the end of July 2000 before making a heartfelt plea to ministers to refrain from bypassing the House. She broke the convention that valedictory addresses should be uncontentious to tell MPs she was troubled by the public's disillusionment with the political process and by the level of cynicism about Parliament. 'The function of Parliament is to hold the executive to account . . . It is in Parliament in the first instance that ministers must explain and justify their policies. Since becoming Speaker in 1992, I have made my views known about that, both publicly and behind the scenes, to both governments. I have taken action to ensure that those who advise ministers should never overlook the primacy of Parliament. This is the chief forum of the nation – today, tomorrow, and, I hope for ever.'

Miss Boothroyd's farewell strictures on the need for ministers to respect the rights of MPs had little lasting impact: within a week of his election as Speaker in October 2000, the first ruling of her successor, Michael Martin, was another reminder that the substance of a statement should not appear first in the news media. Conservative MPs complained about advance publicity ahead of the announcement by the Secretary of State for Defence, Geoffrey Hoon, that two roll-on-roll-off ferries were to be built by Harland and Wolff of Belfast, and that four new amphibious landing ships were to be constructed on the Tyne by Swan Hunter. A press release about the orders was released that morning, and the details had appeared on the website of BBC News Online precisely one hour and fifty-nine minutes before Hoon addressed the House. After conducting an investigation the Speaker confirmed that some 'broadly accurate advance information' did reach the media, but said that he had accepted Hoon's assurance that this was not released by his department. He asked ministers to do far more to ensure that confidential information was protected by the various officials and authorities who were privy to it. 'If ministers were to release information to the press before the House was informed of major policy developments I would regard that as an unacceptable discourtesy.'

Judging by his remarks, Speaker Martin had come to the same conclusion as Speaker Boothroyd that there were too many 'apparatchiks' trying to get publicity for important announcements; and, just like his predecessor, he seemed powerless to protect MPs. In December 2000, after protests by the Conservatives' frontbench spokesman, Gary Streeter, about a 10.30 a.m. news conference to announce the government's white paper on eliminating world poverty, the Secretary of State for International Development, Clare Short, wrote to the Speaker to apologise 'if any action or omission' on her part had been a discourtesy to the House. Her white paper was announced to MPs in a written parliamentary answer that afternoon. A week later the Speaker promised to investigate a complaint by the Conservative MP Dr Julian Lewis that the contents of the government's communications white paper on the future structure of broadcasting had been trailed in both the *Sunday Times* and *Sunday Telegraph* two days before the Secretary of State for Trade and Industry, Stephen Byers, made his statement to MPs. As if to underline the struggle that she knew her successor was facing, Miss Boothroyd used a television documentary programme on her career, *Call Me Madam*, which was broadcast by the BBC the following weekend, to issue a final reminder to Blair to remember that Parliament was 'a forum of democracy' for the country and it should not be regarded as secondary to the government's media presentation.

However much Alastair Campbell sought to brush off journalists' interest in 'processology', the many operational changes that had been made within the information service and the hard-sell techniques adopted by the much-expanded network of special advisers had undoubtedly damaged parliamentary accountability. The procedures which the government had put in place to speed up the dissemination of information had widened considerably the group of people who were in a position to release advance details of new measures to the media, and the repeated rulings by the Speaker were a pointed reminder that ministers remained responsible for their underlings. Yet a reprimand here or there from the Speaker was a small price to pay when set against the considerable tactical advantages the government derived from having created structures which ensured that positive news like orders for hard-pressed shipyards fanned out instantly not just to the news media but also to Millbank Tower, so that the party could relay the information to Labour MPs and their constituency offices. If Labour were to get the full benefit from the favourable publicity that could be generated in evening newspapers and on local radio stations, the media's deadlines had to be met, even if that meant bending the rules over the embargos placed on the release of information.

Soon after the election, Millbank Tower launched the *Daily Brief*, which was faxed to MPs' offices each morning and was subsequently made available by e-mail. It set out the government's responses to the key issues of the day and included news of any major announcements. In February 2000 the daily summary appeared under a new title, *Dividing Lines*, with the declared objective, in preparation for the next election, of setting out 'clear dividing lines' between Labour and the Conservatives. Dossiers on key issues were available from the 'message delivery unit' at Millbank Tower. One of the first to be published was a seven-page document entitled 'Renegotiate or Withdraw', which provided a background brief on the activities of Eurosceptic Tories and the 'Britain Out Brigade'. The strong emphasis on pre-election campaigning was reinforced when the unit launched a new weekly publication, *Tory Watch*, which aimed to demonstrate that the Conservatives' defining characteristics were 'weak leadership and poor judgement' and that the party was driven by 'tactics, not beliefs'.

In collating a summary of the lines that the government intended to take on the main political developments of the day, Labour hoped that every minister, backbencher or party spokesperson would remain on message when speaking to journalists or being interviewed on television or radio. One of the party's most successful innovations during the 1997 election campaign had been to establish a 24-hour media monitoring unit, and it was replicated in government within five months of Labour taking power. After an initial period of operation on a pilot basis with civil servants borrowed from across Whitehall, a permanent unit with a staff of ten was established in the Cabinet Office. Its tasks include informing ministers, special advisers and press officers about the contents of the first editions of the next day's national newspapers, and providing round-the-clock crisis news monitoring so that warnings can be issued about breaking news stories.

Two of the special advisers who worked in the Downing Street press office regularly spent time with the unit, and their presence reflected the significance of the inevitable crossover between government and party work and the obvious political value of newspaper summaries and programme transcripts. There was no longer any excuse for ministers who were caught out during early-morning television and radio interviews: they should have taken the time to read an up-to-date media summary and briefed themselves on the main stories in the morning newspapers before entering the studio.

And yet, though fast and reliable media monitoring was essential for effective rapid rebuttal, and though the defensive mechanisms Blair had established were far superior to anything John Major had ever envisaged, Labour lacked the clout in terms of individual personalities, which the Conservatives had often been able to deploy at times of crisis. After his cabinet reshuffle in July 1995, to prepare for the general election that took place almost two years later, Major was able to call on two doughty performers, the Deputy Prime Minister

Michael Heseltine and the minister without portfolio Dr Brian Mawhinney. Both had cabinet rank and could defend the government across a broad front, although of the two Heseltine had by far the tighter grip on policy issues because of his responsibility in the Cabinet Office for co-ordinating presentation. Blair, by contrast, could command nothing like the same firepower during the first twelve months of his administration. Dr David Clark, the Chancellor of the Duchy of Lancaster, and Peter Mandelson, minister without portfolio, both had responsibility for Cabinet Office affairs and could theoretically have fielded questions across a broad policy range, but neither was as forceful or as authoritative as Heseltine and Mawhinney.

Dr Clark, unlike Mandelson, was a member of the cabinet and could have been used more prominently; but he did not seem comfortable in the cut and thrust of television and radio interviews, and failed to carve out a distinctive position for himself in the heady early days of the new government. Mandelson's great handicap was that he was distrusted by many party members, disliked by most journalists and had no great presence in front of the camera. His shifty demeanour, which made him appear either scheming or menacing, or an even scarier combination of the two, meant that his television appearances had to be chosen with care, and he found it difficult to establish a rapport with viewers and listeners. His one and only attempt to launch himself as an all-purpose, up-front government spokesman ended in disaster. He and the Deputy Prime Minister, John Prescott, had been entrusted with minding the shop in August 1997 when Blair headed for Tuscany on his first family holiday as Prime Minister. Mindful of the forth-coming elections to the Labour Party national executive committee, Mandelson made the mistake of trying to build up his public presence in the middle of the summer silly season, when news-hungry journalists are starved of their usual fare and the smallest gaffe or scandal is likely to be blown up out of all proportion. As the troubles piled up during Blair's absence, Prescott had no diffi-culty looking after himself and he demonstrated his sense of fun at Mandelson's expense with an infamous photo-call on the site of the Millennium Dome at Greenwich. He held up a specimen jar containing one of the Chinese mitten crabs found in the mud at low tide, declared that its name was Peter and then, for the benefit of the television cameras, proceeded to converse with his new-found mate, musing on Mandelson's chances of winning a seat on the national executive. Prescott's devilment underlined Mandelson's precarious position in the party contest, and served as a fitting augury for his ultimate and ignominious defeat at the hands of Ken Livingstone.

David Clark's fall from grace was equally humiliating, but unlike Mandelson he stood no chance of reprieve or promotion. His card was effectively marked during the 1997 election campaign when, despite being an elected member of the shadow cabinet, holding the position of defence spokesman, he was noticeably passed over when Labour chose those who would take prominent front-line positions for television and radio interviews. 'What defence from the invisible man?' was the headline ten days before polling day over Peter Oborne's column in the *Sunday Express*, which claimed that party headquarters had issued instructions that Dr Clark should be barred from the airwaves.

After the election he had responsibility in the Cabinet Office for open government, and Blair charged him with the task of preparing a white paper to honour Labour's manifesto commitment to introduce legislation on freedom of information. His first setback came within a few weeks of the election when he issued a statement regretting his failure as an opposition spokesman to declare the cost of hotel accommodation in Geneva while attending peace talks on Bosnia. His understanding was that the United Nations had picked up the bill. He faced renewed criticism in October 1997 over the cost of first-class flights to the United States, Canada and Australia, which were incurred during fact-finding missions on open government. Dr Clark told the *Newcastle Journal* that details of his travel expenses were leaked as part of a smear campaign. He knew exactly who was behind it and could 'virtually prove' the stories were planted by someone in the government. On hearing that the Sunday newspapers intended to suggest this was a coded attack on his fellow Cabinet Office minister, Peter Mandelson, Dr Clark told his local BBC radio station that while he had no doubt he was being smeared, he did not believe it was a minister who was to blame and thought the information had either been leaked by a civil servant or emerged from somewhere else in the system. Amid mounting press speculation that he was about to be dropped from the cabinet, he had to pull out of a live interview for that Sunday's edition of *On The Record*. Dr Clark said he was unable to take part because of a perforated eardrum and his place was filled by the junior Cabinet Office minister, Peter Kilfoyle, who made the most of his unexpected opportunity and subsequently appeared regularly for the government fielding numerous difficult interviews. The tortuous circumstances surrounding the leak were investigated by the *Observer*'s columnist Roy Hattersley, who reported the following Sunday that Dr Clark had been forced to endure months of 'apparently co-ordinated denigration', which could all have been avoided if the Downing Street press office had taken journalists aside and squashed the rumours that a minister was about to be sacked.

Hattersley's support was to no avail, and hardly a week went by without yet another story suggesting that Dr Clark would lose his job in Blair's first reshuffle. In May 1998 he told the *Guardian* that the whispering campaign against him had been 'relentless'. Although over a hundred Labour MPs signed an early day motion congratulating him on his 'ground-breaking' white paper on freedom of information, the prediction made by almost every political correspondent proved to be correct, and he was dropped from the government in July. Dr Clark's departure after just over a year in the cabinet aroused sympathy among those Labour MPs who felt they had been overlooked by Blair and excluded unfairly from his government. They believed the briefings against Dr Clark were orchestrated from within the government and that it was an unscrupulous tactic used to undermine ministers who were considered to be ineffective or thought to have reservations about New Labour's objectives.

Dr Clark's trashing by unnamed insiders and other anonymous sources was recalled two years later when one of his successors, Dr Marjorie Mowlam, faced a sustained whispering campaign. Shortly before her announcement in September 2000 that she wished to leave the government at the next election, she was the subject of a Channel Four documentary, *The Rise and Fall of Mo*, by Linda McDougall, who wrote an article for *The Times* about her experiences in making the programme. Hattersley was among those she interviewed, and he stated his conviction that a technique of purposely diminishing the work of vulnerable ministers was used to prepare the way for their eventual sacking. Three weeks before Blair's first reshuffle he was writing a profile for the *Observer* and, after contacting Downing Street, was told by the press office that the person he had inquired about was 'a very bad minister, he doesn't get on with his civil servants, his junior ministers are rebelling against him'. McDougall explained what happened next: 'A couple of months later, Hattersley told his story to Alastair Campbell. "It didn't happen," said Campbell. "Pure invention. You are imagining it." Yet this was said in a dismissive, slightly jokey way.' Downing Street issued a statement denying that the remarks were ever made: 'We never engage in negative briefing against a member of the government.' Although Hattersley and McDougall did not name the cabinet minister involved, *The Times* said in a front-page story that it was understood to be David Clark, and when there was no denial of this by either the programme or Dr Clark himself, most newspapers reached the same conclusion.

During the many months of speculation that led up to his sacking I had picked up the odd comment about Dr Clark's lacklustre performance when being interviewed and his alleged reluctance to defend his fellow ministers at awkward moments. The emphasis placed on rebuttal meant that Downing Street and party headquarters had to be able to call on a range of senior politicians who could speak on behalf of the government at short notice and the lack of any big hitters in the Cabinet Office had not gone unnoticed. After the screening of the Mowlam documentary I asked Clark why he had not appeared more frequently on television and radio. He praised Hattersley for having spoken out so strongly against Downing Street's tactics and then acknowledged that his broadcast appearances had been few and far between, but said this was not out of choice. 'Early on I was asked once to do an interview on *Today* but I refused. They wanted me to defend something which was wrong, very wrong, which I felt would have been untruthful. I refused, so did a woman member of cabinet and eventually the interview was done by a junior minister who wasn't very happy about it.

Downing Street were very annoyed with me afterwards. My hunch is that Alastair Campbell was behind it but I was never asked again to go on *Today*.'

Dr Clark's unease reflected the inherent drawback of being put forward as an all-purpose defender of the government, ready at a moment's notice to get stuck in and take on all-comers in what can sometimes be a rather unsavoury business. A fleet-footed fearlessness is the essential attribute for front-line duty on behalf of New Labour's rebuttal unit, and the sole objective is to get across a tightly controlled message for the government while at the same time deflecting and debunking any complaints or allegations raised by the interviewer. Worrying too much about the facts is not always advisable: what Downing Street and party headquarters want is to hear someone sticking up for the government and closing down a difficult story, even if that did mean having to put the boot in. Peter Kilfoyle, who took Dr Clark's place when he pulled out of his *On The Record* interview, had not only the right aptitude for rebuttal but also plenty of experience: he had risen to the top in the rough and tumble of Merseyside politics, where he had spent five years as Labour's regional organiser. Kilfoyle became something of a hero during Neil Kinnock's long struggle against left-wing activists, and in 1991 he won the Liverpool Walton by-election after trouncing Militant's candidate, Lesley Mahmood, who fought the seat as the candidate of Walton Real Labour. His robust opposition to Militant's infiltration of Liverpool City Council was not without some risk, because the by-election had been caused by the death of Walton's MP for the previous twenty-seven years, Eric Heffer, who was prominent on the left and had walked off the platform after Kinnock's explosive attack on Militant at the 1985 party conference in Bournemouth. I covered the by-election campaign, and in my radio reports I made several mentions of the sure-footed way in which Kilfoyle dealt with questions at his morning news conferences. Kilfoyle's campaign was backed by Alastair Campbell, then a political columnist with the *Sunday Mirror*, who did his bit to rally support in the by-election: 'M stands for Mahmood, Militant and maggots . . . Vote Kilfoyle to kill off the maggots.' In subsequent years, when Campbell was installed in No. 10's press office, he worked closely with Kilfoyle, who was later nicknamed Downing Street's 'secret weapon' because of his great versatility in defending the government.

Kilfoyle was one of the first MPs to join Tony Blair's campaign team in the leadership election after John Smith's death in May 1994. Philip Gould, Blair's pollster and strategist, described in his book *The Unfinished Revolution* the moment he arrived for his first meeting with the team and met Kilfoyle, a Liverpool MP with 'impeccable working-class credentials'. One of Kilfoyle's tasks, along with Dr Marjorie Mowlam, was to canvass support for Blair: another Labour MP, Andrew Mackinlay, said he received three telephone calls from Kilfoyle in the space of eight days during the campaign for the leadership, appealing for his vote; but each time he declined. Once Blair had won the leadership, Kilfoyle was appointed an opposition spokesman on education, but he did not join that department after the election and was instead made a junior minister for the Cabinet Office. Nigel Griffiths, whose room at Westminster was next door to Kilfoyle's, said the Walton MP was disappointed not to have joined David Blunkett's team at the Department for Education and Employment because he had spent 'two years going round the country talking to teachers and winning them over for Blair'. Nevertheless, Kilfoyle's skills were soon put to good use as one of his responsibilities as Minister for the Office of Public Service was to answer questions about the work of civil service press officers and the cost of employing special advisers. Shortly before he had to stand in for David Clark, he appeared on *The World At One* to defend the government against complaints from opposition MPs over the enforced departure of eight departmental heads of information. Kilfoyle said the information service had to keep up with a 'modern, modernising government' and he defended Campbell's political role because it was 'open and above board'. He was called on frequently to answer parliamentary questions, and although he was the junior minister he rapidly established his reputation as a forthright performer at the dispatch box as well as at the microphone, in sharp contrast to the two other Cabinet Office ministers, Dr Clark and Mandelson.

In the July 1998 reshuffle Blair promoted Mandelson to Secretary of State for Trade and Industry, and Dr Jack Cunningham moved from agriculture to replace Dr Clark, who was sacked along with the Minister for Transport, Dr Gavin Strang. Dr Cunningham's arrival at the Cabinet Office captured the headlines. He was immediately dubbed 'The Enforcer' when the newspapers learned that Blair had asked him to stem the growing tide of malicious comments about ministers, much of which was blamed on the unattributable briefings that journalists were being given by special advisers. At the select committee hearing the previous month Campbell had assured MPs that the 'vast majority' of special advisers did not have any contact with the press; but he unashamedly contradicted himself when giving a lobby briefing on the reshuffle. He acknowledged that the problems caused by the unchecked speculation that flowed from unattributed conversations between ministerial aides and political correspondents had to be tackled, and he declared himself pleased that a cabinet minister 'close to the Prime Minister and valued by him' had at last been given the authority to end 'this nonsense of spinning, malice, gossip and rumour'. Dr Cunningham's elevation was considered something of a surprise, because there had been some suggestion that he was about to be dropped; but when I met him the morning following his appointment he seemed determined to make the most of the opportunity Blair had given him. I had observed the forceful way he could handle journalists during the 1992 general election, when he was Labour's campaign director, but he admitted he faced 'quite a challenge' if he was to fulfil Blair's request to crack down on the special advisers and stop them gossiping to journalists.

Dr Cunningham was accompanied on his visit to the BBC's studios by the well-respected director of communications at the Cabinet Office, Barry Sutlieff, who was clearly delighted that his department was to be headed by a minister who might be able to match Michael Heseltine's authority. Sutlieff had done all he could to defend David Clark the previous autumn amid the allegations of a smear campaign, and although he had kept his opinions to himself, I sensed that he had struck up a good working relationship with Peter Kilfoyle and admired his combative style and the enthusiasm with which he would bat for the Cabinet Office, however sticky the wicket. Information directors do face problems if the lead minister in their department is reluctant to take on difficult interviews, and Sutlieff gave me the clear impression that he believed Cunningham and Kilfoyle would be ready and willing to speak up for the government across a wide range of issues.

Kilfoyle spent much of the following twelve months fending off continuing criticism of special advisers. In November he assured MPs the government had taken steps to prevent them compromising the political impartiality of civil servants, and the following January, when replying to a debate opened by the Liberal Democrats, he insisted there was still no evidence that government press officers were doing anything other than maintaining a 'studied neutrality'. In March 1999 there was glowing praise in the *Sunday Times* Atticus diary for Kilfoyle's role as Campbell's 'secret weapon' in 'sorting out grisly problems' for No. 10. Whenever Downing Street was in a pickle, Campbell messaged the 'burly cabinet office minister to storm *Today* and other morning programmes, pushing the government's line with steamroller effect'.

Kilfoyle had been used by Campbell with great aplomb the previous July when Downing Street was desperate to defend Roger Liddle, a special adviser in the No. 10 policy unit caught up in the controversy surrounding the lobbyist Derek Draper, whose activities were exposed in the *Observer* by an investigative journalist, Gregory Palast. Draper had introduced Palast to Liddle at a reception in the Banqueting House, and after Palast accused Liddle of offering a commercial client access to ministers, the Conservatives demanded his resignation. Downing Street stood by Liddle's denial that anything improper had happened, and after the *Observer*'s deputy editor, Jocelyn Targett, admitted on *Breakfast News* shortly after 7 a.m. that Palast's conversation with Liddle was not on tape, Campbell swung into action. Although *Today* had been told earlier that morning that no minister was available to be interviewed, Kilfoyle was immediately offered to the programme and when he appeared shortly after 8 a.m. he said the lack of a tape meant Liddle had 'no case to answer' and the matter was closed. Yet despite being ready to ride to No. 10's rescue at a moment's notice, Kilfoyle failed to get the promotion he was hoping for in the July 1999 reshuffle: shifted sideways to become a junior minister at the Ministry of Defence, he lost out to Ian McCartney, who was moved from trade and industry to become Minister of State for the Cabinet Office, under Dr Cunningham.

McCartney, who was a member of Labour's national executive committee and vice chair of the national policy forum, was given a far wider brief than Kilfoyle and effectively had responsibility for maintaining and improving links between the government and the party, an arrangement not unlike that which existed when Dr Brian Mawhinney doubled up as a cabinet minister and party chairman. Kilfoyle was deeply disappointed at having been overlooked and Blair paid a heavy price for having sidelined him in a department for which he had no special interest or affinity. Political journalists were left in no doubt about the extent of his disenchantment and when Tom Baldwin, deputy political editor of *The Times*, was about to report that he was on the point of leaving the government, Kilfoyle faxed his letter of resignation to Downing Street. He told Blair that his job at defence did not represent the best use of his political energies and he wanted to return to the back benches so that he could do more to promote the interests of 'the regions of England and the heartlands of Labour'. Ian McCartney, who represented the nearby constituency of Makerfield, was surprised by Kilfoyle's decision to rush out his resignation letter on Sunday evening, having seen him at a party meeting in Liverpool the previous Friday night when nothing of the kind had been mentioned; but he understood that Kilfoyle was on the point of going public about his disappointment and felt he had to make a statement once he learned that *The Times* intended to publish its story. John Prescott told me was sorry to see Kilfoyle go and thought Blair had a made a mistake in sending him to defence when it was obvious he liked being 'in the middle of things' at the Cabinet Office.

Baldwin said in his report that the resignation of a key Blair loyalist underlined the 'growing disenchantment among MPs representing traditional working-class constituencies', and Kilfoyle's abrupt departure sparked off considerable comment about the government's failure to respond to the concerns of their core voters in cities like Liverpool. Five days after resigning Kilfoyle gave an interview to the *Daily Telegraph* in which he warned that there was a political vacuum at the heart of New Labour because it had no intellectual framework around which Labour's natural supporters could coalesce. Freed from the constraints of office, he had no hesitation in denouncing the massed ranks of Labour's special advisers, describing the ministerial aides he had defended so diligently for two years as nothing more than a 'tribe of spin doctors' who exercised a disproportionate degree of influence over government presentation. 'Minor functionaries give a wholly erroneous impression of what's going on. That does a disservice to the government, to the media and to millions of people around the country who are not getting a factual account.'

Kilfoyle said he could not help being 'naturally bolshie' and, some months later, when I had an opportunity to ask him why had been prepared to remain so completely on message for so long at the Cabinet Office, he agreed it was a fair question. 'Look, I was well motivated. I was part of a team. I was comfortable with what I was saying, so I was happy to go out there, give the interviews and do the business for No. 10.' When I pressed him to say whether he had ever felt uneasy about being under Downing Street's control and told what to say, he paused for a moment before replying. 'The only time I really felt uncomfortable was when I was asked to speak about the arms shipment to Sierra Leone. A Cabinet Office minister was used so as to distance it from Robin Cook, but he was there on the front bench and I didn't feel very comfortable.' Kilfoyle said he had suggested there should be a forum at which junior ministers could put their views to the Prime Minister. 'We got one after eighteen months but it was all top-down. It didn't give us a chance to put our points to Blair. I realised then that a gap was opening up between the government and the party, between ministers and their core supporters, and it was that which finished it for me.'

Shortly after our conversation Kilfoyle was asked by the *Sunday Mirror* to review the BBC documentary *News From No. 10*, which examined Alastair Campbell's role as Blair's official spokesman. Kilfoyle questioned the wisdom of a Prime Minister's press secretary inviting the cameras into Downing Street and allowing the film to suggest he was more assured and articulate than Blair. Campbell knew all the tricks of the trade and must have known he would be portrayed by the programme as one of the most powerful people in the land. 'His body language suggested he was the deputy to nobody, but rather very much in charge of himself and those around him.' In his two-year stint at the Cabinet Office, Kilfoyle had demonstrated the value Campbell had placed on having a troubleshooter at hand who could go round the studios and carry out firefighting for the government at short notice. Despite all the tough words newspapers had written about the likely impact of 'The Enforcer', Jack Cunningham failed to live up to his advance billing. He made no visible impact on the activities of the special advisers, and when it came to defending his colleagues he had nothing like the force or impact of Michael Heseltine. After an early-morning round of interviews at BBC Westminster in the spring of 1999, Barry Sutlieff praised Dr Cunningham's ability to distill a brief and reduce it to a few sentences; but while he had considerable expertise in formulating the message which he wanted to convey, I felt he sometimes did not give the impression of having his heart in what he was saying, and he lacked conviction.

Although Dr Cunningham kept his job in the July reshuffle, he was replaced by Dr Marjorie Mowlam in October 1999 when her job as Secretary of State for Northern Ireland was given to Peter Mandelson on his return to the government. Dr Mowlam said immediately on taking up her new post that she had no wish to be called an 'enforcer' and wanted to be known instead as a 'co-ordinator' whose role was to help improve the presentation of government policy. She had been deeply hurt by her removal from Northern Ireland, and within a month of the reshuffle the *Mirror* revealed the depth of her dismay over the way she felt she had been sacrificed to create a cabinet seat for Mandelson. 'I hate my job says Mo,' was the headline over an exclusive report by the paper's political correspondent, Nigel Morris, which claimed Dr Mowlam had told her pals that she hated her 'meaningless' role at the Cabinet Office and felt she had been the victim of a 'stitch-up' when the job she wanted was Secretary of State for Health, which had gone to Alan Milburn.

Next day she wrote to her staff denying that she was unhappy, but acknowledging her sadness on leaving Northern Ireland and saying she had been laid low with a bout of flu. That Sunday she appeared on *Breakfast With Frost* and insisted that she was looking forward to getting on with her task of trying to simplify government policy and explaining it to the public; but her enthusiastic comments failed to stem newspaper stories suggesting she remained deeply disillusioned. Steve Richards, the *New Statesman*'s political editor, quoted an unnamed 'Blair aide' as saying she lacked the ability to immerse herself in policy detail and was 'on trial' in her new job. Speculation about her true intentions intensified after she confirmed she intended to write a book about her work on the Northern Ireland peace process. Ulster Unionist MPs had been highly critical of what they saw as Dr Mowlam's 'touchy-feely' style of doing business, and for well over a year their leader, David Trimble, had gone straight to Blair rather than negotiate with her. Shortly before she was moved, Ken Maginnis, the Ulster Unionists' home affairs spokesman, said his party had been left with no alternative but to bypass the Secretary of State because she did not read her briefs and did not understand what was going on.

Such attacks on Dr Mowlam, however, only increased her popularity among Labour's rank and file, and her friendly, easy-going style made her a welcome and popular contributor to television chat shows and comedy programmes. Her asides and indiscretions regularly made headline news, and in January 2000 she created quite a storm by admitting that she had smoked marijuana in her youth. One of the specific tasks Blair had given her, in addition to co-ordinating the work of the social exclusion unit, was to head the government's campaign against drug abuse. After the *Sunday Telegraph* reported that the Conservatives planned to 'press Mowlam over her drugs past', she owned up immediately when challenged by Adam Boulton, political editor of *Sky News*. She said she was 'a child of the sixties', although she had not been part of the drugs culture. 'I tried marijuana. I didn't like it particularly. Unlike President Clinton I did inhale but it wasn't part of my life then.' Her intention was to go on telling young people that taking drugs was not within the law and she would continue to fight hard against the drugs that could kill, like heroin and cocaine. Although she kept stressing the importance and seriousness of her work, she remained addicted to publicity and the following month she officiated at a bizarre dog wedding on Channel Four's risqué comedy show, *So Graham Norton*. According to the

Independent she confirmed her reputation as the 'funkiest' member of the government by allowing herself to be escorted on to the show by semi-naked male Cupids; giving away in marriage a bearded collie called Layla; and then admitting to having a penchant for dirty jokes. 'There's no business like Mo business,' was the *Sun*'s headline over a full-page report on how the cabinet minister 'dumped in the political wilderness' by Blair had become the 'darling of the celebrity circuit'.

The light relief provided by coverage of Dr Mowlam's showbiz escapades was in sharp contrast to the steady flow of stories asserting that Blair had lost confidence in her. 'Mowlam is victim of whispering campaign' was the headline over the front-page lead in the *Independent on Sunday* on 30 January, which said 'senior government aides' were concerned that radiotherapy for a benign brain tumour had left her 'without the intellectual rigour' to do the job. At the lobby briefing next morning, Alastair Campbell insisted she had Blair's full support. 'He has huge regard for Mo and thinks she is a massive asset to the government . . . She has got clout. She has got the Prime Minister's ear and his backing.' Later that week Dr Mowlam told *Woman's Hour* that she had been shocked and offended by the sugges-tion she was still dogged by the effects of the tumour and 'not up to the job'. She had received no treatment since 1997 but recognised her illness made a good story. She had stopped reading the newspapers and had no idea who was briefing against her. 'If I did I would stop it . . . There are people who just want to put the knife in and this story enables them to do it.' During the interview she confirmed that Barry Sutlieff, the long-serving director of communications at the Cabinet Office, was leaving, but she denied a report in *The Times* that he had fallen 'victim to her poor publicity' and had been transferred to another job. 'I didn't sack Barry. He has been offered another post and is keen to take it.' Sutlieff had been information director at the Cabinet Office since 1994, and his departure marked the end of an era: he was the last survivor of the seventeen heads of information who were in post when Labour took power.

According to *The Times*, Sutlieff was moving to a new post in Whitehall to train civil servants in the best ways to present the government's achievements. At a lobby briefing two months later in April, Campbell announced that Paul Martin, head of public affairs at the security service MI5, was taking over at the Cabinet Office and said that Sutlieff's future role would be to ensure 'proper co-ordination between policy and presentation' and to 'drive through' the changes recommended by Robin Mountfield. The day after Martin's appointment Dr Mowlam joined other celebrities at the funeral service for the rock star Ian Dury, and the arrival of a new information director did little to stem the constant flow of headline-grabbing news copy about her activities. The following month Linda McDougall's documentary, *The Rise and Fall of Mo Mowlam*, prompted another strong show of support from the Prime Minister. In an interview for *The Times*, he said the claim that Downing Street aides were trying to force her out of office was 'an outrageous and complete tissue of lies'. Dr Mowlam hit the headlines again the following month when she told the magazine *Saga* that the Royal Family should abandon Buckingham Palace and Windsor Castle in favour of 'a palace of the new century' more in line with the modern architecture of London. After Downing Street said the Queen had no intention of moving and the Prime Minister saw no reason why she should, Dr Mowlam apologised for any hurt she had caused. Although Blair had backed her publicly, I noticed that she was rarely being put forward to appear on television and radio news programmes when a minister was needed to mount an all-purpose defence of the government. Some producers told me they were convinced she wanted to do more interviews but Downing Street had refused to field her because she was so unpredictable and could not be relied on to remain on message.

She had certainly started exercising greater care whenever I threw questions at her during doorstep encounters in and around Westminster, and on several occasions she refused to comment, smiled and said I should ask her office for an interview. The *Mirror* was the first newspaper to predict an imminent announcement of her departure from politics: 'Mo: I'll go' was the headline in July 2000 over its exclusive report of an interview in which she revealed that she intended to do more to promote integrated education in Northern Ireland once she left the government. Five weeks later she confirmed that she would be standing down at the next election in order to pursue a career outside politics before she finally retired. I had been amused a few days earlier when Peter Mandelson revealed his irritation with Dr Mowlam for co-operating with Julia Langdon, the author of a forthcoming biography, *Mo Mowlam*. Ms Langdon said that although the book was unauthorised she had been allowed access to Dr Mowlam's friends and family, and in return she had allowed the minister to read the manuscript and change any factual errors. When he heard that the book would suggest he was responsible for co-ordinating personal attacks against ministers, Mandelson did little to hide his annoyance when interviewed on *Today*. He had no sympathy for a fellow cabinet minister who had assisted an author well known for her 'long-standing hostility' to New Labour: 'That's a matter for Mo Mowlam. If she chooses to co-operate with somebody like that and an exercise like that, well, that's her judgement.'

Dr Mowlam was on holiday, so she could not respond immediately, but if she had heard Mandelson's interview she might have been amused by his use of the name 'Mo'. She was one of the first Labour MPs from the 1987 intake to get appointed to the front bench, and when Neil Kinnock promoted her in 1989 to become the opposition's spokesperson on city and corporate affairs, Mandelson advised her to insist on being addressed as 'Dr Marjorie Mowlam' because he considered 'Mo' was 'too fluffy and lightweight' for a rising politician. Needless to say, Mo she remained, and she could never resist the odd cheeky aside about the way Mandelson exercised his authority as the Labour Party's director of communications. His patronage was important for an up-and-coming frontbencher, and he was all-powerful when it came to deciding who would be allocated to prime interview slots on television and radio: programme bids had to go through Mandelson's office. So once when she turned up unexpectedly at BBC Westminster in place of the then shadow Chancellor, Gordon Brown, she told me she could hardly believe her good fortune: 'I really am pleased to be doing this for the BBC. Usually Peter only lets me do *Sky News*.'

Dr Mowlam announced she was standing down from politics immediately on her return from holiday, within a few days of the publication of the first extract from Ms Langdon's book in the *Mail on Sunday*. Mandelson had identified correctly one of the weaknesses of her position: the *Ministerial Code* stated that ministers could contribute to books or newspaper articles only if so doing was not at variance with their duty to 'observe the principle of collective ministerial responsibility', and although she had insisted that the biography was unauthorised and did not represent her views, she did not deny having read the manuscript. Dr Mowlam told *Today* that she had been talking to Blair for some months about standing down; having recently hit fifty, she wanted to do something different.

Given her popularity among party members, she had done the government a favour by halting further speculation about her future almost a month before Labour's annual conference, thus removing a potential source of controversy. At the 1998 conference delegates interrupted Blair's speech to give **her** a standing ovation after he praised her contribution to the Northern Ireland peace process. Perhaps it was only fitting that the first member of the cabinet to pay tribute to her publicly was the minister who, without any public fanfare, had taken on her mantle as the leading all-purpose defender of Labour policy. In the space of a few months the Secretary of State for Scotland, Dr John Reid, had become the ubiquitous voice of the government, ready at a moment's notice to speak up for his colleagues or attack the Conservatives. One of the golden rules of rebuttal is that no opportunity should be missed: television presenters take delight in pointing to an empty chair in the studio if they believe the government or the opposition is too frightened or embarrassed to defend its corner, and New Labour dislikes letting the broadcasters score points so easily. Dr Reid was the natural choice when the party had to provide television and radio programmes with a senior figure to pay tribute to Dr Mowlam. He was warm and magnanimous on *Newsnight*: 'She's never changed. She's always had her feet firmly on the ground.' As Dr Mowlam had retreated progressively from the cut and thrust of topical interviews, Dr Reid had developed into an ideal substitute. He had a reassuring manner and the right temperament: he rarely got flustered on air, however much he might have been annoyed by a bizarre line of questioning or the aggressive attitude of an interviewer. Under devolution, his own workload as Secretary of State for Scotland had diminished, and his task of oiling the wheels of the relationship between the United Kingdom government and the Scottish Parliament and executive was proving far less demanding than he had expected. As a consequence, he had the necessary time to prepare himself across a wide range of policy issues; and, being based at the Scotland Office in Whitehall, he was available for interviews at short notice.

Dr Reid told me that the transfer of power had at times been frustrating because the government was effectively 'giving everything away' to Scotland. He would have liked to become defence secretary in the October 1999 reshuffle, but his role as an instant, all-embracing spokesman at least enabled him to 'keep his finger in the UK pie'. The morning after his *Newsnight* tribute to Dr Mowlam he was on duty outside Conservative Central Office as political correspondents arrived for the launch of the party's draft manifesto. He handed out calculators, urging journalists to complete their own audit of the Conservatives' figures: 'You add them up, we can't.' Unlike most of his cabinet colleagues, Dr Reid rarely seemed to be in a hurry and enjoyed the company of journalists. On the night the gay millionaire businessman Ivan Massow defected to Labour, Dr Reid arrived at the BBC's studios at 11.30 p.m. to give his reaction – calling the loss of a former contender for the Conservative candidacy for Mayor of London 'a devastating blow' for William Hague – and stayed until well after midnight.

Dr Reid reinforced his credentials as a durable all-purpose performer in the face of hostile and provocative questioning in early September 2000 during the mounting protests by farmers and road hauliers over the level of duty on petrol and diesel. He toured the studios to defend the government's handling of the dispute and, after some sustained pressure on *Newsnight*, acknowledged that the government had been caught out by the failure of the oil companies to persuade their tanker drivers to continue deliveries. When challenged repeatedly on *Channel Four News* during the second week of the protests, he told the presenter Jon Snow to stop interrupting him. 'I will deal with your question first and then you can put your supplementary.' Dr Reid had the knack of remaining forthright without being offensive, and he stood his ground equally firmly on *Newsnight* the following week when he was asked to defend the government after the Labour leadership's defeat at the party conference over the demand for increases in the state pension to be linked to the rise in earnings. When Jeremy Paxman made fun of his frequent appearances and taunted him for having become the Minister for Embarrassments, he took it all in his stride. He was a member of a cabinet that believed in collective responsibility and he had every right to speak for the government. However, after he ended his final answer by declaring yet again that he was confident the Chancellor would protect the income of pensioners, Paxman could not resist anticipating the minister's next appearance on *Newsnight*: 'Thank you, we'll wait for the next crisis.'

Dr Reid's new lease of life as a media troubleshooter had attracted the attention of the Crossbencher column in the *Sunday Express*, which noted that 'Jolly John' had rarely been off the airwaves. While the 'wheels fell off the government' he had kept his cool in the television studios and shown that he possessed that 'rare quality among Blairite ministers, a sense of humour'. He was certainly in remarkably good form on arriving in Brighton that weekend in late September, the day before the official opening of the Labour conference. He was holding court in the coffee shop of the Metropole Hotel and clearly relished the opportunity of spending the week as a high-profile party spokesman at such an important gathering. He was on standby that afternoon to give Labour's reaction to the result of the Scottish National Party's leadership election when it became known. When I joked about this being the first time for weeks that he would be answering questions that related to his ministerial responsibilities, he took it all in good part and admitted it had been rather difficult to explain why the Secretary of State for Scotland should be answering questions about the demands of the fuel protesters. He said the most amusing moment was on GMTV when he was asked repeatedly why he was continually being put up as the government's spokesman when he was playing no part in sorting out the dispute. 'I kept explaining that I was the Secretary of State for Scotland and that I was in the cabinet, but it was all very funny, rather like that scene from the film *Annie Hall* where the subtitles show what Woody Allen and Diane Keaton are really thinking. Underneath me it should have said, "That's a bloody good question to a cabinet minister and I'm not sure I know the answer."' At that point Dr Reid's special adviser, Michael Elrick, interrupted our conversation to impress upon me the importance of maintaining contact during the week ahead in case Dr Reid was needed by the BBC. He seemed oblivious to the irony of what he was saying: 'Millbank are keen to use John on whatever story is running at the Labour Conference. They want to use him across the board on anything which comes up at Brighton this week.'

Elrick's honesty was at least disarming, and I noticed that his boss was as pleased as punch to see that his aide had seized the moment and started touting for interview bids. Our conversation reflected the cosy world that can exist at the interface between politicians and the news media. In return for the information I could supply about breaking stories and the access I could provide as a broadcaster, I was in effect being offered a rent-a-quote minister who would perform as required by responding to whatever was in the news. Labour's special advisers and press officers might consider my reaction rather churlish. As a broadcaster I depend on them to provide ministers and party spokesmen at a moment's notice and they know, when deadlines are especially tight, that I will probably be only too happy to take the first person who is available, however loose his or her connection is to the issue or event in question. While I acknowledge that the pressures under which I work as a television and radio journalist do make me dependent on their good offices and grateful for their endeavours, my encounter at the Metropole Hotel only served to underline the reality of the controls that modern political parties seek to impose. Dr Reid was obviously regarded by the government and his party as an ideal frontman: affable with journalists; consistently on message; wary of gaffes; and a reliable troubleshooter. Nevertheless, by accepting him as a substitute for a minister with direct responsibility, broadcasters have in effect submitted to the control being exercised by the party machine. Dr Reid and his ilk are often used to thwart news bulletins and programmes by blocking their attempts to question ministers who have personal involvement in the decision-making process. I accept that other considerations apply: broadcasters are duty bound to give governments and political parties an opportunity to respond; current affairs programmes and rolling news channels need a constant supply of interviewees. Nevertheless, although the deployment of surrogates meets Labour's goal of ensuring that no opportunity is missed, and gives party spin doctors total control over the messages they wish to communicate, viewers and listeners often sense they have been short-changed. They dislike the constant repetition of the same answers and do not have a high regard for politicians who simply parrot the party line. Alastair Campbell claims that the cynicism displayed by today's political journalists is undermining the public's faith in the process of government and doing nothing to counter voter apathy. I would suggest in response that perhaps the contribution being made by the Prime Minister's official spokesman in manipulating and deploying rent-a-quote ministers might have also added to the public's disenchantment with politicians.

PLAYING THE FIELD

'*I went to Alastair Campbell and said: "This is the situation, I don't think we're going to run it, unless Robin Cook wants to talk about it . . ." Alastair came back and said: "I know how you work, run it straight please," which was a fair quid pro quo, and that's what I did.*'

Phil Hall, former editor, *News of the World*, interviewed in the *Guardian*, 3 July 2000

Alastair Campbell's relationship with the lobby correspondents of Westminster has been unlike that of any of his predecessors. We realised from the moment he started work for Tony Blair in the autumn of 1994 that controlling Labour's news agenda would not satisfy him: he would want to go even further and beat us at our own game. The fundamental difference between Campbell and previous Downing Street press secretaries is that he remains in a perpetual state of competition with the political journalists he once worked with. We have no idea where or when he will place his next exclusive: it might be an interview with the Prime Minister, a signed newspaper article announcing a new policy initiative or a tip-off to one of his favoured newspapers. We know that his timing will be impeccable and that the top line will have plenty of political punch. More often than not his initiatives have succeeded in setting the news agenda for the day. I have no hesitation in admitting that his news sense is much sharper than mine, and even if I did manage to match his expertise and spot a story with the same potential, I am sure his opening sentence would be more succinct and his headline far snappier than anything I could write.

While many of my colleagues might be reluctant to be so charitable, few would deny their admiration for his gutsy tabloid instincts and his ability to weigh up within an instant the likely repercussions and future implications of major political decisions and events. The sense of rivalry is as intense as when he was one of us and, once we are all assembled in front of him, he likes nothing more than to find some excuse to poke fun at our story lines, mock our predictions and debunk any attempt we might have made at political analysis. His restlessness is addictive, which explains why most correspondents were genuinely disappointed and distressed when he told the lobby in the summer of 2000 that he wanted to spend more time working on future strategy and intended to scale down his routine of presiding at two briefings a day. In the event his petulant retreat was short-lived and he has continued holding briefings on several days each week, although he has been spending less time overall with the lobby than he did in his first three years in No. 10. Campbell can often be engaging and highly amusing when he joshes the journalists with whom he once stalked the corridors of the House of Commons and in many ways I think he still is a journalist in spirit, although clearly not in practice; I sense that he retains that rush of blood and feeling of excitement that reporters experience close to deadline on a big story. His ability to continue displaying a sense of affinity with those who work in the news media explains why many political journalists have shown little inclination to scrutinise his behaviour, bear down too heavily on his misdemeanours or speak ill of him in public. His trick has been to convince most of my fellow correspondents that he is still 'one of us'.

For the vast majority of political editors and correspondents the lobby's self-interest is the paramount concern: political journalists want to be briefed by a Downing Street press secretary who is in regular contact with the Prime Minister; who can speak knowledge-ably on his or her behalf; and who understands what makes the news media tick. Campbell's authority as Blair's spokesman has never been questioned or doubted. Reporters have complained about his half-truths and evasions, but I know of no instance where he has given inaccurate or misleading guidance about Blair's thinking or inten-tions. Sometimes his jousts with the lobby have become bad-tempered and rancorous, but by and large they are good-natured and Campbell enjoys the bonhomie generated by what is often one of the few occasions in the day when political editors and correspon-dents from the nationals join up with the broadcasters and our colleagues from the regional press, and we all get the chance to catch up with the latest gossip. When Campbell strides into the Downing Street briefing room for the morning lobby, clutching a file of documents and a mug of tea, he has the air of an editor marching into a newsroom ready to allocate his reporters their stories for the day. If he has been annoyed by a report that morning in a newspaper or news bulletin and he can spot the offender, he does not mince his words, and – as I know to my cost – a public dressing-down can be rather wounding. Sometimes Campbell will widen his attack and lambast the editorial line taken by an individual newspaper or a programme. Occasionally he will launch a fusillade at the entire assembled company. I am always struck by the relative good humour with which these broadsides are delivered, as though he is desperate to preserve the matiness of his public relationship with journalists.

However, it is a very different story once he returns to his inner sanctum and the Jekyll of the lobby room becomes the Hyde of No. 10. The anger he tries to suppress at his briefings, and the evident contempt he harbours for the trade he once practised, is vented in a non-stop stream of complaints and criticisms. Anyone from the lowest reporter to the highest editorial executive can find themselves in the firing line as he fulminates at the deficiencies of the news media and the need for higher ethical standards. Newspaper editors and programme producers are rebuked by fax; apologies and corrections are demanded in brusque telephone calls to broadcasters and journalists; letters get penned for newspaper correspondence columns; and the tirade continues in articles, speeches and interviews. As might be expected of a highly skilled tabloid journalist and masterly propagandist, he can spot the weakness in a press report or broadcast item and then use that one mistake or omission to construct a damning indictment of an entire newspaper or programme. His compulsion to cavil or complain at the slightest provocation has made him the Mr Angry of journalism, ready at a moment's notice to lecture all and sundry on the diverse failings of the news media.

Campbell gave his clearest exposition of the shortcomings of today's political reporting in a interview conducted by a former *Daily Mirror* deputy editor, Bill Hagerty, which was published by *British Journalism Review* in June 2000. The recurring theme of their conversation was that lobby correspondents had become spin doctors and the government was 'more spinned against than spinning'. Hagerty found that no matter the avenue down which their discussion turned, it invariably led back to Campbell's belief that the journalists were far more culpable than the press officers of Downing Street for distorting and manipulating the news agenda. What particularly caught my attention was Campbell's assertion that when he reported politics for the *Daily Mirror* and *Today* he used to lie awake at night worrying about the accuracy of his stories and comment columns. 'I think standards have declined a lot. I don't get the sense that journalists lie awake wondering whether they've got a story right or wrong. I've got to be careful because of what I was as a journalist . . . Yes, I was interested in how journalism could be used to debunk a Tory government which had massive support in the media . . . I hold up my hands. I was a biased journalist and I don't make any bones about that. But the bias was so overwhelmingly the other way the whole time, I didn't like it and I was in part responding to that . . . I think there are still a lot of journalists who worry about getting things right. But I think the pressures on them are to get the story regardless; to get the story first, wrong, rather than get the story at the same time as everyone else, right.' Hagerty gave no indication in the report of his interview that he had followed through either of the two fundamental points that Campbell was making: that many political journalists cut so many corners they no longer cared whether their reports verged on the dishonest, and that the pressures under which they worked had become so intense that accuracy had to take second place to speed. I intend to examine Campbell's response on both counts. In his six and half years as Tony Blair's spokesman, what action has he taken to improve the reliability of political reporting and to reduce inaccurate speculation?

Have the new procedures he has introduced for releasing information and promoting government announcements created a level playing field for the news media? Indeed, has his instruction to the government's information service to 'raise its game' done anything to help ameliorate or limit the negative effects of the competitive pressures he identified so clearly for *British Journalism Review*? When Campbell walked through the front door of No. 10 in May 1997 he had an unparalleled opportunity to strengthen the ethical values of the craft in which he made his name. He could, for example, have said that his briefings would be on camera and that a full verbatim transcript would always be made available. I accept that his concern about the effects of falling standards is genuinely held, and I agree with him that in the four years that have elapsed since the general election some areas of political reporting have left a lot to be desired; but he failed to take the radical action that was within his gift. While Campbell does occasionally allow himself to be interviewed about his role as the Downing Street press secretary, he has marked me down as an obsessive whose work is fit only for ridicule. Whenever he spies me writing down anything in a lobby briefing that might relate to his professed pet hates of 'processology' and 'spinology' he pokes fun at my fetish and invariably provokes a laugh from the assembled journalists. If I dare ask a question he raises his eyes heavenwards in despair. My difficulty is that he is usually so quick off the mark in deriding my interest in his presentational techniques that he leaves me trailing in his wake, unable to hit back in time with a suitable rejoinder.

I can always be sure of swift retribution and a snide riposte if I dare refer to his work in one of my television or radio reports. He took particular offence at a jokey aside I made on *Breakfast News* during the government's embarrassment over the leaking of a series of confidential memos written by Blair and his pollster and strategist Philip Gould. They were supplied to *The Times*, *Sun* and *Sunday Times* by an undisclosed source over a six-week period during June and July 2000 – leaked separately so as to create maximum interest. By far the most revealing was Gould's lengthy assessment of Labour's electoral prospects. He considered that 'something has gone seriously wrong' for the party and concluded that the 'New Labour brand has been badly contaminated'. The leak was timed to limit news coverage of the announcement by the Chancellor, Gordon Brown, of his £43 billion increase in public spending. Reports about the contents of the memo filled the first five pages of the *Sun*. One of the last documents to be released was a note from the Prime Minister in which he said the political case for joining the European single currency was 'overwhelmingly in favour'. Blair's memo was published on the day the government announced a five-year plan for the National Health Service. When I was asked about the leaks that morning on *Breakfast News* I suggested to the presenter Sophie Raworth that whoever was responsible for timing their release to the newspapers seemed to have a sharper news sense than Alastair Campbell. She chuckled at my remark.

Later, at the morning lobby briefing, Campbell's deputy Godric Smith told correspondents it was obvious there had been a pattern to the leaks. 'For whatever reason someone is trying to achieve a news blackout of important announcements like the spending review and the health plan . . . We don't know where this news management is coming from but if you look at the timing and content there is clearly selective leaking going on.' Although Smith had substantiated the very point I had made in my interview about the leaks having been the handiwork of someone with a sharp news sense, Campbell had no intention of letting me escape from the afternoon briefing without being put in my place for having made him the butt of my flippant aside to Ms Raworth. Before becoming Blair's press secretary, Campbell had appeared regularly on *Breakfast News* presenting the newspaper review. He looked and sounded assured on screen, and had carved out quite a name for himself as a forthright and provocative political pundit. I knew he retained a soft spot for the programme. As the correspondents stood up to leave the briefing, he shouted out and caught me by surprise: 'Hey, I was watching you this morning with one of my kids and he said to me, "Dad, that bloke is obsessed with you."' I was taken aback by the thought that one of Campbell's two sons, aged twelve and ten, had taken an interest in my early-morning two-way and that my throwaway line might have somehow caused offence at the breakfast table. He had made all sorts of cracks in the past about my interest in his work, but this was the first time he had used one of his children to remind the assembled lobby that they had an unstable obsessive in their midst. As I walked through the members' lobby back to BBC Westminster, I kept thinking about what Campbell had said and decided he must have been having me on. My trouble had been that I had not grasped immediately why everyone laughed: the obvious implication of what Campbell had said was that even his son could spot a nutter. Try as

I might, I could not think of what would have made a suitable rejoinder – until I remembered the interview with Bill Hagerty. Of course, what I should have called out in response was, 'Alastair, how are you going to reply when your son says to you, "Dad, what did you do in Downing Street to try to make sure journalists get the news right and don't make mistakes?"'

Campbell timed his interview for the *British Journalism Review* to coincide with a much wider effort to draw attention to the falling standards of political reporting. In order to demonstrate his point and give the public 'a better understanding of the relationship between modern politics and the modern media', he had decided to co-operate with the broadcaster Michael Cockerell in the production of a BBC documentary. Cockerell was given access over a period of four months and his film, *News from No. 10*, was broadcast in mid-July. It included extensive footage from lobby briefings together with interviews with the Prime Minister, his press secretary and numerous political journalists. In an article for the *Guardian*, Cockerell denied that he had presented 'a sanitised version of Campbell' and believed his film had 'captured the genuine feel of the briefings, which could be bruising encounters'.

Campbell agreed to take part because he wanted to show that the Downing Street press office fulfilled 'a basic, necessary and legitimate function' to distribute a huge range of information in a co-ordinated way and that he and his staff were not the 'horrible, Machiavellian people' as which they had been portrayed. He recognised that the growing use of anonymous quotes from unnamed sources was at the heart of the problem he faced in trying to get Blair's true voice across to the public. One of the changes introduced in November 1997 as a result of Robin Mountfield's report was that journalists were allowed to source Campbell's lobby briefings to 'the Prime Minister's official spokesman'. The move towards clearer attribution began in 1991 when John Major's press secretary, Gus O'Donnell, agreed that his guidance could be sourced to 'the Prime Minister's office' or 'Downing Street' rather than the far more anonymous 'government sources' on which Bernard Ingham had insisted. To underline the fact that his briefings could be considered on the record, Campbell decided that they should be recorded on tape by a member of his staff and that Downing Street would produce a daily summary of the proceedings. He and Blair had both been spending an inordinate amount of time reassuring ministers that quotations attributed to unnamed people close to the Prime Minister were complete nonsense, and he hoped direct sourcing of his lobby guidance would make it easier to refute the 'half-truths and inventions' that were appearing in some newspapers. Campbell admitted on *News From No. 10* that his initiative had failed and that matters were worse than before: 'The papers are still full of "a source", "a friend" and "an insider" says. And in my view a very substantial selection of those quotes are simply made up.'

Some of the journalists were prepared to defend their corner. Michael Prescott, political editor of the *Sunday Times*, denied that lobby correspondents were imposing their own agenda or slanting what they reported. 'We are not spin doctors, we are professional decoders. Politicians speak a strange language and it is up to us to decode it, and that leads to clashes with Campbell.' *News from No. 10* drew heavily on film of the press secretary's hectic life. He was shown conducting lobby briefings, organising news conferences, talking to journalists and at work in his office in Downing Street. Cockerell told the *Journalist's Handbook* that Campbell was anxious to let people see how he dealt with the news media so that they could form their own impressions, which he hoped would shift the perception that he bullied journalists. Campbell seemed satisfied with the feedback he received from the programme, but he gave the documentary only seven out of ten because it failed to do enough to portray journalists as 'corrosively cynical'. Ten days before taking me to task over my *Breakfast News* quip, he called me over to ask for my assessment of the programme. It was the first time he had asked my opinion on anything relating to his work as press secretary and I sensed that, like most performers, he was probably desperate for all the reassurance he could get. I said he must have been pleased so much footage in the film showed what actually happened at lobby briefings and in Downing Street. Campbell acknowledged this and said the response he had been getting about his own performance had been positive. Nevertheless, he was disappointed that the documentary had failed to follow the newspaper journalists more closely and illustrate what happened after they had been briefed. He thought viewers should have been shown some of the stories that appeared under their by-lines. 'The only briefing which the film really stuck with was the one about asylum seekers and I could have produced a hundred stories on asylum seekers which I know the papers have invented.' Campbell was also annoyed that he had not been allowed the chance to refute Michael Prescott's contention that the hardest task for correspondents was to decode Downing Street's lobby briefings. 'If I had been given the chance, I could have shown the programme fifty stories which I think Prescott has made up.'

Having spent four months observing Campbell's work, Cockerell had seen at first hand the problems the government faced in coming to terms with the demands of 24-hour news and the increased competition between print and broadcast media. The pace was frenetic, and he could see why Downing Street thought that, for the sake of accuracy, it had little alternative but to trail the contents of announcements and speeches in advance. Newspapers tended to devote more space to speculation than to reporting events. 'Campbell, knowing the speech will never be reported afterwards, feeds the frenzy by leaking in advance.' Cockerell had been a long-term advocate of opening up lobby briefings to all-comers: in his book *Sources Close to the Prime Minister*, published in 1984, Cockerell and his co-authors, Peter Hennessy and David Walker, had recommended 'the early abolition of the lobby system'. He continued to support those correspondents who thought the briefings should be replaced by televised news conferences, and he hoped Campbell's participation in *Live From No. 10* would encourage him to allow the presence of television cameras on a more regular basis. After observing what happened inside No. 10 he was convinced journalists had to remain on their guard against the pervasive secrecy of Whitehall.

A particular tension that emerged in the film was that in Campbell's relationship with the political correspondents of the Sunday papers. Michael Prescott recalled what Blair's official spokesman said on arriving for his first briefing with the Sunday lobby: 'Why should I waste my effing time talking to a load of wankers like you, when you won't print a word I say in any case?' Campbell was equally forthright when he explained why he had not changed his own opinion of them after three years in government: 'Every weekend I have to deal with stories from the Sunday papers and the only distinction I make is between those stories which are crap and those which are total crap.' In many ways I shared Campbell's reservations about the film's failure to follow through specific examples of news management and political reporting. I thought the programme should have done far more to explore and expose the covert ways in which Downing Street has continued to co-operate with many news organisations under the cover of all-out hostility.

In his interviews for *British Journalism Review* and the BBC, Campbell made much of his utter contempt for the standard of political reporting in the Sunday press, but neither Hagerty nor Cockerell followed this up by asking why Downing Street continued to lavish so much attention on their journalists or was prepared to go to such extraordinary lengths to safeguard the exclusivity of the separate lobby briefings provided for Sunday political correspondents. If Campbell had genuinely wanted to try to curb the flow of unattributed stories appearing in the Sunday papers, he could easily have made a start in November 1997 when he allowed his guidance to be sourced to 'the Prime Minister's official spokesman'. An important first step would have been to end the restricted access he has maintained for Sunday lobby briefings and grant entry to those broadcasters and news agency reporters who also have to report politics at the weekend. Briefings for the Sunday lobby remain the last closed shop at Westminster. They are usually held on Friday afternoon, and reporters from all other organisations are excluded. This is in sharp contrast to the policy adopted during the rest of the week. Correspondents from news agencies that do not report politics at Westminster on a regular basis are allowed to attend the daily briefing each morning and, to his credit, Campbell has encouraged moves to widen attendance and publicise the guidance he gives. However, by continuing to grant special privileges for Sunday correspondents, Downing Street creates immense problems for broadcasting organisations and news agencies that have no way of instantly verifying the many speculative stories printed by the Sunday newspapers.

Competition among the Sundays is intense and they vie with each other to produce exclusive, attention-grabbing stories. A hint of subterfuge is an essential ingredient, and many of their reports are sourced to unnamed government insiders or based on unattributed quotations. Nevertheless, some of their stories do appear to be derived from briefings given by Campbell and other Downing Street press officers. Broadcasters and news agency reporters who are on duty late on Saturday night and early on Sunday morning regularly face an insurmountable task when asked to check the accuracy of the many exclusives on offer, and one of the greatest difficulties is the problem of trying to establish precisely what was said at the lobby briefing the previous Friday afternoon. Although extracts from the twice-daily lobby briefings are available on Downing Street's website, the press office publishes no summary of the briefings for the Sundays. If an official version were made available, say from midnight each Saturday night, Downing Street could safeguard the competitive position of Sunday newspapers while providing other news organisations with a reliable source of information in good time for Sunday morning news programmes. The innovation I suggest would appear to tackle head-on the constant complaint of the Prime Minister and his press secretary that most Sunday newspaper stories are fictitious and that many of them cause considerable grief to those ministers singled out for unsubstantiated criticism. A summary of the briefing would ensure there was at least some guidance for other news organisations as to which of the various story lines on offer had the official stamp of approval, and it would give ministers and government press officers greater authority when fielding reporters' questions.

Regular listeners to Sunday morning television and radio news programmes will be familiar with the difficulties encountered by newspapers reviewers and other guests when they are confronted with conflicting headlines and asked to sort fact from fiction. The three books I have written on the relationship between politicians and the news media have all examined New Labour's close relationship with the Sunday newspapers and the selective briefings that the party has continued to provide for their political correspondents. Politicians have always regarded the Sunday press as a valuable platform on which to float controversial proposals. Because they are in such fierce competition with the dailies, their journalists are willing to co-operate, either individually or in groups, with politicians and political groups who are prepared to supply them with exclusive information on an unattributable basis. In the late 1980s, when Peter Mandelson was Labour's publicity director, he provided Sunday lobby correspondents with unsourced news stories as a way of preparing the party for the policy changes Neil Kinnock intended to introduce. Mandelson and his deputy, Colin Byrne, would spend the latter part of each week giving private briefings to selected correspondents. Their favourite newspaper was the *Sunday Times*, and when I was on weekend duty Mandelson and Byrne would frequently direct me to the work of the paper's political editor, at that time Andrew Grice, who later became political editor of the *Independent*. Although many of his stories were not sourced directly to the Labour Party, I was assured they were reliable. Mandelson understood the important role Sunday newspapers played in influencing broadcasters and in helping to set the news agenda. He believed Labour could not afford to ignore the importance of the political analysis offered by the Sunday press, and his objective was to ensure their reports were accurate. The routines Mandelson rehearsed and perfected have become deeply ingrained: the art of selective briefing is the first lesson that has to be learned by a New Labour spin doctor.

My prying questions have never been welcomed by either the spin doctors or their favoured correspondents, who do all they can to maintain the confidentiality of their relationships. These liaisons are sometimes short-lived: political editors come and go, and various newspapers move in and out of favour, depending on the most recent shifts in their political leanings. Campbell has been reluctant to act in this area because he knows that any move he makes to challenge or undermine the exclusivity of Sunday lobby briefings would weaken and perhaps jeopardise New Labour's long-standing procedures for giving guidance to selected correspondents and columnists. Sunday newspapers have come to be regarded as an invaluable conduit for the many stories that are slipped out in advance in order to trail forthcoming announcements on government decisions and policy proposals. Once the strategic communications unit has agreed the grid that sets out the timetable for statements, speeches and news conferences in the week ahead, the special advisers assigned to each department can consider how they might 'grab the agenda' and secure advance publicity. Examples of Campbell's ability to orchestrate Sunday newspaper coverage to Labour's advantage abound: for instance, he purposely held back news of the defection of the Conservative MPs Alan Howarth and Shaun Woodward so that it could create maximum impact in the weekend papers and cause the greatest possible discomfort to the Conservatives.

When Labour's objective is to damage its opponents, broadcasting organisations are often alerted in advance and told to expect news of a major political development once the first editions of the Sunday newspapers have been printed. A late-breaking story in the Saturday evening bulletins suits the spin doctors because it helps build up interest, and Sunday newspapers hope that the extra publicity might generate additional sales. However, as a general rule, both the government and the party are anxious to let the Sunday newspapers retain their edge over television and radio coverage at weekends because a well-trailed story can help create a favourable news agenda. Whenever I get the opportunity I protest about Downing Street's persistence in continuing to deny broadcasters and news agency staff access to briefings that impact directly on weekend reporting, but my complaints tend to attract nothing more than a loud raspberry. None the less, with the backing of Elinor Goodman, the political editor of *Channel 4 News*, I did instigate some direct action at Labour's 2000 annual conference in Brighton. I was standing with Ms Goodman in the foyer at the Metropole Hotel on the Saturday morning of the conference weekend just as the correspondents for the Sunday newspapers were assembling for their lobby briefing. From what we could gather, Lance Price, the party's director of communications, intended to run through the schedule of the conference week and Campbell, who was still in London, would be connected via a telephone link and answer questions that related to Blair's position on the key events. I was responsible for the BBC's news coverage during the pre-conference weekend, and Ms Goodman was in a comparable position for

Channel 4, having to prepare reports for the newly introduced Saturday and Sunday evening editions of *Channel 4 News*.

We both believed that Campbell's briefing would be of great assistance: we knew we would get an accurate assessment of Blair's thinking and be well prepared for any new stories that might break later that weekend. I admit I did rather egg Ms Goodman on, but she needed little encouragement, and when the Sunday correspondents were called in for their briefing we tagged along, only to find our path blocked by two of Labour's press officers, Steve Bates and Matthew Doyle, who escorted us both to the door. Price did give us a run-down afterwards on the conference timetable, but said he could not answer questions about Campbell's briefing. Sunday's newspapers revealed the story we had missed: 'Blair in U-turn on Dome flop' was the splash on the *Observer*'s front page, and most of the Sunday papers had similar headlines. 'Dome has failed, admits Blair' said the *Mail on Sunday* over its report that the Prime Minister intended to use an interview that morning on *Breakfast With Frost* to express regret and admit for first time that the Millennium Dome had been a failure. Campbell was quoted as having said, in what the correspondents considered was a marked departure from earlier statements, that the Dome had not been 'the runaway success' the government had hoped for, and that the lesson Blair had learned from these 'big, big projects' was that they took a while to settle down. Blair faced a difficult week in Brighton, with the fuel protests of early September fresh in everyone's memory and a possible conference revolt on pensions in the offing. Advance guidance on the conciliatory tone he intended to adopt would have been invaluable in preparing my overnight reports for the morning news bulletins.

Sure enough, Blair's interview delivered the words of regret that had been flagged up by his official spokesman: 'If I had known then what I know now about governments trying to run these types of visitor attraction, it would probably have been too ambitious a thing for a government to have tried to do.' Blair was similarly contrite over the disruption to supplies of petrol and diesel as a result of the fuel blockades that summer: 'It happened on my watch so I take responsibility for it.'

Campbell was well versed in the art of using the Sunday newspapers to pave the way for one of Blair's chastened television appearances. At the height of the row in November 1997 over the £1million donation to the Labour Party by the Formula One motor racing chief, Bernie Ecclestone, he held a Saturday afternoon briefing to alert Sunday lobby correspondents to Blair's intention to use an interview on the BBC's Sunday political programme, *On The Record*, to apologise for not having been more open about the party's finances. 'Blair goes on TV to say I'm sorry' was the banner headline across the *Sunday Telegraph*, and the *Observer*'s front page told the same story: 'Blair: Sorry, we blundered.' When he was interviewed by John Humphrys, the Prime Minister did, as promised, say 'sorry'; but it was hardly the all-out apology Campbell had trailed. Blair chose his words with care: 'No, I am not saying it was wrong to accept the money . . . I apologise for the way this was handled . . . I am sorry about this issue.' Campbell needed no instruction on the importance journalists attached to that one word. If a public figure was at fault in some way, and was finding it impossible to break free from a prolonged and damaging hue and cry in the news media, saying 'sorry' provided a fast escape route. Although there might be embarrassing headlines for twenty-four hours, an apology was usually sufficient to satisfy most newspapers and newsrooms, which, after taking credit for the climbdown, would then redirect their energies elsewhere.

Campbell knew that the apology could not be bettered as a presentational device; but what his former colleagues at Westminster had not grasped was that the Prime Minister's press secretary was about to use the same technique to help engineer world exclusives for the *Sun*'s political editor, Trevor Kavanagh. 'Japan says sorry to the *Sun*' was their first collaborative venture after Campbell attempted to give the Japanese Prime Minister, Ryutaro Hashimoto, a *Sun*-style makeover during Blair's official visit to Japan in January 1998. After Kavanagh suggested to Campbell that Hashimoto might like to write an article for the paper, Blair urged him to take up the offer; once the Japanese had agreed, Campbell said he advised Hashimoto's office on 'style and the way such an article might be expressed'. Kavanagh made the most of his exclusive and claimed that in his 'first article for any newspaper in the world' Japan's premier had made 'an unprecedented plea to *Sun* readers to forgive its atrocities to British prisoners' in the Second World War.

At first, groups campaigning for improved compensation for survivors of the Japanese labour camps thought the *Sun*'s story might have signalled a change of heart by the Tokyo government; but they discovered that on meeting Blair, Hashimoto had simply repeated an earlier expression of 'deep remorse and heartfelt apology'. When correspondents in Tokyo reported Campbell as claiming that Hashimoto had made Japan's first 'official' apology for its wartime misdeeds, there was an immediate protest from Arthur Titherington, chairman of the Japanese Labour Camp Survivors Association. He told the *Independent* that the word which had been used was *owabi*, a much weaker form of apology than *shazai*, which was the expression the veterans wanted Japan to use. Campbell was accused by the *Independent on Sunday* of having encouraged the *Sun* to debase the meaning of an apology in a tabloid public relations stunt; but he insisted in a letter to the *Daily Telegraph* that, given the 'positive effect' that he believed his 'journalistic venture' had on Anglo-Japanese relations, it was worth 'all the effort put into it by the *Sun*'. Yet when the government made preparations the following May to greet Emperor Akihito on his state visit to London, the former prisoners discovered the reality behind the headlines: Blair told them that the British government had no intention of using the visit by the Japanese Emperor to re-open the survivors' claim for compensation. Former prisoners of war, their medals pinned to their chests, stood in The Mall and turned their backs on Akihito as he passed by in the Queen's horse-drawn carriage. The labour camp survivors, most of them in their seventies and eighties, struggled on for another two and half years in a vain attempt to persuade Japan to improve on the compensation payment of £76 it had made to former prisoners of war in 1951. Their efforts were finally rewarded in November 2000 when the British government recognised the futility of their campaign and announced a £10,000 *ex gratia* payment for former prisoners or their surviving spouses. The Ministry of Defence estimated that 16,700 people were eligible; the thanks of the survivors were tinged with the one regret that on their own calculations they were losing their former comrades at the rate of ten a week, and that hundreds had died before the payments were announced.

As MPs heard the news in a statement from a junior defence minister, Dr Lewis Moonie, the focus of the news media's attention was a few miles away at the National Army Museum in Chelsea, where Blair met a small group of survivors. Staff had been alerted to the photo-call the night before, and they were told by Downing Street that the British Legion would arrange for some of the former prisoners to attend. Arthur Titherington considered it had been a great day for the veterans but said he would have been infinitely happier if the compensation had come from Japan and if, after fifty-five years, the Japanese government had felt able to make 'a proper, meaningful apology'.

If Campbell had experienced a recurrence of his sleepless nights on the *Daily Mirror* during this episode, and had lain awake worrying whether the story line of his 'journalistic venture' with the *Sun* in January 1998 was 'right or wrong', and whether it might have added to the distress of the former prisoners of war as they continued their struggle for compensation, it was but a distant memory in October that year when the *Sun*'s editor, David Yelland, alerted news agencies and broadcasting organisations to his paper's latest collaborative endeavour with the Prime Minister's press secretary. 'Argentina says: We're sorry for Falklands' was the headline over Kavanagh's world exclusive.

Yelland's faxed message informing newsrooms that the Argentine President had 'publicly apologised for the first time' was sent out at 9.30 p.m. under a 10 p.m. embargo, which meant it was too late for the BBC's *Nine O'Clock News* but allowed ITN's political editor, Michael Brunson, to break the story on *News at Ten*. In case reporters doubted the authenticity of the story, Yelland took the opportunity to remind rival news organisations of the *Sun*'s special relationship with No. 10 by adding a helpful note at the bottom of the fax: 'Downing Street has a statement ready for release on this matter.' The Campbell–Kavanagh partnership had delivered what was billed as 'another historic apology to the *Sun*': the Argentine President Carlos Menem 'dramatically apologised to *Sun* readers for the Falklands War which cost the lives of 252 British servicemen'. In welcoming the regret Menem had expressed in his signed article, Blair said it showed that the Argentine President, due in Britain the following week on a state visit, would be coming 'in a spirit of reconciliation'. As Yelland had asserted so confidently in his faxed message to newsrooms, No. 10 was proud to be associated with the 'world exclusive' his newspaper had printed. A Downing Street spokesman, quoted by the Press Association news agency, said that after the 'success' earlier that year of the apology written by the Japanese Prime Minister, Kavanagh had asked Campbell to approach the Argentine government for an article and the President had been 'happy to do this as a way of building on the theme of reconciliation'.

Menem's article read like a carbon copy of Hashimoto's apology. The Japanese Prime Minister began by declaring that Britain's Prime Minister was 'a new star on the world stage'; the Argentine President described Blair as 'a great leader' whose 'modernising approach and strong commitment to sound economics are a benchmark in today's world'. Six stylistic similarities in the structure and content of the two articles were detected by Raymond Chapman, Professor of English Studies at the London School of Economics; but it was the repeated misuse of the word 'sorry' that demolished Campbell's second 'journalistic venture' for the *Sun*. Within hours of the paper going on sale, Downing Street's connivance became headline news and the story was turned on its head: 'I'm not sorry for Falklands' said the banner headline on the *Evening Standard*'s lunchtime edition. When asked in Buenos Aires if he had apologised on Argentina's behalf, Menem's denial was emphatic: 'No, saying sorry is something completely different. That is not the way I expressed it . . . The conflict should never have happened, we deeply regret it.'

Godric Smith fielded questions at the morning lobby briefing and denied that Campbell had written the article. However, when he was interviewed that lunchtime on *The World At One*, Kavanagh acknowledged the input of his fellow collaborator and wordsmith: 'Yes, Alastair made a couple of suggestions on stylistic matters but otherwise the views are those of Menem himself.' Yelland was questioned in greater detail next morning on *Today*: 'Yes, Alastair was involved, of course . . . everyone involved in these tortuous negotiations knew that the headline would be "sorry" . . . You can't expect the President of Argentina to get on his knees and say "sorry", this is as near as you are going to get. Menem knew what the headline would be and that is the most important point.'

In seeking to respond to Campbell's charge that political journalists at Westminster have become 'corrosively cynical' in the six and a half years that have elapsed since he was a political editor and columnist for the *Daily Mirror* and *Today*, I cannot underestimate the cumulative effect his collaborative ventures with newspapers like the *Sun* have had on the outlook of the many lobby journalists who have found themselves outside the charmed circle in which New Labour's spin doctors have done their deals. The fallout from the aggressive and divisive techniques he has employed cannot be ignored. By tempting journalists with the offer of special favours and one-to-one interviews, and by playing off one news organisation against another, he has encouraged the superficial coverage of which he complains. Journalists, like the government, also have to cope with the rapid turnover of stories generated by the 24-hour news cycle and the restraints imposed by the tough economics of the news business. The hard-sell tactics adopted by special advisers and government information officers have added to those competitive pressures and do leave journalists fearful of being caught out by a well-placed exclusive story that has the Downing Street imprimatur. I regularly feel a touch uneasy when working on my own during weekend television and radio shifts. Duty press officers in Downing Street and Millbank Tower will often sound reassuring and insist that the government and party have not been giving exclusive briefings on an imminent policy initiative; but it is not until the first editions of the Sunday papers start arriving on Saturday evening that it is possible to know for sure whether Campbell has authorised or inspired a surprise announcement.

He might just as easily have had a role in the latest tabloid sensation involving a Labour politician. His first 'journalistic venture' affecting the personal life of a cabinet minister involved the breakdown in the marriage of Robin and Margaret Cook in August 1997, three months after Labour took office. Instead of telling the *News of the World* that the Blair government intended to have nothing to do with press intrusion into the private lives of politicians, Campbell negotiated with the Foreign Secretary on the newspaper's behalf. I examined the news media's treatment of the couple's break-up and Cook's subsequent marriage to his secretary Gaynor Regan in *Sultans of Spin*, and I do not intend to revisit those events here. None the less, it is relevant to my present purposes in this book to note that, in view of the entirely laudable efforts of Tony and Cherie Blair to protect their children from media intrusion and to safeguard the privacy of their own family life, there does seem a lack of clarity about the duties being undertaken by the Downing Street press office. If Campbell had not done the *News of the World*'s bidding and spoken to the Foreign Secretary at Heathrow Airport, the Cooks might well have caught their plane to Boston *en route* for a planned riding holiday in Montana.

The newspaper needed to speak to Cook before it dared go into print because it had no independent corroboration for its story and was relying on a diary compiled by two freelance photographers and pictures they had taken outside Cook's flat in Victoria. Campbell gave his side of the story to the journalist Kevin Toolis of the *Guardian*, who concluded that the accusation that the Downing Street press secretary had ordered Cook to 'end his marriage and cancel his holiday' was entirely false. 'In reality, Campbell managed to do a deal with the newspaper to buy Robin Cook some time to think – a few hours – before the story inevitably broke.' However, in my view Campbell's willingness to intercede on the *News of the World*'s behalf had been pivotal, and the conclusion I reached in my last book was that the paper's executives must have been 'mightily relieved' when Campbell told them that Cook intended to issue a statement announcing the breakdown of his marriage. My assertion that the story could not have been published without Campbell's intervention was confirmed by the *News of the World*'s editor Phil Hall when he left the paper in June 2000 to become a media consultant with the publicist Max Clifford. Interviewing Hall about the sex scandals the paper had covered when he was editor, Matt Wells of the *Guardian*'s media page asked him if he was justified in printing details of Cook's extra-marital affair. Hall confirmed immediately the critical role Downing Street had played: 'I thought, "I don't know, are we justified here or not?" I went to Alastair

Campbell and said: "This is the situation, I don't think we're going to run it, unless Robin Cook wants to talk about it. But if I don't run it, maybe somebody else will, there's a freelance involved. It's up to you." Alastair came back and said: "I know how you work, run it straight please," which was a fair *quid pro quo*, and that's what I did.'

To his credit, Campbell has not shied away from the role he has sometimes been forced to play as an intermediary between the news media and ministers who have been caught up in embarrassing or distressing news stories. He has argued consistently that there has to be clarity in news management; that sexual disclosures cannot be ignored; and that the Blair government has to be resolute in seeking to avoid the damage inflicted on the Conservatives when John Major was pilloried for his failure to act swiftly after his ministers were caught in extra-marital affairs. None the less, in this instance Campbell was responding to events being dictated by the publishing deadlines of Rupert Murdoch's biggest-selling Sunday newspaper, and the confirmation that the Downing Street press office was ready to arrange a *quid pro quo* might not be of much comfort to the next Labour politician who is about to be exposed by the *News of the World*.

Phil Hall made no secret of the debt he owed to Campbell, or of his view that the Prime Minister's official spokesman had become one of the key figures in the burgeoning world of public relations. 'I think PR is fascinating. In the past ten years it has been transformed by Max Clifford, in particular, but also people such as Alastair Campbell, Tim Bell – they're only doing what Max has been doing for the past twenty-five years. He has made PR fashionable when it was once scorned.' A Downing Street press secretary who is prepared to engage in a 'journalistic adventure' with the *Sun* or settle for a *quid pro quo* with the *News of the World* can hardly be surprised if political journalists treat him with anything other than apprehension. Journalists face an odd contradiction: an official spokesman who considers himself to be a deadly rival of those who look upon him as an information provider. Competition within the media has increased to such a degree that even the most experienced political reporters feel vulnerable. Reliable political judgement and a reputation for accuracy are no guarantee of employment: political correspondents get assessed on their ability to deliver exclusives; they have to make and break news, not just report it. Instead of offering reporters a level playing field and equal access to information about important decisions or policy developments, Campbell and his colleagues have preferred time and again to join forces with selected journalists. Arguably the government's most profound announcement about its relationship with the European Union was delivered by the Chancellor, Gordon Brown, in October 1997, not in a statement to the House of Commons or at a news conference, but in an exclusive interview with Philip Webster, political editor of *The Times*. Brown was roundly condemned at the time for using a newspaper to confirm that Britain had ruled out membership of the European single currency for the rest of the parliament, but the Chancellor's faith in the accuracy of Webster's reporting has remained undiminished. I was informed by the Treasury that his exclusive report in *The Times* in May 2000, which revealed that the Chancellor intended to increase public spending by more than £40 billion, was accurate and could be quoted by the BBC.

Political journalists are under no illusions about the reasons why Campbell and the other special advisers have remained wedded to the techniques they have deployed so effectively for so long. As part of the bargain, the favoured recipients are expected to put the best possible gloss on what they have been told, and the spin doctors hope that an initial favourable interpretation of whatever has been announced will help influence and perhaps dictate the tenor of the coverage that will appear on other news outlets. In such circumstances it is hardly surprising that journalists who spend their time following up a constant run of exclusive stories supplied to their competitors sometimes become overly suspicious and perhaps a little cynical. Our constant preoccupation with 'processology' and 'spinology' is only to be expected when we know that the communications strategy the government has adopted for any given policy has not been a last-minute choice but is the fruit of careful planning and consideration.

The central thrust behind all the changes that Robin Mountfield and Mike Granatt have implemented in the information service on

Campbell's behalf has been to ensure that presentation becomes an integral part of decision-making within the machinery of government and not an afterthought. Therefore, correspondents have to take account of the way in which information is going to be released to the public: it might have had a profound influence on the thinking behind the very decision which happens to be in the news that day. While Campbell cannot be faulted on his determination to take full advantage of the opportunities provided by a 24-hour news cycle, and by his insistence that government announcements must be timed for maximum impact rather than for the convenience of journalists, we know he takes delight in catching us out. If a story that he has instigated has succeeded in upsetting the running order of news bulletins or has necessitated the ditching of coverage that had been planned by newspapers, he savours the moment at the lobby briefing next morning and revels in any tales of the panic and disruption he might have caused. Scoring points against his former colleagues is perhaps one way of retaliating against the media excesses that have caused him so much grief. Nevertheless, the danger of conspiring with a few chosen correspondents and columnists in an attempt to outwit the rest of the news media is that it encourages risk-taking by those excluded from the process. By co-operating with some journalists to the exclusion of others, and by requiring government press officers to adopt the same procedures to 'grab the agenda', Campbell is helping to sustain a media culture that places the greatest value on speculation, exclusives and other devices for manufacturing news, rather than on the reporting and analysis of what has happened. I agree with the assessment he gave *British Journalism Review*: many political journalists are under pressure to get the story regardless; they have to get it first, even though it might be wrong. The question that the Prime Minister and his cabinet colleagues should be addressing is whether techniques like advance briefings for selected correspondents, and the other collaborative ventures favoured by the Downing Street press office, have served the best purposes of either the government or the public. The belief that the state should somehow be in constant competition with journalists, and that the government should instigate stories not simply as a way of informing the public but in order to demonstrate a sharper news sense than that possessed collectively by the media itself, is a concept that is taking root throughout Whitehall; and I would suggest that, rather like Japanese knotweed, once established it will prove virtually impossible to eradicate.

SHARP UPFRONT

'The right way to fight a propaganda offensive is not with more propaganda, it is to tell
the truth, the whole truth and nothing but the truth, and do it as rapidly as possible.
But you need some smart people who can tell you what piece of the truth you are
looking for.'

General Wesley Clark, Supreme Allied Commander Europe, acknowledging Alastair
Campbell's role in the Kosovo conflict, in *Correspondent: How the War Was Spun*,
BBC Television, 16 October 1999

Alastair Campbell's sure touch in shaping and controlling the
image of Tony Blair that has been presented through the
news media has won him plaudits around the world at gatherings of international statesmen. Many a president and prime
minister has forged a working relationship with a former journalist,
but the close bond between these two men has been far stronger and
much more professional than the partnership most other political
leaders have managed to establish with their publicity advisers. At the
height of the attempt early in 1998 to impeach Bill Clinton over his
relationship with Monica Lewinsky, the Prime Minister's official
spokesman enjoyed the notoriety he gained from a succession of
speculative stories suggesting that a transfer deal might be in the
offing and that he was about to be signed up as the new White House
spokesman for a beleaguered President of the United States.
Campbell's flair and imagination in promoting Blair, and his total
dedication in defending him from attacks in the media, was regarded
with wonderment by Clinton's aides, whose loyalties had occasionally been seen to crack under pressure. In October 1998 the White
House press secretary, Mike McCurry, resigned in protest at the way
he felt he had been used unfairly to perpetuate a deception about
Clinton's sexual relations with Lewinsky, and his departure prompted
another flurry of speculation about Campbell's long-term ambitions.
Once it had become evident in capitals across the continent that he
was on the inside track not only in Downing Street but also in

Washington, his authority increased among the advisers and press officers of other European heads of government.

Blair's high regard for his spokesman, and the tight grip he exercised over the presentation of government policy, meant there were few in Whitehall who were prepared to challenge Campbell's authority. After seeing how he outsmarted and outclassed the MPs who cross-examined him when he gave evidence to a televised hearing of the House of Commons Select Committee on Public Administration in June 1998, senior civil servants realised they had better be sure of their ground before attempting to question his judgement. Barry Sutlieff, who as director of information at the Cabinet Office sat behind Campbell during the select committee hearing, told me that he had marvelled at his mastery of his subject and the ease with which he had deflected awkward questions. 'It was like watching the dazzling footwork of a leading footballer, constantly in command of the ball and always on the attack. If Alastair was the lead striker for a top soccer team and not a press officer, it would have required a multi-million-pound transfer fee to sign him up for No. 10.'

I was intrigued by Sutlieff's analogy, because in many ways Campbell's flair and ability were reminiscent of a George Best or David Beckham: he could see an opportunity, seize the initiative, outpace his opponents and grab the headlines before most journalists had realised what was happening. Soccer, of course, is one of the dominant interests in his life: he has been a fanatical supporter of Burnley Football Club since childhood, and one of his friends and heroes is Sir Alex Ferguson, the Manchester United manager and long-time Labour supporter; indeed, because of the constant attention they both faced from the news media, Campbell acknowledged there were many similarities between managing a football club and running the Downing Street press office. In August 1998 he told the *Daily Express* that even the Prime Minister had been getting some tips from Sir Alex on how to keep fit in the highly pressurised job of leading the government, which called for a clear-sighted managerial philosophy, 'sharp upfront, creative in midfield, and tight in defence'. Campbell discussed his love of football and the parallels with politics on Radio Five Live, interviewed by Adrian Chiles on the morning of the Burnley v. Preston match in March 2000. When he was a four-year-old, Burnley were the Football League champions, and although their glory days were a distant memory he had remained a devout fan and regularly took his two sons with him around the country to attend his team's matches in the Nationwide second division. Chiles suggested that being in charge of No. 10's press office was about as frustrating and disappointing as running Burnley, because while he could coach ministers in media presentation, once they went into a television or radio studio he was as powerless as a football club manager sitting on the bench to affect the outcome of the match.

Campbell identified a clearer parallel between his job and that of the Manchester United manager. 'What Alex and I have to do is keep a relentless focus on the things which matter to us both and not what the media want to talk about. Reporters are always asking him about David Beckham and the latest saga involving Beckham's wife Victoria and the Spice Girls . . . So you have this feeling the media are having a kick at us the whole time and our job is to see them off . . . I do talk to Alex about how to deal with reporters and what to do when they always want to get you on to a different agenda.' I was struck by the strength of the comparison Campbell had drawn and his description of how, travelling back to London with his sons, he would go through the match ball by ball like a disappointed club manager. He recalled what happened after one notable Burnley defeat: 'My two sons were with me on the train back and I kept going on about it. "Why wasn't the ball two inches lower?" The kids must have got fed up with me banging on the table every couple of minutes.' I was relieved to think I had not been playing for Burnley that afternoon, because I could just imagine the tirade in the dressing room if Campbell had been the manager and I had missed the crucial goal. Chiles had clearly picked up the same hint about the volatility of his interviewee, because he asked immediately if Campbell ever lost his cool when dealing with the media. 'Yes, I have got a temper and yes, I do tend to lose my temper with journalists.'

Campbell has probably wished on occasion that some of his ill-tempered spats with political correspondents could have been treated like a shouting match in the dressing room and, once washed away in the soap suds, forgotten about next day. Political reporting is far less forgiving: missing the story is one thing, but accusing a journalist of bad practice or inaccuracy is another. His explosive nature when angered by journalists has puzzled government officials, who have told me they have always found him courteous and straightforward. Many of those who have worked with him in No. 10 cannot understand the paradox: why is Campbell highly regarded by civil servants and diplomats but mistrusted by so many journalists? On this particular issue I can write with the benefit of a little personal experience, because I had the misfortune to be the first political correspondent to get a public dressing-down from Tony Blair's newly recruited press secretary. He had only been in the job for a few weeks and was still writing a daily political commentary for *Today* when I caught the full force of his temper at the 1994 Labour Party conference. The air turned blue as soon as I walked into the press centre and he accused me of 'mischievous and unprofessional conduct' over my report a few minutes earlier for *Conference Live*. I had been reporting on reaction to Blair's announcement that he intended to rewrite Clause Four of Labour's constitution and abandon the party's historic commitment to the 'common ownership of the means of production, distribution and exchange'. I had been told by MPs and union leaders who were close to the party's deputy leader, John Prescott, that he had some serious misgivings and had only been won over in the final week before the conference. I told *Conference Live* that Prescott was 'only on board a week ago and did advise against it'. Campbell was furious. He demanded an immediate correction and said the deputy leader had been aware of the decision for several weeks and had been 'fully on board every step of the way'.

At the next appropriate moment I explained on air that the BBC had been supplied with a statement on Prescott's involvement and that he had given his total support to the rewriting of Clause Four. When Campbell was interviewed later in the week by Joanna Coles for *The Late Show* he said my original report had been 'a complete load of nonsense'. However, when I subsequently had time to check with the MPs and union leaders I had spoken to earlier, they assured me my original version was correct and that Prescott was not won round until the final week. Three years later my *Conference Live* report was vindicated in *Fighting Talk*, a biography of the deputy leader written by the political journalist Colin Brown. Prescott said he had been opposed from the start to dropping Clause Four, and he gave a blow-by-blow account of how the wording of Blair's call for a new constitution was agreed only on the night before the speech and how, the next morning, Campbell had telephoned him and he had then agreed as deputy leader to the final revision of the text.

The verbal lashing I was given at the conference taught me a valuable lesson about the need to treat Campbell's statements with care. In some respects his account of what happened over Clause Four matched Prescott's version: discussions had gone on for some weeks; the deputy leader had clearly been consulted; and he had given his approval. Where my broadcast was at odds with Campbell's instant rebuttal was over my contention that Prescott had opposed the move and that it had taken time to win him over. While one can argue about the small print of what we had both said, I would contend that in the light of Prescott's account my original report was a fair and accurate summary, given the speed with which I was having to work at the conference. Needless to say, I realised that I would be well advised to check and check again whenever I reported stories that might provoke a complaint from Campbell. I have also become something of a stickler when cross-checking the statements he has made on media-related issues in his many letters to the editor, newspaper articles and interviews. In my last book, *Sultans of Spin*, I explored how, when giving evidence to the Select Committee on Public Administration, he subtly reworked his account of his contretemps with the lobby in February 1998 after complaints about the accuracy of his briefing on Blair's conversations with the Italian Prime Minister, Romano Prodi. At the time, Campbell challenged any correspondent who thought he had 'lied' to say so, but nobody did. Four months later, when giving evidence to MPs, he inserted the word 'misled' and implied that when he confronted the correspondents he had offered an alternative and less damning charge that had also produced no response from the assembled journalists.

The louder Campbell protests, the more likely he is to rely on those facts that suit his case, and it is only after close dissection that one picks up the omissions and inconsistencies in what he has said.

Journalists are not fools: we know that when statements are volunteered by political propagandists, press officers and public relations consultants there is every likelihood that they will have avoided all reference to matters that might damage their case. However, once challenged, any failure to mention key facts only attracts attention. As Campbell believes his only means of defence is to attack, he does place himself in a vulnerable position and he can hardly be surprised when even his trivial asides get scrutinised.

A shortened version of his interview with Bill Hagerty for *British Journalism Review* about falling standards in political journalism was published in *The Times*. On the day it appeared, 12 June 2000, I discovered that a media training seminar for Labour Party staff from Westminster and the constituencies was to be held at 5.45 p.m. the following afternoon in the grand committee room of the House of Commons. The two main speakers were to be Campbell and the *Independent*'s columnist David Aaronovitch. Admission was by ticket only, and staff had to give their Labour Party membership numbers. Before leaving, party workers were asked to refrain from talking to journalists about the seminar; they should not reveal the presence of either Campbell or Aaronovitch, or discuss the advice they had been given.

The appearance of this pair together on the platform was no great surprise to me. The previous March, in one of his newspaper articles about life in No. 10, Campbell had complimented Aaronovitch for having refused to join other columnists in using their comment pages to 'drop large portions of ordure' on Blair. The current fashion had been 'broadly to dump on him, the more venomous the better'; journalists like Aaronovitch, who dared in any way to support the government, found themselves 'the recipients of peer opprobrium'. In view of this paean of praise, I found it difficult the day before the seminar to reconcile my knowledge that Campbell was about to join Aaronovitch on the platform at a Labour training seminar with his injured protestations in *The Times* when asked by Bill Hagerty if he had ever used certain journalists as his 'mouthpieces'. Campbell was his usual forthright self and did not shrink from naming names: 'David Aaronovitch wrote a piece saying he thinks the government is doing a pretty good job most of the time and got written up as one of our toadies and one of "my people". I could count on the fingers of one hand the conversations I have had with David Aaronovitch since the general election; in fact, I can probably count them on two fingers.' I had no basis for challenging Campbell's recollection of the number of times he had conversed with Aaronovitch but, as he was singled out by name, readers of *The Times* might have felt better informed had they known that the press secretary and the columnist were about to lead a training session organised by Labour's staff network.

Campbell's presence in the grand committee room would also have been of interest to political correspondents, because they had not seen him all week and only an hour earlier they had been told by the deputy press secretary, Godric Smith, that they would be seeing far less of the Prime Minister's official spokesman in future because he intended to scale down his attendance at lobby briefings. Campbell's behaviour had been erratic for several weeks and some of the journalists he once worked with feared the worst: they thought the pressures of the job had become too great, and that he was heading either for the exit or for a showdown with the lobby.

He had made the fatal mistake for a spin doctor of generating more interesting story lines about himself than about the politician he was paid to publicise. Although he liked to pretend otherwise, he craved publicity and enjoyed the notoriety he had achieved as the tough tabloid journalist who probably spent more time with the Prime Minister than any other member of the Downing Street staff. The high profile he had acquired had not been cost-free. By continually promoting stories about himself, Campbell was reinforcing the public's perception that Blair and his party were entirely dependent on spin. The potential damage that that could inflict on Labour's standing with the electorate had not been lost on the Conservatives. Campbell told party workers at the training seminar that they must do all they could to avoid feeding the news media's interest in the work of Labour's spin doctors. He said the constant repetition of the accusation that Blair relied on spin was a deliberate tactic by their opponents and had to be rebutted because it broke down the electorate's trust in the government and fuelled doubts as to whether Labour could deliver what had been promised. Although he would have been far too professional to reveal it, he probably did feel a touch queasy at the seminar on 13 June, because he had failed to follow the advice he was dishing out to party workers, and deep down he must have known it. Campbell had hit a patch of prolonged turbulence and had effectively lost control over the propagation of his own publicity: on some days he was attracting more column inches than the Prime Minister, and whichever way he turned he found it impossible to retreat.

His helter-skelter slide towards the limelight started on 8 March 2000 when he announced that Michael Cockerell was being allowed access to lobby briefings to film for the BBC's documentary on life 'behind the scenes at Downing Street'. On this occasion it took political correspondents only a few seconds to decode their fate: they felt they were about to be cast as villains in a No. 10 production from which Campbell would emerge triumphant, having taken on the massed ranks of the lobby and exposed their dastardly behaviour. Some television and radio reporters felt miffed that this exceptional opportunity had been granted to a broadcaster from outside the lobby; Jo Andrews, an ITN political correspondent, demanded similar access. However, it was the moans and groans from the newspaper correspondents who dominated the group that should have been heeded. Most of the journalists formed the impression there would be further consultations, but at the morning briefing the following Monday, 13 March, Campbell introduced Cockerell and said work on the documentary was about to begin. Having been presented as *a fait accompli* with the news that they were about to be identified on camera, two political editors, George Jones of the *Daily Telegraph* and Trevor Kavanagh of the *Sun*, promptly turned the tables and said that if the briefings were being filmed they would have no alternative but to identify Campbell by name rather than source his guidance to the 'Prime Minister's official spokesman'.

Campbell, clearly caught off guard by this move, seemed to be more interested in impressing Cockerell by demonstrating that he would not be pushed around by the lobby than in thinking through the full consequences of what was happening: 'Yes, you can call me what you want. I don't think it adds up to a row of beans. I speak as the Prime Minister's official spokesman, that is what I am.' Not unnaturally his answer was taken at face value. Next morning the *Daily Telegraph* reported that Campbell had 'finally emerged from the shadows' and agreed that he could be named by reporters when giving his twice-daily briefings. Like other news organisations, the BBC issued instructions that he should be identified in bulletins and programmes. Without having realised it, Campbell had released journalists from their obligation to protect his anonymity: his name would now be attached to countless news stories, giving substance to the charge that he was the real Deputy Prime Minister.

He was ambushed again at the afternoon briefing the following day, 14 March, during a lengthy discussion on the latest projections for the level of taxation through to 2002. The Conservatives had been suggesting for months that the annual tax burden under Labour had been increasing, a claim consistently denied by Blair and Brown. The issue was discussed regularly at the lobby and, after he had gone through the projections issued by the Major and Blair governments, Campbell was asked by George Jones if he acknowledged that the figures were showing that the tax take would be higher than the government inherited. He nodded and then said, 'Yes.' When the *Guardian*'s political editor, Michael White, enquired if his answer represented a change of policy, the Prime Minister's official spokesman seemed to be losing both his thread and his patience: 'It's not a change of strategy. I mean I know you sort of, I know you, oh, anyway, just write what you want.'

His unexpected acknowledgement that the tax burden was forecast to be higher at the next general election than when Labour took office made headline news. In her report for the BBC's *Six O'Clock News*, Carole Walker quoted Campbell by name as having said the tax burden was rising, 'something they've never admitted before'. The story was front-page news next day: 'Blair: The tax burden is up' was the *Daily Mail*'s headline on its report that Campbell had announced 'a fundamental strategic shift' in government policy by admitting that the tax burden at the end of the parliament would be higher than at the start. The *Guardian* went one step further and filled a full page with a verbatim account of Campbell's answers in the briefing, saying it believed relations between the government and the media should be 'conducted in as open a manner as possible'.

Campbell, already alarmed by the way his name had been quoted so freely the day before, had launched an immediate rearguard action in the correspondence columns of the *Daily Telegraph* and denied that he had 'agreed' to be identified by name. In a letter to the editor, he gave his version of what had taken place at the morning briefing on 13 March: 'I said that there was nothing I could do to stop the press from naming me, and that I didn't think it added much to the public's understanding of government if they did . . . But I believe journalists should, and in the main do, see the difference between a one-off film, in which any remarks I am filmed making will not be broadcast "in real time", and twice-daily briefings on behalf of the government . . . I continue to believe that for on-the-record, off-camera briefings, the Prime Minister's official spokesman is a perfectly adequate formulation for both government and the media.' He also wrote a personal letter to political editors appealing to them not to name him on the grounds that both sides had been well served by the previous system; but his attempt to close the stable door was in vain.

Campbell must have realised that his remarks at the two briefings had been foolish and intemperate, because he took immediate steps to limit any further damage or embarrassment by exercising his authority over what was published on the Downing Street website. By withholding an official summary of the two disputed discussions he could limit any wider circulation of his remarks and defend with confidence the accuracy of his version of events, despite the conflicting reports published and broadcast by the news media. Daily visits to the No. 10 website proved my point: Campbell had ensured that any argument about his disputed briefings would have to remain unresolved. The extract on the website for the morning briefing on 13 March made no mention at all of Cockerell's presence, nor did it refer to the disputed exchange over whether the press secretary should be identified by name. Campbell went one step further to protect himself from any more grief over the guidance he had given on the tax burden by ordering that no summary should be published for the entire briefing on the afternoon of 14 March, and the archive on the website, which stored summaries for one month, continued to list no entry for that briefing.

When No. 10 started publishing extracts from the briefings in mid-February 2000, Campbell answered questions online about the policy he intended to adopt. He said the website would be 'updated at least twice a day' with extracts from the briefings. Although the summary would not amount to a full transcript of each briefing, it would go through 'all the main subjects that were covered and some of the questions'. Given these assurances, I failed to see why the 13 March entry made no reference whatever to the issue of his identification, which, judging by his letter to the *Daily Telegraph*, was a matter of considerable importance. Far more serious, in my view, was the omission of the entire entry for 14 March, when the tax burden was discussed. The implication was clear: Campbell had free rein to pick and choose what appeared on a government website that published an official summary of lobby briefings written up by civil service press officers under his direction. Sir Richard Wilson, the Cabinet Secretary, had given MPs repeated assurances that he personally monitored the extracts. I wondered if Sir Richard had noticed that the entry for the afternoon of 13 March had been omitted from the website. Had he ever asked his staff to see if the version published on No. 10's website matched the extracts that were circulated within the government?

I accept that editorial control had to be exercised over the publication of the summaries and Campbell was duty bound to honour the undertakings No. 10 had given to Sir Richard that the website would not be used for party political purposes. Campbell explained online how this safeguard would operate: 'At my briefings I can in some circumstances, quite legitimately, be political. By their nature these remarks could not be carried on the web. That is another reason why there will be extracts of the briefing used on site.' However, careful study of the various entries has revealed that this criterion has been applied in a highly idiosyncratic, not to say cavalier, way, and in my experience it has proved virtually impossible to distinguish the grounds on which Campbell has exercised his editorial judgement. In one respect, there was a uniform pattern: on those occasions when there were political aspects to the briefings and when there has been no mention of them online, the extract available on the internet has invariably listed the other main points of government business that were discussed. I considered reference to the way the press secretary was being identified was of general interest, as were the figures for the burden of taxation. Nevertheless, if the justification for withholding Campbell's comments about the level of taxation was that they were regarded for some reason as party political, why was there no mention of all the other matters that were discussed at the afternoon briefing on 14 March and included in the *Guardian*'s transcript? The conclusion I drew from the omission of this information was that Campbell wanted no reminder on the website of his colourful observations that it did not matter 'a row of beans' how he was described by the news media and that journalists could write what they wanted to about Labour's future tax take.

There were similar contradictions regarding the online entries about the mayoral election in London. The most damaging briefings against Ken Livingstone took place before the website was opened. At that time Livingstone was still campaigning within the electoral college for the Labour nomination. However, after he decided to stand as an independent, there were several additional occasions when he was referred to in critical terms before Campbell announced finally on 30 March that he had 'stopped participating' in the mayoral campaign. His undertaking to refrain from giving 'a running commentary' on the contest was reproduced on the website, unlike two other references earlier that month. On 6 March Campbell told the lobby that Blair believed Livingstone would be 'a disaster for London' and that his transport policies would 'saddle London with billions of pounds worth of debt and would absolutely ruin us'. On 8 March Campbell directed his fire at the correspondents who were reporting the campaign. He accused *Newsnight* of unbalanced reporting and claimed that most of the people working for Livingstone 'carry NUJ cards' (indicating their membership of the National Union of Journalists). In both instances Campbell's references to Livingstone were omitted from the online summaries.

Campbell had been fortunate that neither the 13 or 14 March briefing had been captured on camera. When filming began the following month for the BBC's documentary, the presence of a television crew had an immediate impact. Journalists were aware that they were being scrutinised and their questions tended to be shorter and much sharper. Campbell used the morning briefing on 12 April, during the first week of filming, to underline his commitment to the Labour Party. He said that when the general election was called he intended to resign from his job at No. 10 so that he could join Blair's campaign. This announcement was included in the website summary, serving only to underline the perversity of some of Campbell's earlier decisions on what to include and what to omit.

During the period of filming, Campbell could not be faulted on his attempts at stage management. He went to elaborate lengths at the briefing on 20 April to make sure he was given the opportunity to knock down an exclusive by the *Sun*'s political editor, Trevor Kavanagh, which predicted that Blair was planning a dramatic cabinet reshuffle to replace Dr Marjorie Mowlam with Peter Mandelson. Campbell must have feared he was about to miss his opportunity, so he slipped a note to one of the special advisers sitting next to him. It was passed to a civil service press officer who then gave it to a BBC political correspondent, Carolyn Quinn. On unfolding the note she saw to her surprise that it said: 'We need a question on the reshuffle.' As chance would have it, even before she needed to think what to ask next, another BBC correspondent, Guto Harri, had enquired whether Mandelson was about to return from Northern Ireland to take on the task of planning the election campaign. Campbell responded on cue: the *Sun*'s reshuffle story was 'utter rubbish, garbagian nonsense'. He had come well prepared and proceeded to read out a list of inaccurate reshuffle stories stretching back over the previous twelve months, a welcome opportunity to name and shame his tormentors on camera. After the briefing Campbell walked across to Ms Quinn to retrieve the prompt that had been handed to her: 'I think I had better have that note back.'

Some broadcasters resented their role as props. In an article the previous week for *Sunday Business*, the political editor for *Sky News*, Adam Boulton, said the only reason Campbell had authorised the documentary was because he wanted to take 'another pop at the triviality of the press'. In order to provide some informal footage, Tony and Cherie Blair hosted an evening reception at No. 10 for political editors and their partners. Needless to say there was considerable muttering afterwards because many of those invited had no idea they were about to be filmed. Steve Richards, the *New Statesman*'s political editor, recalled for me the moment when he and his wife walked through the door: 'We knew we had to try to keep out of shot otherwise we were in danger of becoming extras in Cockerell's movie which we could see Campbell was doing his best to control.'

Cockerell was facing fierce competition in his attempt to produce an incisive portrayal of life inside the No. 10 press office: he was up against the impressionist Rory Bremner, who had been hard at work on *Blair Did It All Go Wrong?*, his contribution to a series of Channel 4 programmes marking Labour's third anniversary in May. Bremner used the programme to add a new routine to his impressions of Blair. He was joined for one sketch by the actor Andrew Dunn, who took on the role of a domineering press secretary forever forcing a hesitant, stumbling Prime Minister to learn his lines. 'Come on, more passion,' barks the press secretary. 'But it is my speech, Alastair,' bleats the plaintive premier. 'No, it's not, it's my speech, I wrote it,' says the spokesman. At one point they argue over an article that has been commissioned for the *News of the World*. When told it has been written already, the Prime Minister protests again. Dunn, who had clearly studied his subject, sniffs and then replies with a snarl: 'It doesn't matter what you think. I've written it already.' Bremner told the *Mail on Sunday* he had decided to satirise Campbell's 'hold on Blair and his image, from his policies right down to choice of tie', because it was a relationship journalists were always talking about, and he understood that his depiction of them both 'caught off-camera and unguarded' had ruffled most feathers inside No. 10. Columnists praised the portrayal of the hard-man press aide who contemptuously ordered around his political puppet. Peter Oborne, writing in the *Sunday Express*, said Bremner's sketches reflected the sense that Blair was 'a phoney' and that everything he did was orchestrated by the press secretary who had become his 'invisible crutch'.

Not only was Campbell being assailed by Rory Bremner and Andrew Dunn, he was having to take the blame for a succession of public relations disasters. Philip Webster, political editor of *The Times*, claimed that Gordon Brown's attack that month on Magdalen

College for rejecting the North Tyneside pupil Laura Spence had been 'hatched' inside No. 10 by Campbell. Although I found no way of verifying the accuracy of Webster's assertion, I discovered that Campbell spent much of the following Saturday briefing political correspondents for the Sunday newspapers, assuring them that the Chancellor had not intended to damage Oxford University's world-class reputation. I was on duty that weekend and I was told by Phil Murphy, Labour's director of communications, to expect a call because Campbell was doing a ring-round to insist that Brown's objective was to bring class barriers down, not put them up. Campbell did not speak to me, delegating the task to his deputy, Godric Smith, but as luck would have it I did manage subsequently to have a few words with him. I was on early-morning duty in Downing Street and Bremner's sketch was fresh in my mind as Campbell walked up to No. 10's front door. On attracting his attention I told him how encouraged I had been by his openness in allowing television cameras into the press room to film lobby briefings for the first time. He looked at me suspiciously for moment. Then, I am sure I saw him sniff before he turned on his heel, after delivering the sharp rejoinder: 'The only reason I've done it is for your benefit.'

Cockerell was disappointed that he and his crew were not allowed access to the morning briefing on 7 June, when Campbell had the delicate and difficult task of trying to conjure up a convincing explanation for the indignity the Prime Minister had suffered when addressing the massed ranks of the National Federation of Women's Institutes at their triennial general meeting in Wembley Arena. Blair was interrupted by a slow handclap, an unnerving experience in itself, but an event that was to prove doubly destabilising for his official spokesman. The heckling started when Blair attempted to defend the government's record on the National Health Service, but it was the section in his speech in which he related his reflections on unexpectedly becoming a father again that succeeded inadvertently in turning the spotlight on his press secretary. Leo's birth had helped put Blair's life in better perspective and given him a renewed sense of purpose: 'I think we in government – and that means me – have to trust people more. We don't need to fight over every headline. We should put more faith in people's desire to engage in a conversation about the future.'

For the first time, Blair had revealed publicly a hint of unease about the overriding importance that he and the party's modernisers had always attached to presentation and publicity. The reflective nature of his speech, which had been trailed in advance as the occasion that would mark his return from paternity leave, got lost in a blaze of damaging headlines: the Prime Minister had been jeered by those pillars of the local community, the fearless members of the Women's Institutes. The headline writers had a field day. 'Blair hand-bagged by Middle England' was the *Independent*'s effort, while the *Daily Express*, which said the Prime Minister emerged shaken and crestfallen after addressing his ten-thousand-strong audience, captured the feeling that this was likely to prove an enduring image that the news media would not forget: 'Blair reduced to jelly by W.I.' Campbell had remained in Downing Street that morning, rather than accompany Blair to the Wembley Arena, and had watched the speech on television. As a result the briefing was delayed for about twenty minutes, and Campbell looked ill at ease on having to admit that his assessment of the protest was based on Adam Boulton's commentary on *Sky News*.

When the slow handclap started, and the national chairman of the Women's Institutes, Helen Carey, appealed to the audience to 'let the Prime Minister speak out of politeness', Blair dropped the rest of the section of his prepared text that referred to the health service. 'I knew he would cuts bits out, the speech was about ten minutes too long,' said Campbell. He was sure Blair would not have been troubled by a few protesters. 'I don't believe the speech has backfired . . . We can engage in a dialogue with the nation. Don't forget this is the only government in our lifetime which remains ahead of the opposition in the opinion polls at this stage in the Parliament.' When asked what Blair meant by saying he did not need to 'fight over every headline', Campbell replied that the government had to be open and honest about what it was doing. 'It means not worrying about every headline, not fighting for every headline . . . This government is governing for the long term and we have to do that in a media age.'

If Campbell had been at Wembley Arena, he might have thought twice before volunteering his interpretation, because it was his diligence in trailing the speech so heavily in advance, in an effort to secure favourable headlines, that had sparked off most of the protests. Several newspapers led their front pages that morning with a detailed preview of what was billed as an attempt to reclaim the political middle ground. 'Blair's back with appeal to tradition' was the headline over a report in the *Daily Telegraph,* which said Blair would use his speech to the Women's Institutes, seen by Labour strategists as a 'key audience', to win back the support of 'middle Britain by declaring that he believes in traditional values'. When the television crews and reporters arrived to film the speech, some of the WI members could be heard around them complaining about the media's intrusion for what they feared would be a political speech. Some of the women who walked out, and whose reaction was filmed by the BBC, were extremely annoyed and felt their general meeting had been hijacked by the Labour Party: 'This is just not on. This is the WI' . . . 'It was totally out of order' . . . 'He used this as a party political.'

After watching the lunchtime news bulletins, Campbell realised he would have to mount a fight-back, and he told the afternoon briefing that Blair's staff had been racking their brains to think what the Prime Minister could have said to the WI that would not have been deemed political, other than 'reading out the phone book'. Next morning, when challenged again over Blair's wish to avoid fighting 'over every headline', Campbell denied repeatedly that he had made a presentational mistake by trailing the speech so heavily in advance. The government had not been a victim of its own spin: he had provided political editors with information about the speech the day before, but Downing Street had not briefed the Sunday newspapers. Despite the 'day-to-day babbleology of the 24-hour news media', the Prime Minister's staff did not 'sit around wallowing and navel-gazing'. Nevertheless, despite the strength of his counter-attack, Campbell had been wounded by the WI fiasco, and he gave a hint of the retaliatory action that was to come by threatening to give journalists just ten minutes' advance warning of Blair's next speech so that he could not be 'accused of spinning in advance'. But all

Campbell's defiant bluster in defending himself blew up in his face that weekend when the *Sunday Times* published the second of the leaked memos written by the pollster and strategist Philip Gould.

He had been asked by Campbell the previous Sunday, 4 June, to comment on a draft of the WI speech. Gould thought the language Blair intended to use made him 'look rather sad' and did not feel authentic. 'This is a speech that looks once again like TB pandering, lacking conviction, unable to hold a position for more than a few weeks . . . It leaves the wrong taste, it makes you feel less of him not more . . . TB is not believed to be real. He lacks conviction, he is all spin and presentation, he says things to please people, not because he believes them.' Gould's assessment was devastating and the timing of the leak was just as deadly: it kept the WI débâcle in the news and focused more attention on Campbell's ill-fated attempt to promote a speech that Blair had hoped would put an end to the row caused by Gordon Brown's attack on élitism at Oxford University. A two-page investigation by the *Observer* said that when Campbell prepared to watch the speech on *Sky News* he was pleased that the newspapers had reproduced the line which he had briefed on in advance, that Blair wanted to lay to rest any fears of a renewed class war. 'Campbell's world looked rosy. Thirty-five minutes later came meltdown.' All the bravado Campbell had displayed the previous Thursday, when he insisted that his staff were not sitting around 'wallowing and navel-gazing', evaporated that weekend. Self-doubt seemed to have taken hold; Campbell's role was about to be redefined. His deputy Godric Smith took the Monday morning lobby briefing and refused to answer questions about the memo Gould had sent to Campbell. After he had deputised at the Monday afternoon briefing and the two briefings held on Tuesday, Smith finally confirmed what political correspondents suspected: his boss intended to scale down his face-to-face encounters with the lobby.

Campbell did put in an appearance on Wednesday afternoon, following Prime Minister's questions, and he was quite blunt about the reasons why his duties were being changed: Blair wanted him to spend more time working on future strategy. The two of them had discussed his new role and he felt 'very comfortable' about it. 'Briefing you is only part of a busy day . . . I have a lot more things to do . . . I will continue to see journalists but we will do it our way.' Campbell did little to hide his irritation over the news coverage of the WI speech and the trouble it had caused him. 'It's all been about presentation, pollsters and spin and not what the government is achieving . . . It's time some common sense was injected into this . . . If people are now saying they don't want spin, that's fine, I am happy with that . . . I will still be in charge of communications and co-ordination across government but we will do it in a different way.' Campbell announced another change in direction, too: there would be less advance trailing of speeches. 'On the day before a big event there is a lot of demand from the media but I think, as a general rule, we will not do a briefing and it will be the exception rather than the rule.'

I had rarely heard Campbell speak so openly and in such a matter-of-fact way about the job he performed in No. 10. My conclusion was that Blair must have been desperate to end months of damaging publicity about control freakery and New Labour's reliance on spin; Philip Gould's leaked observation that the Prime Minister was regarded as being 'all spin and presentation' indicated the level of concern there must have been among his closest advisers. Both the *Observer* and *Sunday Times* said that Blair had written the WI speech himself, in longhand, and I thought his promise to 'trust people more' and to stop fighting 'over every headline' reflected his realisation that attempts to influence the news media in campaigns like the one mounted against Ken Livingstone had been entirely self-defeating. By asking his press secretary to hold fewer lobby briefings and adopt a less confrontational role, Blair hoped to lower Campbell's profile and demonstrate that he was genuine about giving up spin. When Michael Cockerell's documentary, *News from No. 10*, was transmitted the following month it confirmed what the lobby had deduced: that Blair had taken the initiative in seeking to stabilise the relationship between his press secretary and the political correspondents. Campbell was interviewed first: 'We had, and I particularly had, got myself into a situation where combat was the only language that was being spoken, which is not terribly sensible either way.' Blair was in no doubt that it had become counter-productive to expect his official spokesman to spend so much time and energy defending himself in such fractious circumstances: 'I decided some time ago that it was sensible for him to step back from doing all the lobby briefings every day, otherwise he can't also look at how we are trying to get the government's message across or what we are saying, in a broader sense.' In their reviews of the BBC's documentary, most correspondents and columnists agreed that if Blair was serious about wanting to lower the state of tension that existed between Downing Street and the news media, his only option had been to place some sort of restraint on his official spokesman.

The obvious solution was to ask Campbell's civil service deputy, Godric Smith, to chair more of the lobby briefings, so as to reduce the political content and make them less contentious. In her column in *The Times*, Mary Ann Sieghart claimed to have inside knowledge and said the Prime Minister had finally put his foot down. 'Blair had been talking to his press secretary since last autumn about taking more of a back seat. "Do one or two briefings a week. Don't do two a day," was his advice . . . Campbell was reluctant, though, to delegate more to his deputy . . . Over the past six months, Blair has been stepping up the pressure. His recurring motif of "I really think you should step back" then turned into a categorical "You've got to do so" after the débâcle at the W.I.' Ms Sieghart was well respected by Blair's inner circle and apparently her insight could not be faulted. Campbell did cut back his briefings to about two a week, although this was tending to increase to three a week by the autumn of 2000.

According to Ms Sieghart's chronicle of the conversations that took place between Blair and Campbell, no attention appeared to have been paid to the press secretary's compulsion to remain an arbiter of press and broadcasting standards. Although the intention was to lessen the degree of conflict in his daily relations with lobby, no attempt was made to restrain Campbell's restless urge to pronounce on the misdemeanours and shortcomings of newspapers and broadcasting organisations: Mr Angry would continue to fire off just as many letters of complaint from No. 10 Downing Street as he had always done. If Blair had expected or hoped for a ceasefire in the open warfare between his official spokesman and the news media, he was to be disappointed.

Campbell had indicated in his inimitable way on *News from No. 10* why he remained impervious to the slings and arrows of journalists who dared question either the motives or the ethical standards of the Prime Minister's press secretary: 'You guys are the spin doctors. We get on and do what we have to do . . . Over time, believe me, the real message and the real record of this government is going to get out, and I will be part of that . . . The stuff about me doesn't worry me, it doesn't faze me. They can pump it out all they want because in the end I do what I do because I believe in it and I think it matters.' Nowhere has that passion and conviction been applied with greater force than over his constant criticism of journalists' distortion when reporting day-to-day events affecting Britain's relationship with the European Union. A fortnight after he scaled down his attendance at lobby briefings, he went into full rebuttal mode on the Downing Street website with a lengthy statement that explained why the Prime Minister believed much of the media's coverage on Europe was 'a joke'. Campbell had refrained on previous occasions from naming names, but this time he had opted for an all-out attack, and his online rebuttal went through the front pages of the newspapers for 30 June 2000 explaining, point by point, why each of their reports was 'rubbish'. Two examples of misrepresentation were the *Daily Telegraph*'s front-page lead that 'Blair comes off the fence to back euro', when the Prime Minister was merely repeating well-known policy, and the *Sun*'s report that 'Blair flies to Berlin for crisis talks', when he was in Berlin for a long-arranged dinner with Chancellor Schroeder. Blair's concern was that the bias shown on an almost daily basis by newspapers was setting the agenda for the broadcasters who 'endlessly repeat the clichés of isolation, division and international conflict'.

Campbell could not be faulted on his tenacity in fighting the Prime Minister's corner, and he rarely missed an opportunity to deride the opinionated news coverage of the Eurosceptic press. While Campbell could point quite correctly to a settled policy over the European single currency in line with the government's commitment to hold a refer- endum after the general election, ministers were constantly sending out confused signals about the speed with which Britain should prepare to join the euro, and most journalists felt the continuing uncertainty made it all the more difficult to keep abreast of the latest twists and turns in what was, after all, a highly political argument.

The attack on biased newspaper reporting reached a new intensity in November 2000 after the United Kingdom committed 12,500 soldiers to a new European Union rapid reaction force. 'Is Blair playing with fire?' was the *Daily Mail*'s headline over a front-page report which said that the 'Euro army' could jeopardise links with the United States, undermine NATO and threaten the safety of Britain. The *Sun* feared that the 'world's most powerful military alliance was at risk' because Britain had signed up to 'a European army'. Blair was in Moscow that day visiting President Putin, and he issued a forthright denial of any suggestion that a rapid reaction force would be a threat to NATO: 'This is a pretty big claim to make but I think even by the standards of parts of our anti-European media some of the coverage in those papers is fundamentally dishonest.'

Campbell briefed the lobby the previous morning, before departing for Russia with Blair, and immediately went on the offensive. He feared that Britain's commitment to support the rapid reaction force would be presented in an 'alarmist way'. If newspapers tried to suggest that it was the European Union that would decide when to deploy British soldiers, their stories would be 'complete garbage' because the Prime Minister would have the final say on the use of our troops. Campbell's tough language against what he and Blair had begun to say was the 'anti-European press' was reminiscent of the campaign he had waged the year before about the way some broadcasters had reported NATO's air raids on Serbia at the height of the Kosovo crisis during the spring of 1999. When the conflict was over, he declared that NATO had 'won the media battle' despite the failure of western journalists to take 'seriously enough the military significance of the Serb lie machine'. Campbell used his lobby briefings during the air raids to criticise British broadcasters based in Belgrade for allowing themselves to be taken in by President Milosevic's propaganda. He wanted television viewers to be told repeatedly that NATO 'did not trust any of the Serbs' pictures of casualties'. In the early days of NATO's campaign, the broadcaster John Simpson was one of those mentioned in a report by Philip Webster, political editor of *The Times*, who quoted an unnamed 'senior official' in No. 10 as saying the BBC's world affairs editor had been 'swallowing Serb propaganda'. Downing Street denied responsibility for singling out Simpson, but in July 1999, in a lecture to the Royal United Services Institute, Campbell showed no hesitation in questioning the ethical standards of long-serving foreign correspondents who had dealt with information from the allies on the basis that it was 'NATO propaganda', whereas 'Serb day-trips to the scene of the NATO crime were treated as a truthful exposé of a flawed air campaign'.

Taking advantage of off-camera lobby briefings to attack British journalists working in war zones was regarded as a step too far by many foreign correspondents, who believed Campbell did himself irreparable damage thereby. So great seemed to be the desire to control the way the conflict was being reported that the Downing Street press office appeared oblivious to the ability of viewers and listeners to filter out propaganda and form their own opinion of the accuracy of news reports from Belgrade. I considered Campbell's conduct had been particularly ill-judged: the allies' air superiority far outweighed Milosevic's capabilities, and the media seemed to be taking the blame for shortcomings of the military campaign. Far from being at a disadvantage in the propaganda stakes, NATO and the Ministry of Defence broke new ground with communication strategies tailored to meet the requirements of 24-hour news services. NATO's spokesman, Jamie Shea, gave seventy-eight televised news briefings during the two and half months of the campaign; there were daily briefings on camera at the Ministry of Defence and the Pentagon, and regular televised appearances by the White House spokesman, Joe Lockhart. Campbell, by contrast, was safe in the knowledge that there would be no publicly available record of the briefings he was giving in No. 10.

Downing Street played a critical role in assisting the allied forces to control the flow of information that was released during the conflict. After it took NATO five days to admit that it had killed up to seventy-five ethnic Albanians when a column of refugee tractors was bombed on the Djakovica–Prizren road during the third week of the campaign, Campbell was sent to NATO's headquarters with President Clinton's support to strengthen the allies' capability in crisis news management. His task was to help NATO 'think strategically' when co-ordinating its response. He paid six visits to NATO's headquarters, and two Downing Street press officers were among those seconded to work there during the military offensive. Shea told me subsequently that Campbell's assistance in helping him obtain information from the allied commanders had been invaluable. 'Campbell could by-pass the military chain of command and by going straight to Downing Street, the White House or the Elysée Palace he could put pressure on the political masters of the allied commanders and get them to tell him what we wanted to know.'

Campbell's role in organising NATO's media operations centre, which was based on a blueprint he prepared for Shea, was examined in a BBC documentary, *Correspondent: How the War Was Spun*, broadcast in October 1999. The presenter, Edward Stourton, said he believed the way in which the world's most powerful military machine had been 'directed not by soldiers but spin doctors' was the untold story of the Kosovo campaign; one White House official had told him it was the media operation that 'ultimately led Milosevic to capitulate'. Stourton set out in an article for the *Daily Telegraph* Campbell's campaign strategy. The tasks to be performed included: 'rebuttal – identifying and responding to misinformation; lines – drafting catchy phrases for Jamie Shea; talking heads – monitoring the views of armchair generals; article factory – writing pieces to appear under the by-lines of NATO leaders'. Another innovation transferred from Downing Street to NATO's media operations centre was the use of 'the grid', which set out the timetable for publicising conference calls and the engagements of NATO's national leaders. Stourton said that the Supreme Allied Commander Europe, General Wesley Clark, got on well with Campbell when they first met at the height of the Djakovica convoy crisis. 'The extent of the general's conversion to the spin doctor's creed may be judged from this astonishing statement: "The right way to fight a propaganda offensive is not with more propaganda," he told me. "It's to tell the truth, the whole truth and nothing but the truth, and do it as rapidly as possible. But you need some smart people who can tell you what piece of truth you are looking for." The truth, it seems, is a little like one of those high-tech bombs his pilots were carrying; it simply needs precision engineering to perform properly. Campbell and his team were not, Clark insists, spin doctors, they were "people who understood which pieces of information were important to provide to the public".'

Military analysts who have tried subsequently to establish the 'truth' about the effectiveness of the air campaign have faced a moving target: NATO's figures for air-strike successes have been scaled down repeatedly. Initially, on the completion of the air offensive, it was claimed 120 tanks and 220 armoured personnel carriers had been destroyed; in September 1999, General Clark reported there were 'validated strikes' on ninety-three tanks and 153 personnel carriers; and in May 2000, *Newsweek* published what it claimed were the suppressed findings of a United States Air Force investigation, which showed that fourteen tanks and eighteen personnel carriers had been destroyed. Authors and historians have faced similar difficulties when trying to establish the facts surrounding the likelihood of a land invasion, and the disagreement between Clinton and Blair over the wisdom of deploying ground troops rather than relying on an air campaign. Blair was portrayed by some British newspapers as the hawk, who alone among the allied leaders was prepared to commit forces on the ground; that certainly was the spin I picked up in Downing Street. Although there is access in archives to the tapes of NATO and White House briefings, the only information available publicly to researchers who wish to examine what Campbell said on the Prime Minister's behalf are the contemporaneous accounts of newspaper correspondents and broadcasters who attended his lobby briefings

Campbell's presence at NATO's headquarters had an electrifying effect on government information officers working for the other European members of the alliance. Their political leaders had admired for some time the effectiveness of the presentational techniques that they had seen being deployed on Blair's behalf at European Union summits. However, if New Labour's spin doctors were to make a habit of marching across the continent, the press officers of Europe had to know more.

Whenever I was asked to discuss Campbell's *modus operandi* at European conferences and seminars I used the Kosovo conflict to illustrate the effectiveness of the communication strategies which Blair's government had developed. My starting point was the simple proposition that if the British people were asked in an opinion poll whether they considered NATO had fought a just war against Serbia, and whether Blair had achieved what he promised, I believed a clear majority would answer 'yes', probably by a margin of 60, 70 or perhaps 80 per cent. When I tried out my thesis on the opinion pollster Robert Worcester, chairman of MORI, during a debate at the London School of Economics in May 2000, he did not demur. The reason why I used this as an illustration was because I knew there was far greater opposition elsewhere in Europe to the use of NATO fire-power against Serbia, and a similar question in an opinion poll in any of those countries might well have produced a very different answer. My argument was that Blair's clarity in justifying the need for air strikes helped to explain the overwhelming support that was evident in Britain. Presentation had been an integral part of the decision-making process. When it came to justifying NATO's offensive, the objective had been limited and straightforward: to ensure the safe return of the Albanian refugees to their homes in Kosovo. If the military campaign had gone wrong, or if the objectives had become confused, the war might have become unpopular, a point that Blair acknowledged once the conflict was over: 'It wasn't just a military campaign, it was also a propaganda campaign. We had to take public opinion with us . . . I felt a bit like, you know, at the beginning of a big political campaign.'

Another important factor had been the effort the government put into reminding the public about the effectiveness of the air offensive. For the British forces involved in the conflict, it was a case of mission accomplished; Serbia had withdrawn its troops from Kosovo and the Albanian refugees had been allowed to return to their homes. Blair's contribution was also seen as having been pivotal. Jack Straw, the Home Secretary, told MPs in April 2000 that if the Prime Minister had not shown the 'statesmanship he did in leading the intervention against the Serbians, Europe would be facing not thousands but millions of refugees'.

My description of the skilful and effective way in which the British government used the news media during the Kosovo conflict was rarely challenged and invariably provoked questions. In view of the evident public support in Britain for NATO's action, some European information officers said they were puzzled by Campbell's harsh crit-icism of the broadcasters reporting from Belgrade. Why, they asked, did the British government not respect the independence of the country's journalists? Their overriding concern as civil servants was to find out more about the way in which information officers employed by the British government had responded to the power and influence that was being exercised by the politically appointed publicity advisers who had been hired by Blair's ministers. In May 2000 I was asked to speak to fourteen information officers from Denmark who were visiting London on what they said was a 'study tour of spin'. Their leader, Morten Boje Hviid, an adviser with a Danish public affairs bureau, told me they feared an invasion of the techniques that had been used by Alastair Campbell and Peter Mandelson. 'Our spin doctors are not as clever as in the United Kingdom. We think we are about five years behind you . . . We are still "virgin" when it comes to political pollsters and focus groups.' My two-hour session with the group was dominated by their wish to explore the potential for conflict and tension between traditional government information officers and what they termed the 'new age spin doctors'. I explained that the rules of engagement were still being written and that I considered the minimal safeguards in place to prevent the politicisation of hitherto impartial civil servants left a great deal to be desired. They listened in silence.

OUT OF CONTROL?

'I would not have made the official spokesman for the Prime Minister a political appointment . . . In these days of a cynical world a dispassionate civil servant, answerable to the head of the civil service for his honesty and probity, can be seen to be more dispassionate than somebody who is not so answerable . . . Therefore, the word emanating from Downing Street would have some independent verification as to its accuracy.'

John Major, giving evidence to the House of Commons Select Committee on Public Administration, 18 July 2000

New Labour's preferred mode of administration was well trailed by the party's modernisers: firm control would be imposed from the centre, and that would require a strengthening of Downing Street's role in formulating policy and coordinating presentation. After nearly four years in power Tony Blair has undoubtedly made a notable impact on Whitehall. He has succeeded in turning the Prime Minister's office into a separate department in all but name, and he has reinforced the steady shift towards a presidential style of government. Not only has Blair increased the size of No. 10's long-established policy unit, he has also brought together an array of specialists charged with the task of integrating the government's work and devising strategies to publicise Labour's achievements. Much of this work has been performed not by civil servants but by a new élite which, in the view of Anthony King, professor of government at the University of Essex, has turned out to be 'quite a different tribe of people' from anything seen before in Westminster.

Professor King told the House of Commons Select Committee on Public Administration in July 2000 that MPs should recognise that Britain was entering 'a new phase of government'. There were now three separate groups of people inhabiting the departments of Whitehall: ministers, career civil servants and special advisers. The emergence of this third category, the new and powerful grouping of political appointees, has not been entirely to the liking of Old

Labour. 'Faceless wonders' was John Prescott's infamous description in July 1999 of the group who worked in Downing Street's much-enlarged policy unit. Blair has sanctioned the appointment of a total of seventy-nine special advisers; twenty-six have been employed in No. 10 and the rest spread around the various government departments. Many of the political aides assigned to individual ministers have been extremely upfront about their work and they have, in effect, become the shock troops for Alastair Campbell in his daily battle with the news media. Professor King had few doubts when asked to give his assessment of the duties being performed by the Prime Minister's official spokesman: he was playing 'a more explicitly political role' than previous Downing Street press secretaries. Campbell, like the other political appointees, has been bound by the terms of a model contract, which has proved to be an inadequate safeguard in the opinion not only of Professor King but also of numerous other expert witnesses who have urged the introduction of a strong code of ethics.

Ever since Blair agreed to give unprecedented executive powers to Campbell and his chief of staff, Jonathan Powell, he has been under pressure to tighten the rules, and he finally agreed, three years after entering No. 10, that action would be taken after the next general election. Ministers set out their proposals in July 2000 in response to a report by the Committee on Standards in Public Life, chaired by Lord Neill, which recommended a separate code of conduct for special advisers; a contract of employment that would require them to 'uphold the political impartiality of the civil service'; and a limit on the total number of such advisers that a prime minister could appoint. As a first step, the government promised that all special advisers appointed or re-appointed after the next election would be asked to sign a revised model contract. Once new legislation governing the work of the civil service was approved in the next parliament, political appointees would be required to abide by a separate code of conduct on which ministers have asked the Select Committee on Public Administration to advise. A report setting out the scope of possible ground rules for the future is likely to be published by the select committee some time early in 2001. However, by allowing the present regime to continue without interruption until after the next election, Blair has entrenched the considerable tactical advantage his ministers have derived from an unparalleled infusion of political expertise.

The appointment of so many special advisers has undoubtedly had the greatest impact at the sharp end of government, where difficult policy decisions have had to be explained and promoted. I hope my investigations for *The Control Freaks* have served to underline the freewheeling nature of the work in which this new 'tribe of people' has been engaged. Political journalists have had to adjust to a new way of doing business: the first point of contact on a breaking news story today is more likely to be a telephone conversation with No. 10's press office or a special adviser in a minister's private office rather than a call to a government information officer in the relevant department.

No previous Downing Street press secretary has enjoyed anything like the power or authority that Blair has vested in his official spokesman, and in my judgement Campbell has failed to honour the undertakings he gave personally to the Select Committee on Public Administration in June 1998. His remarks at lobby briefings about Ken Livingstone and William Hague have constituted the kind of 'personal attacks' that special advisers were told they must not make and that he promised to avoid; his role in arranging and publicising the defection to Labour of the Conservative MP Shaun Woodward breached the condition that stipulated that advisers should not engage in acts of 'political controversy'; and his practice of deciding on a whim what information shall be included in the published extracts of his lobby briefings has turned Downing Street's website into his personal political plaything. The numerous examples I have cited hardly accord with the repeated assurances given by the Cabinet Secretary, Sir Richard Wilson, that the existing guidelines have been properly policed and enforced.

I have also sought to illustrate instances where I consider undue pressure has been placed on civil servants working for the government information and communication service. This was one of the issues highlighted by the Neill Committee on Standards in Public Life, which recommended that a future code of conduct must provide 'greater clarity' about the relationship between special advisers and civil service information officers. The committee was particularly concerned at the absence in the model contract of any duty on special advisers to refrain from asking civil servants to act in ways that might threaten their impartiality, an omission which it said had to be corrected. I felt the committee's recommendation supported the contention in my last book that not enough was done to protect the neutrality of civil servants when Campbell was given the go-ahead in November 1997 to push ahead with his plans to modernise the information service. My conclusion in *Sultans of Spin* was that the working group chaired by Robin Mountfield appeared to 'have done Campbell's bidding and that civil servants were about to become the spin doctors' accomplices'. Mountfield, who was knighted in the 1998 New Year's Honours, subsequently challenged my prediction. In a note that he circulated after his retirement in 1999 he said many of his recommendations had reaffirmed the need to protect the impartiality of the civil service; the permanent secretary in each department had responsibility for policing the relationship between special advisers and information officers.

Sir Robin clearly believed that I had done him an injustice: 'Jones seeks to demonstrate that my report made me a stooge of Alastair Campbell, simply rubber stamping all the changes he had told people he wanted in order to re-inforce his control-freak dominance of the Whitehall information machine . . . On the contrary, much of the report was directed specifically to averting the risk of politicisation . . . The working group, which included senior people quite capable of making up their own minds, made its recommendations because they believed they were right, not because Campbell wanted some of them.'

I did not intend to impugn Sir Robin's integrity in *Sultans of Spin*, nor do I set out to do so here. I agree with him that communication should not be an afterthought but should be an integral part of 'a democratic government's duty to govern with consent', and I support his contention that Campbell's appointment to 'an explicitly political role' has been a more honest position for Blair to adopt. I also accept that he genuinely believed the working group had recommended sufficient safeguards to protect the non-political status of civil servants. Where we disagreed was over the effectiveness of those controls and what I considered was his failure to understand the mechanics of the spin-doctoring techniques that Labour had mastered in opposition. His report made no mention whatsoever of the separate and exclusive arrangements for holding lobby briefings for Sunday newspapers; information officers were told to start 'trailing' government announcements the previous weekend, while being given no clear instructions on how they should avoid breaching parliamentary protocol and annoying the Speaker; and the working group showed no understanding of the way in which civil servants would be asked to play their part in exploiting those news outlets and journalists who, in return for privileged access and information, were prepared to apply the spin the government wanted. At no point had Sir Robin addressed what I believed was the overriding requirement for the communications strategy of a democratic government: the need to provide a level playing field when releasing information to the public, with equal access for all news outlets. None the less I was impressed by Sir Robin's thoughtful observations on the dangers facing a civil service that he believed was still 'genuinely unpoliticised in its upper reaches' but was not 'invulnerable'. If the Blair government continued 'by stealth' and 'without proper consideration and public discussion' to increase the number of politically appointed special advisers, and widen their role, it could lay the 'whole body politic' open to charges of 'patronage and jobbery'.

Sir Robin's frankness was in marked contrast to what I considered was the complacent response of the head of the civil service, Sir Richard Wilson, and his immediate predecessor, Lord Butler of Brockwell. They assured the Neill Committee that a doubling in the number of political appointees did not present a 'permanent threat' to the political impartiality of the civil service, nor did it constitute 'creeping politicisation'. Sir Richard said he did not think the 'senior civil service of 3,700 people is in danger of being swamped by seventy special advisers'. In my view the basis of his comparison was disingenuous; he should have related the body of special advisers to a relevant area of responsibility in the civil service. Although some special advisers have been confined entirely to policy work, on my calculation at least half, and perhaps even two-thirds, of the seventy-nine political appointees have been engaged in briefing the news media and, as a result, they have had to work closely with the information officers based in their departments. Therefore, the question put to Sir Richard should have been far more specific: By employing as many as forty to fifty special advisers whose job it was to influence journalists, was there a danger that the Blair government might end up putting undue political pressure on the 240 civil service press officers based in the eighteen ministerial departments of Whitehall? My investigations suggested that a question framed in that way, focusing on the domain in which most special advisers operated, would have had to be answered in the affirmative; that the unprecedented control which Campbell and his colleagues had been exercising over the flow of information from the government had been politically inspired and did require the support of civil servants.

When the select committee raised this concern with the head of the information service, Mike Granatt, at a hearing in May 2000, he said that if 'a kite is being flown' in news reports from a pre-briefing, it 'has not necessarily come from information officers as the vast majority of their work is on the record, up front'. Again, I felt Granatt, like the Cabinet Secretary, was not as candid as he should have been. I described in *Sultans of Spin* how I had found that government information officers were giving far fewer health warnings than previously about what were clearly speculative news stories. My experience in the two subsequent years, as recounted in this book, would indicate that the process of politicisation has gone much further and that government press officers have been required to endorse exclusive and unattributed stories that have been floated in the news media well ahead of government announcements with no other purpose than to 'grab the agenda'.

By postponing until after the election the introduction of a separate code of conduct for special advisers and a cap on their numbers, Blair and Campbell have retained the freedom to make the most of the current regime during the all-important run-up to polling day. No previous outgoing administration has been in the fortunate position of being able to build up within government, at taxpayers' expense, a ready-made team of press officers and publicists that could be transferred immediately from Whitehall to party headquarters once an election was called. On the face of it, it seems surprising that the likelihood of Labour being able to start the campaign with an election fighting force already in place has not provoked the outraged response that might have been expected from the Conservatives. In fact, the explanation for their compliant attitude is relatively straightforward: they too have managed to build up an election war room, thanks in large part to taxpayers' largesse. While railing in public about Blair's extravagant spending on special advisers, Conservative MPs have had little to say about a handout of £3.4 million their party received from the state during the financial year ending in March 2001. The level of publicly funded assistance for opposition parties was increased dramatically after a report by the Neill Committee in October 1998, which recommended new controls on political funding, including the full disclosure of political donations of over £5,000. Lord Neill was anxious to ensure that opposition parties had sufficient funds to perform their functions effectively in Parliament, and his committee proposed a substantial increase in what is known at Westminster as 'Short money', the financial assistance first offered by a former Labour Leader of the House, Edward Short. The annual allocation to assist the Conservatives to conduct the party's 'parliamentary duties' rose from £1.1 million in 1998/9 to £3.4 million in 2000/01, an increase that the government believed compensated for the increased cost of the wage bill for special advisers, which rose from £1.8 million in the final year of John Major's administration to £4.3 million in 2000/01. Blair has used these figures to silence Conservative MPs when they have attacked him for asking the state to shoulder his official spokesman's annual salary of £96,275. He told the House in June 2000 that the additional £2 million a year for special advisers matched the extra money for the Conservatives and therefore he considered the two parties were 'about even'.

By equating the two increases, but skating over the fact that much of the money destined for the government special advisers has ended up financing the salaries of spin doctors, Blair was simply underlining the step change that has taken place in the state funding of party political work. The Conservatives have made no secret of the fact that much of their Short money has gone on recruiting and training a campaign team ready for the next election. Andrew

Scadding, the party's assistant head of media, told me that Short money had always been used to pay for research assistance for front-bench spokesmen, and the duties of researchers inevitably included briefing journalists and doing other work on presentation. 'The rules say state funds are intended to help the opposition develop and communicate an alternative policy to that of the government, so obviously some of it has gone towards the cost of building up support for the shadow cabinet in the war room.'

Scadding's acknowledgement that state assistance was being directed towards exploiting a wider political agenda, rather than being allocated solely for parliamentary purposes, only tended to reinforce my doubts about the sincerity of the Conservatives' promise to halve the number of special advisers. The pledge to 'restore faith in politics' by reversing Labour's 'massive expansion in the number of political advisers and spin doctors in Whitehall' first appeared in the 1999 *Common Sense Revolution* and was then repeated in the party's 2000 policy document, *Believing in Britain*. None the less, on the basis of my conversations with Tory media strategists I suggested in my last book that once they were back in government the Conservatives would be reluctant to scale down the increase Blair had secured in the overall establishment of political appointees. I still believe that this is likely to be the case, although William Hague's guarantee to make cuts won the support of John Major when he gave evidence to the Select Committee on Public Administration in July 2000. He said he would advise a future Conservative prime minister to cull their ranks 'very dramatically' because, whatever their individual qualities, as 'a collective breed' special advisers caused more problems than they solved. 'I became very disillusioned with them . . . . Advisers these days are too often taken as speaking to their master's voice. There are too many occasions when advisers, who have a certain amount of knowledge, talk to the media, and it is then reported that happens to be the view of their minister, whether it is in fact the minister's view or not . . . I think they were becoming a significant handicap to the government as a whole.'

Major was equally scathing about Blair's decision to appoint Campbell as his press secretary instead of relying on a government information officer. 'I would not have made the official spokesman for the Prime Minister a political appointment . . . In these days of a cynical world a dispassionate civil servant, answerable to the head of the civil service for his honesty and probity, can be seen to be more dispassionate than somebody who is not so answerable . . . Therefore, the word emanating from Downing Street would have some independent verification as to its accuracy . . . I think that a dispassionate view of a civil servant is an advantage to the government, for I think its voice is more readily heard and accepted in that fashion than it would otherwise be.' Major admitted there were some drawbacks in having to rely on an official spokesman who could not operate in the 'grey area between what is party political and what is in the government's interests', but insisted that was far outweighed by the advantage of having 'an independent voice'.

I was present when Major gave his evidence to the select committee and was personally impressed by the strength of his argument; however, some of those who held key positions at Conservative Central Office when he was Prime Minister were not so convinced. Sheila Gunn, a senior press officer with the party, told me that special advisers were essential to a modern government because of their sharp political antennae. 'Civil service press officers tend to go home at around 5.30 p.m. which is just when journalists are hitting their deadlines, and I can understand why Blair's ministers want someone out there, roving around, keeping their finger on the media's pulse. John Major's problem was that a lot of the advisers for his ministers were of a pretty low calibre and nowhere near as sharp as those who have been working for Labour.' Danny Finkelstein, director of the Conservatives' research department, said that although he agreed with Ms Gunn that Major's government had lost some of its sharpness by relying more on civil service information officers than political advisers, it was a difficult balance. 'Blair's problem is that if you have lots of Alastair Campbells, there might be a short-term advantage but their activities can endanger a government's reputation for objectivity, so I have changed my mind. I think Major is probably right, you can have too many special advisers.'

The reaction of Sir Brian Mawhinney, who had been party chairman under Major, was more pragmatic. He thought a newly elected Conservative government would be reluctant to relinquish state funding for such a generous allocation of political appointees. 'I think this would be very seductive once we got into power. Who knows, we might find a million reasons to delay implementation of that particular pledge?' Sir Brian's hunch about the stance an incoming Conservative prime minister might take was shared by Professor Anthony King. He was sure that Blair's successors would take kindly to the idea of having a much enlarged operation in No. 10 and would also want a press secretary who could play a 'more explicitly political role' than previously.

While disagreeing about the number of political appointees that might be needed by a future Conservative administration, Major and Ms Gunn, who served as his personal press officer during the 1997 election, were united in their view that advisers could be a divisive influence. Major was convinced that many of the unwelcome stories he faced about rivalry and disputes between ministers had been fuelled by political advisers, just as he felt Blair had been plagued subsequently by similarly mischievous and unsourced speculation. 'I do wonder how many of the ministerial spats and difficulties that suddenly exploded in the media . . . that unbeknown to me I was at terrible loggerheads with someone I was actually having lunch with . . . came from political advisers.' Ms Gunn believed the personal loyalty advisers owed to their ministers was at the root of the problem. 'We knew what was happening before the last election. Whenever Major's ministers were having a bad time of it, they sent their advisers out to bat for them and their job was to seek out political correspondents and brief them. Obviously the advisers tried to defend their ministers' record, but then they inevitably got drawn into pointing a finger of blame at someone else in the cabinet and that was when the damage was done. An adviser's livelihood is tied to a minister, and in order to survive they have to learn how to spread rumours and to find out which journalists can be trusted so they know who to go to when they want to slip out unsourced information to the press.'

Major's inability to stop special advisers gossiping to journalists had evidently made an impact on Blair: it was apparently one of the problems he mentioned at his very first cabinet meeting on 8 May 1997. A leaked account of the discussion was printed in the *Mail on*

Sunday in November 2000, and it disclosed that Blair urged his colleagues to respect the confidentiality of cabinet proceedings. He intended to come down 'very hard' on leaks and unofficial briefings by junior ministers and special advisers. 'There's much too much chatter . . . Special advisers performed a very good service in opposition, but now we are in a very different position. The last government got into great difficulties over special advisers. I don't want to see them talking to the media now we are in government . . . otherwise newspapers will feed off this type of thing.'

Notwithstanding his initial anxieties, Blair doubled the number of political appointees and – with the exception of his well-publicised doubts about the appointment of Charlie Whelan as personal press officer to the Chancellor – most ministers would appear to have been given a free hand in selecting their special advisers. Whenever the government has been challenged by opposition MPs about the justification for establishing seventy-nine posts, ministers have quoted the view of the Neill Committee that political advisers have 'a valuable role to play'. In a debate in July 2000, the parliamentary secretary for the Privy Council Office, Paddy Tipping, repeated Sir Richard Wilson's assertion that it was inconceivable they could 'corrupt and politicise the senior civil service of 3,700 or a civil service of 466,500'. Aside from these standard exhortations and the government's undertaking to respond after the next election to the Neill Committee's recommendation on the introduction of a separate code of conduct, little has been said publicly by ministers about the need to impose greater discipline. However, within the wider Labour movement there has been a general recognition of the damage inflicted on the party by the loose talk of special advisers. As in John Major's day, the chief drawback has been identified as the unbridled loyalty political appointees have shown to their patrons. A career structure that required special advisers to respond to the needs of the party as a whole, rather than the interests of an individual minister, was an option suggested to me by Councillor Ian Greenwood, leader of the Labour group on Bradford Metropolitan District Council.

He kept an eye on the employment prospects for political students and had noticed a significant growth in job opportunities because of the increased recruitment of researchers for MPs following the trebling in Short money and the improved chances of promotion later to special adviser. 'Some way has got to be found to reduce the political instability which arises when so many researchers and advisers are each totally dependent on an individual politician for their jobs. To reduce their own sense of insecurity they feel they have to feed the ego of their MP or minister, and the only way they can demonstrate that is by promoting their boss in the news media. But a news story which might help a minister climb the greasy pole isn't necessarily going to do the government any favours.' Councillor Greenwood thought the bad-tempered conflict between Alastair Campbell and Charlie Whelan illustrated the inbuilt weakness of the system. 'Charlie was working for the No. 2 in British politics and the only way he could make the Chancellor more successful was to make him No. 1, and that meant Charlie had to try to damage Campbell in order to get at Blair – and Charlie still seems to be doing a pretty good job of it at the moment.' Unless some way could be found to persuade the Campbells and Whelans to show more allegiance to the party than to an individual minister, Councillor Greenwood feared Blair stood little chance of stemming the flow of unattributed stories about personality conflicts within his government. 'By appointing even more of them, Blair has fuelled a system which has ended up feeding the frenetic reporting of politics which he complains about. Special advisers are desperate to talk to the media and political journalists want news of personality splits, so we have a situation where they need each other and it's the good name of the Labour government which gets damaged every time.'

Rather than tackle one of the inherent deficiencies of the special advisers' regime by doing what he could to tighten up the rules on attribution, in the hope of halting the growth in unsourced stories, Campbell has continued to berate the news media and condemn the level of political reporting. The *Guardian*'s response has been to urge its political correspondents to improve standards by being more specific when using quotations from unidentified sources. Alan Rusbridger, the editor, announced in July 2000 that he intended to adopt a stricter code on the use of anonymous pejorative quotes because he wanted to give readers a better chance to evaluate their worth. Attributing remarks to 'one MP' or 'a government colleague' was 'so weak as to be meaningless'. Rusbridger conceded that the stricter editorial processes of American broadsheet newspapers, which insist on stories being supported by direct quotations from named individuals, were harder to apply in the 'ruthlessly competitive world of Fleet Street', but he still considered it was time to break some of the worst customs that had become ingrained in British political reporting. He quoted approvingly from the style guide of the *New York Times* when acknowledging that anonymity should not be used as a cloak for politicians and their aides to attack each other: 'The vivid language of direct quotation confers an unfair advantage on a speaker or writer who hides behind the newspaper, and turns of phrase are valueless to a reader who cannot assess the source.'

I admired Rusbridger's determination to demand tighter rules of attribution; yet no other newspaper indicated that it intended to follow the *Guardian*'s example, and unsourced quotations have continued to proliferate in the press. Much of the in-depth reporting of previous years has disappeared from the political pages. A lighter approach with far less direct attribution has become commonplace, and more space is devoted to interviews, sketch writing, diary columns and other personalised reports, which all tend to be less demanding on the reader. Similar trends can be observed in television and radio. There is more live reporting and many of the scripted reports, in which correspondents reflected on the day's events, have been replaced by the instant two-way in which a presenter discusses the latest developments down the line with a reporter on the spot. Increasingly broadcasters have adopted a conversational style that is not so dependent on direct quotations attributed to named individuals.

Because less space and time are being allocated to considered and well-sourced reporting, inaccurate and loosely attributed quotations tend to get repeated by the many commentators, diarists and celebrity columnists who recycle topical news stories for newspaper supplements and magazines. I have every sympathy with politicians who complain when the same inaccuracies are repeated time after time, and Campbell has every justification for criticising journalists who simply reproduce material from other news outlets and make no attempt to check whether the facts and quotations they are using are correct. However, he cannot ignore his own responsibility to ensure that the flow of information from the Prime Minister's office is beyond reproach. I applaud his decision to publish extracts from lobby briefings on the Downing Street website, but I fail to see why the Cabinet Secretary is prepared to allow a service funded by the taxpayer to be so inconsistent and partial in its coverage. By arbitrarily omitting all reference to briefing sessions that he presumably thought had done the Blair government or himself a disservice or that he considered were too political, Campbell has often left journalists without any means of checking quotations attributed either to himself or to any other Downing Street spokesman. The increasingly idiosyncratic use he has made of the website was best illustrated by the erratic service which Downing Street offered Internet users in late December 2000, when no extracts were published for three consecutive briefings that Campbell gave over the space of seven days. All three sessions omitted had dealt with the government's response to controversial remarks by William Hague linking the fall in police morale to the report by Sir William Macpherson into the murder of the black teenager Stephen Lawrence. Campbell spent time at each briefing outlining the reasons why Blair considered the Conservative leader's conduct had been 'desperate' and 'disreputable', but no extracts were published either on the response to Hague or on the other issues that were discussed. Visitors to the website would have formed the impression that there had been no briefings on the days in question.

The absence of entries for these three dates illustrated the difficulties that faced journalists outside the lobby. At the height of the row over the allegedly racist nature of Hague's remarks, quotes attributed directly to Campbell appeared in most national newspapers, yet the website provided no opportunity to verify what the Prime Minister's spokesman had said. At the first of the three briefings, on the morning of Thursday, 14 December, some time was spent discussing Blair's response to the news from Washington that George W. Bush had been confirmed as President-elect following a ruling by the United States Supreme Court. In reply to questions about Hague's speech, and his suggestion that police morale had been damaged when Macpherson found there was 'institutionalised racism' in the Metropolitan Police, Campbell said he presumed this was the Conservative leader's latest bandwagon. Hague could play that game if he wished, but the Prime Minister considered this was 'pretty desperate and pretty disreputable', a form of words used by other ministers who criticised Hague. Campbell appeared to be quoting from a prepared text, and next morning's *Daily Mail* said the 'vitriolic terms' that the Prime Minister's spokesman had used constituted 'unprecedented abuse' from the Downing Street press office. The absence of any mention of the briefing on the website could be explained by the political nature of his remarks. The language used to attack Hague certainly seemed at odds with the undertaking Campbell gave to the select committee that he would follow the advice of Sir Richard Wilson and refrain from using his briefings to attack the Conservatives with 'bricks and bottles'.

At his briefing on the morning of Monday, 18 December, Campbell dealt first with the steps the government proposed to take to assist the 2,000 workers who were to be made redundant when General Motors closed the Vauxhall car factory at Luton. He then responded to an article written by Hague in the *Sunday Telegraph* in which the Tory leader suggested that the lack of sufficient police officers might have been a factor in the murder of a south London schoolboy, Damilola Taylor. Campbell said he considered Hague should have thought 'pretty carefully before diving into ongoing murder investigations'. Political correspondents were also in the press secretary's firing line: 'I think Hague is getting an extraordinarily easy ride from you guys in relation to the use of his "facts".' No mention was made of this briefing on the website, nor was there any reference to the session on the Wednesday, 20 December, after Prime Minister's questions. Blair told MPs he was not accusing Hague of being a 'a racist' but felt he should adopt a policy of 'stop and think'. Later, at the lobby briefing, when several correspondents asked Campbell if Blair agreed with those ministers who had accused Hague of playing the race card, he repeated the answer given by the Prime Minister. He accused some journalists of having consistently misrepresented the Macpherson Report and there were some heated exchanges, but he stood his ground: 'I will use my words, not yours . . . Blair does think

Hague is a serial opportunist . . . Hague has sought to exploit a murder investigation, he has misrepresented the Macpherson Report as being about racism and the police. He has done it deliberately . . . for clearly opportunist reasons which will backfire . . . The Prime Minister used his words, I will use mine . . . You lot can write what you like, you have done it before.'

Even if Campbell had concluded that his three briefings about Hague were too political for the Internet, there no seemed no justification for omitting extracts about the guidance he had given on Blair's welcome for President-elect Bush and the assistance to be offered to redundant Vauxhall car workers. However, as on previous occasions, he had chosen to make no mention on the website of any of the issues that were discussed, and as a result there was no official record of briefings having taken place on those three days.

A missing entry for the afternoon briefing following Prime Minister's questions on 10 January 2001 revealed fresh inconsistencies. At the morning session, Campbell's deputy Godric Smith was asked about the government's failure to meet two of the five commitments listed on the pledge card the Labour Party issued during the 1997 election campaign. Smith said 'significant progress' had been made on all five pledges, and his lengthy response was published on the website. However, no entry appeared for the afternoon briefing taken by Campbell, although he was quoted extensively in the next day's newspapers insisting that three of the pledges had been met. The government was 'about far more than what is on the back of the pledge card', but it had been 'a very effective method of communicating between a political party and the electorate' and Labour would certainly use 'something like that again' at the next election. If Campbell considered his reply was too political to be reproduced, why had the website published the answers about Labour's pledge card given by his civil service deputy? Internet users were offered no explanation for this apparent contradiction. Political correspondents considered Campbell's answers carried the greatest weight, which explained why his words were quoted; but journalists and commentators outside the lobby had no way of checking the accuracy of newspaper reports despite No. 10's undertaking to publish the 'main points' from the daily briefings.

Ministers, Labour MPs, senior civil servants and sympathetic journalists have all praised Campbell's boldness in deciding to publish summaries of his briefings without apparently realising that the service Downing Street has offered on the Internet has been nowhere near as reliable or as objective as they have implied. I can see no reason why the website should not contain a full transcript of all the daily briefings, including those given to lobby correspondents on Sunday newspapers, together with the questions that were asked and the identity of the journalists involved. If sections have been deleted, or an entire briefing omitted, then this should at least be indicated on the relevant page of the website.

My own strongly held preference would be for all briefings to be televised, a move for which I have argued consistently and which has attracted increasing support. In offering what he described as 'a piece of unsolicited advice' in a column he wrote for the *Independent*, the publicist Max Clifford said Campbell needed to come out of the shadows because he had allowed himself to be portrayed as 'some kind of Svengali, a mysterious and unloved manipulator'. Clifford believed that if the Prime Minister's official spokesman could present himself in a warm and relaxed manner, levelled with the public about what he did and admitted his mistakes, he would be able to counter the spin that the newspapers always placed on political stories. 'If Campbell were to become a successful, respected and popular public spokesperson himself, like presidential press secretaries in the United States, he would take a lot of pressure off Tony Blair.' Clifford had clearly based his argument on the belief that Campbell could withstand the pressure of televised briefings and would have the self-discipline to rise above the petty point-scoring that has characterised so many of his encounters with political correspondents. Most of the briefings that have been omitted from the website have involved bad-tempered exchanges with journalists which Campbell was probably only too anxious to avoid publicising on the Internet. He knew that a sanitised extract would bear little relation to the comments attributed to him by the newspapers, and he presumably assumed the safest course was to ensure there was no published record of a briefing having taken place. If his exchanges with the lobby were to be televised, he would have to curb what Max Clifford considered were his 'bullying tactics' and resist the temptation to ridicule reporters as a way of deflecting their enquiries. His temperament would inevitably become a factor in any assessment of his suitability as a public spokesperson, capable of representing Blair on television and radio, and his combative approach might be seen as something of a liability and unlikely to help win public support for the government.

I believe one of the most cogent arguments in favour of televised briefings is that they do impose a strong sense of self-discipline on the spokesperson: viewers and listeners do not take kindly to gratuitous insults to journalists asking straightforward questions, and a press secretary appearing on camera cannot escape responsibility for whatever might have been said by pretending afterwards that the answers were off the record. Perhaps the most important safeguard is that there are few official spokesmen in Whitehall, Washington or elsewhere who would be prepared to mislead the public on a regular basis if they knew their answers were being televised and were likely to remain a matter of public record. When Mike McCurry resigned from his position as White House press secretary in October 1998 in protest at the way he felt he had been used unfairly to perpetuate a deception about President Clinton's sexual relations with Monica Lewinsky, the fear of being caught out by the Washington press corps for giving an untruthful answer had obviously taken its toll; Howard Kurtz, media reporter for the *Washington Post*, thought it was the chore of getting through the daily briefings that left McCurry 'uncomfortable with the stonewaller's role'. After his resignation, McCurry told *Newsnight* that he had no idea that a 'tortured definition of sex' was lurking behind Clinton's denial of sexual relations with Lewinsky, but he recognised that his failure to give enough information in response to legitimate questions had damaged the credibility of presidential briefings. Nevertheless McCurry made a significant break with tradition when he was appointed in agreeing that his White House briefings could be filmed in their entirety, whereas previously only the first five minutes had been on camera. Howard Kurtz said McCurry believed the five-minute rule set the wrong tone for the briefings and encouraged reporters to 'jump on him with their harshest questions' just before the lights went out.

'Without the rule, he had more control over the ebb and flow of the session and he preferred to take his chances with the cameras.'

The skill and patience with which presidential press secretaries handled televised briefings impressed Campbell, who revealed his admiration for McCurry in an interview for *The World This Weekend* in July 1998. Campbell believed McCurry's strength was that he had the qualities that were needed for an exposed position in the public eye. 'When you talk to him you realise he is a decent, straight bloke. So when Mike is talking to people, communicating with journalists, he is being straight with them. You have to stand there in the White House, as I sit in Downing Street, and you have to take questions from pretty able journalists on any issue under the sun and you have to be able to field them in a way which allows you as the spokesman to communicate the things which you should be communicating and make sure you are not misleading people.' When I heard Campbell speaking so positively about McCurry's ability to handle questions on camera I formed the impression that one day he might respond to persuasion and allow televised briefings inside No. 10. However, so far he has stuck rigidly to the approach he outlined to the select committee in June 1998: that ministers should always present the government's case to Parliament and to the public, and that their position would be undermined if a Prime Minister's press secretary appeared on television and radio. After filming *News From No. 10*, Michael Cockerell believed Campbell had become slightly more amenable to making the switch to on-camera briefings, and I would suggest it remains an option that could prove attractive to a Labour government returning to power with a fresh mandate, anxious to shake off a reputation for having been driven by spin.

If Blair is re-elected I hope he will take some bold initiatives to show that Labour is prepared to deal fairly with all sections of the news media. Televised briefings, a full transcript and the abandoning of the separate and exclusive arrangements for political correspondents on Sunday newspapers would all be important stepping-stones towards the level playing field that I think most journalists would appreciate and that would strengthen the government's hand when challenging the upsurge in unattributed quotations and other unsourced stories. I sense that Blair and his close advisers recognise that while their restless urge to manufacture and manipulate the news might have suited New Labour in opposition, the long-term task of governing the country requires a level-headed relationship with the media. Their relentless recycling of policy initiatives and statistics proved completely counterproductive when it was so clearly out of kilter with the level of delivery being experienced by the public. Journalists could hardly be expected to shoulder all the blame for the cynicism Campbell had complained about.

When Blair told the National Federation of Women's Institutes in June 2000 that the government should not be 'fighting for every headline' he signalled the depth of the uncertainty among his colleagues about the communication strategies the government had been pursuing. He adopted the same contrite approach at Labour's annual conference in September when trying to recover from the protests over fuel prices and the criticism from campaigners for a higher old age pension: 'We get the message . . . I am listening.' The shock of losing touch with the public had magnified other failings and misjudgements which could be laid at the leadership's feet, and I was struck by the uncertainty and self-doubt that had gripped the architects of techniques that had become self-defeating and perhaps redundant.

In an eve-of-conference television interview, Peter Mandelson acknowledged that Labour had to be 'altogether more open, straighter' in communicating with the public. He urged his cabinet colleagues to be less arrogant and admit 'making mistakes'. Alastair Campbell was in a similarly reflective mood when he spoke at a House of Commons press gallery lunch in November 2000 and admitted that Labour's remorseless pursuit of favourable headlines had given the impression that the party was consumed by an unabated desire to control the news agenda and put the best possible spin on the government's management of the country. 'In opposition you really haven't got much to do, other than what you say. You are constantly just trying to get your message out through the media. We just hung on to some of the techniques involved a little bit too long.' Campbell also used this speech to revisit the theme he had developed in his contribution to *News From No. 10*: that today, in contrast to his day on the *Mirror*, *Sunday Mirror* and

Today, political journalists had become 'corrosively cynical' and that some of the reporters working at Westminster did not actually like politics. 'No matter how hard I used to kick the Tories, I always liked the vast bulk of politicians . . . I'm not cynical about politics or politicians . . . I believe in calling on the media to remain sceptical but to avoid cynicism.'

Having observed his work as a journalist and party propagandist over a twelve-year period, I can testify personally to Campbell's liking of politics. His knowledge, enthusiasm and irreverent sense of humour have won him admirers across the spectrum, from the former Labour leader Neil Kinnock through to leading Conservatives like Michael Heseltine and the late Alan Clark. My doubts relate to the depth of his commitment to parliamentary accountability and his failure to recognise his own responsibilities as a temporary civil servant in distinguishing between political propaganda and public information. Repeated instances of government decisions being trailed in the news media before being announced in the House of Commons hardly inspire confidence in Downing Street's belief in the primacy of the political process; grubby manoeuvres to rebut the findings of select committees before their reports have been published sit uncomfortably with the Labour Party's traditional support for parliamentary scrutiny; and while lecturing the news media on falling standards in political reporting, Campbell has offered no explanation as to why he has not been prepared to allow public access to a full and fair account of the information he has imparted to journalists during official briefings held on the Prime Minister's behalf.

Perhaps Campbell might care to reflect on the example of the former NATO spokesman, Jamie Shea, who has had the humility to acknowledge publicly the mistakes he made in the course of the seventy-eight briefings he gave during the Kosovo conflict. Shea told the annual conference of the Society of Editors in October 2000 that after his experience he believed public spokesmen had a duty to moderate their rhetoric and to avoid emotive language. He conceded that he should not have drawn alarming historical parallels or used words like genocide. None the less Shea remained totally committed to the principle of televised briefings. 'A public spokesman should be put under pressure, stuck there like a rabbit trapped in the headlights and forced to give an answer . . . and public spokesmen should acknowledge the truth, that we do all make mistakes.'

And when it comes to casting aspersions on the cynicism of others, perhaps Campbell might care to read John Major's speech to Conservative Mainstream in October 2000, or his valedictory contribution to his final Queen's Speech debate the following December. Major, who is standing down at the next election, thought the Blair government, which had taken office with 'a massive majority and an enormous amount of public goodwill', had contributed to the public's growing sense of disillusion with politics and politicians. 'Labour's deliberate attempt to use sleaze against the Conservative Party because of the behaviour of a few MPs was contemptible, it was contemptible to discredit a whole party.' The former Prime Minister feared the public's distaste of politics and distrust of politicians was likely to lead to a turnout at the next general election that would be 'far lower than for any election in modern times'. Government announcements were in the hands of 'one of the most unscrupulous spin machines Britain had ever seen', and when assessing what of 'real worth' they had achieved, he hoped Labour's 'masters of spin' would reflect on their contribution to the growing cynicism of the electorate and recognise that their practice of bypassing the House of Commons when statements were made to the public had been to the 'disbenefit of democracy and the nation at large'.

In preparing for the final countdown to a general election expected in May 2001, Tony Blair gave the impression that he remained genuinely perplexed about how a Prime Minister should relate to the news media. He revealed the depth of his continuing uncertainty in a New Year interview for *Breakfast With Frost*, when he appeared to question the wisdom of having invested so much effort in seeking to engage in a daily battle with the media that the government always had to try to dominate. He seemed trapped by the aggressive regime he had instituted, as if he realised that some of the questionable routines that had been put in place to control the flow of information and to grab the headlines had developed a momentum of their own and were no longer capable of being restrained. Blair spoke to Frost about the challenges he faced if Labour were returned to power:

'I think the biggest single thing I have learned is that you can't please all the people all the time, but in the end it is less important to be liked than to do the job to the best of your ability . . . I believe that I have the right vision for this country . . . I think we've got to make sure if we are successful in that election . . . then we do the right thing for the country and then I worry less about what is, you know, in the day-to-day wash of the newspapers.'

I was struck by the way Blair kept returning to the theme, which he had first raised the previous June when he acknowledged that he should not be 'fighting for every headline'. His misgivings were understandable, because the main thrust of the interview had served to demonstrate his dilemma. Instead of being able to seize the opportunity to look forward to the election, he had found himself being dictated to by the news agenda and forced to clear up another messy affair made worse by an inept attempt to release only minimal information about the party's finances.

The interview with Frost followed a week of damaging publicity surrounding revelations about three £2 million donations to Labour's election fighting fund. Blair had no hesitation in defending the party's increased reliance on wealthy businessmen. He was proud of the fact that businesspeople, who were 'disaffected Conservatives', were prepared to support his party. Nevertheless, Labour had been on the back foot from the moment news of the first donation emerged on the evening of Saturday 30 December 2000 in the first edition of the *Sunday Telegraph*. 'Labour won't name new £2 million donor' was the headline over the front-page splash, which said the cheque had been banked just weeks before the start in mid-February of new regulations requiring political parties to disclose the source of all donations over £5,000. Next morning, before reporting on the generosity of this mystery benefactor for Radio Five Live and *Broadcasting House*, I checked with the party's duty press officer, Jo Murray, and was given the same response as printed by the *Sunday Telegraph*: that Labour was not prepared to give a 'running commentary' on financial donations, and that donors who had given over £5,000 would not be identified until the following autumn, when their names would be listed in the party's annual report, but without revealing the amounts they had donated.

Several influential Labour MPs criticised the secrecy as unnecessary, and there were accusations that the new rules were being bypassed by a government that continued to point the finger at the financing of the Conservative Party. After three days the government finally relented, and at 12 noon on 2 January 2001 Alastair Campbell alerted lobby correspondents to the imminent release of a statement by party headquarters. It revealed that the donation had been made by the publisher Lord Hamlyn, and in this case there appeared to be an innocent explanation for the delay in releasing the information: he had been seriously ill over the New Year holiday and it had taken time to obtain his permission for naming him. Later that week, when it emerged that *The Economist* was about to reveal the identity of two further donors, Labour immediately announced that the party had received a donation of £2 million from the minister for science, Lord Sainsbury, and another from the financier and philanthropist Christopher Ondaatje.

Much of the newspaper coverage of this episode was hostile to Labour, and most reports referred back to the way the party prevaricated in November 1997 before confirming the receipt of a pre-election donation of £1 million from the Formula One motor racing chief, Bernie Ecclestone. To his credit, Campbell had been consistent in urging greater openness about donations, and was now having to pick up the pieces after some inept news management by the party hierarchy – having himself fallen victim to the control freakery that had become so deeply ingrained in the New Labour psyche. Instead of being straightforward and explaining that attempts were being made to get permission to reveal the identity of the latest benefactor, Millbank Tower had chosen to be evasive. Blair would need to worry far less about the 'day-to-day wash of the newspapers' if journalists could trust the information being released in the government's name. Perhaps a promise to maintain fair dealing with the news media should appear on the Labour Party's pledge card for the next parliament.

THE LAST DEADLINE

'I feel such hurt . . . What an incredibly clever, tendentious and distorted piece of writing . . . You have abused trust and friendship, all because you want to make yourself a media star . . . You have done a hatchet job . . . It's pathetic . . . I hope I never have any contact with you ever again.'

Peter Mandelson rebuking Nicholas Jones, 19 July 1993

One of the recurring themes of this book has been my attempt to explore the often inexplicable risks that Tony Blair's colleagues and advisers have been prepared to take in their dealings with the news media. Peter Mandelson's second resignation from the cabinet, in January 2001, after he gave a misleading answer at the start of what became known as the Hinduja passports-for-cash affair, was the culmination of a fast-moving sequence of events that provided the clearest possible illustration of the brazenly evasive behaviour which has so characterised New Labour's relationship with the press, television and radio. The leading players in this tawdry saga were more concerned with defending their own reputations than in ensuring straight dealing with Parliament and the public. After devoting so much of his political career to the task of trying to influence journalists for the benefit of the Labour Party, Mandelson became a victim of the kind of media pressure he had always sought to control. His hurried departure from the government was followed almost immediately by an unexpected fight-back that in turn prompted savage criticism of their former colleague by a succession of cabinet ministers. For almost a week Labour lost control of the news agenda.

This unexpected bout of blood-letting exposed the ruthless streak in New Labour and provided a salutary reminder of the pivotal role played by the Prime Minister's official spokesman. As my narrative has already demonstrated, Alastair Campbell was well established as the dominant figure in determining what was said on the Prime Minister's behalf, exercising total control over the dissemination of news and information about the government's affairs. Mandelson, the arch-manipulator, was still regarded as one of Blair's closest advisers; but his ministerial duties as Secretary of State for Northern Ireland had tended to keep him well away from Downing Street and Millbank Tower. The twists and turns of the peace process were frustrating and time-consuming, requiring constant attention to detail, and while they gave Mandelson another chance to prove himself as a talented and effective administrator, by the same token they gave him little opportunity to concern himself with his former preoccupations of party presentation and media management. His return to ministerial office in October 1999, less than a year after his resignation from the cabinet for failing to disclose a £373,000 home loan from the then Paymaster General, Geoffrey Robinson, was seen as a mark of Blair's generosity towards his trusted confidant, and Mandelson's additional re-appointment the following month as chairman of Labour's general election planning group, which would have responsibility for the day-to-day running of the campaign, showed that his skill as a political strategist was as highly rated as in previous years. Nevertheless, the events of December 1998 had left him in an exposed and vulnerable position should his veracity be called into question again, and despite the prominence of the positions he held, his name was no longer being mentioned by other ministers, their advisers or party officials with the same awe that had formerly attached to it.

I had started to notice that when journalists wrote about the activities of the inner coterie that surrounded the Prime Minister, Mandelson no longer inevitably figured in their reports. Also, while he was usually assumed to have played a part in most of the more underhand examples of media manipulation that were still blemishing the good name of New Labour, in some cases I could find no actual trace of his involvement. The one arena in which he did still loom large was the European debate, where, driven by his passionate support for the European Union and his conviction that Britain should abandon the pound and join the euro, his behaviour frequently breathed new life into his long-standing feud with the Chancellor of the Exchequer, Gordon Brown, and annoyed some of Brown's Euro-sceptic supporters.

My first real insight into Mandelson's gradual exclusion from the innermost counsels of the government was a conversation with him in July 1999, shortly after he cleared the final hurdle towards his political rehabilitation following the home loan scandal. After a six-month inquiry, the House of Commons Select Committee on Standards and Privileges had upheld held two complaints against him: he should have declared Geoffrey Robinson's loan in the register of MPs' interests; and his application for a mortgage from the Britannia Building Society was 'incomplete and inaccurate and he therefore breached the code of conduct for MPs'. However, despite being the first minister to be found in breach of the Nolan Committee's recommendation that the MPs' code of conduct should apply to 'all aspects of public life', he escaped punishment. The final eight words of the select committee's report had given him the lifeline he longed for: 'We recommend that no further action be taken.'

While waiting for the ruling, Mandelson had rarely been seen around Westminster. Whenever reporters standing outside the members' lobby tried to catch his eye as he hurried by on his way to vote, he remained expressionless, looking straight ahead. Those correspondents who dared to tap him on the shoulder got the brush-off: Mandelson no longer talked to the media. My own inquiring glances were always rebuffed, stony-faced, so I never quite plucked up the courage to have a go myself. In due course, contact was re-opened. As soon as he learned that he had escaped without penalty from the select committee inquiry, he telephoned through a statement to the BBC's newsroom: 'Thankfully for me, the matter is now closed.' He would not be giving any interviews, but did agree to pose for a walking shot. After waiting for eight minutes beneath Big Ben, cameraman Giles Wooltorton and I managed to get a five-second shot of Mandelson walking past the camera with a grin on his face – thankfully, just enough to illustrate a couple of sentences on the *One O'Clock News*. A fortnight later, as I walked through central lobby, he beckoned me over to where he was deep in conversation with the *Guardian* columnist Jonathan Freedland, apparently to ask about my latest book, *Sultans of Spin*. 'What have you been saying about me in your book? I suppose you've said I'm finished, all washed up. I know, don't tell me, Alastair Campbell is your pin-up now. You've transferred all your interest to him, haven't you?'

There had been speculation for some days that, Mandelson having escaped with no more than a rebuke from the select committee, Blair was thinking of appointing him Northern Ireland Secretary, in place of Mo Mowlam. I sensed that Mandelson was anxious to be seen making light of his enforced absence from the government and, on seeing me pass by, had jumped at the chance to do so and at the same time make fun of my work. None the less, his aside about Campbell confirmed my suspicion that he was aware that he had lost his crown as chief media strategist, and was envious of the power and influence now being exercised by the Prime Minister's official spokesman. From then on I decided to make a careful note of any further indications of his possible estrangement from the inner circles of the Blair regime; but once he rejoined the government and took up temporary residence in Belfast there were even fewer opportunities to engage him in conversation, and it was not until July 2000, when he addressed a reception in London held by Britain in Europe, that I had another chance to test out my theory.

Two days earlier the government had been embarrassed by the publication in *The Times* and the *Sun* of a leaked memo in which the Prime Minister urged his advisers to prepare a 'thoroughly worked-out strategy' to regain the initiative on 'touchstone issues' where the government was 'perceived as weak' and needed 'two or three eye-catching initiatives'. Blair had sent the memo to his press secretary, Alastair Campbell; his chief of staff, Jonathan Powell; the head of the Downing Street policy unit, David Miliband; his polling adviser, Philip Gould; and two Cabinet Office ministers, Dr Mowlam and Lord Falconer. On the morning of the reception, *The Times* and *Sun* had published another leaked memo, this time written by Gould, which concluded that the 'New Labour brand has been badly contaminated'. The four recipients were Blair, Campbell, Mandelson and the Chancellor, Gordon Brown. While Mandelson was being filmed with a group of Britain in Europe officials, he told me that he considered the speech he was about to deliver provided an opportunity to align himself with those positive supporters of the single currency who believed economics and not politics drove the case for the euro. Hoping to catch him off guard, I asked him whether he thought there would be any more leaked memos in tomorrow's newspapers. I expected him to dismiss my question with a flick of the hand, but instead he looked straight at me and surprised me by his answer: 'The big question is: "Why haven't I received any memos from the Prime Minister?" There was a time when they would all have been sent to me. The question you should ask is: "Why aren't they being sent to me?" ' He then turned on his heel and had gone before I had a chance to follow up his answer or call across to the television crew to record what he was saying. I always found it difficult to decide whether Mandelson was joking; but he had certainly seemed deadly serious, and had clearly been put out to find that he was no longer on Blair's mailing list for memos on ideas for promoting Labour's achievements.

His apparent lack of input into the government's media strategy surfaced again during the party conference in Brighton in September 2000. Interviewed on the *Jonathan Dimbleby* programme at a point when ministers were still in the throes of recovering from the protests over petrol prices, he conceded that government had got the tone wrong and had come across as 'a bit unsympathetic and a little high-handed'. Mandelson urged his cabinet colleagues to be less arrogant. They should put up their hands and admit 'making mistakes', and be 'altogether more open, straighter' in communicating with the public. On meeting him that evening at ITN's conference reception, I told him how impressed I had been to hear him repenting his previous offences. Caught on the hop by this somewhat cheeky opening gambit, Mandelson did a double-take, but then stopped to give me an answer: 'My remarks were unconsidered.' He paused for a moment, and added: 'They were spontaneous, but genuinely meant.'

These fleeting encounters with Mandelson, which had inadvertently provided me with an instructive curtain-raiser for the disaster that would engulf him the following January, had shown up once again what I considered to be two of his most puzzling characteristics. First, he could rarely resist the temptation of responding to journalists who might approach him; and second, if he did engage in conversation, he loved to talk in riddles. His approach to the media reminded me of a moth fluttering dangerously close to a flickering lamp, but always confident of escaping at the last minute should the flame suddenly be blown towards him. I was particularly surprised when he agreed to exchange a few words with me, because I knew how much he distrusted my work. In the now long-distant days when he was Labour's director of communications he had made numerous complaints to BBC managers and editors about my radio and television reports, and during one argument he pointed out, with only the merest hint of menace in his voice, that I should realise he was having lunch next day with John Birt, then the BBC's deputy director general.

Mandelson was never shy of making the most of his contacts at the highest levels in the media world, and especially in broadcasting; indeed, it was the very breadth and closeness of these connections that had made him so indispensable to Kinnock's Labour Party in its fight to re-establish its credentials as an electable political force. His relationship with John Birt in particular was one of long standing and mutual benefit; and when Mandelson had reaped the reward of his fatal penchant for evasiveness in January 2001, Birt was one of the few among his array of influential friends who were visible in his defence. I was able to confirm the persistence of the links between the two men in the spring of 1993, during the controversy which followed the revelation in February that Birt, on being appointed director general of the BBC, had retained his freelance status and had continued having his salary credited to John Birt Productions, paying less tax as a result. The day after the story broke Birt said he would join the staff, and ten days later he apologised to the rest of the BBC's employees. Much of the early news coverage was extremely hostile to Birt. I thought he was probably getting advice from Mandelson, who had known him since he worked as a researcher and then producer on *Weekend World*, the flagship programme of London Weekend Television where Birt was then director of programmes. Mandelson had also worked briefly for the BBC as a part-time adviser. He took up the post after standing down as Labour's director of communications in October 1990 and offered advice on the future of public service broadcasting before being elected Labour MP for Hartlepool in the 1992 general election. So I took careful of note of my conversation with Mandelson on 3 March 1993, three days after the Birt story broke, at a point when support for the director general seemed to be ebbing away and some newspapers were speculating that he might be forced to resign. I had been asking Mandelson what he thought of the more relaxed approach to the news media that had been adopted by the then Labour Party leader, the late John Smith, when suddenly I changed the subject and put him on the spot by asking whether he thought Birt would survive as director general.

Caught off guard, and clearly without quite realising who he was talking to, he said he had written to the director general and had given him some advice. Birt, he said, had made 'a very bad mistake' in not ending his freelance contract immediately and becoming a BBC employee, but he thought people in public life were judged by the way they acted and Birt had responded well. Even before Mandelson had completed his sentence, I could hear that he was regretting having started it. As a relatively new backbench Labour MP, he would not want his role in advising Birt to be publicised. He was clearly anxious that our conversation should go no further, but equally realised he had no control over the use I might make of the information he had volunteered: 'Look, I am telling you this as a friend . . . I think he will survive as director general, oh, easily. I know John was in the process of changing his position but he was overtaken by events. The moment he became director general he should have changed his status. That was a mistake.'

As was perhaps only to be expected, my habit of squirrelling away detailed notes of our conversations inevitably put me on a collision course with Labour's most eminent spin doctor. Four months later, in July 1993, I wrote an article for the *Guardian*'s media page suggesting that Mandelson, who in his days as the Labour Party's director of communications had been so close to Gordon Brown, was increasingly shifting his attention towards advising the shadow Home Secretary, Tony Blair. Mandelson had told me that he thought Blair, who tended to give far fewer interviews than Brown, and who had adopted a less frenetic approach towards promoting himself, had been 'wise to adopt a thoughtful stance'. I concluded that Blair was intent on establishing himself as the 'more reflective half of the Brown-Blair duo'. My article prompted a torrent of abuse and recrimination of a kind that will be recognised by all journalists and politicians who have had to endure a Mandelson dressing-down: 'I feel such hurt . . . What an incredibly clever, tendentious and distorted piece of writing . . . I now realise that every time I speak to you, you write down our conversations . . . You have abused trust and friendship, all because you want to make yourself a media star . . . You have done a hatchet job . . . You have woven one or two facts and embroidered them into a rich tapestry . . . Your analysis is totally spurious . . . It's pathetic . . . I realise you are a different person to what I thought you were, you are entirely calculated . . . I hope I never have any contact with you ever again.' Needless to say, I considered my assessment for the *Guardian* was quite correct: Mandelson was already in the process of switching his allegiance to Blair, well before John Smith's death in May 1994 and the subsequent leadership election.

Outbursts such as these, among his full armoury of tactics in dealing with the news media, made Mandelson numerous enemies among journalists and broadcasters, and once he was a minister after the 1997 general election some reporters, as well as opposition MPs, tracked his every move. Within a year his purchase of a £475,000 house in Notting Hill had caught the attention of some who were on the lookout for danger signs, and the subsequent investigations into how he contrived to afford this prize piece of property were to lead to his first resignation in December 1998, after serving for only five months as Secretary of State for Trade and Industry. By then the seeds of his second downfall had already been sown.

Mandelson's first job in the government, as minister without portfolio in the Cabinet Office, included responsibility for the construction of the Millennium Dome at Greenwich. Fund-raising for the project had proved particularly difficult, and there was considerable satisfaction within the government in February 1998 when two wealthy Indian businessmen, the Hinduja brothers, wrote to Blair and Mandelson promising to become one of the sponsors of the Dome's Faith Zone, to which they subsequently contributed £1 million. Norman Baker, the Liberal Democrat MP for Lewes, was intrigued by their generosity, and in view of all the furore over the Dome's financing he began to table parliamentary questions to determine the extent of the brothers' links with the government and their connections with Mandelson. Although Baker had no way of knowing it, a question he tabled in early December 2000 would start the countdown to Mandelson's second resignation. A holding answer was issued on 18 December, promising a full reply, and when this was finally released on Thursday 18 January 2001 it seemed relatively innocuous on first reading. Baker had asked for information on the representations the Home Office had received from Mandelson and the Minister for Europe, Keith Vaz, relating to applications by G. P. Hinduja and S. P. Hinduja for British citizenship. Barbara Roche, Minister of State at the Home Office, replied by written answer. She said that Vaz had 'made inquiries about when a decision could be expected'; Mandelson had 'made inquiries about how an application for naturalisation might be viewed given the government's wider policy of encouraging citizenship from long-standing residents who fulfilled the criteria, but did not make representations that an application be granted'.

Mrs Roche's reply was spotted by one of the *Observer*'s political correspondents, Gaby Hinsliff, when she checked through the piles of written answers in the House of Commons press gallery. She drew it to the attention of Baker, who at the time was unaware that his question had been answered. An exclusive story that Sunday by three *Observer* reporters, Antony Barnett, Hinsliff and Luke Harding, revealed that Srichand Hinduja had applied for naturalisation after he and his brother Gopichand had agreed to 'bail out' the Faith Zone and that his British passport was issued in 'a third of the time a typical decision takes'. Subsequent parliamentary answers revealed that Srichand made his application in October 1998 and was granted citizenship in March 1999; Gopichand had been granted a British passport in November 1997. The day after publication of Mrs Roche's written answer the three Hinduja brothers, Srichand, Gopichand and Prakash, who were being interrogated by the Indian police on corruption charges over arms supplies, were granted bail but refused permission to leave India. The *Observer*'s story on what it dubbed the 'passports-for-favours' scandal quoted Norman Baker at length. He demanded an inquiry into why the Home Office had agreed to fast-track Srichand Hinduja's application in 1998 when in 1991 he had been refused a British passport. A brief but carefully worded statement that Mandelson issued to the *Observer* became the catalyst for the subsequent dénouement: 'To the limited extent that I was involved in this matter I was always very sensitive to the proprieties. The matter was dealt with by my private secretary. At no time did I support or endorse this application for citizenship.' So Mandelson had been 'involved', but on the final point he was categoric: he had not lobbied on Srichand Hinduja's behalf.

The next key point in the story was Alastair Campbell's 11 a.m. lobby briefing on Monday 22 January. He stressed that as the written answer and Mandelson's statement to the *Observer* had made clear, the secretary of state had refused to support Srichand Hinduja's application, as was 'proper and appropriate'. Two political editors, George Jones of the *Daily Telegraph* and Trevor Kavanagh of the *Sun*, pressed Campbell for more details – upon which, instead of sticking to his original line, he hardened up Mandelson's statement to the *Observer*. The lobby note on the Downing Street website summarised Campbell's reply: 'Mandelson had not got involved in this matter beyond being asked to be involved – which he had refused to do. Instead, he had asked his private secretary to refer the issue to the Home Office.' Mandelson's original statement had been ambiguous about what he termed the 'limited extent' of his involvement; Campbell, by contrast, was adamant in denying any involvement at all, which was an advance on Mandelson's own statement. On previous occasions when correspondents have persisted in challenging Downing Street's line, Campbell has often been more interested in putting down his interrogators than in thinking through his answers, and in the process he has occasionally ended up saying more than he might have liked. I was not present at the briefing that Monday morning, but the summary on the website captured the flavour of the exchanges: 'In answer to repeated questions from the *Telegraph* and *Sun*, the PMOS said journalists could dance around the issue as much as they liked. The facts were as he had already set out.'

Having thrown down the gauntlet, Campbell could hardly expect journalists to ignore his challenge. Once a briefing has finished, Downing Street staff prepare a full account of what was said which is sent round immediately to all government departments; edited extracts from the summary are published on the website. This service is invaluable for ministers who are preparing to answer questions in the House of Commons and who need to know Downing Street's line on controversial issues. Thus armed, Chris Smith, Secretary of State for Culture, Media and Sport, repeated Campbell's guidance almost word-for-word when Norman Baker challenged him to explain why Mandelson had made enquiries on Srichand Hinduja's behalf. Baker suggested the £1 million had been 'a very expensive entry ticket to the Dome', handed over in order to acquire British nationality. Smith replied that Mandelson's private secretary had dealt with the matter. 'That was Mandelson's sole involvement. He had no involvement in endorsing or supporting the application at any stage.' By repeating Campbell's explicit answer at the dispatch box, Smith had left Mandelson and the government no room for manoeuvre.

By now, however, alarm bells were ringing at the Home Office, and echoing in Downing Street. The first journalists knew of the panicked response at No. 10 was Campbell's 11 a.m. briefing on the Tuesday morning. He said he wished to clarify his statement on Monday that Mandelson's 'sole involvement' was his private secretary's call to the Home Office. That was Mandelson's recollection when he was asked by the *Observer*; but his office had subsequently discovered that in June 1998 Mandelson had had a two minute conversation with the then immigration minister, Mike O'Brien. Although Mandelson had no recollection of the call, O'Brien remembered it and the fact that the conversation took place was noted by an official at the Home Office. Jon Smith, political editor of the Press Association, asked if Campbell was correcting the answer he had given on Monday in which he had said that Mandelson had not been involved personally. 'Yes, that is correct. A call did take place. You must get Norman Baker to ask about this again, as I am sure he will.'

Campbell's correction, and his revelation that Mandelson had spoken to O'Brien on Hinduja's behalf, was headline news. A story that most papers had covered that morning on their inside pages, and that had barely been mentioned on television and radio, was about to lead the lunchtime news bulletins. Mandelson was anxious to give his side of the story, and he telephoned through an immediate off-the-record response. He considered his enemies in Parliament and the news media were 'trying to reconjure' his 1998 resignation. All he had done, as a matter of courtesy, was try to find out whether an application by Hinduja would be affected by the change in immigration policy. He had asked his private office to approach the Home Office. The answer Campbell had given at the Monday lobby briefing had 'unwittingly' stretched the meaning of his statement to the *Observer* to say there had been no involvement, and that he had not spoken to O'Brien, when the Home Office was now saying that he had.

Mandelson's convoluted guidance was followed by an afternoon lobby briefing given by Campbell's deputy, Godric Smith, who had to withstand forty minutes of aggressive questioning. He insisted all questions from the media had been answered in good faith: 'Mandelson has done nothing wrong or improper. The idea that something has been dragged out of us is wrong. Downing Street and Mandelson have been honest and upfront in what we have said. We volunteered the information about the phone call.' Smith said it was decided to issue the clarification after discussions on Monday night between Mandelson, O'Brien and Downing Street. By now the lobby was in full pursuit. Trevor Kavanagh asked whether the Prime Minister thought Mandelson had 'lied through his teeth'. Another correspondent enquired whether Mandelson had offered to resign. Smith found it hard going: 'The Prime Minister's view is that Mandelson is a very talented minister . . . He has done nothing wrong or improper.' Although Smith relayed Blair's apparent show of support for his embattled secretary of state, events had apparently taken a turn for the worse. Late that afternoon Mandelson must have realised his job was on the line; he put himself forward immediately for a series of television interviews and, in a desperate attempt to clear his name, contradicted Downing Street's version of events. 'I made a statement in response to the *Observer*'s inquiry. "Had I been involved?" Yes, I had. The information was already in the public domain in a parliamentary answer. I made clear the nature of that involvement . . . There is no question of me forgetting about anything. Nobody asked me about a phone call on Saturday, Sunday or Monday. Nobody asked me those questions.'

In his rush to defend himself on television, Mandelson had made another fatal error: he had failed again to take the precaution of ensuring that his story married up with the account being put out by Downing Street. In stating so categorically that he had not taken part in any discussion that weekend about the disputed telephone conversation, Mandelson had placed himself on a collision course with Campbell. Next morning's newspapers made grim reading: 'Mandy told a porky' was the *Sun*'s banner headline. On an inside page, Kavanagh claimed Mandelson was a natural born liar: 'Deceit is second nature to him – a tried and trusted weapon in his political armoury.' *The Daily Mail*'s front page spared no punches: 'How many more lies Mr Mandelson?' Still, although most of the leader writers considered Mandelson was unfit for high office, there was no widespread clamour for him to be sacked, and political correspondents arriving for the morning lobby briefing were surprised by the speed with which the drama began to unfold. Campbell was late. One of the BBC's political correspondents, Paul Rowley, told me what happened:

'Campbell walked in at 11.16 a.m. The room was packed. There were fifty-one journalists waiting for the briefing. Campbell told us Blair and Mandelson were at a meeting which had been going on for about twenty minutes. It had been called at the Prime Minister's request to establish the facts. Blair would be answering questions in the Commons that afternoon and there were "a number of points of fact he feels the need to pin down". Campbell was very precise in what he said: "There are a number of difficulties and contradictions over the last few days." Campbell didn't answer when one reporter asked if Mandelson had been lying but he told us what happened: "Yes, I was in contact with Mandelson over the weekend when the story broke . . . Peter was clear with me that he didn't have a recollection of that telephone conversation with Mike O'Brien, as I told you on Monday . . . What Chris Smith said in the Commons on Monday was the line deployed here, and that was wrong." Someone asked if Mandelson would be in a job at the end of the day but Campbell refused to reply.'

After ten minutes most of the reporters were itching to leave the briefing room so they could switch on their mobile phones and report back to their newsrooms. There was no doubt about their interpretation of the guidance they had been given by Blair's official spokesman: Mandelson had misled Downing Street and was on the point of resigning or being sacked. Campbell, too, was in no mood to draw out the session, indicating that he was anxious to return to Blair's meeting with Mandelson. After he undertook to give another briefing, Catherine MacLeod, political editor of the *Glasgow Herald* and the newly elected chair of the lobby, said it was obvious Campbell should rejoin the Prime Minister and the journalists made a hasty exit, not realising they faced a two-hour wait before they would discover the outcome of the Downing Street meeting. 'PM calls in Mandelson' was the front-page headline on the *Evening Standard*'s late-morning edition, which said the Northern Ireland Secretary's future 'hung in the balance'. The lunchtime television news bulletins and *The World At One* had been off the air for only a few minutes when Mandelson finally walked out of No. 10 to announce his resignation to waiting reporters. He admitted giving misleading information: 'I do not accept in any way that I have acted improperly . . . I do accept, however, that when my office spoke to a Sunday newspaper at the weekend, I should have been clear that it was me personally, not my official, who spoke to the Home Office minister. As a result of that reply, incorrect information was given to the House by the Culture Secretary and to the press by the Prime Minister's official spokesman. I accept responsibility for that.' Mandelson said there had been another factor that had influenced his decision to tell the Prime Minister he wished to leave the government. 'As a reading of today's newspapers shows all too graphically, there must be more to politics than the constant media pressure and exposure that has dogged me over the last five or so years. I want to remove myself from the countless stories of controversy, of feuds, of divisions and all the rest, all the other stories that have surrounded me. I want in other words to lead a more normal life, both in politics and in the future outside.'

Still Mandelson had a surprise in store for the news media. Although the lunchtime news bulletins had reported that the Minister of State for Northern Ireland, Adam Ingram, would be at the dispatch box that afternoon, Mandelson said Blair had asked him to answer Northern Ireland questions at 2.30 p.m. before finally resigning from the government. In his first answer to MPs,

Mandelson said that playing a part in the Northern Ireland peace process had been the 'greatest privilege' of his political life. He praised the Royal Ulster Constabulary for embracing change with resilience and professionalism. Norman Godman was the first Labour MP to pay tribute to the Secretary of State's work, noting that his departure would be viewed with 'deep dismay and regret'. David Trimble, the Ulster Unionists' leader, thanked Mandelson for what he had done. By agreeing to take a final session of questions and using it to say his farewells to Northern Ireland MPs and other colleagues in the province, Mandelson had got round the potentially embarrassing problem of having to retreat to the back benches in order to make a resignation statement. Had he chosen to make a formal statement, MPs would have refrained from making any comment; by tradition, a resigning minister is heard in silence. But as Mandelson had sidestepped that option and bowed out at the dispatch box, William Hague had a free hand to respond during the following thirty-minute session of Prime Minister's questions.

Campbell had told journalists that the reason Blair had called Mandelson to Downing Street that morning was in order to establish the facts about the passport application before facing the House that afternoon, and Blair must have feared the worst. In his first answer he paid the 'warmest possible tribute' to a secretary of state who had made 'tireless efforts' to secure peace in Northern Ireland and who had shown 'personal courage and sense of duty' in responding to questions before departing the government. Blair accepted that the reply issued by Mandelson's office to the *Observer* was 'misleading and resulted in the House and lobby being misled'. He had asked the former Treasury Solicitor, Sir Anthony Hammond, to review Srichand Hinduja's application for naturalisation to ensure that it had been 'dealt with properly in all respects'. Hague had no intention of continuing the pleasantries. By sacking Mandelson for 'the same offence in twenty-five months', he asserted, Blair had shown that his 'career-long dependency on Mandelson had been a monumental error of judgement'. Hague recognised that Mandelson had been 'at the heart of the entire New Labour project', but re-appointing a disgraced minister ten months after his first resignation was a demonstration of Blair's arrogance. 'It was Mandelson who picked the Prime Minister out; Mandelson who briefed the press for him; Mandelson who stabbed the Chancellor in the back for him; Mandelson who spun all of his campaigns for him.'

Blair rebuked Hague for failing to 'behave graciously' after the resignation of a secretary of state who had made an enormous contribution. 'Indeed, it is not an exaggeration to say that I doubt whether the process in Northern Ireland would have been sustained so well but for his commitment . . . I also believe he is a bigger man than many of his critics . . . I honestly believe that, in the broad sweep of history, his contribution to the process will be far greater than what has happened in the past twenty-four hours, tragic though it is.' Hague seized on Blair's answer for another onslaught: 'This is not about the broad sweep of history; it is about the conduct of the government – the disgraceful conduct of the government. Has this not told us everything we need to know, not about Mandelson, but about the way in which the government do their business? The Prime Minister said that they would be purer than pure and, as with every other pledge, he has failed to deliver . . . In a government where standards of truth, honesty and integrity have taken second place to spin and smear, is he not truly the first among equals?'

At a lobby briefing immediately after question time, Campbell said that although Blair had asked Sir Anthony Hammond to 'establish what approaches were made to the Home Office in 1998 in connection with the possibility of an application for naturalisation by S. P. Hinduja', the Prime Minister had looked at the relevant papers and was satisfied the matter had been 'handled properly and according to the relevant and appropriate criteria'. When asked if Mandelson had given an explanation for having 'lied', Campbell said he had no intention of going into the detail of conversations that took place in the Prime Minister's office. Blair, in 'a focused way', had been seeking to get to the bottom of the facts and it was clear the facts that had been made available had 'not been consistent'. Mandelson had acknowledged that what had happened was 'not acceptable' and that the account he had given had been 'misleading'. Campbell said he had spoken to Mandelson that weekend but admitted he had not 'felt the need' to ask Mandelson whether he had in fact 'spoken to anybody' in the government about Hinduja's application. Campbell had relied on the statement given to the *Observer*, and it was an official in the Home Office who had alerted him on Monday to the existence of a note about Mandelson's call to Mike O'Brien. Campbell denied there had been 'some terrible row' between himself and Mandelson. They had been friends for many years and their friendship would continue. Campbell assumed Mandelson would now step down from the chairmanship of the team planning Labour's general election campaign. 'I got the very strong impression from Peter today that after this he is thinking about his long-term position . . . I think Peter is clearly looking to wind down his political activity.'

'Goodbye and good riddance' was the front-page headline next morning in the *Sun*, which said Mandelson's 'graceless departure' was an insult to the British press and people. 'He is out on his ear again because he is a lying, manipulative, oily, two-faced, nasty piece of work who should never have been allowed near the government in the first place.' The *Daily Mail* devoted a full page to what it headlined the 'deadly aim of Downing Street assassin' Alastair Campbell, who had 'executed' Mandelson's departure after being misled in the passports-for-favours affair. 'Never has the end of a ministerial career been so ruthlessly signposted – making Campbell the most influential unelected figure in Britain.' Mandelson's failure to be frank with Campbell was said by *The Times* to have been the spark that led to 'an astonishing breakdown of trust' between two of Blair's closest advisers. Siôn Simon, writing in the *Daily Telegraph*, said that on the basis of his experience of working for Labour in the 1992 and 1997 elections, he thought Mandelson's departure would leave a big hole in the party's campaign machine. Simon did not agree with those commentators who thought Campbell's power was 'more over weening than ever'. The reason he was so powerful was because he had become indistinguishable from Blair. 'That's why it is misguided to perceive his influence as sinister. He is neither manipulating Blair, nor even doing his bidding; he is Blair. That is why Mandelson had to go, and it is a phenomenon unaffected by his departure.'

Two of Mandelson's former special advisers chipped in with their assessments of his downfall. Derek Draper, who had been the first parliamentary assistant for the newly elected Hartlepool MP, said he had been warned by his previous boss, the agriculture minister Nick

Brown, that Mandelson would eventually 'implode' because he was 'a political genius tainted with political idiocy'. Draper, writing in the *Daily Mail*, said self-indulgence had triggered Mandelson's self-destruction. 'His insatiable desire to climb the social ladder was almost as great as his desire to climb the greasy pole. He loved mixing with rich, glamorous, exotic people. He seems to go ga-ga when he has anything to do with them.' Benjamin Wegg-Prosser, Mandelson's special adviser from 1995 until his 1998 resignation, said the secretary of state had rung him at 6.45 a.m. on the morning he was called to Downing Street. Mandelson was 'remarkably upbeat' and the 'idea of resignation never arose' in their conversation. 'Peter was annoyed by the *Observer* story, though not unduly concerned . . . I do not believe he deliberately lied to the press; he provided an answer that was at best economical and at worst evasive.' Wegg-Prosser's conclusion was that Mandelson was trying to answer a difficult question in a way that reflected positively on him, but came unstuck. He had been asked constantly why a man in Mandelson's position, with 'precious little political capital', would take a chance like that. 'The answer is simply that Peter is a born gambler. That's why he was able to change the Labour Party, and also why he was never going to survive at the top for long.'

A common theme in much of the damning newspaper coverage of the episode was the firm view that Mandelson should not be allowed to have any significant role in running Labour's election campaign. Geoff Hoon, the Secretary of State for Defence, told *Today* that the Labour Party agreed that this would unacceptable, but he personally thought Mandelson would probably want to play some part in the campaign, 'if only knocking on doors and delivering leaflets'. In fact, at the morning lobby briefing, Alastair Campbell signalled that Mandelson had already been stripped of his position chairing the campaign team: he would perform nothing like the role that had been envisaged. Campbell also understood the former minister was still reflecting on whether to seek re-election in Hartlepool. 'That is another decision he is going to have to take . . . I am not sure he has addressed that . . . I think Peter is making it pretty clear, as he says, he is removing himself from the political scene.'

On this point, the guidance Campbell gave was already out of date: the Prime Minister's official spokesman had been upstaged by an exclusive story to be printed that afternoon by the *Hartlepool Mail*. At ten o'clock the previous evening the paper's editor, Harry Blackwood, had taken an unexpected call that dashed any hopes in the party hierarchy that the disgraced minister might withdraw entirely from politics. 'I was watching Peter Mandelson's resignation on the television news when I found it was him, on the telephone, ringing in for a chat . . . A voice said, "Hello, Harry, it's Peter. How are you?" I said, "I should be asking that question of you." Mandelson said, "I'm fine. I am very resilient. I have been here before" . . . He said to me: "I'm going to concentrate on being a good constituency MP. I intend to fight for Hartlepool and its people." Mandelson told me it was not a difficult decision to make.'

Campbell used the weekly meeting of the cabinet that morning to try to draw a line under Mandelson's resignation. Ministers discussed a range of policy initiatives that he said would be announced during the following month and would show that Labour was delivering on its manifesto. 'Yesterday was yesterday, today is today,' he said. But media interest in the repercussions of Mandelson's ejection was not to be so easily redirected. Photographers and television crews focused their attention on the arrival at No. 10 of Dr John Reid, who had been appointed the new Secretary of State for Northern Ireland. Dr Reid's position as Secretary of State for Scotland was taken by a newcomer to the cabinet, Helen Liddell, formerly energy minister. Photographs of ministers coming and going in Downing Street made front-page news because they all seemed so cheerful, despite the disaster that had engulfed their former colleague. 'We've had a very good cabinet today,' said a grinning John Prescott as he walked out of No. 10. 'Cabinet ministers are united in grief' was the *Independent*'s irreverent headline over a front-page display of pictures showing ministers smiling for the cameras.

Mandelson's resignation had inevitably put the spotlight on the Minister for Europe, Keith Vaz, and much of the newspaper coverage concentrated on exploring his role in making enquiries over Srichand Hinduja's application for British citizenship. 'Passport scandal may claim second minister' was the front-page headline in the *Daily Express*. Answering reporters' questions outside India House, on his way to a reception, Vaz insisted he was 'very confident' about the outcome of the inquiry. He refused to answer questions about the representations he had made on the behalf of the two Hinduja brothers, but was perfectly happy for Sir Anthony Hammond to publish the letters he had written to the Home Office. Vaz detected an unpleasant undertone in the way newspapers were reporting the story. 'You have to remember that the Asian community is a very vibrant, very effective part of our country. The references to the origins of people I think is regrettable, very regrettable, and I hope you won't continue doing so.' Blair, on a visit to his constituency, gave strong support to his embattled minister. 'I can't see anything wrong in him making representations on behalf of the Asian community . . . Having had a look at the papers, I can't see anything wrong.' Blair was equally suspicious of the motives of journalists and thought the coverage was all too predictable once the news media got into 'one of these feeding frenzies'.

Two days had elapsed since Mandelson's resignation, and Blair must have realised only too well that the events of the week would be trawled over again in great detail by the Sunday newspapers. Conflicting accounts of the tortured discussions within the government, over both the drafting of the original written answer and the events that led up to the lobby briefing the previous Monday morning and Chris Smith's reply in the House of Commons that afternoon, had raised many more questions than they had answered. I sensed that the separate lobby briefing that Friday lunchtime for the Sunday political correspondents might well provide another development in the story, and I was slightly amused when the announcement that the briefing was about to take place was relayed on the loudspeaker at the BBC's offices in Millbank; the telephone operator in the press gallery was unaware of the Westminster demarcation line and did not realise that she was announcing the timing of an exclusive gathering that broadcasters were not allowed to attend. On their return to the press gallery the Sunday journalists looked particularly pleased with themselves. They had obviously been told something of significance. All they would reveal was that the briefing had been given by Campbell himself, and not by his deputy Godric Smith.

The last minister who had refused to go quietly after resigning was the Minister for Welfare Reform, Frank Field, who left the government when Harriet Harman was sacked in the July 1998 reshuffle. In order to limit the impact of Field's subsequent attack on the government for failing to persist with his welfare reforms, Campbell had moved in for the kill at an exclusive briefing for the weekend papers. He told the Sunday lobby that Field's talents were 'not best suited to running a government department' and that his proposals 'never took the form of policy capable of being implemented by the government'. Campbell knew precisely what he was doing: he had given Downing Street's stamp of approval to Field's denigration, and had encouraged every unattributable briefer who wanted to trash the former minister to have a go. On seeing the smiles of smug satisfaction on the faces of the Sunday correspondents that Friday afternoon I wondered what was afoot this time. Did Campbell suspect that Mandelson intended to come out fighting that weekend? Was Downing Street determined to get its retaliation in first? Was Campbell preparing to open the floodgates for the character assassination of his friend of such long standing? Late on Saturday evening, the front-page headline on the first edition of the *Sunday Times* provided the first part of the answer: 'Mandelson: I was forced out and now I am fighting back.' In a long, rambling and incoherent article, spread over two pages, the former minister set out to clear his name. The headline said it all: 'I never lied – Downing Street sentenced me to commit political suicide without a fair trial.'

Mandelson said it was just before Christmas when he discovered that Norman Baker, who had been pursuing him 'relentlessly', had tabled a parliamentary question about his involvement in Srichand Hinduja's attempt to be granted naturalisation. He was reluctant to agree to an answer that could be used 'mischievously to misrepresent' his role, and he realised subsequently that he should have got a grip of the facts in early January. A week before his resignation he took a phone call from the Home Secretary, Jack Straw, asking to discuss the drafting of a parliamentary reply. 'Jack said I had had a brief conversation in 1998 with Mike O'Brien, and the answer had been drafted accordingly . . . I should have registered Jack's reference to Mike's phone call, but I did not.' Mandelson said he heard no more until he took a call on his mobile phone the previous Saturday morning while walking around the museum of Asiatic art in Paris. His office had alerted him to an enquiry from the *Observer* about the written answer. 'I dictated a comment, repeating that no representation had been made by me, that I had given no support or endorsement to any passport application, and that the enquiry made of the Home Office was handled by my private office.'

On returning to London next day he was phoned by Campbell. 'I told him the *Observer* story amounted to nothing, that I had given a quote and that No. 10 could use that in response to further press enquiries . . . It wasn't until Monday evening . . . that alarm bells began to ring. Based on his conversations with me, Campbell had said to journalists earlier that day that I had had no personal involvement whatsoever in the 1998 naturalisation inquiry; but Mike O'Brien had contacted him to point out the personal conversation he remembered me having with him that year. I trust Mike and I am sure he acted on the basis of his recollection . . . I agreed that a correction must be made at the following morning's lobby briefing.' Mandelson said that on the Tuesday morning, following the fresh lobby briefing, he was concerned that the story was suddenly being driven to the top of the news agenda. At 4.30 p.m. he was told the story was 'really taking off', and after a quick discussion with Campbell he decided to deal with it himself by giving a series of television interviews. He was annoyed that the suggestion he could not recall his contact with O'Brien was being presented as a convenient lapse of memory. 'I responded to the interviewer that "I didn't forget anything." By this I meant that I didn't deliberately forget to mention it, rather than that I didn't actually recall it.' Mandelson admitted that, in giving these interviews, he had broken his own cardinal rule: 'If in doubt, say nowt.' It was true that he had not originally mentioned to Campbell any conversation with O'Brien, even though Straw had referred to it. 'This was not due to any desire to mislead Alastair but because my dominant recollection continued to be that my private office had handled the original enquiry.'

Mandelson said he woke on the Wednesday morning to 'a shrieking media lynch mob', some whom were labelling him a liar. 'I am not a liar. I did not lie. What I did do was make the mistake of speaking out before establishing all the facts and of rushing into last-minute interviews. This relatively trivial error was turned into a huge misjudgement that led to my resignation.' When he saw the Prime Minister later that morning he was told there was to be an independent inquiry. 'Already the media pressure was mounting, the 11 o'clock press lobby was assembling and a decision from me was required. For the first time, and I hope the last time, in my life, the fight suddenly went out of me. I felt isolated. I knew I hadn't done anything wrong, but I had no time to prove it. I agreed to resign and the Prime Minister – understandably, given the presentation of the facts – did not try to dissuade me. I should have fought for time to allow a fuller examination of the facts.' Mandelson said the following Friday his former assistant private secretary told him that she had a clear recollection of what happened in 1998 and had substantiated his version of events. 'I felt a great surge of relief . . . I decided there and then to start fighting back.'

Mandelson had monopolised the *Sunday Times* with his fightback; but the other front pages were covered with the results of Alastair Campbell's Friday lobby briefing: lurid headlines about the Prime Minister's official spokesman questioning the former minister's state of mind. 'No. 10 says Mandy is a nervous wreck' was the *Sunday People's* headline, over a report that Campbell had told journalists that Mandelson had been 'slightly detached' and 'not as engaged as he normally' was when responding to Downing Street's enquiries about the passport application. In branding the disgraced minister 'an emotional wreck', Downing Street was 'effectively signing his political death warrant'. 'Has Mandy gone mad?' was the banner headline across two pages of the *News of the World*, which reported that Blair's closest adviser claimed Mandelson's resignation was 'prompted by a serious deterioration in his mental health'. Ian Kirby, the paper's political editor, claimed that in the clearest sign yet that the row with the former minister was escalating sharply, No. 10 had said Mandelson's career was 'in tatters' and questioned his state of mind. Kirby quoted Campbell's description of Mandelson's responses: 'In my conversations with him he was curiously detached. He is normally someone who is very focused with attention to detail. I felt this was not normal.' The *Mail on Sunday* said Downing Street had 'twisted the knife' in Mandelson by not only questioning his 'mental condition' but comparing his downfall to that of the former Secretary of

State for Wales, Ron Davies, who resigned in October 1998 after what he said was 'a moment of madness' on Clapham Common.

Simon Walters, the *Mail on Sunday*'s political editor, gave a detailed account of what the Sunday papers had been told that Friday: 'In an extraordinary outburst No. 10 press secretary Alastair Campbell claimed the former Ulster Secretary had been "slightly detached" even before the row over his links with the Hinduja brothers erupted . . . There were aspects of Mandelson's conduct "that Peter can't explain to himself" . . . Asked if Mandelson's state of mind was similar to that of Davies, who quit after failing to explain how he came to be robbed by a man he met at a gay pick-up spot on Clapham Common three years ago, Campbell replied: "I think it was." '

Once alerted on Saturday evening to the sensational headlines appearing in the first editions of the Sunday papers, Campbell issued a statement to the Press Association insisting that he had been misrepresented and that the reports were further evidence of 'the current media frenzy'. He said Friday's briefing had lasted for over an hour. He had set out the facts about Mandelson's resignation and acknowledged that there were parts of this episode that were difficult to explain and understand. 'I do not deny saying the words attributed to me, but that has not prevented their misrepresentation . . . I said that he was "curiously detached", by which I meant, as I explained, that he did not see the *Observer* story as a great problem, that he was not focused on the detail . . . To present that as an attack on his state of mind, let alone a knifing, is absurd . . . The only references to Ron Davies during the briefing came from journalists and the only assertion being put to me that I agreed with was that there were some elements of the past week that I could not fully explain, as was the case then.' Campbell said the claim that he and Mandelson were 'somehow at war' was undermined by the fact that when newspapers carrying these headlines hit the streets on Saturday night, Mandelson was at his home in north London attending a family birthday party. Whatever the difficulties of the previous week, 'he was, is and will continue to be a friend'.

Campbell's attempt to disclaim responsibility for the interpretation placed on his briefing itself provided a fresh twist to the Mandelson story and attracted considerable comment. I considered he had been as ruthless as he was in July 1998 when paving the way for the denigration of Frank Field. Campbell knew from his own time as a political editor that it was most unusual for a Downing Street press secretary to make highly personal references about a prime minister's close colleagues. His use of the phrases 'slightly detached' and 'curiously detached' needed no decoding for political journalists. In May 1986 Margaret Thatcher's press secretary, Bernard Ingham, undermined the then Leader of the House, John Biffen, by describing him as 'a semi-detached member of the cabinet'. Ingham was widely condemned at the time by politicians and commentators alike for having used a lobby briefing to attack an elected politician. By using the word 'detached' twice in his own briefing, Campbell had provided a highly charged quote for the correspondents and given any minister or Labour MP who might be interviewed that weekend on television or radio the green light to attack Mandelson's account of the events that led up to his resignation.

I also considered that Campbell's action in spending over an hour in an exclusive conversation with Sunday journalists, offering his version of Mandelson's downfall, demonstrated his readiness to engage in cynical manipulation of the news media. He had said time and again that he distrusted the Sunday lobby and, at a briefing the previous day, he had criticised the reporting of Mandelson's resignation, calling much of it 'complete garbage' and 'so fictitious as to be not worth reading'. None the less, here he was, talking freely and at length about Mandelson's conduct, knowing that he was feeding the Sunday papers with quotes that were ambiguous and obviously open to misrepresentation and lent themselves to sensational headlines. There could hardly have been a clearer example of the double standards that have become the hallmark of New Labour. In his constituency that Friday morning the Prime Minister had condemned the reporting of Mandelson's resignation as a media feeding frenzy; yet, at a briefing that lunchtime, his official spokesman was doing his bit to breathe fresh life into the story.

Journalists had been told repeatedly that the government was anxious to avoid prejudicing the outcome of Sir Anthony Hammond's inquiry and that the media should await his report; the

Downing Street press secretary, it seemed, was bound by no such constraint. Campbell knew full well that he was talking to a small, self-contained group of journalists; no broadcasters or news agency reporters were present; and, as it was not one of the regular twice-daily briefings, no trace of his guidance would appear on the Downing Street website. In my view, both his Friday briefing and the short session on Wednesday morning, at which he announced that Blair had asked Mandelson to see him in No. 10, should have been televised. Both briefings were key moments in the unfolding drama and if, in his position as a temporary civil servant, Campbell was prepared to make statements on behalf of the Prime Minister about the fate of a cabinet minister, he should have done so in a manner that was open and accountable. His long-standing argument that briefings could not be recorded or televised because they might pre-empt proceedings in the House of Commons had no relevance on this occasion. Here was an unelected public servant making personal and highly contentious remarks about the conduct of a secretary of state in a way that could not be accurately or independently verified.

Several of the correspondents who belonged to the Sunday lobby stood by the stories they had written. Colin Brown, political editor of the *Independent on Sunday*, who had described Campbell's 'extraordinary private briefing' as 'a damage limitation exercise' by the government, told *Broadcasting House* that he had a clear shorthand note of the proceedings. 'At one point Campbell went off the record when talking about Mandelson's handling of his personal affairs . . . The word "detached" has a special resonance at Westminster. It is not a word you would use lightly . . . What Campbell was doing was saying in effect that Mandelson was no longer a key figure and Labour would move on without him.' Kamal Ahmed, political editor of the *Observer*, defended the assertion in his report that by using the words 'unfocused' and 'detached' Campbell had suggested that Mandelson had 'a problem with his state of mind'. In a follow-up article for the *Guardian*, Ahmed said the phrase 'slightly detached' had the same ring of longevity as 'psychological flaws' or 'moment of madness', and did seem to sum up the mood of the moment.

He described the scene in the Downing Street briefing room at 1.30 p.m. that Friday lunchtime: 'Campbell was ten minutes late, clasping

THE LAST DEADLINE / 263

as usual a Burnley FC mug of tea . . . He had obviously come prepared for a lengthy discussion because after each question he gave long and frank answers – so long, in fact, that he had to send out for another cup of tea . . . There was an implication throughout the briefing that Mandelson had not been focusing on the political issues in the way that he usually would . . . Campbell said he had noticed it for some time . . . Campbell is not someone who just breezes into meetings and says the first thing that comes into his head. He chooses his words carefully.' Michael Prescott, political editor of the *Sunday Times*, who claimed the purpose of the Downing Street briefing had been to 'destroy Mandelson once and for all', told BBC television news that the journalists did not have to force lines like 'slightly detached' out of Campbell. 'This was absolutely volunteered by the man and we can all wonder about his motivation.'

By issuing his Saturday evening statement confirming that he had used the phrase 'curiously detached', Campbell had, as I suspected, gone even further in giving ministers the green light to wade in behind him in and rubbish the credibility of Mandelson's fight-back in the *Sunday Times*. Clare Short, the Secretary of State for International Development, told *The World This Weekend* that Mandelson had resigned because he had problems with the truth. 'It is saying that you didn't ring up when you did . . . He wasn't accurate, didn't speak the truth, let himself down and the government . . . He is one politician. There is a world out there . . . Peter Mandelson is over.' The Home Secretary, Jack Straw, who was interviewed on the *Jonathan Dimbleby* programme, added his voice to the combined assault on a former cabinet colleague: 'There is no doubt by his own admission that he told an untruth . . . I am personally sad. I regard Peter as a very good colleague and minister but if you depart from the standards which Parliament and the public expect, resignation is inevitable . . . The answer that was given by Barbara Roche, but with my full approval, was as accurate as we thought it was. So by defini-tion, all of us were satisfied on the evidence before us that the conversation had taken place.' By being so forthright in denouncing Mandelson, Straw drew attention to his own role in the lead-up to Blair's decision to confront the Northern Ireland Secretary. 'Straw the Destroyer' was the *Daily Mail*'s headline over a report which said the

Home Secretary's telephone calls to Mandelson and Blair had torpedoed his cabinet colleague and cut him adrift. 'Mandelson: now the knives go in' was the front-page headline in the *Daily Telegraph*, which said Campbell had denied engaging in 'smear tactics' at his Friday lobby briefing.

Despite having contributed to the weekend's news coverage in such a calculated and provocative way, at the Monday morning lobby briefing Campbell laid on a bravura performance. His hands were clean; he was not responsible for every feeding frenzy the news media whipped up and wished to keep going. Blair wanted Sir Anthony Hammond to get on with his inquiry, and although that might be inconvenient for journalists, it was a common-sense way to proceed. 'You may not want to move on but the government has a lot to do . . . I don't intend to get into a position where, when a line appears here or there in a newspaper, we have to suspend the business of government.' Campbell denied that either Jack Straw or Clare Short had put the boot in against Mandelson, and he insisted he had no reason to reproach himself for his Friday briefing. 'I am afraid, if you had really had as much experience as I have of the Sunday press . . . This briefing was not a secret. There is no mystery about the words. I used them. The question is what interpretation you put on them.' At this point Campbell dismissed further enquiries, saying he was not going to answer any further questions about the 'process' of briefing the news media. I had heard Campbell take this line time and again, always using the same escape route; by refusing to get drawn into a discussion about 'processology' or 'spinology', he contrived to block any attempt by correspondents who wished to challenge the honesty and transparency of the process.

Campbell made no mention at the briefing of the alarm expressed by Sir Anthony Hammond about the outspoken and potentially prejudicial remarks made by himself, Straw and Short. The first journalists heard of the edict by Sir Anthony that ministers should make no further comment on the Hinduja inquiry was in response to telephone calls that Monday morning to Straw's special adviser, Ed Owen, whose office said ministers had been told to 'cool it'. Margaret Beckett, the Leader of the House, confirmed to MPs the following Thursday that Sir Anthony had asked ministers to avoid making comments that appeared to prejudge any aspect of his inquiry. I regarded Campbell's strong support at the Monday lobby briefing for the interventions made by Straw and Short as further evidence of the importance ministers attached to following the line put out by the Prime Minister's official spokesman. Chris Smith had used the press secretary's guidance as the basis for his original, incorrect reply at question time, and most ministers took great care to make sure they were in step with what Downing Street was saying. One minister who regretted having followed Campbell's advice was Ron Davies, whose resignation had been compared with Mandelson's hurried exit. Davies told the *Daily Telegraph* he thought the Northern Ireland secretary had been placed under unfair pressure to quit. 'The story which Mandelson has told rang very, very true to me. I know the pressure. You are facing this bloody welter of stuff at the time . . . you just think you cannot go on.' In his own case, Campbell had written a resignation letter for him and he was persuaded to sign it, although it was not until weeks later that he 'even read the bloody thing'. Davies told the *Sunday Times* that it was Campbell who had coined the phrase 'a moment of madness', which he used three days after resigning in a BBC interview. When Davies was told what to say, he had not slept for three days. He knew he had to apologise for what had happened, and he went into the interview with the word 'sorry' written in red ballpoint on the back of his hand. 'I saw the phrase "a moment of madness" as a lifeline. Now I know it is a noose around my neck.'

The mini-reshuffle that followed Mandelson's departure provided another telling example of how far Campbell's writ ran. One of the resulting changes involved a sideways move for the Foreign Office Minister of State Peter Hain, who replaced the Minister for Energy, Helen Liddell. When asked at the morning briefing the following day whether Hain's move was a demotion, Campbell said it was not a downgrading: 'In energy, there are issues which require attention to detail, like miners' compensation, gas prices . . . You should not see that as a downgrading. As for Peter, a domestic job is no bad thing for him.' When Hain was interviewed that afternoon by BBC Wales, he parroted Campbell's line precisely: 'Actually the Prime Minister's official spokesman said this was not a demotion but if anything a promotion into domestic politics. I am thrilled to be doing bread and butter political issues like miners' compensation.' Campbell was equally effusive about Dr John Reid's switch to the Northern Ireland job, even though it meant the press secretary had lost a minister who had often been deployed at short notice to defend the government across a wide range of policy issues. Dr Reid's ability to hold his ground during difficult television and radio interviews had not gone unnoticed in Downing Street. 'The Prime Minister felt John was the right guy because John is someone, as I know from my job, who can absorb a brief incredibly quickly.' Dr Reid's role as a sure-footed troubleshooter for the Blair government drew a waspish rebuke from the former Scottish trade unionist, Jimmy Reid. The two men knew each other from their early days in the Communist Party in Scotland and Jimmy Reid, writing in the *Guardian*, said he believed his former comrade was tailor-made to be a front man for New Labour. If Blair was ever under fire, Dr Reid was sent on television to do battle and put the nation straight. 'No matter how absurd the brief he never blushed but instead looked intently into the camera and delivered the message – with absolute certitude.'

In some respects it was hardly surprising that Campbell had escaped virtually unscathed from the Hinduja saga. In my conversations with other political correspondents, I found that most lobby members thought he had enhanced his reputation by acting so swiftly to correct his first mistaken briefing over Mandelson's involvement in the passport application. He had clearly been anxious and determined to put the record straight, and for that he was seen as something of a hero by some journalists. His guidance on the morning that Blair asked to see Mandelson had been invaluable, especially for broadcasters, who predicted with growing confidence that lunchtime that the secretary of state's resignation was imminent. Campbell was taken to task by some commentators and leader writers for having described Mandelson as 'curiously detached', but his briefing had been a welcome lucky break for the Sunday lobby and provided them with a stunning new angle on the Mandelson story.

Not everyone was so impressed, however. In his weekly column in the *Independent*, the Mayor of London, Ken Livingstone, said he thought Campbell's action in briefing against Mandelson was a repeat of what had happened to him the previous year during the controversy over the selection of Labour's mayoral candidate. Livingstone considered that for a second time Campbell had broken his undertaking to present the government's case 'without, frankly, briefing against anybody'. The problem was the unaccountability of the lobby system and the impossibility of obtaining verbatim transcripts. 'If Mandelson's sacking was meant to expunge any impression of sleaze, the reported attacks on him emanating from the Friday lobby briefing have damaged Labour as much as the original misdemeanour.'

The loyalty shown towards Campbell by most political editors, and their reluctance to speak out publicly against him, infuriated not only Livingstone but also those Conservative MPs who believed the Prime Minister's official spokesman had become a Labour Party propagandist paid for by the taxpayer. The Chichester MP Andrew Tyrie, who was a member of the Select Committee on Public Administration and was one of the Tories who had challenged Campbell on his appearance before the committee in June 1998, made a point of monitoring published accounts of the daily lobby briefings. Tyrie believed the Cabinet Secretary, Sir Richard Wilson, needed to be far tougher in policing what was said by Downing Street and he thought Campbell should be reprimanded on those occasions when he ignored Sir Richard's instruction to refrain from going 'over the top' and attacking the Conservatives with 'brick and bottles' during lobby briefings. On the morning Campbell corrected his briefing about Mandelson's involvement with Srichand Hinduja, he was keen to mount a diversion and launched an unprovoked attack on the spending plans announced the previous evening by the Conservative leader, William Hague. Campbell said the Conservatives' proposals to match the government's spending commitments on the police, defence and transport were incredible. 'They're a joke. If Labour put this forward, you guys would kill us . . . You are talking about an insult to Mickey Mouse and the envelope it was written on and, having insulted Mickey Mouse, they're now insulting the back of an envelope.' Campbell could hardly stop laughing to himself as he completed his tirade, which, perhaps not surprisingly, was not included in the extract published on the Downing Street website. Staff at Conservative Central Office found details of the 'Mickey Mouse' briefing on an Internet news service provided by Gallery News and, after he had seen a report in the *Daily Telegraph* about the Conservatives' policy being described as 'a joke', Tyrie asked the Leader of the House, Margaret Beckett, whether Campbell's briefing breached Sir Richard Wilson's guidelines. Another Conservative MP, Tom King, said that if Campbell was using his position to start the Labour Party's election campaign he should be removed from the public payroll. As Mrs Beckett was not prepared to give an assurance at the dispatch box about the press secretary's future conduct, Tyrie wrote to Sir Richard demanding that Campbell be asked to resign from his position as a special adviser for having engaged in 'blatant' party political activity in the run-up to an election. The Conservatives stepped up their pressure the following week after the Prime Minister acknowledged at question time that it was wrong of Campbell to compare Conservative economic policy to that of Mickey Mouse. Blair made light of the Conservatives' complaint about the briefing given by his official spokesman. 'I want to make it clear that he has been reprimanded strongly for that. We are a fan of Mickey Mouse.'

When asked about his conduct at the lobby briefing that afternoon, Campbell spoke confidently of Blair's support: 'The Prime Minister is happy with the role I play.' Sir Richard's reply to Tyrie's letter was published two days later, and although it revealed that the Prime Minister's official spokesman had been warned about his future conduct, the Cabinet Secretary intended taking no further action. Instead, he would rely on Campbell's undertaking to resign as press secretary as soon as the general election was called. 'I attach a lot of importance to ensuring that the resources of the government are not used for party political purposes. What is, and is not, acceptable is sometimes a grey area where difficult distinctions have to be made, but rules still have to be observed. I have reminded Alastair Campbell that it is particularly important to be careful as a general election draws closer and he has assured me that he understands this.'

Most of the news coverage during the second week of the Hinduja affair concentrated on the role of the Minister for Europe, Keith Vaz. There were fresh disclosures about his personal and business affairs on an almost daily basis, and ten days after Mandelson's resignation the Foreign Secretary, Robin Cook, protested about what he said was the 'unjustified hounding' of his colleague by the anti-European press. Cook had seen nothing in the stories that was not 'innuendo and guilt by association'. Reporters were urged to await the outcome of the government inquiry, which Sir Anthony Hammond expected to complete by the end of February.

Some of Peter Mandelson's friends began a concerted campaign to help him clear his name. The writer Robert Harris was at the forefront of the fight-back and told *Today* that he believed the sacked minister had been unfairly 'branded the biggest liar in Britain'. He claimed that the only record of the alleged phone call between Mandelson and Mike O'Brien was a scribbled note of three words: 'Mandelson, Hindujas, naturalisation'. By the following Sunday, Mandelson's supporters had produced fresh evidence to back up his assertion that the enquiries on behalf of Srichand Hinduja were made by a civil servant in his private office. Both the *Sunday Times* and the *Independent on Sunday* quoted from a leaked memo written by Mandelson's personal secretary in the Northern Ireland Office. It suggested that a week before the Secretary of State's resignation Mike O'Brien did not 'remember how precisely' Mandelson had raised the issue of the passport application. Mandelson, who had been abroad for several days, spoke on the telephone to the *Independent on Sunday*'s editor, Janet Street-Porter. He told her that he intended to co-operate fully with the Hammond inquiry because all he wanted to do was clear his name. 'Nothing I do will ever be designed to harm the government or the party . . . I am not seeking revenge on anyone. I am simply seeking the truth, because I know I didn't mislead people. I know I didn't lie.' The *Independent on Sunday* said Robert Harris had been joined by Lord Birt, the former director general of the BBC, in seeking to rally support for Mandelson. Lord Birt had been appointed the previous year to advise Blair on crime policy, and although he was reported to have spent several hours in Downing Street lobbying on Mandelson's behalf, No. 10 made no response; a spokesman said the press office never commented on advice given to the Prime Minister.

I was struck by the timetable Harris had put together for Mandelson's final few hours as a minister. He said that while

Mandelson was being questioned by Blair, the secretary of state's former principal private secretary was calling No. 10 to say that the enquiries on behalf of Hinduja had been handled by a former deputy private secretary. She had subsequently come forward to substantiate this. 'It was unfortunate that the whole affair turned on having to say something to the 11 a.m. lobby briefing. If that briefing had been postponed, maybe for an hour, the information that a private secretary handled the whole thing would have been in the Prime Minister's hands. Mandelson's former principal private secretary was calling Downing Street, telling No. 10 that Mandelson is telling the truth, but this information was never passed upstairs. I think the whole thing was being driven by a media deadline.' As I listened to the account Harris gave on *Today* I almost had to pinch myself to make sure I was not dreaming. He could hardly have conjured up a more fitting epitaph for New Labour's ultimate control freak: Sacrificed for a media deadline.

DON'T GET CAUGHT

*'Alun, it's now a very good day to get out anything we want to bury.
Councillors expenses? Jo.'*

E-mail from Jo Moore to Alun Evans, director of communications, Department of
Transport, Local Government and the Regions. Subject: media handling.
Date: 11 September 2001, 14:55:12. Copied to: Robin Mortimer, Dan Corry.

A global television audience of unprecedented proportions
watched the unfolding drama that followed the terrorist
attack on the twin towers of the World Trade Center in New
York on 11 September 2001. For a few hours it seemed the United
States of America was spinning out of control. In his first, hurried,
response, while visiting a secondary school in Florida, President Bush
announced a 'full-scale investigation to hunt down and find those
folks who committed this act'. After the Pentagon too had been hit
and the US authorities realised the scale of the threat they were
facing, the President's safety became the prime concern of the
security services. There seemed to be no-one to whom the television
networks could turn to make sense of what was happening. Tony
Blair had mastered the art of seizing the moment to get maximum
media exposure and, within just over an hour and a half of the first
plane hitting the north tower, while President Bush was incommuni-
cado in the safety of a US defence base, Britain's Prime Minister
became the first world leader to speak coherently and with real
authority about the dangers that mass terrorism posed to democratic
nations.

Blair, who was preparing to address the annual conference of the
Trades Union Congress in Brighton, abandoned his planned speech.
After his staff had given sufficient advance warning to the broadcasting organisations, so that television stations in Britain and
around the world could link up with the television pictures from
Brighton, he walked on to the platform. No other western prime
minister or president had developed a better understanding of the

demands of the electronic news media and, with the help of his long-serving press secretary, Alastair Campbell, newly promoted to the government's director of communications and strategy, he demonstrated his unquestioned ability to exploit the tremendous reach, and consequent impact, of live television coverage around the globe. Blair's instant attempt to address the challenge facing democratic nations in responding to the devastation that their citizens were witnessing can hardly be bettered: 'This mass terrorism is the new evil in our world today. It is perpetrated by fanatics who are utterly indifferent to the sanctity of human life and we, the democracies of the world, are going to have to come together to fight it together and eradicate this evil completely from our world.' Blair's words seemed at the time – and still seem – to be the embodiment of what millions were thinking as they watched the horrifying events taking place in New York.

Later that day, from Downing Street, the Prime Minister spoke again to reporters, and his call for solidarity with the United States was replayed time and again on American television: 'This is not a battle between the United States of America and terrorism, but between the free and democratic world and terrorism. We therefore here in Britain stand shoulder to shoulder with our American friends in this hour of tragedy. We, like them, will not rest until this evil is driven from our world.' Blair had catapulted himself to the forefront of world attention and his responses were making the headlines. In an age of non-stop news coverage, we need our elected leaders to be able to relate to what is happening and to guide us through unfathomable events. The rapid expansion in continuous news services, and the relentless demand for new story-lines, has put politicians under tremendous pressure, and any failure to respond can be seen as a sign of weakness or indecision. The heartbeat of the twenty-four-hour news media is as strong in the United Kingdom as in the United States, due to the dominant position of world broadcasters like the BBC and Sky News, and in many respects the journalistic pulse rate is probably faster in London than in either Washington or New York, given the enormous influence and reach of the British press. The expertise which the Blair administration has developed in facing up to this challenge is the envy of many other governments, especially in

Europe. The speed with which Blair reacted to the World Trade Center attack, and his innate ability to speak in tune with the emotions of so many people, provided further illustration of the British government's position at the cutting edge in the development of techniques to withstand and manipulate the enormous power of the global, twenty-four-hour media.

Blair was in the process of checking through the original text of his speech to the TUC, which was due to begin at 2.45 p.m., when more and more television channels dropped their scheduled programmes and started switching to the live pictures from New York showing the north tower on fire after it had been hit by the first hijacked plane at 1.46 p.m. EST After a second plane was flown into the south tower at 2.02 p.m., and it seemed certain there had been a co-ordinated terrorist attack of devastating proportions, Blair decided to abandon his prepared address. However, he was in two minds as to whether to speak briefly to the conference or cancel his appearance altogether and return immediately to Downing Street. As the horror of what had happened became apparent, he realised he could not leave Brighton without responding to the terrible scenes which were being watched in stunned silence by groups of delegates and observers at every available television set around the outside of the conference auditorium. In the media centre, where I was standing watching, transfixed, with other journalists, Nigel Stanley, the TUC's head of campaigns and communication, kept assuring us that although the Prime Minister had decided to abandon his set speech, he would shortly have something to say to the delegates. Behind the scenes, Blair's staff were trying desperately to get as much information as they could about the horrific events in New York.

Isobel Larkin, the TUC's parliamentary officer, who saw what went on at first hand, told me how impressed she had been to observe the Prime Minister in action at a moment of such high drama. 'Blair was desperate to get back to Downing Street but he knew he had to say something before leaving. We realised that most of the delegates in the hall didn't know the severity of what had happened. There was a lot of rushing around among members of his staff to make sure the facts were correct. Alastair Campbell was there, right in the middle of things, but it was Blair who was in command and who clearly wanted to get what he was going to say to the conference exactly right.' Blair delivered his short statement at 3.28 p.m. and told the delegates he knew they would want to join him in sending their 'deepest condolences' to President Bush and the American people for 'the terror and the carnage' which had resulted from 'two hijacked planes being flown deliberately into the World Trade Center'. After restrained applause for his expression of sympathy, the Prime Minister left the platform almost immediately in order to catch a train back to London. Brendan Barber, the TUC's deputy general secretary, told me he thought it entirely appropriate that Blair had delivered a short statement before departing. 'He really captured the moment and the mood. He realised he had both an audience and an opportunity. He hit the right tone and in a few short sentences he pulled together both for the delegates and the viewers the terrifying events which were unfolding in America.' Nigel Stanley, with his long experience of watching union leader and politicians react to sensational events, was just as impressed by Blair's ability to seize the moment. 'It really was spontaneous on his part. He just went for it.'

John Edmonds, the TUC vice-president, told me there was an element of luck about the timing. He was sitting on the platform with the president, Bill Morris, and the general secretary, John Monks. 'We'd heard Blair was thinking of going back to London without speaking. John sent Blair a note advising him he shouldn't leave without saying something and in the event he handled it brilliantly.' The praise for Blair's deft touch at a moment of great uncertainty was shared by the rest of the TUC leadership. They had seen with their own eyes how important it was for a prime minister or president to give a lead when, for a few hectic hours, it seemed the events in the aftermath of the hijackings were being driven solely by the pace of the coverage on the rolling news services. Democratically elected politicians had to show they were in command; and inevitably the first world leader who was able to speak coherently on television would have real credibility and be the focus of enormous attention.

Campbell left the conference centre without talking to reporters, so I had no chance to find out any more details about the preparations which had gone on behind the scenes. However, after his success in working with the White House in developing NATO's media response to the air strikes against Serbia during the Kosovo crisis, Campbell would have known instantly how to make contact with the information staff working for President Bush, and I sensed that he realised only too well that the live television coverage already planned for Blair's speech to the TUC had provided the Prime Minister with an unparalleled opportunity to speak directly to a world audience.

An event of such mammoth proportions as the destruction of the World Trade Center would, by its very nature, obliterate almost all other news stories and wipe out any plans the government might have had to influence the domestic news agenda. Campbell needed no guidance on how to respond: his task was to ensure that Blair's authority was enhanced, however tragic the circumstances. His thought processes were being replicated in ministers' offices and government departments across Whitehall by a network of former Labour Party press officers and sympathetic ex-journalists who were also having to come to terms with the fact that the news agenda had been turned topsy-turvy by the attacks in New York and Washington. Unexpected events, which dominate the media's attention for days if not weeks on end, present a constant challenge to the publicity staff of any organisation. Most of Campbell's colleagues, although shocked by the devastation they were seeing on their television screens, would probably have felt a slight tinge of disappointment: they knew that long-planned events or press launches, which could not be postponed, were likely as a result of these cataclysmic events to get little or no publicity; months of work had probably been wasted. In some embattled departments, such tragedies can have a silver lining, because they divert journalists' attention away from difficult or embarrassing stories and provide a welcome opportunity for ministers to announce unpopular decisions safe in the knowledge that they will receive scant attention.

The hand-picked team of special advisers who had become the personal spin doctors to members of the cabinet, and whose appointments had all been approved personally by the Prime Minister, were well versed in the various routines that would come into play. Campbell had drilled into them the importance of understanding how to respond to the vagaries of twenty-four-hour news coverage. The rapid turnover in headlines had to be exploited to the government's advantage, and no chance should be missed to minimise or dispose of negative story-lines. One highly respected, long-serving New Labour apparatchik was about to make a fatal mistake and put her instructions in writing. Jo Moore, special adviser to the Secretary of State for Transport, Local Government and the Regions, Stephen Byers, had done what was clearly second nature to her. Like Campbell, within minutes of hearing the news, she had thought through the options which were likely to present themselves and had realised instantly how the catastrophic events taking place on the other side of the Atlantic provided an unexpected opportunity to make life easier for her much troubled minister. Her infamous e-mail, sent just over an hour after the first plane hit the north tower, revealed the dark underside of Blair's media machine. Ms Moore's folly would not become public knowledge for almost a month; but her injudicious instruction to the department's director of communications, Alun Evans, that it was 'a very good day to get out anything we want to bury', was destined to blow up in Byers' face and give the lie to the Prime Minister's repeated assurances, since his government's landslide victory in the general election of June 2001, that Labour had turned its back on spin.

There could hardly have been a clearer example of the unacceptable pressures which Blair's web of political appointees were applying to civil servants. Ms Moore's e-mail epitomised the true nature of the manipulative techniques which the Prime Minister had sanctioned, and its significance was magnified by the fact that it was the knee-jerk response of a true Blairite, who had been schooled by Labour's arch media manipulator, Peter Mandelson. New Labour had spawned a new breed of aggressive media managers who had moved effortlessly from the party's headquarters at Millbank Tower to the inner offices of cabinet ministers. Ms Moore had spent almost her entire working life as a press officer assisting Labour politicians, and from what I could discover it appeared there were numerous occasions when she believed she had put her career on the line for her party. However calamitous her mistake, she could not be discarded lightly; she was part of the New Labour tribe and her years of unstinting loyalty had to be taken into account. Byers was ready to make a stand on her behalf; her unswerving support since he had become a cabinet minister had to be repaid. Blair could hardly ignore

Byers' wishes, although Alastair Campbell believed she had to go. Against his own better judgement, Blair had allowed the Chancellor, Gordon Brown, to retain the services of his controversial special adviser, Charlie Whelan, for far longer than either he or Campbell had wanted. Ms Moore had served under three party leaders – Neil Kinnock, the late John Smith and Tony Blair – and she had risen to become Labour's chief press and broadcasting officer, winning promotion early on during the long and testing lead-up to Labour's 1997 general election victory.

I had spoken to her regularly since she joined the party's public relations department in 1989, when Mandelson was Labour's director of campaigns and communications. He was impressed by the offensive she had waged against left-wing control of the National Organisation of Labour Students, of which she was elected vice-chair, and by her subsequent support for Neil Kinnock and the modernisers on becoming a member of Hornsey and Wood Green Labour Party. After joining the staff of the London Borough of Haringey as a press officer she switched to a similar job at Islington Council, at which point she was recruited to work at party headquarters by Colin Byrne, who was then head of the press office and Mandelson's deputy. Byrne described in an article for the *Observer* why she had been hired by the party: 'She was tough as old boots, not overly worried about personal charm, took no crap from journalists – all of whom seemed to hate Labour – and ate Trots for breakfast.'

I probably played a small part in the steep learning curve which she must have negotiated in coming to terms with the vicissitudes of her new life as one of Mandelson's propagandists. My television and radio reports in September 1989 about a dispute over the demand for the creation of separate black sections within the Labour Party obliterated news coverage of a survey of increases in council house rents which had been prepared by the party's shadow housing minister Clive Soley and which was launched at one of the first press conferences to have been organised by Ms Moore. Mandelson was furious about interviews which I had filmed on the steps of the party's headquarters with two of the supporters of black sections, Mark Wadsworth, a journalist from Thames Television, and Nuowamba Kuonga, a party activist from Bristol, who wore his hair in dreadlocks. On finding that Ms Moore's positive story on housing had effectively been 'buried' by what he believed was my hostile reporting of an internal party dispute, Mandelson complained to the BBC. Labour's publicity supremo would no doubt have been anxious to demonstrate to his newest recruit the full panoply of measures which could be used to intimidate errant journalists: after the relevant programme editors had been informed of Labour's displeasure, the individual miscreant should be notified personally of the harm that had been done. In a hand-written letter of complaint, Mandelson told me how he was 'very disappointed after all the help' he had given me that my report should have been 'constructed almost entirely' from the standpoint of the black sections campaigners and that I had delivered the 'familiar, stereotypical "Labour row" story'.

Ms Moore always struck me as being highly competent and extremely reliable, especially from the party's point of view. She had a no-nonsense approach when dealing with media enquiries and little time for small talk. Unlike some of her colleagues, she responded promptly to pager messages and often accepted telephone calls at home, even during those weekends when she was off duty, which was much appreciated by political correspondents like myself. On New Year's Day 1991, when I had been unable to contact the party's duty press officer, she did what she could to help me obtain a Labour response to an interview on *The World At One* by the then Conservative Chancellor of the Exchequer, Norman Lamont. The shadow Chancellor, John Smith, was unavailable and eventually I had to phone Labour's trade and industry spokesman, Gordon Brown, who told me he could not do an interview because he was 'laid up with flu and feeling terrible'. I had never known Brown turn down the chance to comment on the Conservatives' economic record. He promised to look through his notes and ring me back with a quote, which he duly did an hour later, saying Lamont's 'complacency bordered on the irresponsible'.

My first lengthy encounter with Ms Moore came in June and July 1991 during the Liverpool Walton by-election, which turned into something of a trial of strength between Neil Kinnock and the rump of the Militant Tendency, which had decided finally to break cover and field a candidate under the banner of Real Labour. The by-election followed the death of the Labour MP, Eric Heffer, and Ms Moore, who was press officer for the campaign, won praise for her part in what turned out to be a comfortable victory for Labour's candidate, Peter Kilfoyle. In many respects the by-election was a heaven-sent opportunity for Kinnock, who had sanctioned a wave of expulsions and was now anxious to demonstrate publicly that he had finally rid the party of Militant infiltrators. Liverpool had been one of their chief strongholds, and the selection of Kilfoyle to fight the seat represented another head-on challenge to the Broad Left grouping on Merseyside. Kilfoyle was a former north-west regional organiser for the party and had been regarded locally as a scourge of Militant, so he relished the chance to take on the Real Labour candidate, Lesley Mahmood. He told me that he asked for Ms Moore to be his media handler for the by-election because he had seen her in action and knew how effective she could be.

She realised that a great deal was riding on the result: a general election was less than a year away and it was hoped the contest would provide an ideal platform for some high profile visits by Kinnock and members of his shadow cabinet, including the environment spokesman, Bryan Gould, and the shadow employment secretary, Tony Blair. Ms Moore had to arrange daily news conferences in the Goodison suite of Everton Football Club and, in marked contrast to the harsh sloganising of the far left, she was determined to soften Labour's image. Each morning there was always a fresh posy of red roses on the table in front of Kilfoyle and that day's visiting front-bencher; the platform party also wore red roses in their buttonholes. Much to Ms Moore's annoyance, I drew attention to the presence of the roses in a feature for *Today* in which I included an interview with a local florist, Sue Davis, whose job it was to prepare the flower arrangement each day. I was chided for wasting the BBC's airtime on something as inconsequential as roses when it was the local politics which mattered; Ms Moore was already well versed in the Mandelson dictum that journalists should be discouraged from writing about the packaging and presentation of New Labour. She demonstrated her political judgement two days before the by-election when giving me her prediction of the result: she said that Kilfoyle would walk it and that Militant's share of the vote would be well under 10 per cent. 'If that's all they can get in the birthplace of Militant, it's going to be derisory. We forced them to stand as Real Labour and they've played into our hands. Now we've got them out into the open we can deal with them; they're on the run.' Her forecast was right on the ball: Kilfoyle held the seat on 53.1 per cent of the vote and Real Labour, taking 6.5 per cent, finished third, behind the Liberal Democrats (but ahead of the Conservatives). She was equally sure-footed in having hinted at further disciplinary action against Militant sympathisers. Within a fortnight of the by-election Labour suspended fifty-eight party members who had been observed by regional officials giving their support to the Real Labour candidate.

Ms Moore was made chief press and broadcasting officer in the autumn of 1993. Her promotion was ridiculed by *Labour Briefing*, which dubbed her 'Haringey's witless right-wing witch-hunter' and claimed she had got the job because no candidate with 'real journalistic experience' would touch it. Nevertheless she was an efficient and effective organiser, and her dedication impressed Joy Johnson, who was Labour's director of communications for eleven months from February 1995. Ms Johnson told me she was taken aback by Ms Moore's calculated approach in deciding which stories to exploit. In December 1995, a month after delivering his Budget, the Chancellor, Kenneth Clarke, said he doubted whether the poorest 10 per cent of society were really as badly off as they suggested. He told the Commons Treasury Select Committee that this bottom 10 per cent 'always drives me up the wall' because they were an unreliable guide to living standards: some of those who declared no income had 'very good accountants' and there was 'a high level of smoking' among low-income groups. Ms Johnson described Ms Moore's response when she asked Labour's press officers to do all they could to exploit the insensitivity of Clarke's remarks: 'We were all together in the newsroom and Jo challenged me. She said: "There aren't any votes in the poor." I know what Jo meant but I was struck by her single-minded approach, just like the New Labour policy of only targeting winnable seats. But what she said really was appalling. It seemed some of the apparatchiks around Blair were second-guessing the leadership and had forgotten what Labour was about. I know Gordon Brown definitely wanted a war on poverty.'

Labour's move of its headquarters from Walworth Road to Millbank Tower during 1995 marked another stage in the build-up of the party's media operation; and, as chief press and broadcasting officer, Ms Moore played a key role in organising day-to-day relations with journalists during preparations for the 1997 general election. Her team of press officers worked alongside a much-expanded unit for monitoring the news output of television, radio and the press, and they had to do all they could to assist a newly established rebuttal unit. After the election, like so many of her fellow party workers, Ms Moore found that Labour's landslide victory had turned her into a highly attractive proposition for the public affairs and public relations consultants who were keen to recruit former Millbank insiders with extensive contacts inside the new government. Within six months of the election she announced she was joining the lobbyists Westminster Strategy. She was being assigned to the public relations side of the business, and she told me she understood her clients would include the Law Society and the Premier League.

During the run-up to the election I had not personally had as much contact with Ms Moore as in previous years, but since her promotion to chief press officer I had noticed that she had begun adopting a rather haughty attitude and could on occasions be quite curt, with even less time than before for pleasantries. Her imminent departure from Millbank earned her a mention in the *Daily Telegraph*'s 'Peterborough' column, which said Labour's 'toughest spin doctor' was 'off to make money' with Westminster Strategy and, in return for 'a suitably handsome salary', would shortly be 'bending government ears with all the robust efficiency she employed on journalists'. She evidently regarded the write-up as a compliment, because the invitation she sent out for her leaving party in December 1997 referred to the 'Peterborough' story and urged journalists to turn up at the Westminster Arms to say goodbye to 'Labour's rather scary' chief press officer.

One subject which was decidedly taboo at Ms Moore's farewell was the role she had played the previous month in trying to limit damage to the party's reputation following newspaper reports which linked the government's decision to exempt motor racing from the ban on tobacco sponsorship to a million-pound donation from the Formula One boss Bernie Ecclestone. For the first time since becoming Prime Minister, Blair was having the word 'sleaze' thrown at him by his political opponents; and instead of making a clean breast of it when approached initially by reporters, Labour's tactic was to bluster and prevaricate in the hope of concealing the facts. Many questions about the party's relationship with Ecclestone and the fund-raising techniques being used by staff at Millbank Tower went – and have remained – unanswered. Jo Moore was named as the point of contact on the press release, issued on 13 November 1997, which contained a letter from the party's general secretary, Tom Sawyer, stating that Ecclestone had made a 'substantial personal donation' the previous January and had 'offered a further donation' since the general election in May 1997. Labour was forced to publish Sawyer's letter after journalists obtained a leaked copy of the reply he received from Sir Patrick Neill, chairman of the Committee on Standards in Public Life, who advised Labour to return the first donation and to refuse to accept the second.

When making enquiries for *Today* next morning I challenged Ms Moore about the accuracy of Sawyer's letter, because in an interview for the *Mirror* Ecclestone had said the suggestion he had offered Labour a second donation was 'a million per cent nonsense'. To begin with she was defensive; but she then admitted that while Labour's fund-raising department had made a fresh approach to Ecclestone's advisers, there had 'never been any arrangement' for a second donation – and therefore she accepted Ecclestone's denial was correct. In my report for *Today* I said the amended version of events which I had just obtained was of considerable political significance because it suggested that at the same time that ministers in the newly elected Labour government were considering a possible exemption from the tobacco sponsorship ban for Formula One, staff at party headquarters were in the process of soliciting a second donation from Ecclestone. My enquiries confirmed my suspicion that we were still probably aware of only the bare outline of the story. Ms Moore clearly knew a great deal about the secret fund-raising which had helped finance Labour's 1997 election campaign and it was only as a result of pressure from the news media that any information was released. Two days after my report for *Today*, Blair gave an interview to *On The Record* in which he regretted the way the whole affair had been made public. He said Labour had been entirely justified in taking Ecclestone's first donation of £1 million and insisted that it had had no influence on the government's decision to exempt Formula One from the sponsorship ban. 'I apologise for the way this was handled . . . I am sorry about this issue . . . I think most people who have dealt with me think I am a pretty straight sort of guy, and I am.'

I lost track of Ms Moore while she was employed by Westminster Strategy. Then, fifteen months later and rather to my surprise, I discovered in March 1999 that she had renewed her links with the Labour Party and become a part-time special adviser to Stephen Byers, who had taken over as Secretary of State for Trade and Industry after Peter Mandelson's resignation. A year later, in March 2000, she was again caught in political crossfire when Byers was accused of a cover-up over secret negotiations by the German car company BMW to sell off Rover, its ailing British subsidiary. After considerable criticism of his handling of the future ownership of the main Rover car plant at Longbridge, Byers attempted to clear his name by publishing the confidential departmental minutes of his meetings with BMW; Jo Moore was listed among the names of those who were on the internal mailing list for copies of the relevant documents.

By sheer coincidence, at the height of the furore over the collapse of Rover, I shared a platform with Matt Tee, director of news at the Department of Trade and Industry. We had both been invited to contribute to a seminar organised by the Council of Europe on how to make the best use of the news media; and, as we waited for our turn to speak, Tee assured me that BMW's decision to sell Rover had come 'entirely out of the blue'. Byers had 'no inkling' of it and had been left in 'a difficult position because BMW had not taken him into their confidence'. In his address to the seminar, Tee was quite open in acknowledging that, immediately after the 1997 general election, Labour cabinet ministers had expressed their disappointment about the level of expertise in the government's information service. Although he made no mention of Jo Moore by name, he explained that one of the two special advisers in his department 'does help Byers with his press work', and he described the pressures which this could place on civil service press officers. 'Ministers do desire a high profile and this does throw up questions of what a politically impartial civil service is required to do . . . Sometimes special advisers are trying to get a bigger political advantage from a story than is permissible and that is a tension; that is a tension which is there.'

Needless to say, remembering Tee's account of the difficulties he faced at the Department of Trade and Industry, I had a sense of *déjà vu* on 9 October 2001 when reading a front-page exclusive in the *Independent* which reproduced the e-mail Ms Moore had sent to Alun Evans, director of communications at the Department of Transport, Local Government and the Regions, where Byers had become Secretary of State in the cabinet reshuffle which followed the 2001 general election.

Copies of her instruction that it was 'a very good day to get out anything we want to bury' were sent to Robin Mortimer, a senior civil servant in the department, and to Byers' other special adviser, Dan Corry. Although the *Independent* gave no clue as to how it had obtained a leaked copy of the memo, unidentified Whitehall sources were quoted at length describing their fury at the way civil servants had been asked to trawl through sensitive government material for embarrassing stories that could be released and thus 'buried' under news coverage of the attack on the World Trade Center. 'It shows such insensitivity looking for party political advantage at a time when thousands of people had clearly been killed,' said one Whitehall insider.

The *Independent* claimed that it was well known at Westminster that Ms Moore, who was thirty-eight, married with two children and worked for Byers three days a week, had experienced a 'difficult' relationship with civil servants at the two departments where she had been employed; and it said Alun Evans, the main recipient of the e-mail, had 'since left his job after clashes' with her. The story-line pointed to one fairly obvious conclusion – she had been shopped by a disgruntled civil servant – and I thought at the time that this was the likeliest explanation, given the astute timing of the leak, at a moment which would inflict the maximum political damage on Blair and Byers. A flurry of interviews that morning on *Today* provided a foretaste of the criticism which was about to be heaped on the head of the Secretary of State and his hapless adviser. Ms Moore was accused of being 'absolutely cynical and heartless' by the shadow transport secretary, Theresa May; the Liberal Democrats' transport spokesman, Don Foster, said she had 'plumbed new depths' even for a Labour Party spin doctor. Sensing a rough passage at the morning lobby briefing, Tom Kelly, one of the Prime Minister's two official spokesmen who had taken on Alastair Campbell's former duties, came well prepared. He told the assembled correspondents that Byers was made aware of the e-mail the previous evening and had told Ms Moore it was 'an error of judgement'. She accepted she had been at fault and, although she had been reprimanded by Byers, he wanted it to be known that she had given him very good advice over a long period of years and that as Secretary of State he continued to value her 'skills and experience'. Kelly then read out a statement which Ms Moore had asked to be released: 'I would like to sincerely apologise for the offence I have caused. It was wrong to send the e-mail and I accept responsibility for doing so. It was clearly a mistake I regret.' Tony Blair, who was said by Kelly to have 'a very high regard' for Byers and 'trusts his judgement', shared his Secretary of State's view that Ms Moore had made a mistake. As she had been reprimanded and had subsequently apologised, the Prime Minister hoped the whole matter could be kept in perspective.

If Blair and Byers had thought Ms Moore's contrite apology might draw a line under the story, their hopes were dashed when Kelly reported back to Campbell on the savaging he had received at the hands of the lobby. He had to endure half an hour of hostile questioning as political correspondents went through a long list of stories which they believed the government had attempted to 'bury' in the month which had elapsed since the World Trade Center attack. Top of their list was the announcement which Byers made on the morning of Sunday 7 October that he intended to force Railtrack into receivership by seeking a High Court order to place the company in administration. Shock news of Railtrack's demise was dwarfed within hours by the confirmation that the United States and Britain had begun a massive air attack on Afghanistan.

I was among the reporters waiting in Downing Street that Sunday afternoon for the start of a news conference at which Blair told reporters that cruise missiles had already been launched from British submarines in the Gulf. While queuing up to go through the No. 10 front door, I was joined by Sarah Smith of *Channel 4 News*, who had just left the Department of Transport after a briefing on Byers' plans for Railtrack. Her account of what had been said about the background to the company's collapse already seemed to be old news the moment we saw senior ministers filing in behind Blair for the announcement that the government had authorised the use of the United Kingdom's military forces. The point put repeatedly at the lobby briefing two days later was that it looked as if Byers had still been following Ms Moore's advice that Sunday because he appeared to have used the cover of a declaration of war against the Taliban and Al-Qa'ida to reveal that he was taking legal action to wind up Railtrack. Kelly insisted that the Secretary of State's decision had been driven by 'hard financial facts' about the rail industry. Trevor Kavanagh, the *Sun*'s political editor, would have none of it: the decision to dissolve Railtrack was clearly 'a political act which had been brewing for months', and as the timing of it had taken the chairman and his directors 'completely by surprise', it looked as if Byers had used the 'cover of war' to 'smuggle out' the announcement. Kelly refused to reveal whether Byers was among the 'relevant people' who knew in advance about the planned military offensive and, as the questioning continued to get nowhere, it was obvious the Secretary of State for Transport had become a marked man: if he dared appear in public to give interviews defending his decision to put Railtrack into receivership, he would be dogged by questions about Ms Moore and her advice to 'bury' bad news.

Kelly had an equally hard time trying to convince journalists that other announcements during the previous month had all been part of the 'normal business of government'. He denied that the government had acted in an underhand way when announcing that plans for a new athletics stadium at Picketts Lock in north London had been abandoned, or in giving British Nuclear Fuels the go-ahead for a new reprocessing plant at Sellafield in Cumbria. 'You cannot put all government business on hold.' He was greeted with disbelief when he asserted that a consultation paper on travel and subsistence allowances for councillors, which was published the day after the World Trade Center attack, had been 'due for release anyway' on 12 September. In her e-mail, Ms Moore had mentioned 'councillors' expenses' as the one item of news which it should be possible to 'bury'. The fact that the department had released it in line with her advice was one of the issues explored by *The World At One*, which obtained a statement from Dan Corry, the other special adviser assigned to Byers. He said he was 'in a meeting' with the Secretary of State at the time Ms Moore sent her e-mail and had seen it only 'some time later'; and, as no-one knew that evening precisely what was going on in New York, it was 'neither here nor there'.

The programme's main interviewee was Tony Wright, chairman of the House of Commons Select Committee on Public Administration, which in February 2001 had recommended the introduction of a new code of conduct for special advisers and a cap on their numbers. As a first step towards meeting the committee's concerns, Blair had approved a new model contract for special advisers, which was published in July 2001 and which reminded ministerial aides that they had to act in a way which 'upholds the political impartiality of civil servants and does not conflict with the civil service code'. Wright told *The World At One* that the attitude Ms Moore had displayed was 'incompatible' with public service, and that if there was a culture of 'such deep cynicism among a raft of people' who were paid for by the taxpayer to service ministers, it had disturbing implications for the way Blair was running his government. That evening he told *Newsnight* the e-mail was 'far worse' than an error of judgement. Wright thought it should not be possible for 'a minister or anyone else' to survive what was a failure by Ms Moore to think through her role in the political system.

Damning headlines in the next day's newspapers underlined the devastating consequences of being caught red-handed trying to manipulate the news media. Byers had effectively been forced into hiding at a critical moment, unable to mount a defence of the government's controversial decision to take control of Railtrack for fear of being forced into an embarrassing corner over the e-mail; Ms

Moore had pressed the equivalent of the self-destruct button because she knew that if she dared speak again to any self-respecting journalist her call would a become a story in itself and would almost certainly inflict further damage on the government. 'Sin Doctor' was the *Mirror*'s headline over a report by its commentator Paul Routledge, who said journalists 'very rarely get cast-iron evidence' of the lengths to which New Labour were prepared to go to spin the facts and bamboozle the public. 'Bye bye Byers' was the *Sun*'s take on Trevor Kavanagh's report on the pressure Blair was under to sack a Secretary of State who had 'completely lost the plot'. It said that in future no journalist would be able to trust a word said by Ms Moore, who drew 'a hefty salary – as much as £50,000 a year – from the taxpayer.'

The *Independent* followed up its exclusive with a strident editorial which declared that Ms Moore had discovered to her cost that electronic mail could be a 'treacherous medium'. Instead of delivering her 'disgustingly ill-conceived' advice by 'a quiet, untraceable word in her minister's ear' she had shown herself to be guilty of 'gross political ineptitude'. For the second day running Tom Kelly faced awkward questions from lobby journalists who were anxious to probe the way in which Byers had dealt with Ms Moore. It had emerged late the previous evening that the permanent secretary in the department, Sir Richard Mottram, had invoked civil service disciplinary procedures and given her an official warning. Why, asked the correspondents, had Byers issued his reprimand and then decided to retain Ms Moore's services, when the matter should have been examined first by Sir Richard? Kelly insisted the correct procedures had been followed and refused to elaborate any further on the action that had been taken. The question No. 10 wanted journalists to address was whether sending an inept e-mail warranted destroying her career. But Downing Street's plea for tolerance fell on deaf ears when fresh allegations emerged suggesting Ms Moore had had a role in Alun Evans' sudden departure.

The main thrust of the story was that Byers had dispensed with the services of his director of communications after Evans refused to allow his staff to take part in a dirty-tricks campaign against London's transport commissioner, Bob Kiley, during the long-running dispute over the future of London Underground. Ms Moore was accused of having asked the department's information officers to help undermine Kiley's opposition to the government's public–private partnership plans for the tube by briefing the press on a non-attributable basis. One of the civil servants who objected to this request went to Evans and obtained his support. After voicing his concern, Evans was called in by Byers and asked again to ensure that his staff co-operated. When he refused to comply, he was informed he had lost the Secretary of State's confidence and was moved to a new post.

Although Ms Moore made no comment on the circumstances surrounding Evans' ousting, much of the story was corroborated by his trade union. Jonathan Baume, general secretary of the First Division Association of senior civil servants, told the BBC he was aware of the allegation that Evans had been involved 'in a row' with Ms Moore about briefing the media. He believed there had been unacceptable political pressure. 'Our sources in Whitehall say that Alun Evans was moved after he was asked to undertake an act which he felt was improper. He felt that it was political; he refused. There are clear rules setting down what is proper and improper for government press officers.' Bob Kiley told reporters he was convinced that he had been the victim of a campaign of 'personal vilification' for having fought so hard to keep control of the tube, and he admired Evans' refusal to get involved. 'He did the right thing and I hope he's not punished as a result of it.'

After having attempted the day before to keep a safe distance from the story, Downing Street now changed tack and tried to rebut the worst of the latest allegations: Evans' departure was not connected with Ms Moore; he was a senior civil servant who came from a policy background and, after two years as a director of communications, was moving back to policy work and would be heading up the secretariat to assist the inquiry into the outbreak of foot-and-mouth disease. When asked whether Ms Moore had tried to force Evans to brief against Kiley, No. 10 equivocated. Journalists should not be surprised that the government disagreed with Kiley about the future of the tube; the job of the communications staff within Byers' department was to 'state where it had policy disagreements and they had done so . . . pointing out where you disagreed with someone does not amount to personal vilification.'

Once the government's line had been approved and issued to the lobby, Byers broke his silence and agreed to give interviews to the transport correspondents of BBC, ITN and *Sky News*. It was the first time for three days that he had appeared in front of the news media, and his decision to limit himself to three carefully controlled interviews rather than answer questions at a press conference was criticised by the newspapers. Railtrack's disgruntled directors had exploited Byers' withdrawal from the public arena to switch the focus of press coverage to the plight of the company's shareholders, many of whom were their own employees. Byers, who looked like a minister under siege, stuck rigidly to the replies which had been formulated in Downing Street. He said that he understood people's anger over Ms Moore's 'terrible error of judgement' but that it had been 'an isolated mistake'; both the Prime Minister and the permanent secretary felt it would be 'inappropriate' to sacrifice her career because of it. Byers denied he had authorised a 'dirty tricks' campaign over the tube: Evans had left for 'a very important' job, not because of 'a conflict' with Ms Moore. 'We did brief on the London Underground. We were rebutting arguments put forward by Bob Kiley and that response was highly appropriate.'

Downing Street's careful orchestration of Byers' reappearance was too late to stem the growing tide of damaging disclosures about the activities of one of the government's most experienced special advisers. Stephen Pound, the only backbench Labour MP prepared to speak up publicly in Ms Moore's defence, beat a hasty retreat after one brief radio interview. He told *Today* that she had been 'incredibly unfortunate' in having stupidly used the word 'bury' half an hour after the planes were flown into the World Trade Center, at a point when no-one could have guessed how awful it would be when the two towers collapsed. 'Hindsight gives you perfect vision . . . I think Jo Moore acted at the time in the light of the information she had. It wasn't remotely as terrifying and awesome as it subsequently turned out to be. To try to crucify her now is absolutely outrageous . . . People are pursuing a separate agenda against Stephen Byers via Jo Moore.'

Although Pound gave no further interviews to support his assertion that there were some extenuating circumstances which helped explain Ms Moore's conduct, I did succeed in obtaining a fuller account from Phil Woollas, the assistant government whip for transport and local government. Woollas had been a producer for *Newsnight* and *Channel 4 News* before becoming MP for Oldham East and Saddleworth in 1997. He worked with Ms Moore as a Labour press officer during the 1992 general election and he was well versed in New Labour's news management techniques. He told me it was her great misfortune to be in the wrong place at the wrong time and to do the wrong thing. 'Jo heard about the attack on the World Trade Center on the car radio. She had gone to pick up her kids. She sent the e-mail from home on her own computer. She hadn't seen it happen on TV. Obviously she wouldn't have done the same thing an hour later when the towers had collapsed; that's why it was all so unfortunate for her.'

Byers' attempt to draw a line under the affair simply accelerated the flow of stories suggesting that the Secretary of State and his special adviser were serial offenders when it came to 'burying' awkward stories and applying political pressure to government information officers. The *Express* reported that several Labour MPs had complained about being included without their approval in a list of parliamentary supporters of Byers' plans for the London Underground; the *Sunday Times* claimed that, twenty-four hours before Byers had seized control of the rail network, Ms Moore told the paper's reporter 'that he would "look like a f***ing idiot" if he wrote that Railtrack was bankrupt and was being taken over by the government'. Newspaper columnists tried to outdo each other with lurid anecdotes about Ms Moore's youthful exploits. The *Mirror* claimed she was known as 'Stalin's granddaughter and was frequently squabbling with Trotskyites' during her time with the National Organisation of Labour Students; the *Sunday Telegraph*'s political editor, Joe Murphy, recalled that after volunteering to help in the 1987 general election she had told the annual conference that 'one of Mandelson's pet hates, the party's in-house newspaper, *Labour Weekly*, was a waste of money'; and the *Guardian* diary quoted an anonymous former colleague from Labour's press office who remembered that she wore a 'silver ice-pick charm during those heady days of Militant expulsions' in order to provide a chilling reminder of the weapon used to murder Trotsky. Charlie Whelan, who worked with her during the 1997 general election, joined in the chorus of disapproval. In an article for the *Sunday Telegraph*, he admitted that as 'a former practitioner of the black arts of spin', he had used the same ploy; he had found that late Friday afternoon was a good time to release a story potentially damaging to the government. In his view, New Labour's news management had become 'compulsive and amoral', and although he was no longer Gordon Brown's spin doctor, having resigned in January 1999 at the height of the Mandelson home-loan scandal, he knew only too well that the methods 'masterminded' by Alastair Campbell were 'still used throughout the government, and the manipulativeness remains boundless'.

Next day most newspapers ran stories based on anonymous quotes from a Downing Street source which said that Campbell intended issuing fresh instructions to special advisers to remind them that the Prime Minister had been 'anti-spin' since his re-election and wanted the government to be judged on the 'delivery of public services rather than presentation'. An editorial in the *Independent* said that only a government which had 'lost all sense of self-awareness could announce the "end of spin" by means of an unattributed briefing'.

Byers left it until Monday 15 October, almost a full week after the *Independent*'s original story about the offending e-mail, before making a statement to MPs to explain why the government was no longer prepared to give Railtrack a blank cheque. Ms Moore was absent from the bench in the press gallery reserved for special advisers. Eric Pickles, the Conservatives' transport spokesman, called for the resignation of a Secretary of State who 'clings to office with his despised spin doctor'; they should, he said, both do the House of Commons and the rail industry 'a favour, by quitting today'. Byers defended his decision to retain Ms Moore, insisting she had been 'dealt with through the official disciplinary procedures'.

The next day, having spent the previous week keeping out of the public spotlight, Jo Moore returned to work; and that afternoon, in a bid to start again with a clean state, she made an emotional public apology. Four television crews and several journalists arrived at the headquarters of the Transport Department hoping to gain access, but she insisted on staging a controlled media opportunity and in the event only one television cameraman, reporter and photographer were invited to an upstairs room. Jenny Percival, of *Sky News*, said Ms Moore looked pale and strained when she emerged from her office; she was nervous and barely audible when she read out her statement. She wanted to 'again sincerely apologise for the huge offence' her e-mail had caused. 'I can well understand the disgust people will feel with what I wrote. I very much wish I hadn't written it. In fact I find it difficult to believe that I did write it. But I did write it and that's something that I'm going to have to live with for the rest of my life. I can't take back, much as I wish I could take back, that error of judgement, but I hope people will accept that my regret is genuine and heartfelt. Equally, I hope that people will accept that we all do things we regret in life, but the most important thing is to learn from them . . . and I'm grateful for another chance.'

Ms Moore's public apology, which was an unprecedented step for a special adviser, was necessitated in part by the House of Commons timetable. Blair had to answer questions next day, Wednesday 17 October, and she realised that if she was prepared to say 'sorry' publicly, however humiliating her ordeal, it would make it easier for the Prime Minister to try to draw a line under the affair. His support for Byers' decision to stand by her had to be repaid. Sure enough, Peter Luff, Conservative MP for Mid-Worcestershire, had a well-primed question: What was the Prime Minister's response to the Anglican vicar who believed Ms Moore's infamous e-mail was 'basically burying bad news . . . under the bodies of six and a half thousand people'? Blair did not refer to the public apology of the previous afternoon, but he would have recognised that she had done her best to help close down the story. Most of the national newspapers published photographs that morning of what *The Times* said was a chastened special adviser with her 'lips pursed, eyes lowered and hands clasped in contrition' as she stood waiting to express her regret. In any event, the Prime Minister had little difficulty in disposing of Luff's question: 'I do not defend in any shape or form what Jo Moore said, which was horrible, wrong and stupid. I do, however, defend the decision that to sack someone and end their career was too heavy a penalty. That was the decision taken. I supported it and regard the matter as closed.' The same line was taken at the lobby briefing: No. 10 was 'moving on' and had nothing further to say. Newspaper reports suggesting that Campbell had told Byers to sack Ms Moore were 'absolutely not the case'. We were reminded that Charlie Whelan's departure had shown that when special advisers 'became the story it became impossible for them to do their job'. However, as Byers had decided Ms Moore would continue to work for him, 'albeit not in the public eye because of the sheer logistical problems the media exposure and interest in her had caused', Downing Street believed she would in time be able to 'resume her work in the normal way . . . and continue to brief the media'.

Next morning the leader writers expressed their incredulity. 'Let Jo go, Mr Blair,' said the *Sun*, which declared the Prime Minister was wrong to protect 'a key cog in New Labour's political wheel'. The *Daily Telegraph* recalled the way Ms Moore had hung her head in 'well-choreographed shame' at her photo-opportunity. 'The sombre black suit, the silver heart necklace, the trembling lips with just a hint of gloss. Jo Moore spun out her remorse . . . But as soon as she thought the cameras had gone, she gave a triumphant grin. That smirk buried a thousand apologies.' The strength of Ms Moore's determination to fight on was evident the following morning, when she brushed away questions from journalists who had been waiting outside her home: 'I thought you lot would be bored by this now.'

For all her own defiance, there was to be no escape from the spotlight of publicity. MPs, like political journalists, were in hot pursuit, and a flurry of questions appeared on the House of Commons order paper. Some members of the Public Administration Select Committee believed she had breached the recently introduced code of conduct for special advisers. When the Deputy Prime Minister, John Prescott, was called to give evidence, he was questioned at length about the supervisory role of the Cabinet Secretary, Sir Richard Wilson. Tony Wright, the committee chairman, who had said repeatedly that he believed Byers should have sacked Ms Moore, asked what would happen if 'any special adviser were found to be prevailing upon civil servants to do things it was quite improper for them to do'. Prescott said Ms Moore's e-mail was an error of judgement of the 'worst kind' but it had been dealt with in 'a professional manner' by Byers and the permanent secretary, Sir Richard Mottram, who did not intend holding a separate investigation into the circumstances surrounding the departure of Alun Evans, the department's director of communications. Tony Wright failed to elicit an answer to his question about the penalty facing special advisers who went too far in directing civil servants and who had displayed an approach which was 'inconsistent with any notion of public service'.

A week later, on the eve of an opposition debate calling on the Secretary of State to dismiss Ms Moore, Byers used a parliamentary written answer to explain the circumstances surrounding her attempt to persuade a civil servant to brief against London's transport commissioner. He said one of Bob Kiley's assistants had proposed changes to a consultants' report in order to make it more critical of the public–private partnership for the tube and an information officer was asked to 'make the media aware' of this. In the event, however, the department did not release the document. In moving the Conservatives' censure motion, the shadow Secretary of State for Transport, Mrs Theresa May, argued that by trying to persuade a junior civil servant, whom she named as Charlotte Morgan, to leak information to journalists aimed at discrediting Kiley, Ms Moore had broken the code of conduct. Her action, Mrs May claimed, typified 'a culture of spin that says whatever the issue, spin matters more than substance'. Byers told MPs that there was no truth in the suggestion that he was responsible for orchestrating an attempt to damage Kiley: the covering letter written by one of the transport commissioner's assistants stated that quotes which were 'not particularly helpful' had been eliminated from the consultants' report. 'The report was supposed to be independent. I felt people had a right to know; no dirty tricks, no attack on Bob Kiley. When opposition MPs read what actually happened, they will wonder who embarked on a dirty-tricks campaign.' Byers was equally robust in refuting the idea that his department had been influenced by Ms Moore's e-mail. He did not see it on 11 September and was indeed not shown it until 8 October, the day before it appeared in the *Independent*. He said the announcement on councillors' expenses, issued the day after the World Trade Center attack, had been planned the week before. 'There was no news management.'

Byers' explanation failed to satisfy the father of the House, the

Labour MP Tam Dalyell, who said Ms Moore's e-mail was 'a moral lapse' which demonstrated the 'aggressive cynicism of a media-management culture'. And her refusal to acknowledge the damage which she had inflicted on the government worried a former colleague, the Labour MP Sion Simon, who had worked with Ms Moore as a press officer at Millbank Tower. 'She is a most unusually single-minded and unsentimental woman. I think Ms Moore's own interests would have been better served had she chosen to apply to her own expendability the same sense of ruthless pragmatism for which she has been so much admired professionally by so many of us for so long.' At the conclusion of the debate Labour MPs rallied to Byers' support, and the Conservatives' motion was defeated by 340 votes to 167; but the deep sense of unease resurfaced the following month when the Cabinet Secretary was questioned by MPs on the Public Administration Select Committee, who tried again to establish the penalty for a special adviser who made 'a partisan request to a civil servant'. Sir Richard Wilson's response on the general point was emphatic: such action was not proper because their role was not to 'line manage civil servants or give them instructions'. It had been 'entirely proper behaviour' on the part of Alun Evans and the department's information officers to decline to brief the media about the way Bob Kiley's staff had amended the consultants' report. 'The document was not a government document and therefore it was not an appropriate thing to do. I think they were entirely right and I support them . . . I am glad they declined to do what they were asked to do.' Because the matter had been referred 'up the line' nothing wrong had happened, and he could assure the committee that Evans' move to the foot-and-mouth inquiry was 'already in play' and was 'not the direct result of this episode'. He did, however, acknowledge that Ms Moore's action had exposed 'a grey area' because, instead of seeking the advice of Byers' private secretary or the department's permanent secretary, she had 'gone down the line' to an information officer who was not clear about the force of her request.

Sir Richard accepted that civil servants did worry about their own position in relation to their minister if they decided to 'rock the boat', but said that they should have the confidence to raise matters with senior managers and be given the assurance that their concerns would be supported. Sir Richard said Evans and his staff would have been within their rights to make an official complaint about the 11 September e-mail but they had not chosen to do so. 'I do not want to go on about the Jo Moore episode any more because I think she has been punished horribly by the degree of vilification from all quarters, but the thing about that episode which dismays me is the sense that it weakens the trust of the public in what goes on inside government.' The public were entitled to feel that public servants could be trusted and had a set of values which people could identify with and regard as proper. Notwithstanding the weight of criticism attached to Ms Moore, it gave him no pleasure when civil servants leaked documents and then spoke anonymously to the media. 'I think both sets of behaviour go against the public sector ethos which I would like to see in the civil service.'

However, the Cabinet Secretary refused to speculate on the ways in which Byers' permanent secretary, Sir Richard Mottram, might seek to punish another special adviser who made improper requests. 'I think it would be wrong for me to anticipate the department's disciplinary process in relation to somebody else.' Sir Richard admitted that as head of the civil service he had 'no role in relation to specific disciplinary issues relating to special advisers' other than those attached to ministers in the Cabinet Office. He made no secret of his dissatisfaction with this general lack of clarity: he thought there should be a wider awareness and understanding of the code of conduct, and he hoped the Prime Minister would honour the government's commitment to introduce a Civil Service Act to give a statutory footing to rules governing the ethics and behaviour of special advisers and to provide for a cap on their number. There should be an opportunity 'once and for all' to discuss their role outside the political arena and to stop treating the issue as 'a political football'.

Sir Richard had rarely been so explicit about the tension which could arise when political appointees made improper approaches to civil servants, and the depth of his evident unease about the danger this posed to the public service ethos reflected the wider concern within Whitehall about the impact of Tony Blair's decision to appoint twice as many special advisers as John Major. Although he had been forthright in defending the information officers who had objected to Ms Moore's e-mail, and to her attempt to get the Department of Transport to brief against Kiley, the hearing had shown that to all intents and purposes the Cabinet Secretary was powerless to discipline special advisers who retained the confidence of their minister and who also had the backing of the Prime Minister. The committee did not ask Sir Richard to explain why Ms Moore had survived when Charlie Whelan had been forced out, but the answer seemed pretty obvious: she continued to enjoy the support of her political masters whereas Whelan had had no alternative but to resign once Tony Blair had finally lost patience with him and Gordon Brown was no longer prepared to defend him. No special adviser had previously been subjected to the kind of parliamentary scrutiny which Ms Moore had attracted and, in retaining her services, Byers had made himself an easy target for opposition MPs and the media, who were suspicious of his every move and ready to exploit any opportunity to accuse him of continuing to try to 'bury' bad news.

By having to admit that at the end of the day there was little he could do to control the activities of ministerial spin doctors, Sir Richard had in effect thrown down a gauntlet which the lobby correspondents, those self-appointed guardians of political standards, were only too happy to pick up; the chase was on. Although Ms Moore must have known she was a marked woman, and that whatever she did on Byers' behalf would inevitably go on being seen as a news story, she was no faint-heart; she confounded her critics and rose to the challenge. Byers used an interview on *Breakfast with Frost* on Sunday 25 November to express his confidence in her judgement. She would continue to work for him alongside the department's new director of communications, the former BBC Moscow correspondent Martin Sixsmith, who had returned to government service after a brief period with GEC-Marconi.

Two days later Ms Moore was headline news once again: she was accused of having taken advantage of Gordon Brown's pre-Budget report to the House of Commons to slip out the minutes of a controversial meeting between Byers and the Railtrack chairman, John Robinson. Copies were faxed to the offices of *The Times*, *Financial Times*, *Guardian* and *Independent* while the Chancellor was giving

MPs details of his spending plans, and the four named recipients were the correspondents who were later described by the government as having taken the closest interest in the story. Next morning, Brown's warning that taxes would have to rise to pay for 'a world-class health service' had to share the front pages with the latest twist in the Railtrack saga. Both Byers and Ms Moore were back in the dock: there was nothing in the minutes to substantiate his claim that he had been warned that Railtrack would go bust unless it received more government money, and she was accused by the Conservatives of pulling off a real-life example of 'burying bad news'. Selective briefings are sometimes effective; by supplying the minutes to four carefully chosen newspaper correspondents, Byers must have hoped there was a fair chance of gaining favourable coverage on what was, after all, a busy news day. The danger in such blatant manipulation is that it can anger other media outlets and ultimately produce far worse coverage than if all news organisations had been treated in the same way. In this case, political journalists who had been excluded from the exercise were hell-bent on revenge, and Tom Kelly had to bear the brunt of their wrath at the morning and afternoon lobby briefings.

He said the minutes were published on the same day as the pre-Budget report in order to meet a deadline set by the Transport Select Committee. Byers' department chose to send copies to the four news-papers which were 'following the story most closely'. When asked why it had been left to a special adviser like Jo Moore to determine how the minutes should be released, Kelly seemed anxious to do all he could to distance Downing Street from the Department of Transport. 'I don't recognise the course of events you describe . . . You must talk to the department concerned. It is not for Downing Street to approve it or not.' Some of the correspondents were deter-mined to press home their advantage: they claimed they had seen their colleagues being briefed by Ms Moore. Jon Smith, political editor of the Press Association news agency, said he was convinced that the whole point of the exercise had been to 'bury' the minutes and to make sure the damaging evidence they contained did not detract from coverage of the Chancellor's statement in the news bulletins that evening. Kelly struggled to hold the line for No. 10: 'I have not made direct enquiries along the lines you have asked . . . My information is that it was not Jo Moore . . . it was the department that did the briefing.' Although my own enquiries failed to identify the precise chain of command, there seemed to be every justification for the claim by some reporters that Ms Moore had been involved. Civil service information officers in Byers' department told me that they were asked to contact several named journalists; they faxed the minutes, as instructed, to the four newspapers; and they insisted that the method and timing of the document's release had been a 'political decision'.

Their account indicated that the responsibility lay either with the Secretary of State or with one of his special advisers. 'Byers rebuked for "contaminating" big day' was the front-page headline the following day in *The Times*, over an exclusive report which said the Secretary of State had been sent a 'stiff letter' of complaint by Downing Street's strategic communications unit for having released the minutes during the pre-Budget report. Tom Baldwin, the deputy political editor, said the minutes were faxed to *The Times* at 3.35 p.m., five minutes after Brown started speaking, and the Department of Transport was told the decision to release the document that afternoon was bound to 'attract negative media coverage' which had inevitably 'contaminated' news reporting of the Chancellor's statement. At the lobby briefing later that morning Downing Street was again on the defensive. Godric Smith, who doubled up with Tom Kelly as one of the Prime Minister's official spokesmen, was adamant that reports suggesting Blair was distancing himself from Byers were 'rubbish'. He had no intention of answering any further questions. 'I don't intend to feed what has become a processological orgy of who said what, where and when . . . The Prime Minister believes Byers has taken exactly the right decision in terms of modernising our railways. Railtrack is a company that has a reverse Midas touch, delivering a deteriorating standard of service and sucking in public money . . . We are moving on.'

Smith's bravado was No. 10's only line of defence in the face of a damning interview by Jonathan Baume, leader of the First Division Association. He told *Today* there was a mechanism through which Alastair Campbell and the strategic communications unit reprimanded those departments which departed from the grid of events dictated by No. 10. As far as his union was concerned there was 'no doubt' that the decision to release the minutes had been taken at a political level, and he appealed to the government to allow the 'very, very experienced' civil servants within the department to sort out the future of Railtrack. 'My advice certainly to Jo Moore would be to stand to one side and let the professionals get on with the job and then perhaps the Secretary of State would be better served than he has been recently . . . There's a great deal of frustration in the department once again . . . There's a very experienced head of information, who's just been appointed, and I do think people like that should be left to get on with the job.' A week later, on 3 December 2001, the Conservatives sought to step up the pressure by moving a House of Commons motion which deprecated the government's 'pursuit of cynical news management'. Byers did not reply to the debate as he was opening a new bridge in his constituency of North Tyneside. His absence from the chamber was exploited by Tim Collins, the Tories' spokesman on Cabinet Office affairs, who said that as long as Blair allowed Byers to remain Secretary of State for Transport, he would 'like a snail produce a trail of slime leading across Downing Street and right up to the door of No. 10' – a jibe which the Speaker forced Collins to withdraw.

Anne McIntosh, one of the Conservative MPs on the Transport Select Committee, told the House she had read with interest that *The Times* was faxed its copy of the Byers' minutes at 3.35 p.m., having received hers at 5 p.m. 'If that is not an example of cynical news management, I do not know what is.' The Liberal Democrat MP Paul Tyler said his party had tried without success to obtain a list of the conversations which Jo Moore had had with journalists that day. Under their code of conduct special advisers were 'supposed to record all contacts with the media', but questions addressed to Byers had met with 'blank obstruction'. Clive Soley, the Labour MP for whom Ms Moore had worked when he was shadow housing minister, thought she had 'ruined her career' because of her 'incredibly insensitive' e-mail. He suspected it was the 'constant tug of war between civil servants and political advisers' which had resulted in her getting into so much trouble. Ministers needed the assistance of special advisers in 'a modern, complex Parliament' and he wanted to see them accommodated within the system in a way which recognised the importance of their job as political appointees but stripped them of their status as civil servants.

The name 'Jo Moore' had become synonymous with spin, and in their reviews of the year almost every national newspaper included her e-mail as one of the most memorable quotations of 2001. Her photograph stared out from the *Sun* in a montage of the 100 faces whose lives had been changed for ever since 11 September. In the London *Evening Standard* Ms Moore was nominated as 'villain of the year' by the publicist Max Clifford, who said she had broken the most important rule of public relations: 'Don't get caught.' Subsequently Clifford told me that once the e-mail had been leaked she should have stood her ground. 'What Jo did was only human nature for anyone in our business; it's just like a journalist who is forced to make a correction and wants to bury it on a busy news day.' In what the *Independent* described as its list of 'smear of the year' awards, Bob Kiley suggested she should get the prize for the 'murkiest' smear.

The denigration of Ms Moore proved too much for one *Guardian* reader. In a letter to the editor, David Ross of London objected to an end-of-the-year editorial which said cynicism about politicians and politics had been reinforced by the refusal of Byers' special adviser to resign over her 'grossly tactless "bury bad news" tip'. Like Max Clifford, Ross believed most journalists and press officers would have made a comparable calculation: 'Everyone in public communications had to decide similarly on what action to take. Three months after the event, is it not time for the humbug to stop?' While I accepted that there was a considerable degree of hypocrisy about the way many commentators had chosen to pillory Byers' spin doctor, I felt Clifford and the *Guardian*'s letter-writer had overlooked one salient point. Ms Moore enjoyed the status of a civil servant, and she had demonstrated on more than one occasion that she had few inhibitions about giving highly questionable instructions to government information officers. If she had been working as a political propagandist at Millbank Tower or Conservative Central Office – or, for that matter, as a public relations consultant for a tobacco company – it might have been easier to excuse the cool and calculated way in which she instructed her staff to exploit the World Trade Center attack. However, different considerations applied to the dissemination of information about affairs of state, and the public rightly expected higher standards. I shared the assessment of another of Ms Moore's former colleagues, Ian Willmore, who knew her from her days as a party press officer. In an article in *The Times* he described how, as members of Hornsey and Wood Green Labour Party, they had tried to fight off attempts by the far left to gain seats on Haringey Council. Willmore thought she had 'a deserved reputation as an exceptionally tough political organiser' but he doubted whether those attributes served her well working for a Labour government. 'She grew up in a political culture that is now dead. To confront the idiocies of the far left in the London Labour Party in the early 1980s took persistence, endless effort and personal courage. But it made her – it made all of us – hard . . . And that hardness has infected the party we fought so hard to save and threatens to rob it of its soul.' Willmore thought Ms Moore's talents could be better employed elsewhere, and he suggested she become a campaigner for a non-governmental organisation. 'She is fearless, clever and determined. A government or large corporation facing her would certainly think twice.'

I knew from my own dealings with Ms Moore that she shared Alastair Campbell's deeply held conviction that the Labour Party could never afford to ease up in its constant battle against media misrepresentation. They both regarded the struggle as never-ending: Tony Blair's re-election in June 2001 had changed nothing: the party had to remain on a permanent campaign footing and that meant that, if necessary, risks had to be taken in defending the Prime Minister and his cabinet. Ms Moore's single-minded determination to see off her critics reflected the strength of her long devotion to the Labour cause.

WRECKERS AND
RESIGNATIONS

'You spoke about possibly making this announcement on Friday. We should not do it on
Friday, as that is the day on which Princess Margaret is being buried. There are too many
connotations to the word "buried" for us to do anything on that day.'
E-mail from Martin Sixsmith, director of communications, to Stephen Byers, Secretary
of State for Transport, Local Government and the Regions. Subject: rail performance
indicators. Date: 2 February 2002. Copied to: Ian Jones, Jo Moore.

Having withstood three months of vilification following the
publication of her 11 September e-mail, Jo Moore had
demonstrated beyond all doubt that she was a worthy
honours graduate of the Mandelson–Campbell Institute for
Manipulation. Resilience in the face of unrelenting pressure was an
essential prerequisite for a New Labour spin doctor and, as she had
been advised by her two most eminent tutors, she knew that the best
tactic in the face of a prolonged media onslaught was to keep cool
and play it long, in the well-founded belief that journalists usually
have a short attention span and might eventually tire of whatever
story they have been pursuing.

Tony Blair was a class act when it came to riding out a feeding
frenzy and rising above the murky, manipulative world inhabited by
Alastair Campbell and the rest of the political appointees who did
daily battle with the news media on his behalf. After telling MPs in
mid-October 2001 that he accepted Ms Moore's apology and
regarded the matter as 'closed', the Prime Minister succeeded,
against all the odds, in fending off further questions about her
attempts to give civil service information officers instructions which
the Cabinet Secretary, Sir Richard Wilson, had subsequently deemed
unacceptable. However distasteful it might have seemed to the
public, her 'bury bad news' e-mail symbolised the expertise which
Blair had done so much to encourage, and he had simply turned a

blind eye to the tensions which had been created through the impo-
sition of routines more akin to the dictates of political propaganda
than to the delivery of public information. In the face of little or no
resistance from Sir Richard and the departmental permanent secretaries, Campbell and his network of special advisers had managed
to exert ever greater control over the flow of news from the
ministries of Whitehall.

Nevertheless, the opposition which was being encountered at the
Department of Transport showed that the headline-grabbing culture
which had served Labour so well in opposition could not always be
replicated quite so easily in government. Not long after the various
end-of-the-year reminders of her infamous e-mail had begun to fade
away, and it seemed she had been able to survive a maelstrom of her
own making, Ms Moore found herself back in the headlines. 'Byers
in new furore over spin, politics and Moore,' said the *Independent*'s
headline on 21 January 2002 over a front-page report claiming that
the Secretary of State's 'disgraced spin doctor' wanted to get a top
job for one of her friends in order to help her 'politicise' Byers' information staff.

An unidentified union official was quoted as saying there had
been tension and ill-feeling because the appointment of a new head
of news for the Department of Transport had been blocked for seven
weeks as a result of a disagreement between the Secretary of State
and his recently installed director of communications, Martin
Sixsmith. Byers wanted the job to go Ann Wallis, who was a friend
of Ms Moore, but Sixsmith favoured the department's assistant
director, Ian Jones, whose promotion had been recommended by a
civil service appointments panel. Ms Wallis was a civil servant in the
rough sleepers' unit, which was attached to Byers' department, and
she had responsibility for media presentation. She and Ms Moore
had previously worked together for the lobbyists Westminster
Strategy.

Once news of the disagreement appeared in the morning papers,
there was some swift footwork behind the scenes and late that afternoon the department confirmed Jones's appointment. Initially
Downing Street suggested that there had been no hitch and that a
seven-week delay in announcing an appointment was not unusual.

Then, at the afternoon lobby briefing, the line suddenly changed: Tom Kelly said an announcement was imminent. The only inference which could be drawn from the rapid turnabout was that either Blair or Campbell had intervened; when the department confirmed Jones's promotion an hour later, most correspondents concluded that Byers must have been overruled, an interpretation which Downing Street did little to dispel. Jonathan Baume was pleased that No. 10 had intervened. His union had been dismayed to discover that Byers had put the appointment 'on hold' for so long, and he hoped there would be 'no further attempts at manipulating the appointments process'.

Because of the unwelcome publicity her presence attracted, Ms Moore had rarely been seen in action during the previous three months, and she usually kept in the background when broadcasters and newspaper reporters visited the department to interview either the Secretary of State or one of his junior ministers. Now, despite another batch of unfavourable headlines, she was determined to put in an appearance at party events and demonstrate publicly that she could provide Byers with the support and back-up which he needed. She chose the weekend of Labour's local government and women's conference at Cardiff in February 2002 as the occasion at which to make her comeback and give her first up-front briefing for political correspondents. Byers was one of the main speakers, and, after handing out advance copies of his speech to the journalists waiting in the media centre, Ms Moore stayed for a few moments to answer questions. There was considerable interest in what Byers planned to say because ministers saw the gathering as a valuable opportunity to defend the government's private finance initiative. Three of the biggest trade unions, Unison, the T&G and the GMB, had other ideas and were determined to use the conference as an opportunity to step up their campaign against the privatisation of public services.

Byers' text showed that he intended to describe the argument which was taking place over the government's agenda for modernisation and reform as 'a battle between the reformers and the wreckers'. In response to our questions, Ms Moore agreed that the 'wreckers' included not only the Conservatives but also those trade union leaders who were resisting Labour's plans to step up the use of private finance. The first speech of the morning session was given by the

Unison general secretary, Dave Prentis, who was warmly applauded when he voiced his unease about the way the 'New Labour aristocracy' kept reassuring themselves that 'involving private companies is not privatisation.' From the standpoint of Unison's members in the hospitals and local authorities, the involvement of private companies was 'just as much privatisation as compulsory competitive tendering was under the Tories'. Byers was also applauded early on in his speech when he declared that he was in no doubt that taking control of Railtrack had been 'the right thing to do' – but there was nowhere near the same enthusiasm for his remark about 'wreckers' or his warning that ministers would not let 'vested interests' stand in their way. When interviewed by the *PM* presenter Carolyn Quinn and asked if the 'wreckers' included union leaders like Prentis and John Edmonds of the GMB, Byers readily agreed with her: 'If people stand in the way of change we have got to take them on and explain to their members why change is necessary.' Ms Moore's briefing, and the Secretary of State's subsequent confirmation that some union leaders, as well as the Tories, were his opponents, set the scene for an explosive reaction at a lunchtime rally of public service workers.

Byers, one of New Labour's most enthusiastic modernisers, had caused offence among the trade unions in previous years: at the 1996 TUC conference, he told a group of journalists that it was time the party prepared to sever its links with the union movement. Now, the fight-back at the rally was hard-hitting: Edmonds argued that Labour's future in power was at stake unless ministers heeded the lack of public support for privatising public services. 'This government had better be very careful, because it has invented totally unnecessarily its own poll tax, its own electoral disadvantage, its own imploding policy, which is going to drag down its support.'

In my reports for BBC radio, I said Byers' attack on the 'wreckers' had fuelled 'a display of angry name-calling' between ministers and the unions, whose opposition to the use of private finance was becoming increasingly vocal. We then discovered, late that afternoon, that in his closing speech to the conference the following morning, the Prime Minister proposed to use the same theme: that the modernisation of public services had become a battle of 'reformers versus wreckers'. On being asked at a news briefing whom Blair had in mind when speaking of 'wreckers', the party's chief press and broadcasting officer, Matthew Doyle, told us that it obviously included all those who were opposing reform, 'from right to left'. We thought the line was clear – that union leaders were included among the 'wreckers' – but Doyle must have had second thoughts, because he spent the rest of the afternoon and evening reminding journalists at every opportunity that the advance quotations which he had read out from the speech indicated that Blair was talking about the Conservatives when he used the word 'wreckers'. Alastair Campbell, who was still in London, confirmed that the Conservatives were the Prime Minister's target in that particular section of his speech; pitching the government's agenda as a battle of 'reformers versus wreckers' was the agreed theme for speeches that weekend. Nevertheless, Campbell did not seek to challenge or correct what Ms Moore or Byers had said in extending this categorisation to include the unions.

In closing the conference next morning, Blair's address followed the advance text: the Tories were intent on destroying the public services. 'Our strategy is to build up the public services. Theirs is to knock them down. Reformers versus wreckers. That is the battle for this Parliament and it is one we must win . . . for just as we must take on and defeat the big "C" Conservatives who want to undermine public services, so we must defeat in argument the small "c" conservatives who believe the old ways will do and who resist reform.' Later in his speech Blair widened his attack still further to include those on the 'far left' who tried to accuse Labour of privatising public services when the government's intention was to be 'creative in public service solutions'. He appealed to the party to 'hold firm' against the opponents of reform and, just as with Neil Kinnock's push against Militant, he said he was ready to 'fight every single inch of the way' against those who accused the leadership of betraying Labour's principles. Campbell, who stood at the side of the platform watching the speech, had applauded enthusiastically when Blair vowed to beat the 'wreckers'.

Afterwards Campbell stopped briefly to speak to reporters and told us we would be quite correct in assuming that the attack on 'small "c" conservatives' and the 'far left' did include those union leaders who opposed the modernisation programme. 'Some on the left are saying you can't invest and reform. Union leaders say it's privatisation when it's not. We have had this at every major step change. The cry of betrayal goes up when you are using modern means . . . Yes, we are going to stand firm.' Campbell could not have been clearer: although Blair had not linked the word 'wreckers' directly to the unions, he obviously considered they were proving just as destructive as the Conservatives and was equally determined to take them on. In an interview that evening for *The Westminster Hour*, the TUC general secretary, John Monks, rounded on Blair for having been 'absolutely destructive' in condemning public service workers who were voicing their concern about the government's plans. He was mystified by the Prime Minister's motives because, in a speech in Newcastle the previous week, Blair had said those who chose to work in the public services deserved respect. 'One week we were warmly praised . . . This week's theme is a "wrecking" innuendo. I think it is bizarre what is going on. It is erratic and it is not worthy of the government to indulge in such juvenile terminology.' Bill Morris, the T&G's general secretary, told *Today* that the 'wreckers' were the 'spin doctors who tried to bury bad news' and who used their spinning to conjure up enemies for the government. Next day the unions took full-page advertisements in the national newspapers to ram home their response. 'Is she one of the "wreckers" Tony?' said the caption for the GMB's ad, which showed a photograph of a nurse caring for a baby in a hospital incubator. Unison used a picture of a home help combing the hair of an elderly woman and asked the same question: 'Is she the wrecker?'

On looking back at the course of events in Cardiff that weekend, I was not at all surprised that Ms Moore had been in the thick of it and had, without hesitation, played her part in trying to influence the news agenda in favour of the modernisers. Byers had used the word 'wreckers' the previous week to describe those unions that were opposed to the private finance initiative for the London Underground, and in her briefing in advance of his speech to the conference, Ms Moore had no qualms in giving journalists her guidance on the thrust of his attack. I thought she had shown considerable courage in facing the media when she knew full well that her presence beside Byers as he talked to delegates, and then when he toured the conference exhibition area, was bound to attract the attention of photographers and television crews. As I listened to Blair's speech in Cardiff I had to marvel at his audacity in turning the headlines provoked by Ms Moore's briefing about the 'wreckers' into one of his regular tirades against the media. 'The rubbish comes in and out. There it is, swirling around, whether you read it or not, but all that disappears with next day's news. All that remains is the vision and the values and the ability to take tough decisions and get the job done.'

Less than a fortnight after relaunching herself at the Cardiff conference, Ms Moore was forced to resign. Her demise was just as swift, savage and spectacular as Charlie Whelan's hurried exit at the height of the home loan scandal which forced Peter Mandelson's first resignation from the cabinet. By admitting the previous December in his evidence to the Select Committee on Public Administration that Byers' special adviser had been in the wrong on at least two occasions, but in failing to do anything about it, Sir Richard Wilson had given rank and file civil servants every excuse they needed to exact their own punishment; and the political journalists, who had been such eager recipients of the information which she had been able to impart to them over the years, were waiting in the wings, ready and willing to act as accomplices in her downfall. 'Moore Shame' was the *Mirror*'s front-page headline on Thursday 14 February over an exclusive story which it shared with the *Daily Express* about another audacious attempt to 'bury' bad news. Yet again there had been a leak from within the Department of Transport's media office; both papers claimed that the director of communications, Martin Sixsmith, had sent an e-mail to Ms Moore accusing her of having planned to use Princess Margaret's funeral the following day, Friday 15 February, as the moment to release damaging rail statistics. The *Mirror* went one step further than the *Express* and reproduced a copy of what it said was Sixsmith's message: 'Dear Jo, there is no way I will allow this department to make any substantive announcements next Friday. Princess Margaret is being buried on that day. I will absolutely not allow anything else to be.'

An unidentified source within the department was quoted by Patrick O'Flynn, the *Express*'s political editor, as saying that Sixsmith had been alerted the previous Monday, the day after Buckingham Palace announced the date of the funeral, when information officers first heard of Ms Moore's proposal at a routine discussion on the timing of the week's press releases. Paul Routledge, the *Mirror*'s commentator, claimed that Ms Moore's 'grotesque behaviour' had disgusted civil servants. 'They are so incensed that they blew the whistle to the *Mirror* – and thank heaven they did . . . the only funeral tomorrow will be that of a much-loved Royal. The interment of Jo Moore's reputation should follow very soon thereafter.' When other newspapers tried to follow up the story after the first editions had been published, Byers' department issued a firm denial: 'There is no story. It is a fictitious e-mail.' Ms Moore was just as forthright when approached by the Press Association. She said she had not proposed the release of any 'bad news' to coincide with the funeral; an announcement about new indicators for rail performance, which had originally been pencilled in for Thursday or Friday of that week, had been postponed until the following Monday. 'This is a very hurtful accusation which is completely untrue . . . the reported e-mail is completely made up.' Next morning, as she left for work, Ms Moore told the same story when an ITN reporter showed her the *Mirror*'s inside spread which, alongside her photograph, had the bold headline: 'Her last mistake'.

Later that morning, at the 11.30 a.m. lobby briefing in Downing Street, Godric Smith was as definite as both the Department of Transport and Ms Moore had been in rebutting the story: 'The e-mail between Martin Sixsmith and Jo Moore doesn't exist. It's a fabrication . . . You can say what you like about us, but we don't lie.' Smith did reveal that earlier in the week Sixsmith had 'alerted' Byers to the 'possible misconstruction' which could be put on the release of railway performance indicators on the same day as Princess Margaret's funeral, and the announcement had been rescheduled to the following Monday. However, Downing Street had no intention of elaborating on 'every bit of internal communication' in Byers' department just because of the 'totally erroneous construction which had been put on a fictitious e-mail'. An hour later, at business questions in the Commons, the Leader of the House, Robin Cook, told MPs he could give them a 'categorical denial' of the story. 'The e-mail that appears in the *Mirror* today is a fabrication; there was no such e-mail . . . there was no disagreement on the matter between Sixsmith and Moore.' Downing Street seemed to have succeeded in killing off the story: little attention was paid to it on the lunchtime television and radio news bulletins, and most journalists would probably have accepted the denial had it not been for a mid-afternoon newsflash from the Press Association's political editor, Jon Smith, saying that he had learned authoritatively that Ms Moore 'did receive an e-mail' from Sixsmith warning of the danger of 'burying bad news' on the same day as Princess Margaret's funeral. This e-mail was not identical to the one published by the *Mirror*, which the Press Association said had allowed officials to deny its existence, but it 'did contain the words "Princess Margaret", "Friday" and "buried".'

Lobby correspondents realised immediately that the country's leading news agency would have made sure it was on firm ground before putting out a story which contradicted what Downing Street and a cabinet minister had just said. From the moment the newsflash arrived on journalists' computer screens at 2.43 p.m., the press gallery was agog with speculation. Word spread rapidly that Sixsmith was anxious to put his side of the story, and at 4 p.m., when correspondents gathered for Godric Smith's afternoon lobby briefing, they had a pretty clear idea about what they thought had happened. The general consensus was that Sixsmith must have felt Downing Street had gone too far in dismissing the story as 'a fabrication', because there seemed to be little doubt that he had sent an e-mail to Byers. His message would almost certainly have been copied to Ms Moore, with whom it was known Sixsmith had been at loggerheads for weeks, and the assumption was that he felt so aggrieved about the way she was being exonerated by Downing Street, after he considered she had tried yet again to interfere in the department's news management, that he was determined to make sure his version of events was not ignored. Reports of Sixsmith's anger had obviously reached Downing Street, because Godric Smith opened the afternoon briefing with an unprecedented personal statement.

Ever since the 11.30 a.m. lobby briefing he had been taking calls from journalists who were convinced the e-mail existed and who felt they had been misled. Therefore he wanted to set the record straight and explain the steps he had taken to make sure his original briefing was accurate. Earlier that morning he had spoken to both Byers and Sixsmith, and Sixsmith had assured him that the e-mail reprinted in the *Mirror* was 'a fiction' and that 'an e-mail from Sixsmith to Jo Moore' did not exist. As he had explained that morning, Byers had been advised by Sixsmith that the rail announcement should not be made on Friday; this communication had been made by e-mail but there was no e-mail from Sixsmith to Ms Moore. Therefore, Smith said, he stood by the account he had given at the time, and did not take kindly to being accused of telling an untruth. 'If anonymous sources want to dispute that they can, but they should have the courage of their convictions and come out and say so . . . There are clearly people in the Department of Transport who will hide behind anonymity and do everything possible to undermine Jo Moore and in doing so undermine their own department and the Secretary of State . . . As a member of the government's information service I find that pretty unacceptable . . . If you behave in that way, maybe you are in the wrong job.' When Smith was asked if his remarks were directed at Sixsmith, he avoided giving a direct answer: 'I am not pointing the finger at anyone. I am not saying that.' None the less he agreed there seemed to be 'civil war' between Byers' media advisers. 'Clearly there is a game going on here, but I am not prepared to have my integrity and credibility put on the line because they are something which I value and which are precious to me.' Downing Street would not tolerate having a briefing by one of the Prime Minister's official spokesmen countermanded anonymously by leaks from within a government department and Smith said a stern reminder was being issued to all information officers. Mike Granatt, head of the government information and communication service, would be writing to Sixsmith and other heads of information 'deploring in the strongest possible terms' what had happened and reminding both them and their staff that there were proper channels through which complaints should be made.

Despite the apparent severity of Granatt's reprimand for Sixsmith and renewed demands by the Conservatives for Ms Moore to be sacked, Smith refused to comment on their possible fate; but most correspondents had little difficulty reading between the lines and concluded that the resignation or dismissal of one or both of them seemed likely. Next morning the two newspapers which broke the story were determined to hammer the government for having traduced their reporting. 'Liars' was the one word splashed across the *Mirror*'s front-page lead, which said that Downing Street, Byers' department, Robin Cook and that 'Whitehall vamp', Ms Moore, had all been 'exposed as liars'. Headline writers for the *Daily Express* took the same line: 'You liars' were the two words which appeared above front-page photographs of Ms Moore, Byers and Godric Smith, who were each taken to task for having denounced the paper's original story as 'fictitious'. Paul Routledge, the *Mirror*'s columnist, claimed that lying had become second nature to New Labour. 'They lied. Through their teeth. Through their spokesmen. Through their media machine. Through every avenue available to escape guilt for their own big lie.'

Sixsmith must have taken some encouragement from the vilification of Ms Moore in the morning newspapers because he put on a brave face when interviewed on his way in to work. 'This whole story is a complete nonsense. Worse than that, it's a distraction. My only job and Jo Moore's only job is to help Stephen Byers sort out public transport in this country, make it fit for the twenty-first century; that's all I'm interested in doing and that's all Jo is interested in doing.' Sixsmith's bravado belied the seriousness of his position. Journalists had been given a copy of the letter which he had been sent and it underlined the degree to which he was being held personally responsible by Mike Granatt for the leaks and confusion which followed Downing Street's initial briefing. 'For that to be undermined by an anonymous, inaccurate briefing apparently from the DLTR, is unacceptable . . . I will not defend any member of the GICS who acts in this way . . . anyone who feels so strongly that they wish to act outside the civil service code should do the honourable thing and resign.' Godric Smith's turn of phrase at the Friday morning lobby briefing sounded just as ominous. Having been stripped of his own anonymity as one of the Prime Minister's 'official spokesmen', and having had his name and photograph splashed all over the newspapers, Smith looked somewhat chastened as he opened the proceedings with what he believed was the definitive account of the week's events.

When Byers' media team held their Monday morning meeting to discuss future announcements there was no mention of Princess Margaret's funeral; Ms Moore did not suggest 'taking advantage' of the funeral; and it was only when someone had 'quite sensibly' alerted Sixsmith to the possible misconstruction which could be placed on releasing rail statistics on the same day that he sent an e-mail to Byers which was then copied to Ms Moore and another civil servant. 'People have spun this and twisted this for a certain agenda. In the end I hope people will look objectively at the facts.'

As he had done the day before, Smith refused to give a direct answer when asked if the Prime Minister still had confidence in both the information director and the spin doctor. 'I am not going to get into a running commentary . . . There are issues which are going to have to be looked at and sorted out by Stephen Byers and his permanent secretary, Sir Richard Mottram.' After having made so much fuss about not using the occasion of Princess Margaret's funeral (held at 3.30 p.m. that Friday afternoon) as a cover to smuggle out unpopular government announcements, we all realised that Byers was hardly likely to make any further comment while the service was taking place at St George's Chapel, Windsor. However, check calls to the No. 10 press office early in the afternoon confirmed that action of some kind had been taken. By mid-afternoon, when television crews reported that Sixsmith and Ms Moore had already left the department, it was clear there had been a dramatic outcome; and at 4.40 p.m. the BBC was told by Downing Street that they had both resigned.

From what we could piece together it seemed there had been conversations that morning between Byers, Alastair Campbell, Mike Granatt and the Cabinet Secretary, Sir Richard Wilson. Ms Moore had apparently offered her resignation to Byers after they had agreed the previous evening that her position was untenable, and there was a general consensus that in fairness to Ms Moore, and in recognition of her loyalty, Sixsmith should be told by Sir Richard Mottram that his position was untenable and that he should be asked to resign too. In the words of Downing Street, this was the only way to ensure that there was a 'fresh start' for the Department of Transport's information staff. One development which was confirmed publicly that

morning was that Byers intended to reshuffle his department's information staff and establish a separate team who would work at a
'secretary of state' desk and be assigned the task of helping to rebuild
his media image.

Finally, at 5 p.m., Byers issued his own statement, which was brief
and to the point, about the poisonous ill-feeling which he had
allowed to fester for so long: 'It is clear that there has been a breakdown of trust within the department. This could not be allowed to
continue. Both Martin Sixsmith and Jo Moore have done the right
thing by offering their resignations. The department faces major
challenges to deliver our ambitious programme. It will need the undi-
vided attention of ministers and civil servants. As a result of these
changes we should be in a far stronger position to meet these challenges.' Byers gave a series of television interviews and repeated his
belief that his special adviser and information director had both
'done the right thing by tendering their resignations'.

However, the Secretary of State was careful to avoid taking sides
or apportioning blame. Ms Moore felt under no such constraints,
and released a copy of her resignation letter, addressed 'Dear Steve',
which she used to attack her opponents within the department and
to underline the depth of her commitment to the Labour government.
She had hoped all along that her 'genuine, heartfelt apology' after the
11 September e-mail would have been accepted by the civil servants
with whom she worked, but it had become increasingly obvious that
was not the case. 'Clearly there are some individuals in the department who are not prepared to work with me and are even prepared
to invent stories about me as they have done this week. I have devoted
most of my adult life to working for the Labour Party because I am
committed to achieving a fair and just society. I do not want to be an
obstacle to achieving this goal. Yet stories like the one this week,
despite the fact they are totally untrue, are allowing opponents to
denigrate the real achievements of the government and are a distraction from our priority of investing in and reforming key public
services like railways and the London Underground. It therefore
seems to me the right thing to do is resign.'

David Hill, who had been Labour's director of communications
when Jo Moore was chief press officer, was one of the few party

spokesmen to rally to her defence that evening. He told *News 24* that while her position had become untenable, he suspected the events leading to her hurried resignation were 'a set-up' designed to force her out. Hill was convinced that there was a place in government for special advisers, but he accepted there had to be changes and thought that in future ministerial appointees should be based in a clearly designated political unit attached to each Whitehall department.

Jonathan Baume told *News 24* he regretted Sixsmith's resignation but felt he had acted honourably. Information had been leaking out of the media office in the Department of Transport over a period of months, which had led Downing Street to question Sixsmith's loyalty. 'What this whole episode has shown is the need for everyone to stick to the rules. Civil servants must not leak.' Baume had little sympathy for Ms Moore, who had done 'immense damage through her failure to respect the judgement of civil servants'. His union was convinced Alastair Campbell had wanted her sacked for months, but No. 10 had not been prepared to defy Byers for fear of weakening his position.

'On Your Bike, Jo' was the *Mirror*'s headline over a two-page report next morning, which featured a photograph of Ms Moore cycling to work. As Paul Routledge remarked in his comment column, it had turned out to be 'a good day to bury bad news after all', and most of the newspaper headlines were a variation on that theme. Sixsmith was hailed as the hero of the affair by the *Daily Mail*, which believed he had paid a high price for his integrity. The axe had fallen on the one man who 'dared to question Ms Moore's sickening lack of ethics', and clearly any other civil servant who revealed the 'cynical corruption of Blair's propaganda machine' would be similarly destroyed.

My task that Saturday morning was to assess for *Today* the likely fall-out from yet another illustration of the way in which Blair's government was being damaged by a regime which gave the highest priority to presentation and spin and allowed political appointees the opportunity to exercise ever greater control over the flow of information to the public. Tony Wright, chairman of the Select Committee on Public Administration, told me it was Byers' refusal to sack Ms Moore after her 11 September e-mail which had precipitated this latest 'fiasco'. He believed the two resignations had strengthened the hand of his committee in demanding that the code of conduct for special advisers be put on a statutory footing in a new Civil Service Act, which Blair had promised before the 2001 general election. Once the code had the force of law, aggrieved civil servants would be able to raise their concerns through a proper complaints procedure if they considered ministerial spin doctors were exercising political control or issuing instructions which endangered civil service neutrality. Wright was backed by Gwyneth Dunwoody, chairman of the Transport Select Committee, who put the blame on 'a small coterie' of unelected special advisers in No. 10 who were interfering in the work of the individual departments by demanding strict adherence to the weekly grid of future announcements issued by Downing Street's strategic communications unit. 'They are interfering not on the basis of agreed cabinet decisions but because they say, "Well, you must only do this or that at a particular time." There isn't a lot of point in having a civil service if you are immediately going to up-end everything they do.' Andy Wood, a former director of communications for the Northern Ireland Office, who was among the heads of information ousted soon after the 1997 general election, agreed with Wright and Dunwoody. Special advisers like Ms Moore had 'picked up on a mood set by ministers' about what they thought they could 'get away with', and their influence had to be curtailed. Barbara Roche, Minister of State for the Cabinet Office, told *Today* that the code of conduct already provided a 'perfectly proper' procedure for complaints, but she indicated the government would be consulting shortly on the legislation to be included in a new Civil Service Act.

Within a few days of what journalists had been sure was the grand finale to the Jo Moore saga there were hints that Byers had not seen the last of the troubled legacy left by her infamous e-mail. Both the *Financial Times* and the *Independent* carried reports suggesting that although Sixsmith had been forced out of his job at the Department of Transport, he had not resigned from the civil service and was having discussions with Sir Richard Mottram about the possibility of being found another posting within the information service. Nothing more was heard of these negotiations until the following Sunday, 24 February, when the *Sunday Times* revealed that Stephen Byers had blocked a deal under which Sixsmith hoped to be exonerated and moved to another position. 'Byers "lied" over press chief's resignation' was the headline on a front-page report which was based on an 18,000-word dossier compiled by Sixsmith. It included contemporaneous notes of all his phone calls and conversations during the previous two weeks and was said to have stripped away 'the veneer of Whitehall to reveal a pervasive rot caused by the politicisation of the civil service'. Not only had Sixsmith 'not resigned', in contrary to Byers' statement on Friday 15 February, but Mottram had 'given his word that he would not be forced to quit' because he had 'not done anything wrong'.

Sixsmith told the *Sunday Times* that he learned of his own 'resignation' through a radio news bulletin on Friday afternoon after attending an appointment at the Chelsea and Westminster Hospital. 'Before Byers made his announcement, the permanent secretary assured me they accepted there was no suspicion of misconduct against me . . . Mottram said: "I will not sack you" . . . I was therefore amazed to hear they had unilaterally "resigned me" . . . Very senior people, including ministers, MPs, journalists and union officials found themselves being misled into providing on-the-record reaction to this false story . . . As far as I'm concerned, I still have a job in the civil service.' Sixsmith's dossier included a vivid description by an unidentified senior civil servant of Mottram's reaction when he heard that a 'low-grade twerp' in Downing Street had deliberately leaked news of the two resignations before he had a chance to speak to Sixsmith. 'He found the permanent secretary in a terrible state, shouting: "We're all f*****. I'm f*****. You're f*****. The whole department's f*****. It's been the biggest cock-up ever and we're all completely f*****." Then Mottram pulled himself together and apologised for the language.' Sixsmith also revealed details of his subsequent conversations with Alastair Campbell as he tried to reach agreement with Mottram on a compromise deal under which he would 'resign retrospectively' from the department and be found another job, possibly working on the Queen's Golden Jubilee.

Campbell explained why he was so concerned about Sixsmith's demand for an 'unequivocal statement exonerating' him: 'The papers are portraying you as the shining example of civil service probity in all this . . . and people like Jo and me as the dirty, underhand political advisers. So if we now announce that you have been exonerated and reinstated it just becomes another excuse for the media to dump on us and on Downing Street.' The following day, fearing that he had been 'stitched up' by his civil servants, Byers refused to accept a deal that was designed to clear Sixsmith's name. Campbell outlined the difficulty he had encountered: 'The problem is that Steve is very sore. The wounds are very fresh. He promised Jo that if she went, you would go too.' Later, it was 'intimated' to Sixsmith that he might get a year's salary of £100,000 if he agreed to go quietly.

His vivid tale of Whitehall double-dealing was sensational in itself; but he had timed its publication with devastating precision, because it coincided with Byers' pre-arranged appearance in front of a studio audience in Newcastle on LWT's Sunday political programme, *Jonathan Dimbleby*. Downing Street's rebuttal unit had clearly been hard at work agreeing the line which ministers should take and the previous evening, after the *Sunday Times* first editions had been circulated, reporters who contacted Byers found he was in a combative mood, warning them that they had better not repeat the claim that he had lied.

Helen Liddell, Secretary of State for Scotland, who was a guest on *Breakfast with Frost*, was the first minister to be asked to respond to Sixsmith's allegations. She immediately attacked the BBC's judgement for thinking that a story about 'a spin doctor negotiating his exit strategy' was the major news item of the day. Byers was 'a straightforward man' who was told by his permanent secretary that Sixsmith had resigned. 'It was part of Jo Moore's going that he had to go as well . . . the media department was dysfunctional and we needed a new start.' Two hours later Jonathan Dimbleby found that Byers was firm and resolute in rebutting the allegation that he had lied. As a Secretary of State he did not get involved in personnel matters, which were the responsibility of his permanent secretary. Byers denied that Ms Moore had demanded that Sixsmith should be forced out in return for her own resignation or that it had been his view that his director of communications should 'inevitably go' because she was going. 'No, no conversation of that kind at all . . . she'd basically had enough, and she wanted to go and it really was as simple as that. I also felt that in order to have a fresh start in the department because confidence had been lost, there wasn't the trust that needed to be there, that it would be good if Sixsmith went as well.' Byers insisted he had merely repeated what he had been told when he made his statement on the two resignations. 'Sixsmith agreed with Sir Richard Mottram, the permanent secretary, that he Martin Sixsmith would resign from his post as director of communications on 15 February, that's the situation, that's the situation which is agreed and stated by Sir Richard, those are the facts.'

When Dimbleby put it to Byers that Sixsmith considered the Secretary of State's use of the word 'resigned' constituted a lie, he again stood his ground: 'I'm not sure Sixsmith is accusing me of lying, I think there is a certain connotation that was put on by a national newspaper, in inverted commas, by the way.' Byers was just as unshakeable when denying Sixsmith's allegation that he had blocked a compromise deal under which his director of communications would resign retrospectively and be moved to another civil service post: 'No, these are personnel issues between Sixsmith and the department and they're dealt with by Sir Richard as his employer.' Dimbleby tried again: 'And you had no conversation about that with Sir Richard?' Byers: 'No, these are personnel matters . . . Oh, I was being kept informed of the developing situation, but I do not get involved with personnel matters.' Throughout the programme Byers did not depart from what appeared to be a firmly agreed line, but he looked drawn and uncomfortable, especially when the studio audience challenged his reasons for having retained the services of his special adviser after her 11 September e-mail: 'I've said this publicly before, that the Jo Moore e-mail was horrid, it was wrong, but should you sack someone because of one mistake and the balance of the decision was . . . [protests and shouts of 'Yes'] . . . and some people have that view, I understand that.'

Sixsmith responded immediately to Byers' interview and put out a statement challenging each of the minister's denials. 'If you resign from your job it is probably something you would remember doing. If I had indeed resigned, why did they spend a week trying to offer me a deal to keep quiet and why did they offer to pay compensation if I would agree to sign a retrospective letter of resignation? . . . I know for a fact that Byers has been involved.' Next morning's newspapers gave considerable space to Sixsmith's accusations and put the Secretary of State firmly in the dock. The front-page headline in *The Times*, '"Liar" Byers fights for political life', was tweaked rather humorously in the *Sun*'s version: 'Liar Byers . . . pants on fire.' The *Mirror* was alone among the nationals in turning the spotlight on Sixsmith himself, who was accused of having led a 'secret Whitehall plot to oust spin doctor Jo Moore'. Paul Gilfeather, the paper's Whitehall editor, said he felt 'forced to tell the truth' and reveal hitherto off-the-record conversations because Sixsmith had 'misled the *Mirror* and sanctioned senior colleagues to do the same'. An inevitable consequence of his action in publicising his claim that Byers was blocking his move to another job was that Sixsmith had exposed himself to further scrutiny. One of the documents in his dossier, which was reproduced in the *Sunday Times*, was his version of the e-mail he sent to Byers about the release of 'rail performance indicators'. Copies went to the Department of Transport's head of news, Ian Jones, and Jo Moore. It said: 'You spoke about possibly making this announcement on Friday. We should not do it on Friday, as that is the day on which Princess Margaret is being buried. There are too many connotations to the word "buried" for us to do anything on that day.'

In releasing his e-mail Sixsmith provided Paul Gilfeather with the vital information he needed when reconstructing the enquiries he had made for the *Mirror*'s original story about Ms Moore's attempt to use Princess Margaret's funeral to 'bury' bad news. Gilfeather accused Sixsmith of having misled him into believing Ms Moore was the 'main recipient' of the e-mail and that its wording was 'savagely critical' of her when the *Sunday Times* version showed this was not the case. 'From the start of our conversation he wholeheartedly joined a carefully constructed plot to end Ms Moore's disastrous reign . . . This was no kamikaze operation by Sixsmith to snuff out his rival. He meant to finish her off and take total control of the department's press operation.'

The *Mirror*'s revelations about Sixsmith's role in trying to bring about Ms Moore's downfall were seized on with relief by Godric Smith when he faced a barrage of hostile questions at the 11 a.m. lobby briefing the next day, Monday 25 February. Downing Street stood firmly behind the account which Byers had given: Sixsmith had agreed to resign when he was seen by Sir Richard Mottram, and that decision was communicated immediately to Byers, No. 10 and the Cabinet Secretary. Instead of giving a direct answer when asked repeatedly whether No. 10 knew if Byers had played a part either in forcing Sixsmith to resign or in vetoing his move to another civil service posting, Smith took refuge behind the same response: discussions about Sixsmith's future were still 'a live issue' and it would be inappropriate to comment. Instead, Smith took the opportunity to explain why he believed that he too had been misled, just like Gilfeather of the *Mirror*.

At an 8.30 a.m. meeting in No. 10 on the morning of Thursday 14 February, the day the story first appeared, Sixsmith left Smith with the firm impression that the 'false allegation' being made about Jo Moore did have some substance. 'Twenty people left that meeting with the impression that it was a question of "same offence, different e-mail" . . . I spoke to Byers at cabinet. He said Moore had categorically denied suggesting the announcement should be made because it was Princess Margaret's funeral and he said the e-mail in the *Mirror* was a fabrication. I spoke to Sixsmith just before the 11.30 a.m. briefing and he replied 'yes' when I asked if she had suggested making the announcement on Friday. Again he gave me the impression that it was a case of "same offence, different e-mail", an impression which I only discovered later was false.' Because there were these two differing versions, Smith said, he was left in 'a very difficult position' and was unable to give a comprehensive account to the lobby on the morning of Thursday 14 February, which would have been his preferred course of action. 'Moore said she didn't do this; the impression I got from Sixsmith was that she had. To say, as I did, that there had been a communication between Sixsmith and the Secretary of State was the right thing to do but I didn't know the facts for certain and if I had said there was an e-mail, I would have damned Jo because of what the newspapers were saying.'

Smith denied he was guilty of attempting a 'spin too far', but his account of the risks he had taken in rubbishing the whole story by stating so categorically that the e-mail reproduced by the *Mirror* and *Daily Express* was 'a fabrication' and did not exist had a familiar ring to it. The rush to rebut had become an endemic fault-line in Downing Street's news management, and a similarly misleading briefing had been one of the factors that had triggered Peter Mandelson's second resignation from the cabinet in January 2001 during the Hinduja passport affair. When that story first broke, Alastair Campbell told the 11 a.m. lobby that Mandelson had 'not got involved' in making representations over Srichand Hinduja's application for British nationality. This was a firmer line than Mandelson had intended, and Campbell was forced to issue a retraction next day after the immigration minister, Mike O'Brien, said he remembered taking a telephone call from Mandelson. Twenty-four hours later – again up against the same deadline of the 11 a.m. briefing – Campbell told correspondents that Tony Blair was still trying to pin down 'difficulties and contradictions' over Mandelson's role. It was the 'mounting pressure' to make a follow-up statement to the lobby, in the face of 'a shrieking media lynch mob', which Mandelson said subsequently was the factor which forced his resignation.

A year later, history had repeated itself: yet again it was a hasty, declaratory briefing in Downing Street which had provided the spark for another damaging conflagration. In adopting Campbell's favourite tactic of taking a robust position, and by hardening up the line he had agreed with Martin Sixsmith, Godric Smith had not only left the government little room to manoeuvre but had also failed to anticipate the possibility that his briefing might spark a response from Sixsmith and could rebound on No. 10 – an eventuality which he was foolish to have ruled out, bearing in mind that he had known all along that an e-mail had been sent to the Secretary of State and copied to his special adviser.

There seemed to be little doubt that the counter-briefing against Downing Street by unidentified sources within the Department of Transport had been precipitated by Smith's decision to push the official line further than had been agreed; and, as in Mandelson's case, it was the aggressive stance adopted by No. 10 which was setting the pace of the story. Despite Byers' point-by-point rebuttal of Sixsmith's allegations in his interview with Jonathan Dimbleby, Smith's convoluted explanation about the inadequacy of his initial lobby briefing gave correspondents an insight into Downing Street's growing discomfort about the many inconsistencies and contradictions surrounding the events of the previous ten days. Sir Richard Mottram made the first move to clear up the confusion when, late that Monday afternoon, he took the unprecedented step for a permanent secretary of issuing his own account of his conversations with Byers and Sixsmith. His earlier failure to be more assertive in disciplining Ms Moore over her 11 September e-mail had angered the First Division Association and some commentators thought it had damaged Mottram's chances of succeeding Sir Richard Wilson as Cabinet Secretary. He set out his version of events in a written personal statement which ran to two pages and gave a step-by-step account of his actions after Sixsmith took 'the unusual step' of e-mailing the Secretary of State to advise against the suggestion that the announcement on rail performance indicators should be rescheduled to the day of Princess Margaret's funeral. 'It would appear that one or more officials chose to make mischief by describing a fictitious e-mail and a made-up story about these events to two national newspapers.'

Sir Richard said the same thing had happened on the day of the Downing Street briefing, when one or more officials advised the press that the line put out by the Prime Minister's official spokesman was incorrect. 'It was clear to me that this situation could not continue and that Moore and Sixsmith should both leave their posts, because relationships within the department and with its ministers had broken down. I discussed this with Byers. He agreed with my proposal. We agreed he would talk to Moore and I would talk to Sixsmith.' Sir Richard had two conversations with Sixsmith on Friday 15 February. 'He was reluctant to resign, arguing to me that he had acted in a manner appropriate to his responsibilities. My own strong view was that his position was untenable. He agreed that he was willing to resign on three conditions: that Moore should also resign; that he and I agreed the terms in which his resignation would be presented in a manner which did not blame him; and that he needed to understand the financial terms under which he would leave, although he said these were unlikely to be a difficulty for him. I told him that Moore would be resigning. We agreed to meet again . . . At this stage I informed the Secretary of State and the Cabinet Secretary that Sixsmith had agreed to resign.' Sir Richard had expected to see Sixsmith again at 3.30 p.m. but he did not return from a hospital appointment until two hours after the agreed time. Because of a leak about the imminent departure of Moore and Sixsmith, the official announcement was made earlier than had been planned, at a time when the detailed terms of his resignation had not been finalised or put in writing. 'I met Sixsmith at 5.30 p.m. that evening. At that meeting he argued that he had never resigned. He said that the release of the announcement without his agreement changed everything.'

On first reading, it seemed Sir Richard's statement had gone some way towards clearing Byers by confirming the version of events he had given in his television interview: Sixsmith had offered to go, although his resignation was announced by Sir Richard before the details had been agreed to. Headlines in the teatime news bulletins tended to favour Byers rather than Sixsmith, but the reports all drew attention to the many loose ends in the story, and the general conclusion was that the Secretary of State was still in deep trouble. 'Byers is hung out to dry' was the headline in later editions of the *Evening Standard*, which chose to highlight Downing Street's pointed refusal to go as far as endorsing Byers' declaration that he played no part in Sixsmith's dismissal. By now Conservative MPs were in hot pursuit and, during a series of points of order that afternoon, the former Conservative chairman, Sir Brian Mawhinney, said he could not remember a weekend when a minister was alleged to have told so many untruths.

The newspaper front pages next morning, Tuesday 26 February, reflected the sense of uncertainty among journalists as to precisely where the story was going. 'Civil servant breaks silence to back Byers' was the headline over a report in *The Times,* which said Sir Richard and Downing Street had 'combined forces in a desperate rearguard action' to save his career. Other newspapers were convinced that Sir Richard's unprecedented intervention had not offered a lifeline to the Secretary of State: 'Byers is sinking,' said the *Mirror.* Under the headline, 'Byers: and still the lies go on', the *Daily Mail* said Sir Richard had dealt him a 'hammer blow' by confirming that the announcement about Sixsmith's resignation 'had been false'. Of all the headlines, perhaps the most ominous was in the *Financial Times,* which declared: 'Byers lied over sacking, claim senior officials.' Its political correspondent, Cathy Newman, said the Secretary of State was under sustained pressure from his most senior civil servants, who had privately 'accused him of lying' for having told Jonathan Dimbleby that he had no role in 'personnel matters'.

Sixsmith sensed his tactical advantage and, given the almost universal criticism that morning about the inadequacy of Byers' denials, he used an interview on *Today* to back up the story he had given to the *Sunday Times*. On the central point of whether Byers had intervened to force him out and then blocked his transfer to another job, Sixsmith was adamant: 'Having got to the end of his tether, I suspect, with Jo Moore, Byers decided he would accept Jo's resignation . . . I was told that Jo would go but the quid pro quo for that was that I had to go as well . . . Mottram told me he'd spoken to Byers about this and the decision was that it had to be a symmetrical resignation.' Sixsmith said that when the 'face-saving compromise' to give him another job fell through he decided to go public, although he was warned by friends in Whitehall that if he did so Downing Street would be vindictive and mount a smear campaign against him. 'I didn't believe them . . . but I've had national journalists, well-respected journalists from well-respected newspapers, ringing up and saying that sources close to No. 10 are saying, "Ring Martin and try and find out something about his property portfolio" . . . Absolutely bizarre; I own a flat in Paris, what's the secret about that?'

After his prolonged and bruising set of exchanges with the lobby, Godric Smith must have been mightily relieved when the Prime Minister's other official spokesman, Tom Kelly, stepped forward to take the 11 o'clock briefing that morning. He said he could 'deny categorically' that there was an 'authorised smear campaign' against Sixsmith. To the surprise of the assembled correspondents, Kelly announced that Byers would be making a statement to the Commons that afternoon and it would take the form of 'a departmental statement' from the front bench. If he had chosen to make a personal statement, this would have indicated to the journalists that Byers was perhaps on the point of resigning; but Kelly insisted that the Secretary of State had volunteered to make the statement and retained the Prime Minister's full confidence. However, during lengthy questioning, Kelly failed to give a straight answer when asked on five occasions whether Downing Street was convinced that Byers had told the truth in denying that he had blocked the compromise deal for Sixsmith. Byers had expressed himself 'in his own way' during his television interview and Downing Street intended to leave it to the Secretary of State to respond in his own way in his statement to the Commons.

Political correspondents left the briefing speculating about the precariousness of Byers' position. Nick Robinson told the BBC's *One O'Clock News* that it seemed Downing Street had 'pulled the rug from under him'. Tony Blair was absent from the front bench when Byers rose to make his statement but the Deputy Prime Minister, John Prescott, was there together with the Chancellor, Gordon Brown, and the Secretary of State for Health, Alan Milburn. Opposition MPs were not quite sure what to expect, but the massed ranks on the government benches behind the despatch box suggested the House was about to hear a spirited fight-back. Byers had Sixsmith firmly in his sights as he explained the lead-up to the two resignations. The e-mail published by the *Mirror* was 'clearly false', and yet his own director of communications had verified its authenticity by telling the *Mirror*'s reporter: 'Every aspect of your story is correct. I'm happy with it.' The following morning, 'one or more officials' from the Department of Transport began to brief the press that the Prime Minister's official spokesman was incorrect to have suggested that the e-mail was a fabrication and did not exist. 'At least one official appears to have spoken on the basis that he was ringing on behalf of Sixsmith. So what we had was a concerted attempt by a very small number of civil servants in the press office to undermine the department.' Byers set out the sequence of his conversations with Sir Richard Mottram and explained why he had told Jonathan Dimbleby that he believed both Ms Moore and Sixsmith should resign. He had not met his director of communications since his resignation.

'I made it clear to Mottram, however, that in my view – this view is strengthened by the events of the past few days – Sixsmith should not be given a job elsewhere in government. Ultimately, I was not in a position to block any arrangement about his future employment elsewhere in the civil service . . . It was because, in the end, this decision about his future beyond his leaving my department was not for me to take that I sought to make it clear on the Dimbleby programme that I was not personally involved in the discussions . . . But if my answers on the programme gave the impression that I did not put forward a view or make clear my views to others inside and outside the department, this is obviously something that I regret and I welcome this opportunity in the House to clarify matters . . . I believed that Sixsmith should not be given another job. I did not see the Dimbleby programme as a suitable place for detailed discussion about a personnel issue. Indeed, it is with some regret that I stand here now making clear what my views of Sixsmith actually are . . . What is at issue is whether one or two unnamed officials, acting quite contrary to the traditions and ethos of the civil service, can be allowed to disrupt and undermine the vital work of a department of state.'

Initially Byers' statement did not attract the outcry which might have been expected from Conservative MPs, and the significance of his apology, for having given a false 'impression' about his opposition to Sixsmith's possible move to another job in the civil service, seemed to have escaped the attention of the shadow transport secretary, Theresa May. Instead of picking up on the fact that Byers had just admitted to having lied during a television interview, she ploughed on with a previously prepared response, challenging the accuracy of some of his earlier denials. Mrs May did face sustained barracking by Labour MPs, but Byers, who had given her a copy of his statement some minutes before he rose at the despatch box, could hardly believe his good fortune and immediately chided her for having delivered a response which had obviously been 'prepared a little earlier'. In answering supplementary questions, Byers did go some way towards explaining why he had become so suspicious about the conduct of his director of communications and why he believed his employment as a senior civil servant should be terminated. 'Sixsmith sent an e-mail to me at my personal e-mail address rather than, as is normally the case, to a private secretary . . . The implication was that I, after Princess Margaret's death, had approached Sixsmith and said that I wanted to change the date of an announcement to the Friday. That is totally inaccurate. Anyone who read that e-mail would have drawn the same conclusion as I did. I do not know why Sixsmith sent the e-mail in that form, but, without any explanation behind it, it clearly had the potential to put me, as Secretary of State, in a difficult situation.'

Immediately after the statement, Tom Kelly told the assembled lobby correspondents that the Prime Minister had asked Byers and Sir Richard to see him at No. 10 later that afternoon. The purpose of the meeting was to provide 'an important signal' of Blair's personal support for the Secretary of State and his permanent secretary and to 'draw a line' under the whole affair. Kelly said Byers' conclusion that his director of communications was no longer fit to remain a senior civil servant had been reinforced by the events which had followed Sixsmith's decision to publicise his case in the *Sunday Times*. The allegation contained in Sixsmith's e-mail, which was not his usual way of communicating with Byers, was 'designed to destroy' the Secretary of State; and the culture which had been allowed to develop among a small element within the Department of Transport's press office, which believed it was 'OK to leak against a minister', was 'disgraceful'.

If Byers thought the strong show of backbench support which had been orchestrated on his behalf by the Labour Party's whips had made a favourable impression on the news media, this was immediately dispelled by next morning's headlines. 'Spinocchio' was the one-word headline on the front page of the *Mirror* over a photograph of Byers on which had been superimposed an elongated nose, to which had been added the caption: 'The lie keeps growing and growing . . . until it's as clear as the nose on your face.' Under the headline 'Byers apologises – and escapes again', the *Independent* used a picture of him smiling in conversation with Sir Richard Mottram on the back seat of a ministerial car as they were driven away from their meeting with the Prime Minister.

The *Daily Telegraph*'s headline, 'Byers admits lie and gets pat on back from Blair', provided a handy line for the Conservative leader, Iain Duncan Smith, at Prime Minister's Questions that afternoon. He accused Blair of having reneged on the undertaking he gave before the 1997 general election that he would expect ministers in a government he led to resign if they lied. 'It is bad enough that such a cabinet minister does not resign, but last night the Prime Minister rolled out the red carpet at No. 10 and congratulated him. Is it any wonder that the public's trust in politicians has fallen so low when the Prime Minister is too weak to root out dishonesty?' Blair retaliated by accusing Duncan Smith of trying to divert attention from the Conservatives' 'botched privatisation' of the rail network. 'One agenda – that of the Conservative Party and parts of the media – is to do with scandal and gossip, day after day. The other agenda is about the economy, living standards, jobs, the NHS, education, crime and the real issues of transport. He can concentrate on the first; we will concentrate on the second.' Despite a complaint from the Liberal Democrats' leader, Charles Kennedy, that using a ministerial statement instead of a personal statement to make an apology was an 'abuse of Parliament', Blair put the seal of approval on his backing for Byers by insisting to MPs that the House had been given 'an absolutely full' account of what had happened and that it was time they judged the Secretary of State on real issues to do with transport.

In the four days which had elapsed since the *Sunday Times* revealed the breakdown in negotiations over Sixsmith's resignation, much of the press comment had focused on the apparent deterioration in the working relationship between senior civil servants and Blair's enlarged band of eighty-one politically appointed special advisers. I had made a small contribution to this debate the previous week with an article in the *New Statesman*, written jointly with Professor Stuart Weir, director of the Democratic Audit at the University of Essex, in which we examined the impact that political appointees were having on the traditional neutrality of the civil service and the public's access to information. After taking regular soundings among political correspondents, I calculated that thirty-seven of the advisers either were primarily employed to promote the image of the government and their ministers or were prepared to do so. I estimated that the duties of almost half of the twenty-six political appointees assisting Blair in Downing Street involved briefing the news media, and that for most of this group it was their primary occupation. I considered my findings were of interest because they helped explain the origins of the conflict between Jo Moore and Martin Sixsmith and were an indication of the wider concern about the way control over the flow of information from government departments was being exercised increasingly by political appointees rather than civil servants. My estimate of the number of ministerial spin doctors was far higher than the figure which Downing Street had supplied to the Select Committee on Public Administration. In evidence he gave in June 1998, Alastair Campbell said the 'vast majority do not have any contact with the press whatever', and as late as December 2001 the Cabinet Office had informed the committee that only eleven of the eighty-one advisers were 'employed primarily in the area of communications'.

Once my findings had been published I was invited, together with Professor Weir, to give evidence to the committee at a hearing arranged for Thursday 28 February, the day after Blair had defended Byers at Prime Minister's Questions. The committee's interest in the government's dependence on unelected political advisers had been heightened in January 2002 when Downing Street released an organogram setting out the way staff were organised in No. 10. It showed the division of responsibility between the Prime Minister's three leading special advisers: the chief of staff, Jonathan Powell; the director of communications and strategy, Alastair Campbell; and the director of government relations, Baroness Morgan. Two units, each run by a special adviser, reported to Campbell: strategic communications, headed by Peter Hyman, and research and information, led by Philip Bassett. A week after publishing the organogram, No. 10 announced another extension to Campbell's remit: Carol Fisher, chief executive of the Central Office of Information, had been appointed the government's chief adviser on marketing, press and television advertising, and had been told that in future she would be reporting directly to Downing Street's director of communications. As we pointed out in the *New Statesman*, the importance of 'this last addition to Campbell's kingdom' could hardly be overstated, because the COI was the Whitehall agency which handled campaigns and promotions for government departments. In effect, Campbell had become Blair's 'minister of information'; yet he remained an unelected party political adviser.

Fortuitously, our appearance before the committee was preceded by evidence from Mike Granatt, head of the government information and communication service, whose letter deprecating leaks from within the Department of Transport was an early indication of the seriousness of

Sixsmith's position. Granatt was responsible for the professional standards of the thousand civil service information officers employed by the government, and he was questioned at some length about the degree to which their work was being influenced by special advisers like Jo Moore. He said an adviser was entitled to take a view on how a press release should be cast, but a question about whether the final product met the rules was his responsibility as head of the GICS. When asked how many of the eighty-one advisers were doing information work, Granatt estimated that 'about half of them advise on presentation and talk to the media . . . we are talking about forty people, but as I say, that is an imprecise figure'. He acknowledged that the 'general thrust' of the government's communication programme and 'day-to-day guidance' came from Alastair Campbell. 'To take an analogy, he is on the bridge, he is steering the ship in the direction of the Prime Minister: I am making sure the engine room and the machinery works properly.'

Granatt's explanation about the nature and extent of the information work being done by special advisers was followed up by the Conservative MP Michael Trend, who wondered whether their influence had been underplayed. 'If we take your figure, which I thought was fair, of forty people, these are up on the bridge with Alastair Campbell and the thousand people who are down in the boiler room with you, then the forty people up on the bridge can have a hugely disproportionate effect on what actually happens.' Granatt accepted that Trend had made a fair point, but he thought that generally there was a strong working relationship in Whitehall between special advisers and the information staff.

When it came to my turn to answer questions from the committee chairman, Tony Wright, I picked up immediately on the fact that, contrary to the government's previous evidence, Granatt had conceded for the first time that around forty of the advisers were doing media-related work. When Wright enquired whether I thought the clash between Ms Moore and Sixsmith indicated a systemic breakdown in relations, I suggested this interpretation was correct because there had been a similar 'root and branch feud' in the autumn of 1997 involving Gordon Brown's former special adviser, Charlie Whelan, which resulted in the forced departure of the Treasury's head of communications, Jill Rutter. The point I stressed was my belief that because No. 10 had been 'in denial' for so long about the conduct of Ms Moore and some of her colleagues, the committee had failed to appreciate the transformation which had taken place and did not understand the conflict which could arise in a system which allowed political appointees in Downing Street, backed up by a network of ministerial spin doctors, to dictate to Whitehall departments and civil service information officers what they 'can and cannot say'.

Our evidence session was eclipsed by a headline-grabbing denunciation of Ms Moore's behaviour by Jonathan Baume, who told the committee that he felt he had no alternative but to take the painful course of re-opening the wounds surrounding her resignation. Soon after she was appointed as a special adviser in March 1999, when Byers became Secretary of State for Trade and Industry, information officers started to realise they had a 'serious problem' on their hands. 'My perception is that Jo Moore was forceful and aggressive to the point where she bullied and victimised civil servants both in the press and in related policy areas. Her behaviour as described to me was an almost classic textbook case of bullying. She appeared to me to have no grasp whatsoever of the concept of political impartiality in the civil service or, if she had, she ignored it . . . It was completely unacceptable. The problem was that it was never tackled.' Baume told the committee he would not be putting his own credibility and that of the FDA on the line unless he was 'absolutely convinced of the truth' of what he was saying.

Aggrieved civil servants failed to raise their concerns through the normal procedures because they did not think any action would be taken as they believed Byers had offered her 'absolute loyalty and trusted her'. As a result, information officers had 'voted with their feet' and left for other departments because they did not wish to confront her or to embarrass the Secretary of State. Baume described the pressure which built up within the Department of Transport in the autumn of 2001 after the previous head of information, Alun Evans, was 'forced to move', which was the point when he accepted the FDA should have intervened on behalf of its members. 'I will be honest, the FDA failed in that, it is down to me . . . a small minority of individuals clearly began to leak. I do not believe this was an attempt to undermine the department in the round or the Secretary of State himself, but it was obviously an attempt to undermine Jo Moore . . . it is patently obvious that people were leaking because I believe they were desperate, they believed the system was failing to protect them and they did not see why they too should not vote with their feet. It was a collective failure. It was a failure by the Secretary of State to recognise the damage that his special adviser was doing to him and to the department, to recognise how unacceptable her behaviour was.'

Baume sought to reassure the committee that FDA members felt 'enormous goodwill' towards the Secretary of State; they were anxious for him to succeed and were ready for 'a fresh start' in the department. But soothing words about the need to rebuild relationships had little impact on the news media, and next morning's newspapers showed the extent to which the committee's hearing had injected fresh life into the story. 'Terror reign of "textbook bully" Moore is revealed' was the *Daily Mail*'s headline over a report which claimed that Baume's 'unprecedented attack' on the 'disgraced spin doctor' confirmed that Byers' 'loyalty to Ms Moore had blinded him to the problems she had caused'.

Three days later, on Monday 4 March, the turmoil within the Department of Transport appeared to have claimed a third victim: the head of news, Ian Jones – Sixsmith's deputy – was suspended on full pay pending further investigations into the allegations that civil servants had leaked information in an attempt to undermine Byers and Ms Moore. The decision to suspend Jones, after a report by security officials, was taken by Sir Richard Mottram, whose own conduct in the whole affair was about to be put under the spotlight at a further hearing of the select committee on Thursday 7 March. Sir Richard told the MPs that 'a tightly defined' inquiry into who might have contacted the *Mirror* and *Daily Express* showed that Jones had a case to answer; he expected the investigation would take some weeks to complete. If information officers had been 'leaking to the media' with the aim of 'getting Jo Moore', that was 'completely unacceptable' as it had created chaos and seriously damaged his department's reputation. When asked if such conduct could lead to dismissal from the civil service, Sir Richard was cate-

goric: 'If it could be proved that they had committed gross misconduct, yes.'

Most of the committee's hearing was devoted to a detailed recon-
struction of his management of the department during the preceding
six months; rarely had a permanent secretary been subjected to such
forensic questioning about the day-to-day rapport between a secretary of state, a special adviser and senior civil servants. Rather than
ask Ms Moore to leave, once he realised the difficulties she was
causing, Sir Richard had tried to find ways to 'manage' her relationship with the rest of the department and ensure that she understood
the importance of working with others. One of the tensions had been
that she thought a few of the information officers 'were not the
greatest thing' she had ever come across. 'All of that is manageable
and it is not rocket science to do it. Why am I sitting here squirming
if it's not rocket science? Why didn't I pull it off? The answer is events
sometimes catch you out.' Sir Richard said Ms Moore's 11 September
e-mail had been 'widely disseminated' within Whitehall before being
leaked, and when Byers had asked him to invoke the disciplinary
procedures, and make a judgement on its wording, he considered it
represented an error of judgement rather than gross misconduct. A
special adviser was appointed personally by the Secretary of State so,
as permanent secretary, he had no power to hire or fire Ms Moore;
he did not know whether or not it was true that after the leaking of
the e-mail Byers thought she should go, but Tony Blair had ordered
that she should stay.

However, once the e-mail about Princess Margaret's funeral had
been leaked to the *Mirror* and Daily *Express*, and Ms Moore was
again being doorstepped outside her home, she knew that it was the
'final confirmation' that it was impossible for her to remain. 'She was
the story . . . She was the innocent party who had been leaked against
. . . but she was the story. Why did I recommend that she should go,
which I did do? Because, in my view, what had now happened was a
confirmation of something that in a way we knew and we had been
trying to manage our way through – that it was almost impossible for
her to operate without the media turning it into a story about her and
a story about an e-mail. Her effectiveness, and I am not being
personal about her . . . her position was becoming very, very difficult

. . . She did not have to go, she resigned.' Sir Richard took the committee through the events which led on, inexorably, to her departure. Charlotte Morgan, the junior information officer who had refused to comply with Ms Moore's instruction to brief against London's transport commissioner, Bob Kiley, did so for 'very good reasons' because the task was not appropriate for a civil servant. Ms Morgan had left the department for another job in Brussels without a cloud hanging over her. 'I have the highest opinion of her . . . Far from rebuking her, I said, "Yes, you did the right thing."' Sir Richard sought to correct a similar myth about the departure of Alun Evans, who took up Ms Morgan's complaint and who had been intending to stand down as director of communications.

Evans had been hired by the Deputy Prime Minister, John Prescott, when he had had responsibility for transport; Prescott wanted a head of information who was strong on management and strategic planning and who would tend to 'downplay any spokesman role'. When Byers took over responsibility for transport, he asked for a director of communications who was stronger on managing the news media. 'Alun Evans was a career civil servant who could be readily deployed somewhere else . . . He has no journalistic background . . . I don't think Alun would ever argue that he is the greatest briefer of journalists that the world has ever seen.' Martin Sixsmith won an open competition to succeed Evans and had the different blend of skills required by Byers. In response to a question from the Labour MP Kevin Brennan, Sir Richard agreed that Prescott did not want 'a spin doctor' but that Byers did. 'Sixsmith's clear intention, openly expressed to me, was to make a success of his relationship with Jo Moore . . . For various reasons, that did not work out very well latterly. That is a civil service euphemism for "it went belly up".' Sir Richard invited Sixsmith to resign because his position had become untenable as a result of the way his part of the department had conducted itself during the week of Princess Margaret's funeral. 'A number of ill-judged things were done for which he was personally responsible . . . Not that he had necessarily done them but not that he had necessarily not done them . . . We received a rocket from the head of the government information and communication service which was couched in really quite extreme terms.'

Sir Richard felt it was 'a bit of a pity' that Sixsmith had taken his dossier to the *Sunday Times* when he had been hoping to see him again the following Monday to discuss a proposition that he should leave on mutually agreed terms. 'I was not taking shorthand records . . . Perhaps some of my conversations with him were meant to be jollying him along in what were difficult circumstances when I did not actually expect that everything . . . would appear in the Sunday newspapers.' Sir Richard conceded that Sixsmith's account of the bad language he had used was accurate; he regretted the words attributed to him which appeared with asterisks in the *Sunday Times*. 'They were uttered in private to one person, with one other person in the room and they were quite clearly over the top, not least in describing the nature of the crisis we were engulfed in . . . In previous incarnations I have dealt with life and death matters . . . for things to do with nuclear warfare . . . and whatever one thinks about the events that Friday they are not in that category. I much regret the thing was so over-hyped.' Sir Richard also regretted the need to draft and publish his own personal statement challenging Sixsmith's version of events, which was 'an accurate' account neither of their own conversations nor of Sixsmith's dealings with others whose confidence had been ignored. 'I was very reluctant to do that . . . because for constitutional reasons I think it is very inappropriate for the permanent secretary to make a statement . . . When asked if I would do this, I said I would do it.'

Sir Richard denied having volunteered his statement simply to serve the interests of the government; he did not think the civil service had been politicised; but he did provide the MPs with a pointed critique of the problems which permanent secretaries faced when trying to manage the increased number of special advisers who concentrated 'wholly or largely on media relations' and whose briefings for journalists overlapped substantially the press work of the official machine. Departments were quite effective in telling their own story about what the government had achieved, but he recognised that increasingly ministers wanted their special advisers to put 'political spin' on what they were saying. 'If there is not clear openness between the special advisers and the machine, then you have great scope there for muddle. One of the favourite games that civil servants play . . . is you spot who briefed about what. You can spend five minutes doing this each day and you can see bits that come from ministers and bits that have come out of one bit of the machinery and then the bits that come out of another bit of the machinery. If you are not controlling that process – control is probably the wrong word – if that process is not coherent the government can go through quite a muddle . . . I think this is the case also in relation to Jo Moore; this is not simply an issue about the competence of special advisers, it is also an issue about the competence of government information officers, they have to be credible, they have to be able to do the business.'

Sir Richard advocated improved procedures for the induction and training of special advisers, followed by an appraisal of their work, a theme which was enlarged upon at a session of the committee the following week, on 14 March, when it was the turn of the Cabinet Secretary, Sir Richard Wilson, to give evidence. The select committee's hearings had attracted considerable interest, and the appearance of the head of the civil service was preceded by stern warnings from a succession of former Whitehall mandarins. They believed that, before his retirement in the summer of 2002, it was incumbent on Sir Richard to give a clear signal to Tony Blair that the civil service wanted to claw back some of the ground which had been lost to political appointees. Lord Armstrong, who was Cabinet Secretary for most of Margaret Thatcher's premiership, urged Sir Richard to press for 'unmistakable clarity' about the duties and responsibilities of those special advisers who were concerned with news management, or 'what is now known as spin'. In an article for the *Spectator*, Lord Armstrong set out the reasons why he believed there should be a limit on the number of 'often relatively junior people' who were appointed because they shared the political precon- ceptions of the party in power. 'There has never, in my experience, been a time when considerations of political spin did not enter into the business of news management; but it seems to me that the balance has now swung too far in that direction. What the practi- tioners of this black art sometimes fail to recognise is that the main casualty is their own credibility; people are increasingly reluctant to accept what they put out as gospel truth.'

I was struck by the fact that among the former permanent secretaries lining up to give their advice was Sir Robin Mountfield, whose report in 1997 paved the way for what I considered at the time was Alastair Campbell's master stroke. Within six months of Labour taking office, the rule book for government information officers was rewritten in order to meet Campbell's demand that they should 'raise their game': for the first time civil servants were instructed to 'grab the agenda' and were told to confirm the speculative stories which the special advisers were feeding to journalists. Although Sir Robin insisted in an article for the *Independent* that his recommendations on new working practices had 'reasserted the conventional neutrality' of government press officers, he was concerned about the dismissal of Martin Sixsmith and other, pre-1997, heads of information and he thought senior civil servants were being sidelined. 'This government has used special advisers far more intensively than its predecessors in press communication, side-stepping the official machine . . . At the heart of government, the position of special advisers is becoming more powerful and potentially dangerous, particularly in No. 10, the Cabinet Office and the Treasury. The effect is not so much interference in civil servants' impartiality, as the virtual marginalisation of orthodox civil service advice.'

After a short opening statement to the select committee, Sir Richard Wilson was asked by the chairman, Tony Wright, if he agreed with the collective assessment of Butler, Mountfield and Mottram that the civil service was in 'new territory' because half the special advisers did press work and had assumed a dominant role in the news management of their departments. Sir Richard conceded that the role of the news media was stronger than it used to be; the selection of a head of information was 'particularly important' to a secretary of state, as was the choice of a special adviser to brief journalists. He assured the committee that the government's long-promised Civil Service Act would clarify the boundaries within which special advisers could operate and propose a cap on their number; the Centre for Management and Policy Studies had already been asked to lay on training courses. Sir Richard was also anxious to ensure that the legislation provided a more accessible grievance procedure for discontented civil servants and, in a speech on 26

March, he would lay out what he hoped would be new ground rules to protect their neutrality. The first step should be to bring the special advisers 'in from the shadows' and put them on a proper footing. A Civil Service Act should state 'clearly and firmly' what these political appointees could and could not do: they must not 'behave illegally or improperly'; ask civil servants to do anything which was 'improper or illegal'; undermine the political impartiality of the civil service; or have any role in the 'recruitment and promotion of permanent civil servants, or in their line management'.

His remedies sounded like a tailor-made prescription for all the ills revealed during the Moore–Sixsmith saga and although he identified no one by name, there was no doubting the identity of his final target: responsibility for the selection and behaviour of special advisers 'should rest with the minister who is accountable to Parliament for them'. Unless these boundaries and responsibilities were clarified and Parliament placed a limit on the number of advisers, Sir Richard feared the 'grey areas' which were left unattended would only 'fester'. A legally enforced grievance procedure would help tackle the problems caused by unauthorised leaks against the government of the day. If the civil service commissioners had responsibility for ensuring there was a better and more effective avenue of redress, and if the process for making a complaint was not 'too daunting', there would be less temptation for disaffected civil servants to leak information to the press or the opposition.

Sir Richard's speech, and his plea to the Prime Minister to clarify the frontiers of the shadowy world inhabited by the special advisers, was a far cry from the position he had adopted in 1999 when both he and his immediate predecessor as head of the civil service, Lord Butler, gave evidence to the Committee on Standards in Public Life. At that time they both spoke in glowing terms about the value of special advisers and saw no need for further safeguards. Lord Butler, who as Cabinet Secretary instigated the 1997 order in council providing Alastair Campbell with executive power over civil servants, was confident these ministerial aides presented no 'permanent threat' to the political impartiality of the civil service; he was comforted by the knowledge that 'in the end, the odds are stacked in favour of the civil service.' Sir Richard was similarly effusive about the role which could be performed by special advisers and he too was satisfied that a doubling in their numbers did not amount to 'creeping politicisation'.

Needless to say, having been one of the journalists invited to hear the speech in which Wilson beat a hasty retreat from his earlier optimism, I could not resist the opportunity to compliment him afterwards on having finally acknowledged the inherent danger in allowing Blair's cadre of political appointees to seize control over the flow of information from the state to the public. The communications network which issued instructions from Downing Street, and which was under Campbell's control, was able to dictate the news agenda across Whitehall; and, as events at the Department of Transport had demonstrated, there was considerable unease within the information service about the ethical standards of New Labour's media techniques. Sir Richard agreed with me that it was impossible to ignore the increased number of ministerial spin doctors, and what he said was the impact of the heightened political pressure to maintain 'a permanent level of campaigning' between general elections. 'I wanted to grasp this nettle, to bring this problem out of the shadows, not deal with it by stealth . . . Yes, I do hope my speech will build up a momentum towards tackling this as openly and as quickly as possible.' In view of his impending retirement, and his wish to see legislation on the civil service included in the Queen's Speech in the autumn of 2002, I sensed Sir Richard had been keen to go as far as he could in setting out his own checklist of desirable safeguards.

He promised his speech would be followed by a consultation process which would take into account any proposals made by either the Public Administration Select Committee or the Committee on Standards in Public Life, which announced on 4 March that it intended to mount a fresh investigation into the role of political advisers and review the effectiveness of the regulatory framework which it recommended in January 2000. At a news conference to launch its consultation paper, *Defining the Boundaries within the Executive*, the committee's chairman, Sir Nigel Wicks, indicated there was every likelihood that both Sixsmith and Ms Moore would be summoned to give evidence. The Wicks committee had drawn up a list of thirteen questions which it hoped would establish a clearer definition of the functions and accountability of special advisers.

Blair and his cabinet colleagues were being assailed from all sides for having allowed their personal appointees to wield so much power over career civil servants, and the announcement of the two inquiries provided the Conservative leader, Iain Duncan Smith, with an opportunity to put forward his own proposals for greater transparency in Downing Street and Whitehall. A future Tory government would reduce the number of special advisers by 'at least 25 per cent' and revoke the order in council which allowed Alastair Campbell and Blair's chief of staff, Jonathan Powell, to command civil servants. Duncan Smith set out his plan to 'clean up' No. 10 in an article for the *Sunday Telegraph*: there was every likelihood he would follow the example of Margaret Thatcher and John Major and appoint specialists to advise ministers in any administration he formed, but the regulations had to be tightened. 'We will tackle the Hydra-like mass of over-mighty special advisers created by this government. Jo Moore may have gone, but a whole host of her colleagues remain . . . We will legislate to make it unlawful for anyone other than a Minister of the Crown or a more senior civil servant to give instructions to officials about the conduct of their duties.'

In laying down a marker on behalf of the civil service, Sir Richard Wilson had called for 'a broad consensus of cross-party support' for future legislation. Although the Cabinet Secretary was desperate to ensure that the debate about the number and role of special advisers did not become 'a political football', the legacy of Jo Moore could not be overestimated. She had done her bit to ensure that the word 'spin' would go on being linked inextricably to that of the Labour Party – and that was a target which was likely to prove far too inviting to be ignored by either the Conservatives or the Liberal Democrats.

SPIN IS DEAD . . .
LONG LIVE SPIN

'No one is going to believe a word that he says about waiting lists or anything else when the National Audit Office report today shows that the government have put systematic pressure on doctors and hospital managers to fiddle the waiting list figures . . . the Prime Minister is to blame for everything in the report . . . It is his culture of deceit that has forced the health service to manipulate these figures.'

Iain Duncan Smith challenging Tony Blair at Prime Minister's questions,
19 December 2001

'We need to be more direct, more convincing and possibly more honest . . . If the government . . . convincingly puts that sort of age of spin behind it, which I believe the government should do, and from the media we elicit a response which is . . . more responsible and accurate . . . then I think we have the basis of a new and different settlement . . . from the government greater openness, and from the media a greater sense of proportion in reporting and analysing politics.'

Peter Mandelson interviewed by *On The Record*, 24 March 2002

Tony Blair's second landslide victory in June 2001 followed a general election campaign which provided another vivid demonstration of Labour's continued superiority as a political fighting force. Once polling day was announced, the party was able to call on a ready-made team of propagandists. Alastair Campbell and other key publicity staff moved out of their offices in Downing Street and Whitehall and instantly took up their places inside Labour's campaign headquarters at Millbank Tower.

No previous party, whether in government or opposition, had been able to draw on such a wealth of talent and experience in media presentation. Blair's decision in 1997 to double the number of special advisers had paid handsome dividends. He had created a pool of ministerial aides well schooled in the art of manipulating newspapers, television and radio, and once the campaign began this tightly knit team of political appointees helped to produce a constant flow of press releases and policy initiatives which fostered the impression that the election was being fought by a team of experienced cabinet ministers who were waiting impatiently to resume work.

There were some embarrassing headlines. Blair was mocked for delivering the opening speech of the campaign during afternoon assembly at St Saviour's and St Olave's Girls School in south London, not least because the 650 pupils were too young to vote. And two unscripted events all but obliterated news coverage of the launch of Labour's manifesto: Blair was ambushed outside the Queen Elizabeth Hospital in Edgbaston and forced to endure a tirade of criticism from Sharron Storer about the lack of government support for the medical staff treating her partner for cancer; and, when confronted by an egg-throwing protestor at Rhyl, the Deputy Prime Minister, John Prescott, responded with a straight left jab to the chin of his assailant, Craig Evans, which provided the most memorable television footage of the entire contest. But apart from the odd stumble, the rest of Labour's campaign went like clockwork.

I had expected much more from the Conservatives and thought they would find ways to dominate the news agenda and keep Labour on the defensive. In the event journalists waited in vain for a hard-hitting critique of Blair's first four years in government or for the release of new and challenging information about Labour's failure to deliver improved public services. By placing so much emphasis on his party's 'keep the pound' campaign, the Conservative leader, William Hague, effectively disengaged himself from the kind of contest which political journalists had expected him to fight and simply retreated from what we had assumed would be the battlefield. The outcome of the 2001 election became notorious for the wrong reason: five million fewer voters went to the polling stations than in 1997, a turnout which shocked MPs and which I felt reflected a level of engagement among journalists which was much lower than in previous elections. An overall majority of 167 was far larger than many in the party had anticipated, but it was not quite the ringing endorsement which Blair had hoped for: he had to reconcile his historic achievement of being the first Labour Prime Minister to be assured of a second full term with the depressing news that four out of every ten voters had stayed at home. The average turnout of 59.4 per cent was only a fraction ahead of the 58.9 per cent recorded in 1918, and some analysts suggested it was the lowest level of participation since the general election of 1885. Various reasons were advanced for the massive drop in interest: the seeming inevitability of the result; a healthy economy; a general feeling of well-being; and what was seen by some pundits as a growing sense of disenchantment with the whole political process.

Falling election turnouts had been mirrored by flagging party membership, and in the months which followed the poll there was considerable soul-searching within the New Labour élite. The modernisers recognised that the public were becoming increasingly cynical towards politicians and that many potential voters disliked modern political campaigning. Blair's long-standing personal pollster, Philip Gould, was the first insider to question the effective-ness of the government's communication techniques and to challenge Labour's heavy dependence on presentation. Voters had not been inspired or engaged by the 'total campaigning' style of 2001, which had been 'rooted in message' and in the party's determination to 'defend itself against attack at speed'. His prescription for future elections was 'participatory campaigning': Labour had to find ways to meet the upward pressure for greater political participation and recognise that voters regarded themselves as empowered citizens; political parties had to be less defensive and the media less intrusive and cynical. 'If we want a society that is more participatory, we need a media that is more constructive and politicians who can respond with openness.'

There was clearly a concerted move afoot to provoke a debate because within days of Gould publishing his ideas in the *Independent* in January 2002, his call for a rethink was supported by Douglas Alexander, the party's campaign co-ordinator for the 2001 election. Alexander, the minister for e-commerce, used an article in the polit-ical journal *Renewal* to argue that Labour's tried and tested campaign techniques had left voters 'feeling that political parties are talking at them rather than with them'. Labour should never run another centralised campaign from Millbank Tower because, he feared, it would create 'an increasingly arid interaction that leaves journalists ever more frustrated, the politicians ever more wary and the public ever more cynical'.

The coded language used by Gould and Alexander did little to lessen the strength of their underlying argument: that the name 'New Labour' had become synonymous with spin, and that many of the media routines which Peter Mandelson and Alastair Campbell had drilled into their troops were becoming counterproductive. Labour ministers and MPs had become figures of fun for refusing to give direct answers to questions; for their dogged persistence in remaining on message; and for their refusal to depart from the official 'line to take' however ridiculous their replies might sound. Advance trailing of government decisions by leaking them to compliant media outlets was no longer a sure-fire way to grab the agenda or secure favourable headlines; Labour's political opponents had found ways to counter the party's famed reputation for instant rebuttal; and an increasing number of political correspondents were reluctant to tolerate the manipulation to which they and their colleagues had been subjected for so long by ministerial spin doctors. Hostility was becoming deeply entrenched in some sections of the media, and journalists had proved far more effective than opposition politicians in stoking up the furore generated by the publication in October 2001 of Jo Moore's infamous e-mail. Any hint that the government was trying to smuggle out an embarrassing or unpopular announcement was invariably seized upon by political reporters as another example of ministers trying to 'bury' bad news.

A heavy reliance on soundbites and photo-opportunities, coupled with the government's continued practice of seeking to present as 'new money' spending allocations which had already been announced, provided plenty of opportunities for the newly elected Conservative leader, Iain Duncan Smith, to repeat William Hague's well-worn taunt that the Prime Minister remained 'all spin and no delivery'. A succession of public relations disasters preceded the plea by Gould and Alexander for a communications strategy that was more open and less confrontational. Perhaps the most serious was a report published in December 2001 by the National Audit Office, which revealed that nine National Health Service trusts had been engaged in 'systematic manipulation' of hospital waiting lists in an attempt to make their performance 'appear more favourable'. Cutting waiting lists by treating an extra 100,000 patients was one of the five early pledges made by Labour in the 1997 general election. The NAO found that the nine trusts had 'inappropriately adjusted' their waiting lists, in some cases over a three-year period, and the objective had been to 'understate the overall size of the waiting list so as to facilitate meeting targets'. When challenged at Prime Minister's Questions, Tony Blair agreed it was 'entirely unacceptable' for any trust to manipulate its waiting list figures, but pointed out that only 6,000 patients had been misallocated and that had to be compared with the 25 million operations performed over the same four- to five-year period.

'Doctored lists' was the *Mirror*'s headline that morning and damning press coverage about the secret massaging of figures to meet one of Labour's most important election promises presented an open goal for Duncan Smith. He told MPs that Blair should personally take the blame: 'No one is going to believe a word that he says about waiting lists or anything else when the National Audit Office report today shows that the government have put systematic pressure on doctors and hospital managers to fiddle the waiting list figures . . . It is his culture of deceit that has forced the health service to manipulate these figures.'

A month later, the high-pressure media routines which Labour had perfected pushed the Prime Minister into another embarrassing corner from which there was again no retreat. Some of the government's most aggressive techniques were the result of pioneering work done immediately after the 1997 election by Joe McCrea, Frank Dobson's special adviser at the Department of Health. McCrea spent Labour's three final years in opposition 'developing and honing' a rebuttal system at Millbank Tower which he replicated within the department so that 'inaccurate attacks' could be 'instantly shot down' by Dobson; two years later McCrea moved to the Cabinet Office to establish the 'knowledge network', an electronic database for ministers and civil servants. On becoming Secretary of State for Health in October 1999, Alan Milburn and his special adviser, Darren Murphy, inherited the rebuttal unit which McCrea had introduced. Attacks on the health service by political opponents and the news media were logged and challenged; aggrieved hospital patients who took their complaints to the newspapers could expect no mercy if their criticism was considered unjustified.

While such procedures might have some merit for a political party struggling to make its mark against the might of an overbearing administration, attempts to micro-manage the news reporting of individual complaints can present nothing but pitfalls for the government of the day; ministers who get bogged down in the intractable minutiae of a who-did-what dispute can find there is no easy escape route, especially if they have been caught out trying to second-guess the decisions being taken by local managers. After the London *Evening Standard* published a front-page report on Monday 21 January 2002 alleging that a woman of ninety-four had been left for three days 'unwashed and caked in blood' in the accident and emergency department of the Whittington Hospital in Highgate, Milburn, instead of calmly promising an investigation and acknowledging the inevitable distress experienced by elderly hospital patients and their relatives, chose to fight back. When interviewed on *Today* the next morning, armed with a brief from his rebuttal unit on the 'lines to take', Milburn denounced the *Evening Standard*'s coverage: 'When we are dealing with these problems, let's talk fact, not fiction . . . she was not abandoned in Casualty, she didn't wait three days for an NHS bed, she was not left caked in blood.'

Milburn's combative performance might have drawn a line under the story had it not been for the fact that the patient's daughter, who had taken her complaint to the *Evening Standard*, was a constituent of Iain Duncan Smith. The ensuing argument over the treatment received by Rose Addis dominated the news all week and proved as embarrassing for Labour as the party's ill-judged 'Jennifer's ear' election broadcast in 1992, which had illustrated all too clearly the danger of focusing so much attention on one problematic case history.

The early-morning rebuttal mounted by the health secretary was a tribute to the speed with which his department could react to hostile reporting: his response was based on a letter written by the Whittington Hospital's chief executive, Trevor Campbell Davies, which had yet to be published by the *Evening Standard*. But when the patient's relatives heard that the Secretary of State had suggested they were liars for having complained about her treatment, Mrs Addis's daughter, 72-year-old Mrs Zena Gold, made another appeal to Duncan Smith for assistance. Tony Blair's preparation that morning for Prime Minister's Questions was as thorough as the briefing given the previous day to Milburn, but the resulting spat across the despatch box did little credit to either the Prime Minister or the Leader of the Opposition. Many Labour and Conservative MPs said afterwards they felt decidedly uncomfortable hearing their respective party leaders trying to score political points at the expense of a woman in her nineties. Blair defended the Whittington by quoting from a letter written by the hospital's medical director, Professor James Malone-Lee, who accused the *Evening Standard* of 'misleading and inaccurate' reporting and for having derided health staff for 'a callousness of which they are innocent'. Duncan Smith retaliated by quoting what he had been told by his constituent: 'Mrs Addis's daughter said to me: "If my poor mother had been a dog she would have been treated better" . . . [Labour protests] . . . That is what the Labour Party does: it shouts down people who have a problem in the health service.'

I was surprised that the Prime Minister made no attempt to commiserate with the family. Although he obviously considered the case of Mrs Addis was being exploited unfairly by Duncan Smith, it did reflect the experience of anxious relatives who found hospital accident and emergency departments were sometimes seriously understaffed and often had difficulty treating distraught and confused elderly patients. Yet even after the unedifying exchanges witnessed on the floor of the House, there was to be no let-up: Downing Street remained in full rebuttal mode, and five minutes later one of the Prime Minister's official spokesmen, Tom Kelly, was telling the lobby that for 'guidance purposes' he wished to draw correspondents' attention to the fact that Mrs Addis had been 'confused . . . and had not allowed the staff to undress her until her daughter had arrived, hence the delay'. Kelly was equally forthright in rebutting the *Evening Standard*'s account of the Whittington Hospital's treatment of another elderly patient, 88-year-old Sidney Hockley, who was said to have spent five days waiting to be moved from the accident and emergency department: he had been washed and changed by nurses 'on the occasions he had been incontinent'. When asked whether Downing Street had obtained the families' permission to brief the news media on the confused state and incontinence of these two patients, Kelly said it was not No. 10 which had decided to 'publicise these cases in the first instance' but the relatives, and this had put the government in an 'invidious position'. If newspapers made allegations which smeared the 'integrity and professionalism' of medical staff, it was inevitable that both hospitals and government would have to get into a far more detailed discussion than ministers would wish.

Downing Street's briefing was a green light to the Whittington to continue an all-out offensive against both the *Evening Standard* and the patients' relatives. In an interview that evening for *Newsnight*, Professor Malone-Lee said Mrs Addis's clothing had not been changed for two days because she 'would not receive treatment from the sort of nurses working in the department'. On being asked by *Newsnight*'s political correspondent, Martha Kearney, if viewers should assume he was referring to ethnic nurses, Malone-Lee replied: 'I can imagine people could deduce that.' Next day the Prime Minister's spokesman, Godric Smith, was as robust as his colleague Tom Kelly had been the previous afternoon. The idea that Downing Street was breaking patient confidentiality was 'wholly spurious and bogus' as the facts were already in the public domain. Under guidance issued by the last Conservative government in 1996, NHS trusts were told that although the overall 'duty to confidentiality' still applied, they could respond publicly when a patient 'invited the media to report his or her treatment'; any response should 'confine itself to factual information or the correction of any misleading assertions'. Therefore there was no reason why the Whittington Hospital should not 'come out fighting' and 'knock back the attacks' on the professionalism of its staff. Journalists were told that the Prime Minister had mounted a spirited defence in cabinet: the government was engaged in 'a full-scale battle' to defend public services and to say hospital patients were treated 'no better than dogs' was to denigrate staff who were 'fed up with hearing individual cases used – in this case wrongly – to run down NHS services'. Blair was just as forthright that lunchtime on *The Jimmy Young Show*: he was not going to have doctors and nurses abused in this way.

However, after four days in the spotlight, the management of the Whittington were counting the cost of having been a standard-bearer for the Department of Health's rebuttal unit and, in a bid to end hostilities, the hospital's chief executive apologised for the suggestion that racism on the part of Mrs Addis might have hampered the staff. He said Malone-Lee had not intended to imply she was racist and the Whittington recognised that to suggest 'there was any racist overtone might be seen as a slur on the family'.

The Whittington's retreat followed intense media scrutiny of the medical director's possible motives for adopting such a high profile. Journalists' suspicions were alerted during Prime Minister's Questions, when Blair quoted at length from Malone-Lee's letter, which not only defended the Whittington but also referred to the problems caused by 'years of under-investment' in the NHS and welcomed the fact 'that this is changing'. After he accused Iain Duncan Smith of using 'very spiteful and defamatory language', Malone-Lee ended up in the firing line, having to answer questions about his own political affiliations. It emerged that he had been a Labour Party member for twenty years; in the 1992 general election he was one of nine clinicians who supported Robin Cook at a news conference; and in the 1997 election he joined fifty-nine hospital doctors and consultants in signing a letter to the *Mirror* which warned that the 'NHS will die' if the Conservatives were re-elected. When he appeared again the following evening on *Newsnight*, Malone-Lee insisted that he had kept his political beliefs separate from his work as a professor of medicine, but his assurance was rejected by the Conservatives' health spokesman, Dr Liam Fox, who claimed the events that week revealed the extent of the 'politicisation of health professionals' under Labour. Duncan Smith took the same line next morning on *Radio 5 Live*: the government's spin machine had gone 'into over-drive accusing the old lady of racism and having a neglectful daughter . . . now the hospital has backtracked; it will be talking to the relatives; and has apologised to them . . . nothing would have happened unless I had raised this.'

Tony Blair used a speech in Newcastle to put the government firmly on the side of hospital workers: it was the Conservatives who were denigrating the NHS by saying the hospitals were 'lousy' so that people felt the health service was 'hopeless, that nothing works, and that any investment is just wasted money'. Blair did not refer directly to the hiatus over Rose Addis but, as so often in the past, he put the blame on the news media. 'To the newspapers, a real-life NHS story is today's frenzy and tomorrow's fish and chip wrapper. To the nurse and doctor it is their reputation, their integrity.' Yet again Blair had turned a blind eye to the possibility that the government's media strategies might have fuelled the feeding frenzy of which he complained. His post-election promise that Labour would be 'anti-spin' in its second term seemed to have made no impression on either the Department of Health's rebuttal unit or the Downing Street press office. Whenever they were challenged at lobby briefings about No. 10's role in orchestrating questionable or distasteful media offensives, Godric Smith and Tom Kelly simply parroted Alastair Campbell's well-worn riposte about being bored by correspondents' questions over the 'process' of disseminating news; it was policy and delivery which interested the public.

I regarded Blair's protestations about spin as no more than a cover for Campbell, whose pivotal position in No. 10 had been strengthened following his promotion to director of communications and strategy. Although he had withdrawn from lobby briefings and no longer put in an appearance on the press officers' bench in the press gallery during Prime Minister's Questions, he held firm to the discipline which he had helped to instil in the party and the government: there could be no easing up in Labour's daily battle with the media. Among those who had worked at the sharp end, devising the communication techniques which had served Blair so well for so long, there was none of the self-doubt which Philip Gould had voiced in the wake of the furore over Rose Addis; nor was there any concern about the effectiveness of rapid rebuttal. Colin Byrne, Labour's chief press and broadcasting officer in the late 1980s and early 1990s, sprang to Campbell's defence in an article for the *Evening Standard*, praising his continued success in promoting the message of New Labour. Byrne had made a name for himself in corporate public relations, having become joint chief executive of the Weber Shandwick communications consultancy, and as a communicator who had cut his 'teeth in the Mandelson–Blair revolution', he was convinced that their strategies had 'revolutionised corporate communications', which was why big business was queuing up to learn from New Labour's approach. 'It is that battle-hardened experience of transformed reputation, media rebuttal and constant, proactive media management that we seek to share . . . The story of New Labour is not the triumph of spin, as its critics would suggest, but is a textbook case study of focused and disciplined communications reconnecting a brand with its "consumers" . . . Every day is a mini campaign you have to win – whether it's for votes, market share or confidence in your stock . . . Communications is not just about winning in a competitive environment, it is about staying in the lead.'

Byrne's hard-nosed assessment of the achievements of his former colleagues was endorsed a few weeks later in March 2002 when a panel of public relations professionals, brought together by the magazine *PR Week*, hailed the brutal effectiveness of the gruelling offensive masterminded by Peter Mandelson. Labour's media management since the mid-1990s took first place in a list of the twenty most effective public relations campaigns because it had developed a brand which 'sought to shed the image of a spendthrift, inflationary and union-dominated party, and create one that suggested it was in touch with the people'. By an odd coincidence, the week before the award was announced *PR Week* organised a conference which discussed the degree to which the profession's reputation was being damaged by the government's obsession with news management and spin. I was asked to give the opening speech, and my central point was that I believed the standing of the public relations industry was being impaired by the practices which New Labour had developed in opposition and subsequently adopted in government; the danger for the profession was that the conduct of political spin doctors was being mimicked in other sectors such as financial public relations. Speakers from the floor expressed their concern about the impact of a lowering of standards following the revelations about Jo Moore, and data prepared by Echo Research showed a marked drop in positive mentions for public relations; half the negative news coverage was driven by unfavourable reporting on politics and spin.

There was considerable discussion about the steps being taken by the Financial Services Authority to secure the 'full, accurate and timely disclosure' of price-sensitive information. In December 2001, the FSA obtained powers to prosecute listed companies which engage in what is known as the 'Friday night drop': the practice of withholding a major profits warning or similar announcement until after the close of the Stock Exchange and then supplying information about it to one or more Sunday newspapers in the hope of obtaining positive news coverage. Buckingham Palace has authorised a similar initiative aimed at providing 'equality of access' for royal correspondents in the hope that this might encourage a more responsible attitude by the news media. As from April 2002, information about the Queen's Golden Jubilee celebrations was released daily on a website to which accredited correspondents could gain access by means of the password given to each of them. Simon Walker, the palace's communications secretary, told me that the Queen wanted television, radio and the newspapers, whether national, regional or local, to get the same information at the same time. 'She's very keen that every news outlet should have a fair crack of the whip . . . yes, we believe that by giving journalists a level playing field, we might get a positive response.'

Again I am sure it was only coincidental, but three days after the PR Week conference, Peter Mandelson reflected on the wider unease about New Labour's preoccupation with spin when he was interviewed by On The Record. He supported Philip Gould's thesis that politicians and the press had to find ways to forge a new settlement that allowed political parties to be less defensive. 'We need to be more direct, more convincing and possibly more honest . . . if the government . . . convincingly puts that sort of age of spin behind it, which I believe the government should do, and from the media we elicit a response which is . . . more responsible and accurate . . . then I think we have the basis of a new and different settlement . . . from the government greater openness, and from the media a greater sense of proportion in reporting and analysing politics.' I have no doubt that Mandelson's plea was genuine – he had warned before about the way some of his techniques had proved counter-productive – but he held back from suggesting what initiatives the government might take to develop a new relationship with the media.

The lead given by Buckingham Palace and the FSA has demonstrated that organisations which have control over the flow of

356 / THE CONTROL FREAKS

information are best placed to take the first step. Tony Blair could follow the Queen's example and order that henceforth his ministers must create a level playing field for lobby correspondents by ensuring that information supplied to the news media is made available simultaneously to all political journalists rather than provided on a selective basis. If announcements were released on a controlled basis through a system guaranteeing instant access to government websites, and Downing Street were forced to provide transcripts for all lobby briefings – not simply those which No. 10 deemed important – there would at least be some stepping stones towards the new settlement which Peter Mandelson and Philip Gould have advocated.

SLOWLY BUT SURELY, COLLAPSING

'We have got to be less buttoned up, far more open, far less worried about what you guys are going to write.'

Alastair Campbell, Downing Street director of communications and strategy, telling senior political journalists of his plans to start dismantling the Westminster lobby system, 2 May 2002.

No sooner had I completed the paperback edition of *The Control Freaks* and it was on the point of being printed, than I found that I had been upstaged by Alastair Campbell: he announced that another step was about to be taken towards dismantling the much-discredited lobby system at Westminster. As I should have guessed, news of this emerged in the typical hole-in-the-corner fashion which has become the hallmark of Tony Blair's government.

Most political correspondents were taking it easy on the afternoon of Thursday 2 May, polling day in the 2002 council elections, knowing they would be busy that evening once the results came in. Just after lunch, James Hardy, the lobby chairman and political editor of the *Daily Mirror*, was given ten minutes' notice to round up a group of senior correspondents who were asked to meet Campbell in Downing Street. No. 10 had discovered that Tom Baldwin, deputy political editor on *The Times*, was about to reveal that the Prime Minister's office had a plan to scrap the lobby system and switch to the American practice of holding televised briefings for political correspondents. Campbell told Hardy's delegation that he wanted to inform lobby officers of his proposals before news of them appeared in *The Times*.

His aim was to open up the lobby and allow many more journalists to attend the morning briefings in Downing Street. Once a new and larger venue had been found to replace the basement briefing room in No. 10, these sessions would no longer be exclusive gatherings for the lobby. Specialist correspondents, covering fields such as health, crime and transport, would have the right to be present; so too would foreign correspondents.

Another innovation which Campbell hoped might also take effect in the autumn of 2002 was that in future ministers, including Blair himself, would take the lead at the morning briefings; these were the sessions which he intended should be televised. James Hardy and his colleagues needed only a few minutes to decode what No. 10 was up to: by breaking the political correspondents' stranglehold over access to Downing Street briefings, Campbell would be able to weaken the lobby's ability to pin down the Prime Minister's official spokesmen and, if there was a move towards more general news conferences, No. 10 would hope to exercise far greater control over the day's news agenda. Needless to say, the senior lobby correspondents who had been called to Downing Street feared the worst.

Ever since it was first established in 1884, in the days of the Liberal Prime Minister William Gladstone, the lobby had been dominated by newspaper journalists, and from the late 1980s onwards they had been mounting a rearguard campaign to fight off a succession of attempts both to undermine the exclusive nature of their organisation and to erode what they considered was their right to obtain information from the government of the day on a non-attributable basis.

Blair had gone much further than his predecessors in seeking to by-pass the political correspondents at Westminster by going direct to television and radio studios, but in the early years of his government the manipulative nature of the lobby system had proved invaluable to Campbell. Labour's spin doctors used every trick in the book to exploit the highly competitive nature of the modern news media and this constant obsession with presentation, despite the government's overwhelming parliamentary majority, dismayed many party stalwarts and was said to have contributed to the increased sense of public cynicism about the trustworthiness of politicians.

The Conservatives had tried to make the most of Blair's vulnerability. Iain Duncan Smith had proved as tenacious as William Hague in seeking to hang the word 'spin' round the Prime Minister's neck with the same enthusiasm which Labour had pinned 'sleaze' to John Major. My own position could not have been clearer: I believed Labour's addiction to spin had caused immense damage to the good name of the Labour government and the distaste this aroused within the party was fuelled in large part by Campbell's continued use of the lobby's cloak of secrecy to manipulate journalists and play the media at their own game. I set out my arguments in favour of Downing Street allowing all lobby briefings to be televised in my book *Soundbites and Spin Doctors*, published in 1995. My conclusion at that time was that I was confident that 'the whole edifice of the unattributable lobby briefing was indeed, slowly but surely, collapsing.'

During the intervening years I have welcomed a series of moves, which have been taken by both Conservative and Labour administrations, to ensure that there is more precise attribution and wider dissemination of the guidance on offer. I hope these latest changes will stiffen the resolve of broadcasters to continue campaigning for all briefings to be recorded and televised. Once the presence of cameras has been accepted, even though this might only be on limited occasions to begin with, I am convinced the pressure on Downing Street will intensify and that the clamour for greater transparency will become impossible to ignore. Campbell's furtive behaviour on the day he released news of his intention to break the lobby correspondents' closed shop was a perfect illustration of the straitened circumstances in which he has been forced to operate. His post-election promotion in June 2001 to the new post of director of communications and strategy marked his final retreat from the media front line. Campbell had started reducing his appearances at lobby briefings the previous summer, after finally acknowledging that his combative stance often generated greater coverage than the policies he was supposed to be promoting; for example, his mere presence on the press officers' bench in the reporters' gallery at Prime Minister's Question Time could be enough to provoke another round of critical news stories. Campbell realised that he had little alternative but to lie low and stay away from the press gallery if he was to stand any chance of limiting the damage which Downing Street's reputation for control freakery and spin had inflicted on Blair's government.

Instead of being open and upfront with journalists, he decided to operate behind the scenes and, whenever possible, he wanted to ensure his name was no longer mentioned in news reports. Perhaps the clearest illustration of the handicap he was working under emerged at the height of the second instalment of the Jo Moore affair, when he was said to have admitted that if the government was forced to make a statement exonerating Martin Sixsmith from blame, it would only encourage the news media to 'dump' yet again on Ms Moore and himself and step up their denigration of Blair's 'dirty, underhand political advisers'. Although he remained a key figure at No. 10, he recognised that when it came to trying to foster good public relations on behalf of New Labour he had in effect become a liability; therefore he could not risk having his name linked to his hastily arranged off-the-record meeting in Downing Street. After telling James Hardy and his colleagues of No. 10's plan to open up lobby briefings and allow televised sessions with ministers, Campbell pleaded for anonymity; the Press Association's political editor Jon Smith complied with his request, and the news agency sourced its report to 'a Downing Street spokesman'.

Campbell's explanation of the reasoning behind the decision to change the lobby's status was that it was part and parcel of Blair's instruction to his government colleagues to spend less time fretting about next day's headlines: 'We have got to be less buttoned up, far more open, far less worried about what you guys are going to write', he said, but he left it to Godric Smith, one of the Prime Minister's two official spokesmen, to provide an on-the-record account of what Downing Street was proposing.

Smith told the afternoon gathering of political correspondents that the government was not attempting to 'scrap' the lobby system but simply open up No. 10's briefings to others. Blair wished to hold press conferences on a regular basis and these sessions would be on-camera, as would any briefings given by other ministers, such as the Secretary of State for Defence, Geoff Hoon, who, it was suggested, might well have briefed journalists on the recent deployment of British troops in Afghanistan. 'We want the authentic voice of the politician to be heard more than the voice of the spokesmen . . . It's all about focussing more on the elected politicians.' On some days, However, No. 10 intended to ask senior officials to answer journalists' questions; these briefings would remain off-camera, as would those with the Pime Minister's two official spokesmen. Smith cited the example of the aftermath of the World Trade Center attack as an occasion when it might have been appropriate for Blair's foreign policy adviser, Sir David Manning, to brief correspondents. Alternatively the government could have asked the British ambassador to the United States, Sir Christopher Meyer, to brief the media. In such cases, the guidance that was given could be attributed to a named official. When challenged as to whether the presence of a large number of foreign correspondents asking questions about unrelated matters might dilute the effectiveness of questioning by political reporters, Smith said this argument did not stack up. It was nonsense to suggest that the lobby would prefer to harry the Prime Minister's spokesman rather than put questions to a directly elected politician.

No. 10 was quite prepared for the lobby chairman to preside at the morning briefings so that Downing Street could not be accused of having total control over who was allowed to ask questions. Afternoon briefings would remain the exclusive preserve of political correspondents so the Prime Minister's two official spokesmen would continue to be available on a daily basis. Smith said opening up lobby briefings had to be seen in conjunction with the announcement the previous month that the Prime Minister was ready to be questioned every six months by the chairmen of the House of Commons select committees. Given that he had such a large majority and there were currently none of the knife-edge votes of previous administrations, Blair believed his government had a special responsibility to look at different ways to refocus attention on Parliament: 'It is clear there is an issue relating to voter apathy and disconnection. We believe one of the ways to counter that problem is to make sure the voices of those who are elected are heard more often, rather than focus on the reported words of those speaking on their behalf . . . Despite the fact that lobby briefings are now on the record, there is still a feeling amongst parliamentarians and the public that the system is a "secret garden". If we can introduce measures to help it become even more open, then surely that would suit everybody.'

The gradual process of opening up the closed world of lobby briefings began in earnest in 1991 when John Major's press secretary, Gus O'Donnell, agreed that his guidance could be sourced to Downing Street; in 1997, Alastair Campbell announced that all his briefings on behalf of Blair would be on the record and could be attributed to the Prime Minister's official spokesman; and then in February 2000 the

No. 10 press office started publishing extracts of lobby briefings on the Downing Street website. Although these steps were welcomed by MPs from the across the political spectrum, opposition parties continued to demand far greater accountability.

Charles Kennedy was the first party leader to call for all lobby briefings to be televised. He told a press gallery lunch in December 1999, within a few months of winning the Liberal Democrats' leadership election, that at a time when there was a move towards greater freedom of information it was no longer tenable to have the 'nods and winks' of a system which allowed the government to go 'on and off the record' at will.

In setting out his party's plans to 'clean up' No. 10, Iain Duncan Smith declared in March 2002 that an incoming Conservative government would want to 'shine a light into the deepest, darkest recesses of Downing Street's power.' He promised not only to make a 25 per cent reduction in the number of special advisers but also to discuss with media outlets whether the daily briefings in Downing Street could be broadcast on both television and the Internet. Writing in the *Sunday Telegraph*, Duncan Smith said there had to be greater transparency. 'It is increasingly absurd to see political editors of the main television channels standing in the middle of Downing Street repeating what they have just heard, rather than being able to run verbatim clips of it. I am attracted to the way they work in the United States.' The strength of Duncan Smith's challenge to Blair to tackle Downing Street's control freakery and abuse of the lobby system was underlined in a clutch of damaging opinion polls in the first few months of 2002; they suggested potential voters sensed they were being misled.

Questions about Labour's reliance on spin were being linked increasingly to the wider subject of political sleaze, which had remained a regular topic for opinion surveys; the replies pointed to a growing level of dissatisfacton over Blair's failure to deliver on his promise to 'clean up politics'. Two YouGov polls for the *Daily Telegraph* in April 2002 illustrated the extent of the damage which had been inflicted on Labour: 59 per cent of respondents in surveys conducted on the Internet believed the government had 'too often been manipulative and less than straight-forward in its dealings with the news media and the public'. and 52 per cent considered Blair relied 'too heavily on PR men and spin doctors'.

A poll by ICM Research for the *Daily Mirror* found that 64 per cent of those who replied believed Blair was 'too interested in image'. Most political commentators concluded that these grim findings from the opinion pollsters, so close to the fifth anniversary of Labour winning power, must have had some influence behind the scenes on the concerted moves which Blair was making to demonstrate a new sense of openness about the government's activities.

Some columnists were disappointed that Downing Street was tweaking the lobby system rather than scrapping it altogether. Jonathan Freedland, writing in the *Guardian*, argued that Blair had failed to make a clean break with a style of politics which had had its day. 'Abolishing the closed, secretive system of the lobby would have sent a signal that, after five years in power, this government wants a new way of doing business. It could have banished the old order and promised that, from now on, official Downing Street would always speak in the open and on the record. That would have meant a new start, and the press would have had to respond.'

Lining up on the other side of the argument were those who believed Campbell's real objective was to reduce the lobby's ability to mount surprise attacks on the government. Michael Jones, a former *Sunday Times* political editor, said the larger the news conference, the harder it was for troublemakers to ask questions. 'The lobby's strength lies in its refusal to be fobbed off and in its bloody-minded persistence.' The *Daily Mail* had reached the same conclusion: this was New Labour's 'most determined move yet' to manage the news; the only detailed grilling of the government, on a daily basis, tended to come from the political correspondents. Now, sustained questioning would no longer be possible and the lobby's 'ability to winkle out the facts' would be reduced. Although he had been careful to avoid addressing political journalists en masse to defend his plans to shake up the lobby, once the dust had settled Campbell gave an exclusive interview to Tom Baldwin, the deputy political editor of *The Times*, who had been on the point of breaking the story the previous week.

Baldwin gave no indication of the terms on which he was allowed to question Campbell but the limited nature of the quotations suggested that the part of the conversation which was on the record was restricted to the subject of reforming the lobby. He was told that the moves to widen attendance at the presently closed briefings should be seen as a genuine attempt to encourage 'a spirit of honest inquiry' in holding the government to account. The squeals of anguish from lobby traditionalists about control freakery and the presence of outsiders were proof of the media's introspective nature and the 'trivia-obsessed' attitude of the cynics who worked in the press gallery at Westminster. Campbell agreed that he had become 'part of the problem' in the steadily worsening relationship between the government and the media which was why he had stopped conducting lobby briefings. Nonetheless there had been fault on both sides: Campbell was prepared to be contrite and he acknowledged for the first time that some of the media routines which both he and Peter Mandelson had adopted when the party was in opposition did not necessarily suit Labour in power.

Their aim initially had been to make sure that Blair did not suffer from the 'vicious' treatment in the press which Neil Kinnock was forced to endure. 'In the end the story of how we managed the media became something of significance in itself. For a while that was seen as a positive, because the Tories had always had a monopoly on professionalism and presentation. And in opposition all you have is words; you can devise policies but you can't change people's lives. But when we came into government, if I were honest about the thing, we hung on to some of the techniques and ways of opposition for too long.'

Campbell's soul-searching had evidently been wide ranging: he agreed that tactics like the constant re-announcement of policies, a plethora of new initiatives and the double-counting of spending pledges had proved counterproductive; the government had persisted in using such devices because of the need to feed the insatiable appetite of rolling news on television and radio and to cater for the relentlessly competitive newspaper industry. 'I don't know whether it could have been done differently to prevent the whole spin thing becoming so huge. All our relations with the media have now become defined in that context.' Tom Baldwin concluded that Campbell seemed entirely confident about the path he intended to follow in Labour's second term: the government did not need to 'spin any more – or, at least, so much.' In future Blair could point to 'a body of experience, reality and achievement' and Campbell felt that ministers who had spent too long worrying that no one would read about their arguments 'unless there is some new wheeze or angle attached' should take comfort from the fact that voters knew more about what the government had done than what it had said.

Campbell shared the desire of Blair's personal pollster, Philip Gould, to see if the government and the media could find ways to develop some common ground so that the coverage of politics could be made less of 'a game' and more relevant to people's lives. 'The way politics is being reported is just aiming off all the time. Everything has to be a "massive scandal" – never a minor scandal – or it has to be the "worst crisis yet". You want to report everything as if it's 100 miles an hour in the fast lane, but most people are living in the middle lane and don't want to go that fast . . . We need a more grown-up and honest understanding between government and the media that there will not be a new policy every day.'

Campbell's plea for an 'honest understanding' with the media echoed the words used by Peter Mandelson in his *On The Record* interview in March 2002. The positive and constructive tone taken by *The Times* towards Campbell's overtures was another demonstration of his ability to avoid detailed scrutiny while managing to publicise himself. He had made a point of giving relatively few interviews but each one was tightly controlled and he always took care to vet the likely line of questioning. One issue which Baldwin might well have wished to discuss was Blair's unprecedented decision the previous month to lodge an official complaint with the Press Complaints Commission.

The Prime Minister's office had sought to invoke the PCC's code of conduct on the accuracy of news reporting in protest at the failure of the *Spectator*, *Mail on Sunday* and London *Evening Standard* to correct articles which 'falsely alleged that Downing Street sought to change the arrangements of the lying in state of the Queen Mother in order to enhance the role of the Prime Minister.'

No. 10 said the story was 'a complete lie', and although Downing Street tended to ignore 'a lot of the stuff' which was not true, occasionally there were stories which were 'just plain wrong and offensive' and had to be corrected. The two journalists who claimed to have unearthed the story, Peter Oborne and Simon Walters, had to understand that No. 10 had the 'right to challenge' them and seek redress. Nevertheless taking a complaint to the Press Complaints Commission hardly accorded with Campbell's declaration that Downing Street intended to be 'less buttoned-up' with the media. (In a humiliating climbdown for No. 10, the complaint was subsequently withdrawn.)

The dispute over Blair's role in the Queen Mother's funeral was one of the issues which Campbell insisted could not be mentioned when he appeared on Radio Five Live's breakfast programme in order to debate the threat posed by the British National Party in the May 2002 council elections. The point of the interview was that Campbell wanted to stress the danger which would face his home town of Burnley if any of the BNP's thirteen candidates were elected to the borough council. He told the programme's presenter, Brian Alexander, that the BNP were 'a bunch of racist misfits' and if the town woke up to find that it had elected BNP councillors, it would be 'disastrous for jobs in Burnley, investment in Burnley and all the rest of it.' In the event three of the BNP's candidates were elected.

This was the second BBC interview which Campbell had given about his home town and his life-long support for Burnley Football Club. In March 2000, he told Radio Five Live's listeners that he had been a devout fan for forty-one years and regularly took his two sons with him when he attended the team's matches around the country. This interview aroused my interest because Campbell told the programme's presenter, Adrian Chiles, that he considered there were many similarities between managing a football club and running the Downing Street press office. After writing (in chapter 7) about the clear parallels which Campbell identified between his job and that of the Manchester United manager Sir Alex Ferguson, I discovered subsequently that the Prime Minister's official spokesman left nothing to chance before a Five Live interview. Chiles told me the inside story: Campbell had taken inordinate precautions to avoid being caught out on air. So as to help compile a series of trivia questions about Burnley Football Club, Chiles contacted a group of supporters known as the London Clarets. 'As a result I was able to work out in advance what I wanted to ask Campbell and, as expected, when I got to No. 10 to record my interview, he insisted we could only talk about football. When I let slip that I intended to test him out with some trivia questions about Burnley, he exploded. He refused to let the interview go ahead unless I told him what the questions were. I had to back down and tell him, but when I recorded our chat, although he knew full well what I was going to ask him, he pretended not to know. He hammed it up, thinking out aloud and then gave listeners the impression he wsa answering the questions ad lib. I have admit it was a damn good performance.'

Campbell's sympathetic interview with *The Times*, like his carefully contrived radio appearances, was designed for a purpose: he wanted put across his argument in favour of developing a new accord with political journalists and to prove to the public that the government was intent on encouraging 'a spirit of honest inquiry'. Unfortunately his timing could not have been worse, because on the very day he gave his interview to Tom Baldwin, the Department of Transport published an abject state-ment which finally exonerated Martin Sixsmith and contradicted the statement which Stephen Byers gave in the House of Commons on 26 February in an attempt to draw a line under the Jo Moore affair. Campbell's protestations to Baldwin about the cynicism of the lobby and his endeavour to blame political journalists for being 'obsessed by trivia and process' looked rather hollow alongside the government's contrite retraction of the inaccurate statements which Byers and Downing Street had issued on the fate of the Secretary of State's former director of communications. Sixsmith was leaving 'by mutual agree-ment' at the end of May after it had taken his trade union, the First Division Assocation, two months to secure him a £180,000 pay-off.

The wording of the apology was a testament to the hard bargaining which had taken place with civil service officials:

> The department accept that Martin Sixsmith has remained in their employment since his contract began on 19 November 2001. He did not resign on 15 February 2002. The department regrets that, while acting in good faith, they announced he had resigned on what turned out to be an incorrect understanding of earlier discussions that day. Because of views expressed by the Secretary of State, Sixsmith felt that he had good reason to take his story to the *Sunday Times*. He regrets in hindsight that this exacerbated a breakdown in working relations between him and the Secretary of State. Both parties accept that this now makes it impossible for Sixsmith to work effectively in his post at the DTLR . . . Were it not for these unfortunate events, for which no blame is being apportioned, he would continue to be a successful director of communications in DTLR.

The size of the compensation payment, and the fact the agreed statement turned on its head the explanation which Byers had given from the despatch box, produced a barrage of protests from opposition MPs. Both the Secretary of State and Downing Street were accused of double dealing: the shadow transport secretary, Theresa May, called on Byers to make an immediate apology for having misled the House of Commons. At the afternoon lobby briefing, No. 10 insisted there was 'nothing new' in the statement setting out the terms of Sixsmith's departure.

In his statement of 26 February, Byers had referred to a statement issued the previous day by his permament secretary Sir Richard Mottram, who had acknowledged that his understanding of Sixsmith's resignation had 'turned out to be incorrect.' Therefore Byers had drawn attention to the fact that there had been 'an incorrect understanding, in good faith, of the earlier discussions . . . that, as a matter of law, there had been no enforceable agreement to resign.' Journalists left the briefing dumbfounded by No. 10's audacity: there could hardly have been a clearer example of the way in which Downing Street, rather than the lobby, had ended up dancing on a pin head. Next morning's newspapers were unanimous in castigating Byers for yet again having been economical with the truth. The Hansard report of his statement to MPs was headed 'Resignation of Martin Sixsmith' and the transcript showed that he had used the words 'resigned' or 'resignation' a total of fifteen times. Blair had a rough ride defending Byers at Prime Minister's questions that afternoon, and although he tried to argue that Byers' statement was made 'in good faith', he made little headway in the face of a sustained attack by the Conservative leader, Iain Duncan Smith. After Blair insisted that Byers had been told by Sir Richard Mottram that Sixsmith had agreed to resign but that it had been made equally clear to MPs that Sixsmith 'disputed that he had resigned', Duncan Smith (mis)quoted Sir Walter Scott: 'O what a wondrous [for "tangled"] web we weave, when first we practise to deceive!'

The outcry that followed forced Byers to return to the despatch box next day, and he again sought to assure MPs that he had not misled the House: there was no conflict between his statement on 26 February and the agreement reached over Sixsmith's departure; he had acted 'in good faith' in announcing Sixsmith's resignation on what turned out to be an 'incorrect understanding' of the discussions there had been with Sir Richard Mottram. 'There is therefore nothing new here, and indeed nothing that was not a matter of record at the time of my statement on 26 February.' However, Byers did acknowledge that his own precipitate announcement of Sixsmith's 'resignation' on the evening of 15 February was a factor in triggering the botched finale to the Jo Moore affair: 'The release of that announcement without his agreement changed everything.'

I could not help noting the irony of the occasion: here was a beleaguered secretary of state admitting that it was the government's action in chasing the headlines which had allowed Sixsmith the opportunity to blacken Byers' name and walk away with a six-figure pay-off. The headlong rush to rebut unfavourable stories, and the need to meet Campbell's dictum that the government must 'grab the agenda', had tripped up Downing Street once again. The whole sorry saga surrounding Sixsmith could be pinned directly onto the front door of No. 10. It was a briefing by one of the Prime Minister's official spokesmen, Godric Smith, who claimed the story about Sixsmith's e-mail concerning Princess Margaret's funeral was 'a fabrication', which prompted the counter-briefing by unidentified officials in the Department of Transport and which, in turn, led to the final escalation in the Moore–Sixsmith feud.

Again it was Downing Street which grabbed the headlines and preempted the tense discussions involving Sir Richard Mottram by announcing at 4.40 p.m. that afternoon that Sixsmith had 'resigned'; it was that inaccurate and premature disclosure which prompted Sir Richard's memorable observation that, 'We're all completely f*****'. There could have been no clearer illustration of the need for greater transparency in Downing Street. If the Prime Minister's official spokesmen were forced out in the open, if their statements were recorded and televised at lobby briefings, perhaps No. 10 might find that the need to be upfront with political correspondents would induce a sense of caution and encourage a more honest accord between the government and the media. I considered the final twists and turns of the Moore–Sixsmith debacle – which culminated in the resignation of Stephen Byers on 28 May – made my case: those who control the flow of information have a duty to act with complete propriety, and with the ever-shortening deadlines of the media-driven age in which we live, no government can afford to ignore the importance of its reputation for straight dealing.

INDEX